Across the Divides:
Chile. A Different Perspective

For Robin + Jan
with very best wishes
Gill A Smith
March 31st 2008

Gill Williamson Smith

Published by

MELROSE
BOOKS

An Imprint of Melrose Press Limited
St Thomas Place, Ely
Cambridgeshire
CB7 4GG, UK
www.melrosebooks.com

FIRST EDITION

Cover designed by Tanya Fukes

ISBN 978-1-906050-49-8

Printed and bound in Great Britain by:
Biddles, 24 Rollesby Road, Hardwick Industrial Estate,
King's Lynn. Norfolk PE30 4LS

Foreword

This is the story of how one woman, with her family, heard and responded to the call of God to go out beyond their safe boundaries to the other side of the world.

I have often been surprised at a funeral, by the picture painted of a good friend that I thought I knew quite well. As with God himself, there is always more to discover. Gill is very much alive. These pages have opened my eyes to another dimension to her life that I never really knew before. We can have a pre-conceived idea of what being a missionary is all about. This book will put the record straight.

This gifted and passionate author has entrusted her readers with a full, intimate and engaging account of what is involved in obeying the call of Christ to go and communicate the Gospel by life and by lip. She, with her clergyman husband Ray, and their 3 small children, packed up their home and life in this country to move to Chile, serving over a period of 9 years.

At times the reader is left breathless with the energy and courage they showed in the pursuit of their calling to live and minister in a foreign country. From beginnings of ministry in East London, they crossed cultures to a beautiful country, at times dangerous with life-threatening erupting volcanoes, earthquakes, tsunamis and the breaking up of glaciers.

There were political challenges too. The author recalls the moment that she became more politically aware. It was while sitting in the dentist's chair of a Chilean communist. This new awareness served them well as they lived under two opposing political extremes of Presidents Allende and Pinochet. They were there during the detention and torture of Dr Sheila

Cassidy. Earlier food had become scarce. People were gunned down under both regimes, and fear took hold. But Gill and her husband remained faithful and undeterred.

Gill kept a diary and had access to letters and other writings which makes this story so detailed and honest. She writes with the artistry of a painter, the courage of an explorer, the skill of a midwife, the love and sensitivity of a mother, and the pastoral care of a priest. She is all of those things. The reader is often transported through her vivid descriptions, to imagine being in the country with its vibrant colours, its sun-soaked summers and noisy bustling cities.

An unashamed Christian, Gill has a burning desire to reach across divides. Personal stories of conversion to Christ are shared with her readers with some candour. Their friends and colleagues in Chile include people from across the denominational and political divides. Her gaze is always focused on her Lord, which throws man-made divisions into relief. Those divisions became relatively unimportant, though respected, and surmounted in the service of Christ.

It is clear that the Smith family have gained a love for Chile and the friends they made while they were there. This is no 'hit-and-run' story. Friendships have continued. They include some of the converts who have gone on to serve Christ themselves in their own country and in different parts of the world. That Gill has dedicated her book to her children is an indication of her love and respect for their part in the risk that she and Ray took in responding to God's call as a family.

'When God calls He enables.' Gill Smith and her family are living proof of the truth of that statement to this day.

Grace Sheppard
Wirral
Oct 2007

Dedication

To Naomi, Andrew and Julian whose continual presence not only helped in bringing normality in far from normal years, but also lightened up grey days with the sunshine of laughter.

Acknowledgements

In the six-year journey of writing this book there have been fellow travellers, without whom I would have long given up.

My two *constant* companions over these years have been my husband and my sister; Ray, whose patient encouragement held me steadfast when on more than one occasion I was ready to quit; Elaine, who although due to physical limitations was unable to verbalise her impressions yet nevertheless entered into the whole process. I read each chapter to her as it progressed and she was able to relive her own visit to Chile. It is a very special thanks to Elaine for the finances she has put into the whole project.

The first year's literary travel began under the tutelage of Dr Elizabeth Bray and companions from the Writers' Workshop of the Cambridge University of the Third Age. I am extremely indebted to them for the many tips, constructive criticism and affirmation given. Other Cambridge friends include Barbara Priestly, Mary Hall, Canon John Lowe and Dr Dorothy Lowe – each playing a part in the whole venture.

My grateful thanks to Keith Haskell, acting UK Ambassador to Chile on the recall of Ambassador Reginald Secondé, for checking the political events; Grace Sheppard for much encouragement, and writing the Foreword; Susan Hare for the initial proof reading; Nigel and Jimena Strang for checking my Spanish; Julian and especially Sarah Angier giving unstintingly of her time when having IT problems often at short notice – and husband Keith for releasing her.

Without the input from so many friends scattered over the world and especially from Chile itself, this book would have little relevance. It is not so much my story as together our story.

Introduction

'You two should write a book!'

How often my husband, Ray, and I have had this remark made to us over many years and several continents.

Writing has always interested Ray: not me, however. So what changed my mind?

Writing his memoirs for the family, Ray suggested I should write a chapter or two on our years in Chile. It didn't take long for me to realise this would never work as our styles would be very different.

'But I do feel passionate about Chile and the years we spent there.' Listening to my heart, with its passion for Chile and its people, and picking up the gauntlet laid down by those many friends, were the stimuli needed to embark on a literary journey. This journey, like any journey, has involved companions on the way, reference maps in the form of a personal diary and nine years of letters sent home, as well as other reference points. At times the way has led through a desert, void of imagination, only to emerge from the barrenness into an oasis of inspiration. The journey has presented challenges to scale literary mountains almost as formidable as the Andes themselves. Emotion has erupted as pressure has mounted in a volcano of frustration with a misbehaving computer. Family and other life events have led at times to a cooling off of the trail as cold as the glaciers and icebergs. More important still than images of fire and water, snow and desert, verdant green valleys and lofty mountains that make up the land of Chile are the people themselves.

To say that our lives were and still are being enriched by those who touched them in the years we lived there is an understatement. The hardships encountered in what became the most turbulent years in Chile's history played no small part in that enrichment.

In a country torn apart politically we found ourselves facing divides that had to be crossed, not only between people on opposing sides, but within ourselves and our own preconceived ideas. As Christians our priority was to meet people where they were, be they rich or poor, Marxist or rightwing, atheist or God-convinced, and accept them regardless. The passion that fired our hearts was to introduce them, even if in small measure, to Jesus, who through a life given in sacrifice has brought reconciliation between humans and their creator God. This book will introduce the reader to some who in discovering their own need for forgiveness and reconciliation with God were able in turn to forgive and be reconciled to those on the other side of the divide.

God's call to us was full of surprises and what seemed to be a reversal of expectations, both our own and others'. From working in London's East End among the less privileged in a developed nation, within a comparatively short time we were to be working among the affluent in a developing nation. But human needs remain the same. We were to discover that among the affluent there was at times a poverty of spirit that material wealth was unable to satisfy. In today's obsession with consumerism and celebrity status we can perhaps learn from this.

My desire in writing this book for those of faith or no faith is best summed up in the words someone in the publishing world wrote on reading extracts. In his opinion one of the qualities was that in reading this book 'it may start the casual reader to think less casually.' If that is the case then I think the literary journey has been worth travelling.

Gill Smith

Contents

Chapter 1   Fearful Rumblings..1

Chapter 2   Early Influences: Heroes and Heroines...................9

Chapter 3   The Call: A Reluctant Follower.............................17

Chapter 4   Overseas on Hold 24

Chapter 5   G.M.T. … but not Greenwich...............................29

Chapter 6   Living among the Cockneys 46

Chapter 7   South America on the Horizon.............................56

Chapter 8   Frantic Frinton 66

Chapter 9   Discoverers and Conquerors 83

Chapter 10 Captain Allen Gardiner: Pioneer.......................93

Chapter 11 Chile's Uniqueness 100

Chapter 12 Chile: A Stressful Beginning 111

Chapter 13 First Impressions 118

Chapter 14 The Marxist Experiment...................................137

Chapter 15 'Enemies' Become Friends................................150

Chapter 16 Strategy 162

Chapter 17 The Worsening Economic Situation...................181

Chapter 18 Some Welcome Respite: Going South 200

Chapter 19 The Political Temperature Heats Up 219

Chapter 20 Some Welcome Respite: Going North 232

Chapter 21 Change of Direction 242

Chapter 22 Radio Rumblings of a Political Tremor 253

Chapter 23 Last Three Weeks in Allende's Chile 262

Chapter 24 Going Home...273

Chapter 25 Catching Breath and Catching Up 301

Chapter 26 New Beginnings 323

Chapter 27 Pinochet's Chile...334

Chapter 28 A First Harvest 350

Chapter 29 Out from the Comfort Zone...............................367

Chapter 30 Family and Extended Family 383

Chapter 31 Treacherous Waters 402

Chapter 32 A Second Harvest 429

Chapter 33 A Diplomatic Crisis 444

Chapter 34 An End of a Chapter 456

Chapter 35 Passing on the Baton 463

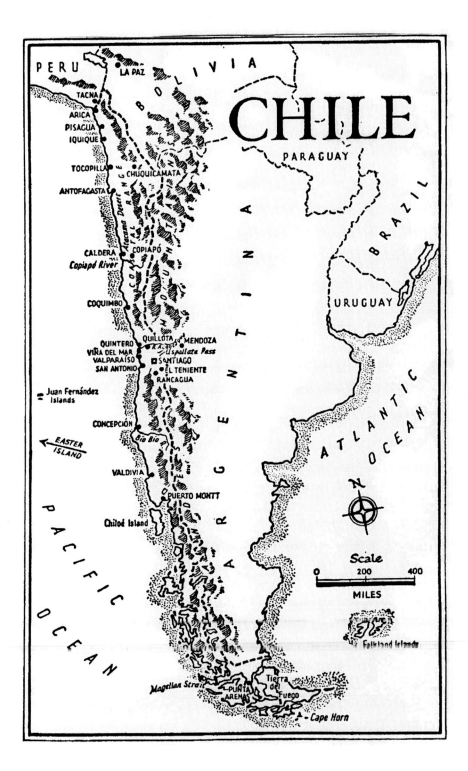

Chapter 1
Fearful Rumblings

It was July 8th 1971, three minutes past 11.00 pm. Without any warning we heard rumblings as of an approaching underground train. The fact was we were not underground, neither were we waiting at a station for a train to arrive.

The underground rumblings within seconds gave way to a mighty roar as the ground beneath our feet began to shake violently. I should have been in the bath, fortunately I wasn't. Our next-door neighbour had called round unexpectedly. As a result the bath water was decidedly lukewarm. I called to my husband, 'Ray, I'll just run in some more hot water.' It was while reaching for the tap that IT happened. There was no warning. It was as sudden as a mighty bomb explosion.

Within seconds the glass in the whole corridor of french windows of the bungalow in which we lived rattled in an ever-increasing crescendo. There were twelve in all. Simultaneously with these noises came those of various objects as they tottered, then fell from their pride of place. We, with our three little children, had been in Chile a mere four months. To add to the drama of moving ground beneath our feet, which we could not control, we were suddenly plunged into darkness as the electricity automatically cut out. Perhaps this was for me the most fearful moment as I shouted to Ray above the noise and commotion, 'It's an earthquake!'

The *terremoto* (earthquake) registered 7.3 on the 1-12 Richter scale and its duration the longest on record. Below 7.0 is a *temblor* (tremor). We later discovered that the epicentre was at La Ligua, approximately 100 kilometers north of Quilpué, where we were living. Quilpué was then a large, sprawling village, hardly a town, situated inland from the coastal resort of Viña del Mar (Vineyard by the Sea). For many Chileans living in the capital, Santiago, this was a favourite place to gravitate to for the weekend.

We had been told that in the event of an earthquake the safest place to shelter, if inside a building, is under the overhead beam of the doorway or under a table. Many injuries and deaths occur from flying objects of masonry. However, as we were living in a bungalow with plenty of surrounding land, not being overshadowed by other buildings, we had devised our own plan of escape. I would exit by the back door, keeping close to the adjacent side of the bungalow and under the protection of the eaves of the roof. Then I would make my way to the two bedrooms, next door to each other, in which our three children slept. Meanwhile Ray would go into the first bedroom and pass the first child out to me through the window. Then, the same strategy would follow for the remaining two until we were safely sheltering in the orchard – all very well in theory, worked out in the cool light of day!

Ray and I have very different ways of facing problems, and distinct coping mechanisms. I anticipate them before they happen and try and work out some strategy – at times wasted effort because they never happen! Ray, on the other hand, waits for the crisis to occur and sometimes is caught totally unprepared. On the plane to Chile I ended up with a terrible headache, terrified about living in an earthquake prone country when we hadn't even arrived! I remember picking up our three-year-old Naomi's Ladybird book, *David and Goliath*, and feeling somewhat rebuked when I was showing such little trust in the Almighty to deliver me from my 'giant' of fear. Having subsequently experienced a real rather than an imaginary 'quake, I lost much of my fear. For me it was a case of the old adage, 'Better the devil you know than the devil you don't.' For Ray, his face was to change, for several weeks to come, from its usual ruddy colour to an ashen white every time we felt tremors.

(There were plenty of these. We were at a dinner party, years later, with Professor Robert White from the Bullard Laboratories, Cambridge University, and on hearing about our experience he sent me more detailed information. The earthquake of July 8th was at a depth of 40 kilometers, followed by 'a whole string of smaller earthquakes … the biggest was 6.3 … on 11th July.')

In addition, my nursing and midwifery training gave me some advantage in reacting to an emergency. On that never-to-be-forgotten night, I shot out through the back door with hardly a second thought. On reaching the first bedroom the wooden shutters were still shut and refused to open. With Ray inside, presumably having unlocked the shutters, the only conclusion I reached was that they had become jammed, which can happen as a result of shifting ground and displaced foundations.

I panicked. As I tried to wrench them open, superficially tearing off the skin of my knuckles, Ray staggered out through the back door with Julian, fourteen months, in his arms. In his panic he had forgotten the plan! I took Julian from him and, placing him well away from the house, shouted, 'Quick, through the window!' One minute later we were all safely under the apple trees in the orchard. The *terremoto* had lasted four and a half minutes.

Writing home, Ray described the noise in graphic terms. It had reminded him of a visit made in 1958 to a boys' camp with a friend: *'We were welcomed to an evening meal in the school dining hall by over a hundred boys drumming on the tables with their mugs, plates and cutlery – the noise was uncomfortably deafening!'*

On that climactic day of July 8th, the noise of the ground in turmoil was soon to be replaced by human screams, howling dogs, and the wailing sirens of the emergency services. The full moon on this mid-winter night radiated its incandescent glow over the dancing trees. It could not have been better choreographed were it not for the reality of the unfolding tragedy. The rising dust obliterated the moon within minutes.

In four minutes 221,000 houses were made uninhabitable and over 100 people had died. More deaths and structural damage would have occurred, we were told, had the seismic movement been more horizontal rather than vertical.

When it was relatively safe to go back into the house, Ray collected blankets and we remained in the garden reassuring the children who, by now, were fully awake. They had slept through most of the initial drama. Andrew, a two-year-old toddler, and his older sister, Naomi, were more bemused than frightened.

'Why are we in the garden in the middle of the night and in the middle of winter and in pyjamas?'

Brian Skinner, our earlier visitor, came to see if we were all right and the five of us left with him to join the rest of his family next door. We camped out in the open, four adults and seven children huddled round a portable gas fire. The ground was still shuddering. We waited for the next big shock wave. It didn't come.

We read together Psalm 46, the following words taking on new meaning for us:

'God is our refuge and strength,
An ever present help in trouble.
Therefore we will not fear, though the earth give way
And the mountains fall into the heart of the sea,
Though its waters roar and foam
And the mountains quake with their surging.'

The majestic Andean range is shared by the Western Republics of the sub-continent of South America and forms the spinal column of Chile. The mountains twitch and tremble and in their convulsive state, attempting to push the landmass into the Pacific.

We were comforted by the visit of our Anglican Bishop, David Pytches. With the area in total chaos he personally managed to visit most of those in his pastoral care to check that we were all safe. All telecommunications were non-operational. So it was impossible initially to speak to our families back home.

My diary entry the following day reads, '*It was 2:10 am (9th) and I noted that my father would be listening to the 7 am news at home – so we prayed for God's peace*' as the news broke. With little information getting through to us within Chile itself we tuned in on our battery operated radio to the BBC World News later that day. Chile was the second item.

'President Allende has declared a state of emergency in Central Chile after a severe earthquake, in which sixty people died and hundreds injured. In Valparaiso (largest seaport serving the capital) twenty-five are dead, a possible 300 injured, forty percent of homes damaged. The roof of the cathedral has fallen. The effects of the earthquake were felt in Argentina. President Allende is personally directing the relief.'

After Bishop David left, it was decided that the eleven of us, for what was left of the night, would sleep in our bungalow. For the next two nights we lay on our beds fully clothed in case one of the continuing tremors would build up to another 'quake. Over the following six weeks more than five hundred tremors were recorded on the seismograph.

Two days later the electricity supply had been re-established, as had gas and water. The bath I never managed to take on the night of the 8th was put to good use in supplying us with water over those days. After another couple of days we were able to take baths but in very muddy water.

News filtering through told us of a local family of four killed when their house caved in on them. The more modern buildings in towns and cities fared better than those of the *campo* (countryside) or those inhabited by the poor of Chile. These are often made of *adobe* (hard baked mud and straw, plastered over). The house belonging to the next-door neighbour of the Skinners was made of *adobe* and the wall of one room fell out on to the street. The elderly occupant was in bed at the time.

On the 12th our diary tells of our walking around Quilpué surveying the scene. We '*noticed very few corner houses had escaped damage… It was obvious that the poorly constructed homes and those made from poor material, adobe, suffered the most. Many tiled roofs were also damaged and garden walls had caved in. Some people were seen packing up home and shop as their accommodation was no longer safe to live in… the fire brigade and demolition workers were busy demolishing two homes (one very large) which had fared badly.*'

The next two weeks saw a steady stream of colleagues wanting to make use of our water supply to do their washing and to have baths. The Bishop's family had had no tap water since the 8th. Unfortunately they had inadvertently left their taps turned on.

5

On returning home from a day out they were met by a cascade of water running down the stairs and out through the front door! With wry humour they told us that only that morning in the daily newspaper there had been a cartoon of a similar occurrence with the caption *'María, el agua llegó!'* ('Mary, the water's back on!') David Pytches' wife's name is Mary!

This 'cascade of water', controllable by human means, contrasts with the uncontrollable flood of water that at times accompanies earthquakes. Tidal waves have all too often followed in their wake. Chile is no exception to this other frightening act of nature.

John Gunther in his classic book *Inside South America*, writing about help received from outside Chile remarks on how 'sardonic' the relief can be. To support this he quotes from a Santiago newspaper reporting on aid sent after the 1965 earthquake:

'Until the close of this edition, the following aid had been received (for the earthquake victims): Estados Unidos-35 tons of yo-yo's; 35 promises of loans from the Inter-American Development Bank, 6 more from the International Monetary Fund, and 139 notices of loans overdue for previous earthquakes, plus an autographed photo of President Johnson 18 x 24 cms. Soviet Union-25 radio-controlled rockets; 15 agitators; 32 bazookas; 5 cases of vodka, and one spy with camera. Cuba-5,000 copies of "Guerilla Warfare" by Che Guevara; 72 tons of extracts from the speech made by Fidel Castro on the inauguration of children's games at El Guajarito. Argentina-Their deepest sympathy; a long-play (sic) record of the latest creations of Alfredo de Angelis; and an autographed letter from the Foreign Minister Miguel Angel Zavala Ortiz, stating that "the earthquake is one proof more of unbreakable Argentine-Chilean friendship".' [1]

In 'our' earthquake the sea level of the port of Valparaiso dropped approximately twenty centimetres.

Over the next nine years we were to experience many more *temblores* but thankfully no further *terremotos*. An amusing situation arose while living in the capital a little later on. I was vacuuming the sitting room, when the plumber, who had been

---

[1] John Gunther: *Inside South America*, Hamish Hamilton Ltd. p. 281

fixing a leak in one of the pipes, staggered into the house from the direction of the garden. Trembling, his face ashen, he said, '*Señora,* didn't you feel it?'

'Feel what?' I replied.

'*El temblor,*' he answered.

In his concern to escape himself from impending disaster, it seemed he was quite content for the '*Señora*' to continue her cleaning! She, however, was quite oblivious of the more sinister vibrations than those of the vacuum cleaner!

We have, at times, been asked how our children reacted to tremors occurring fairly frequently. We don't remember them being particularly frightened. However, we do remember one morning when we were just about ready to get out of bed and a tremor started. We lay still for a few seconds with bated breath. Would it get stronger? When it did we decided to go to the children. By the time we opened the door of the boys' bedroom it had subsided. Andrew was playing on the carpet with his much loved Matchbox cars. As we entered, he looked up and, with a big smile on his face, said, 'Mummy, Daddy, the floor went like this,' moving his arms in a wavy motion, 'just like a boat on the water.'

It was to be more than twenty years before we felt another 'quake, this time in London. We took our then five-year-old grandson, Daniel, to the Science Museum. Here, together with the curious, we endured a two minute simulated earthquake. Daniel was impressed that 'Nana and Grandpa and Daddy' had felt a 'real' and not a 'pretend' one.

The fearful rumblings of July 8th 1971 were to move into the background as rumblings of a very different nature were heard over the radio on June 29th 1973. An Argentinian friend living close by 'phoned us to tell us to switch on our radio as it seemed there were serious events taking place in the city centre. The 'rumblings' were those of heavy armoured tanks as they made their way down the streets of the capital. The initial reaction was that it was an attempted coup. However, this was not the case as facts later emerged.

Just over three months later the rumblings of tanks were to

be heard. On September 11th a political 'earthquake' of great magnitude hit Chile. This was an authentic coup d'état or referred to in Chile as *'un golpe del estado'*, which would leave in its wake the demolishing of democracy for many years to come.

Even as I write this first chapter another September 11th has occurred, the epicentre of this 'quake being New York. The 'shockwaves' from the bombing of the twin towers of the Trade Centre have been felt worldwide and the foundations of the fabric of freedom itself have been shaken to the very core.

Geological earthquakes are perhaps easier to accept than political, the one 'an act of God', the other 'an act of man.'

Chapter 2
Early Influences:
Heroes and Heroines

The first time I was aware of a land called Chile was in my early childhood. A family from the Baptist Church we attended had left England to go as missionaries to a distant land 'at the end of the earth'. A call that for them was every bit as challenging as that Jesus gave in his farewell commission to his disciples before his ascension to heaven.

According to a specialist writer on Latin America, George Pendle, the name probably comes from the language of one of the old Indian tribes who lived in the Andes whose word 'Chilli' means 'where the land ends'. To a child of eight or nine the name of this country conjured up not so much its geographical location but rather a country more likely to be known for its cool climate and frosty welcome. Nothing could have been further from the truth, when this child, now a young mother of thirty-one, together with her husband and family of three left for the country 'where the land ends' in March 1971.

Ray and I, long before we met one another, had been influenced by the exploits and adventures of men and women down the years, who had left the comforts of home and family to obey this commission to the Christian church. The fictional books I enjoyed reading were real 'cloak and dagger' stories: books like Baroness Orczy's *The Scarlet Pimpernel* and Alexander Dumas' *The Three Musketeers*. I always did have a very vivid imagination.

It was when I was eleven years old that this vivid imagination was rewarded with the meeting of a real live heroine. It was February 4th 1951.

My childhood home was a large corner shop in Leicester. It had fairly spacious living quarters. We were a family of four, mother, father and older sister, Elaine, although for a brief six months we were five. In the downstairs of the premises a largish entrance hall separated the shop from the living quarters. At one end of the shop was the post office, together with the stationery and greeting cards section. Next to the General Post Office in the centre of the city ours was reputed to be the second busiest, a claim well proven especially in the war years and throughout the forties and early fifties.

Three sides of the shop counter formed a continuing line following the contours of the rectangular shaped shop. On the fourth side was the entrance from the street into the shop and on either side of the entrance were the two principal display windows. To the left of the left hand shop window, as you walked in from outside, and also directly facing you, was what my parents referred to as the 'private' part of the shop in contrast to the 'public' section which comprised the post office.

The shop counter that spanned this area was in turn broken up at its right-angled corner by sweet shelves. Immediately next to these was a very large 'fridge at counter level leading to a continuation of the counter into the 'public' section to the right ending at the right hand shop window. Just before the 'private' part finished and the 'public' one started was, to all appearances, more shop counter. In fact it was a lift-up flap, which in the family was referred to as the 'trap door'. Only family, friends and employees used this. On entering it was directly facing you across the wooden shop floor. The most usual way to go from the shop into the house was to lift up the 'door' on its hinges, at right angles to the counter. While still small enough, Elaine and I would walk underneath. When we were taller, we would just bend down and crawl through.

Large, tall rectangular glass jars were stacked in rows on tiered wooden shelving. These contained all sorts of sweets that to two children were a constant source of temptation – something Mummy in particular was concerned about. During these early wartime years Daddy was away serving his country. It was left to our mother to set the boundaries. As a special treat we were allowed to have any left over sweets, which lay at the bottom of the glass jars.

One story that became an oft-repeated family anecdote was when I crossed the boundary line, the temptation having proved too much.

I went missing and the cry went up: 'Where's Gillian? Has anyone seen Gillian?'

The shop assistants (there were at least two) joined mother and no doubt five-year-old Elaine in the hunt for the missing two-year-old. It wasn't long before the culprit was found. 'Here she is.' The search was called off. There to the right of the 'trap door', sitting under the shop counter, was a tiny blonde child thoroughly engrossed in the task at hand. The 'task' in both dappled brown hands was the demolition of a large box of chocolate whipped cream walnuts. The well-contented face, matching in colour the brown stained hands, soon changed from focused concentration to fearful consternation at being caught in the act. The problem wasn't only the fact of rationing but that none could be salvaged. Instead of eating one at a time I had taken a bite out of each!

Once our father was home and we were old enough to have weekly pocket money we were able, on a Friday night, to weigh out and buy our own chosen delights.

The 'Glory Hole' was a small stock room and, after a fresh delivery, was filled to capacity with boxes full of bars of chocolate, sweet lollipops, groceries and at one period, children's toys. Once the War was over, the large 'fridge began regularly to fill up with Lyons ice cream. Lyons was the rival to Walls at that time. In addition the shop had tinned and packaged groceries. It was also a tobacco shop, which, with today's health enlightenment, would never have been my parents' decision.

A door at the other side of the 'trap door' led into the hallway of the house, thus dividing the living quarters from work. Downstairs was the sitting-cum-dining room, large pantry and kitchen. To the left of the door leading from the shop were the stairs.

Upstairs were three bedrooms and a good-sized lounge, the bed-sofa converting for overnight guests when needed. My room was the small box room overlooking Slater Street. The bathroom was next to Elaine's bedroom. Both were large. Above the entrance hall was the landing covered by linoleum. We used to play in this large area. Our favourite game was climbing into the huge cardboard boxes in which scores of cigarette boxes had been stored prior to being stacked on the shelves. The empty boxes became 'boats', the polished 'lino' (linoleum) floor the 'sea'. The squeals of delight as we 'sailed the sea' would inevitably give way, at times, to squeals of annoyance and arguments, following the capsizing of one 'boat' after a collision.

It was a happy childhood, marred only by the sadness of losing a baby sister, whom I had so looked forward to loving. Stephanie Ann was born on May 24th 1950 with a heart condition. She lived only six months.

One day my mother announced that we had a very important visitor coming to tea. It was a Sunday and this important person was speaking at the evening service. She lived in China. This previously unknown woman was to become so well known that many books would be written about her. One of these books would be made into a feature film starring Ingrid Bergman as the 'small woman'. The film was *The Inn of the Sixth Happiness*, the 'small woman', Gladys Aylward. Her story was later broadcast in the BBC's 'Undefeated' programme.

By three o'clock the tea table was laid, the best bone china sitting on the lace tablecloth. The sandwiches had been made, as had the delicious sponge cake. Wafting in from the kitchen was the familiar smell of Mummy's famous scones – always cooked at the last minute so they were at their freshest. The excitement was mounting as the hands of the clock moved towards three-thirty. By a quarter to four the tension was almost unbearable. Then the doorbell rang. Daddy went to the front door. Mummy followed. As voices were heard in the hall, Elaine and I looked at one another with the sheer excitement of anticipation.

Both my mother and father were tall. Mother was five feet eight inches tall and my father six feet. As the door from the hall to the sitting room opened, Mummy led the way, followed by our visitor. Daddy brought up the rear. Then came the first surprise. She was so diminutive, no taller than I was. She wasn't even five feet. Then came the next surprise. What were those strange clothes she was wearing?

In a short time we were sitting at the table, the little lady in her mandarin-collared brightly patterned silk jacket, seated on my left. I sneaked little sideways glances at her as we ate our tea. She seemed very prim. Two thin brown plaits, firmly secured on top of her head, framed her plain face. The dark-rimmed glasses seemed much too big for her small sharp features. She looked like an owl. I was not impressed – that is, until she recounted her story that evening. Because of her height she would have disappeared in the pulpit were it not for a wooden box on which she stood. She held us riveted. Such authority, courage and compassion flowed powerfully from this 'small woman'.

A cocktail of courage, determination bordering on stubbornness and sheer grit resided in this austere little lady. It was this mixture of personality that wouldn't take 'no' for an answer, when she was turned down by a mission society for work in China. She was a domestic servant working in London at that time. It was her stubborn determination and sheer grit that saw her some months later crossing the wastelands of Siberia by train on her way to China. It was 1930. Her courage would be put to the test again and again. However, Gladys Aylward, above all, had an unshakeable sense of God's call to go to China. Added to the cocktail of personality was a childlike trust in God's provision and protection.

The story for which she will always be remembered was how she led a hundred Chinese children to safety across the mountains to the Yellow River. They were fleeing the Japanese army, which had invaded northeast China.

Perhaps, being a child rather than an adult, the amazing feat of this undertaking didn't stand out in my memory or perhaps she didn't refer to it that Sunday evening. What I do remember hearing from the pulpit was her graphic description of another incident.

She had fled a Chinese city (Tsenchow), the Japanese soldiers in hot pursuit, with a price on her head (a hundred dollars reward was offered for her capture).

Outside the city wall was a graveyard, she sped through it and headed towards the moat. Bullets ricocheting around her, she fell to the ground, the rising dust and grit from where the bullets struck stinging her eyes and filling her nostrils. She felt a thud in her back followed by a burning sensation. She had been hit, but it was fortunately only a superficial graze: the thickly-padded jacket had taken the brunt. Wriggling out of it, she noticed a number of bullet holes. Using her large Bible, which she had grabbed as she fled, she placed it under her front, and, using it as a sledge, dragged herself along the ground. She fell down into the moat just as a further spray of bullets hit the now empty jacket.

The early years of exposure to missionaries would shape both Ray's and my life independently in the years ahead.

Ray's childhood was spent in Essex. He was the eldest of five children – his father a busy GP, his mother a wonderful homemaker. Their large home, ' St Breock', was open to all for hospitality. Like my mother, my mother-in-law was a wonderful cook. Included among the many visitors to the home were missionaries home on leave. Out from the chaos of the kitchen would emerge a veritable feast of delights. Not so delightful for Ray and his father was the huge pile of washing up his mother was noted for, needing to be tackled!

In early adulthood, before meeting one another, Ray and I read biographical books of men and women like Hudson Taylor, Amy Carmichael, John and Betty Stam, and five young American men. John and Betty Stam were murdered in China, the five American men in Ecuador. The young widow of one of the men and the sister of another remained in Ecuador. Within a few years a church was established. Among the early converts to Christ were the very Auca Indians who had thrown their spears into the men's bodies.

Some time later, when I was studying theology and mission, I shared a room with a Welsh nurse and midwife. Margaret was a second year student while I was in my first. She left England to work in a mission hospital in Thailand in the sixties. Several years later news came that terrorists, to look after their wounded, had abducted two western missionaries. Many months went by with little news reaching the outside world. One day in the seventies (by now we were living in Chile), the wife of the British Consul, both regular members of our church, approached me.

'Gill, I think you should see this.' With that she thrust a newspaper cutting into my hand. Two female skeletons had been found in the jungle, a single bullet through each head. They were the remains of Margaret and Minka.

A book I found very challenging was *The Cambridge Seven*. These seven graduates were all from very privileged backgrounds. Among them was a baronet's son, the son of a major general, three Etonians, and a former stroke-oar of the Cambridge boat. C. T. Studd, the famous cricketer, was also one of the seven. W. G. Grace paid tribute to Studd by describing him as 'the most brilliant member of a well known cricketing family' and that 'from 1881-1884 he had few superiors as an all-round player.'

John Pollock, the author, gives a vivid description of the last night the 'Seven' spent before leaving for China:

'On 4th Feb., 1885, a wet winter's night in London, a large crowd was making its way into the Exeter Hall in the Strand. Inside, the hall was rapidly filling with men and women of all ages and ranks. Well-dressed ladies, in silks and jewelry, whose carriages would be waiting afterwards to carry them back to Belgravia or Mayfair, mingled with flower-girls and working women in plain dark dresses who had found their way on foot from East End slums. Smart young men were sitting beside drab shopmen and kindly rogues who, on a superficial glance, might have seemed more at home in the gallery of a music hall.' [1]

He goes on to recount how one by one the 'Seven' platform speakers told how in the past eighteen months God had called them to renounce their careers to serve him overseas:

'The Cambridge Seven struck with force the consciousness of

---

[1] J. C. Pollock: *The Cambridge Seven*. Inter Varsity Press

a generation which set much store on social position and athletic ability.'

At the time of reading this and other biographical books I had no idea how in the future we ourselves would not only face the challenge of living cross-culturally but also crossing social divides.

Far into the future Ray and I would be making the big jump between East Enders and Embassy personnel, the former living in ugly tenement buildings, the latter in luxurious houses and near-mansions. Once again nursing training paved the way. The tramp admitted one day to the hospital ward I was working on received equal quality care as that given to the university professor in the bed opposite.

Spanning the divide of culture and social class was, for us, the bridge of God's call but our response initially was to be very different.

Chapter 3
The Call: A Reluctant Follower

I am starting this chapter the morning after returning to our home in Cambridge from five days spent with our three grandchildren (their new brother or sister due this week!). Common to all small children is an in-built reluctance to break off from the all-absorbing task of the moment to follow a call to what is perceived as a more boring alternative. The call, 'It's time to go home' will often result in a running in the opposite direction. The slide on the far side of the playground looms even more compelling than it did on arrival! A later call to bedtime produces the result, 'I'm just finishing my dinosaur puzzle,' no matter that only a few minutes previously it had been discarded as 'too difficult'. Our three 'little treasures' are no exception to this innate tendency.

God's call to me would initially meet with the same response as that of my grand children: the fact was, however, I was no longer a child.

By now I was happily fulfilling a long-held desire to follow a nursing career. One day at the age of four I had announced to my parents, 'When I grow up I want to be a nurse.' Like most little girls I had a doll. My doll, however, was dressed in a nurse's uniform with a bold red cross on the front of a white triangular shaped hat. My parents thought this was just a childhood phase I would grow out of. There were no known relatives who had followed either a medical or nursing career! They were wrong.

This 'momentary-childhood-diversion' in fact proved a reality. At the age of sixteen, after 'O' levels, I began a two-year pre-nursing course. We were known as cadet nurses. Then followed three years training for State Registration.

It was during these three years that the call of God came and, like the reluctant grandchild, I didn't want to be diverted from the all-absorbing task of the moment. It was a Sunday evening. I was nineteen years old. The preacher in the Evening Service was a missionary doctor.

I don't recall where he was working or what he said, but what followed on the way home was to become life-changing in the long term if not in the short. An inner voice, 'Gill, would you be willing to serve Me overseas?' came out of the blue. Try as I would I was unable to silence the 'voice' as I continued on my way home.

I was 'nights-off' and had chosen to spend my free time at my parents' home rather than the Nurses' Home. It was a thirty-minute walk. It seemed much longer. The more I tried to shut out this unwelcome invasion of mind the more persistent it became. I reached home.

Regularly, on Sunday evenings, a small group of University students would congregate at home. The usual trio from my parents' church was John, his brother Adrian, and John's friend Gordon. They were such great fun. John in particular had a dry and wicked sense of humour while maintaining an incredibly serious facial expression. We would often play table games. Our home would resound with a great deal of laughter as well as animated discussion on these Sunday evenings. The latter were usually of a theological nature. Mummy and John especially enjoyed the stimulation of these discussions. They would often be locked in serious debate. As I entered the sitting room it was obvious such a discussion had been in full flow.

The first words I heard were my mother saying to John, 'You know, John, sometimes God asks of us something we would rather He didn't!'

That remark hit home like a sharp arrow. I mumbled something about having a bad headache and would they excuse me if I went to my room. Later I undressed and got into bed. Before turning the light out I reached for my Bible. As I was turning to the passage I was currently reading, the pages fell open unexpectedly at the end of Mark's Gospel. There in front of me were these words of Jesus to his disciples: 'Go into all the world and preach the good news to all people.'

I slammed my Bible shut, wouldn't pray and for the next three months tried to run away from God. But like Jonah in the Old Testament and very many reluctant followers ever since, I was to discover that God wouldn't let me off the hook that easily! After all I had chosen to be a Christ follower from early adolescence with no coercion.

The next months were not happy. It wasn't long before I realised one can't run away from God and be at peace.

Why was I so reluctant? The honest answer lay in a false perception of the nature of God. This had its root for me, at that time, in an equally yet understandably wrong impression of what a missionary was like. The majority I had met were single women, decidedly frumpish and apart from the 'Little Woman' deadly dull.

An outstanding example was a maths teacher at the Grammar School I went to. She had straight hair that never changed its pudding-basin style, and inevitably wore grey or brown. Her feet were decked in traditional Clark's sandals and ankle socks, but even more important than her appearance, which could be overlooked, was her awful reputation.

I don't ever remember seeing her smile, nor give a kind word of encouragement. Every thing about Miss Smith (not her real name) was negative. Sadly in those days it wasn't unusual for some to hold the idea that Christians shouldn't enjoy themselves or follow fashion, certainly wearing make-up was frowned upon. The impression at times was that God himself was a killjoy.

This thankfully wasn't the view in my childhood home, although my parents, especially my mother, set standards that in Christian families today would be considered off beam! Life was to be enjoyed and we did just that. There was lots of laughter and good fun in those early years. At nineteen, I liked nice clothes and I certainly wanted to fall in love and marry one day. Missionaries to me were not normal.

Perceptions of what a missionary is have been mixed over the years. While admiring the educational and medical input they have brought, often at great personal sacrifice, criticism has been levelled at many for apparently changing the cultural background of those to whom they go. This criticism of 'westernising' can be justified and sensitivity hasn't always been respected. However, in taking the message of the Gospel, the good news of Jesus Christ, a higher mandate is adhered to and becomes the motivating factor. The Great Commission of Jesus to his disciples has motivated men and women for nearly two thousand years. It was this that was the driving force in the lives of the Saints – Augustine, Cuthbert, Aidan and Patrick – and resulted in Christianity taking root in our own Islands.

Much has been learned from past mistakes and mission today is not seen as one way, that is, 'the West to the Rest', but rather as a partnership between the developed and the developing nations. The Christian church in the developing world is thriving and vibrant in many countries. It is also growing in many others against a background of persecution. Increasingly it is becoming a sending church. Accompanying this 'sending' is a reciprocal concern for a Western impoverished society, where spiritual values are all too easily jettisoned for material ones. The world events following the destruction of the Twin Towers of the World Trade Centre have highlighted and called into question some of these values. Many a thinking person, especially young adults, are questioning these values. The 'Have-nots' have much to teach the 'Haves' if only we would listen!

At the end of three unhappy months of trying to silence the inner voice of what God might be asking of me, I stopped running away. It was one night in the solitude of my room in the Nurses' Home that I got down on my knees and prayed, 'Lord, I'm not willing, I would be a hypocrite to say I was, and I can't even make myself willing, but I'm willing to be made willing.'

The peace that filled my inner being at that moment is difficult to describe. I had a sense of the presence of Christ himself, alongside me in that little room, the memory of which remains as vivid today, forty-four years later. It was life changing. Over the next few years, instead of avoiding all things missionary, which I had done for those three months, I started avidly to read the biographies referred to in the previous chapter.

After qualifying as a midwife and practising for a time, I went on to study theology, comparative religions and mission at what was then, in 1962, the Mount Hermon Missionary Training College in Ealing, London. It later amalgamated with its brother college, now All Nations Christian College.

It was during this time that Ray and I met each other. On both occasions we were attending conferences, one held at the University of Cambridge, the other at Oxford. I well remember the spartan conditions of the students' bedrooms in the early sixties. The furniture was basic, a bed, table, upright chair and a cupboard for clothes. I can't remember if there was even a chest of drawers. In the centre of the stone floor was a medium sized rug. It was so cold during the night that I picked it up and put it on top of the bedclothes.

Coiled up on top of the windowsill was a rope. Was this the chosen method for a forbidden lover to rendezvous with his beloved? But no, nothing so exciting. It was the means of a fire escape. Given the minimum of furniture and furnishings, I felt it would be safer and quicker to exit by the bedroom door in the event of a fire than to shin down the rope. I didn't have the athletic prowess that a number of students claimed! The cold and the chiming of the College clock kept me awake most of the night.

It was at the Oxford conference, September 1963, that I found myself meeting up with Ray. I was walking across the quadrangle on my way to the Refectory for breakfast. A tall dark-haired man in his early thirties drew alongside and engaged me in conversation. It was only a considerable time later, in fact two years later, that I discovered this meeting had been contrived!

Ray had first set eyes on me the previous spring at Cambridge, which was hardly surprising as my right leg was in plaster following a fracture of one of the metatarsals. According to his later confession he couldn't believe his luck when his eyes alighted on me that early autumn morning and this time without a 'white leg'! It was during breakfast I discovered he worked in the NHS specialising in haematology and bacteriology.

Over time the friendship developed. We were to discover many influences in our lives in fact ran parallel: a working life in the NHS, a move from the church denominations of our younger years into the Anglican Church and for both of us a facing up to the call of God to serve overseas.

It was at the Keswick Convention as a young man of eighteen that he responded to the challenge of God's call to be willing 'to go anytime, anywhere'. His response was not with a reluctance that mine had been initially. Also unlike me, Ray came from a family background of both medical and nursing careers.

While working as a medical laboratory technologist at the London Hospital, where his father had qualified as a doctor in 1928, Ray met Dr Andrew Forbat, who was visiting from India. As a result of this encounter, he applied for a post in the Ludhiana Christian Medical College. The post was to head up the laboratory team and more importantly to train Indians in pathology technology. There were two applicants for the job. In the end the other was appointed.

Interest in South America came later. There was an opening to work as an assistant to a doctor in Paraguay. This doctor's surgery, laboratory and dispensary were conducted from a motor launch. He travelled up and down the River Paraguay visiting the sick Indians in the tiny riverside settlements along the riverbank. However, this too wasn't to be. Instead Ray's life took a completely different direction. God's call led him into the ordained ministry in the Anglican Church. At the time no one was more surprised than Ray himself.

While continuing his laboratory work at the London Hospital, Ray was living in the community of the Mayflower Family Centre in London's Docklands and helping in the youth work. The Warden was David Sheppard: he was one time Captain of the English cricket team and became known as 'the Cricketing Parson'! For me then, he was only the incredibly handsome face that appeared as the 'Agony Uncle' of the *Woman's Own* magazine! Later he would become the Bishop of Liverpool.

Perhaps his greatest contributions to the church were his writings, his concern for the underprivileged and marginalised of society, and reaching across the divide of Roman Catholic/ Anglican relationships, notably with the late Derek Worlock, the then RC Archbishop of Liverpool.

With David's encouragement, Ray began the process towards ordination. David and his wife, Grace, would become good friends in the ensuing years and David would play a significant part in my own life very many years later.

It was while Ray was studying theology at the then London College of Divinity (LCD), now St John's, Nottingham, that we were to meet again at another conference, this time in London in January 1965. I was with a fellow student from college. Margaret and I had met up with some young ordinands we had been working with on a mission project from our respective colleges two years previously. It so happened their college was LCD. Interrupting the flow of conversation as we gathered in the foyer was a voice that came from behind me. 'Well. Well. Well, Gill, how nice to see you.'

I turned round and there was the dark-haired man, last seen over breakfast in Oxford! After we exchanged pleasantries, Ray said, 'I bet you can't guess what I'm doing now?' and before replying, he continued, 'I'm training for the Anglican Ministry!'

This next meeting was the beginning of our friendship blossoming into romance and later, love.

Chapter 4
Overseas on Hold

It was while I was working as a midwife, before meeting Ray and before starting theological training, that I became a worshipping member of the Anglican Church. It wasn't a sudden decision. Circumstances and a sense of God's direction over the previous year contributed to this.

In the late summer of 1962 I exchanged the delivering of babies for learning how to deliver sermons! September saw me installed in Ealing, London, at Mount Hermon Missionary Training College. The College was housed in a very large old house with extensive grounds, some of which had been reclaimed to provide space for the addition of a modern annexe. We numbered approximately thirty-plus students, with a resident staff of around five. Many of our lecturers were non-resident. It was during my first term that I had shared a room with Margaret, one of the heroines referred to in my second chapter. Margaret was from Glamorgan. She was quite short, with a character as gentle as her Welsh voice.

The curriculum consisted of Old and New Testament theology, Christian doctrine, church history, comparative religions, and Christian ethics. A few students, in addition, studied New Testament Greek. We also had a subject called homiletics. Here, once a term, we would have to present to the student body a talk, carefully prepared, and using established principles our lecturer had demonstrated. These principles were under three headings: Manner, Method and Material.

In the first we had to be aware of any potentially distracting habits: the taking on and off of glasses, the repetitive use of 'err' or 'umm', the fiddling with a necklace, or the constant changing from one foot on to the other, etc.

The second 'M' was how we actually presented the talk. What was the aim? Did we reach the goal? Was the introduction arresting? Were the headings for the main points clear? What about the application? Was the conclusion appropriate?

Three students, chosen at the beginning of the lecture, were allocated one of these headings. Their task was to offer constructive criticism of the talk under their assigned 'M'. This at times was a nerve-racking experience, but laid a good foundation for the future.

In addition to the academic side of training, each student was given a 'placement' in a church representing the different church denominations. This would enable us to have some small insight of the challenges faced in church leadership.

Alongside the curriculum were very practical tasks assigned, sometimes, from our angle, far from what we thought our training was all about! Getting up extra early to help on the breakfast team for one term, wasn't so bad, but cleaning out the dustbins once a week another term, well that was another story! At such times we encouraged one another with the words 'Well, it's all good GMT' (Good Missionary Training)!

About half of the students would later serve with mission societies abroad. Others would find their future in a variety of different openings in this country: teaching RE, youth work, joining the staff team of a church, administration in a home-based mission society. Some would find themselves marrying an ordained minister. Others would return to the lives they had left behind, the richer for their time at college.

There were certain requirements which, taken at face value, seemed unreasonable. Notable among these was that we were not to wear sleeveless dresses! I balked at this until it was explained that in a number of cultures some of the students would be going to, a woman completely baring her arms in public would be looked upon as immoral. Most of the time we would accept such reasoning with the comment 'GMT', sometimes said with a question mark intonation, at other times with an exclamation, depending on our own personal agenda! However, learning to be culturally sensitive was a good lesson to learn.

One student who has made a lasting impression on me was Maureen. She also trained as a nurse and midwife. I remember a particular afternoon we spent time together. I was Senior Student and she asked if we could have a chat. One look at her face warned me that not only was she unhappy, but she was also angry. I was right on both scores. She was rebelling at the restrictions certain rules in college life had imposed upon her and was threatening to leave. I don't remember now which particular ones they were or what I said. Being a bit of a rebel myself, I lent a listening ear. She didn't leave.

Maureen right up until recent years worked in Uganda and must hold the record for being the longest serving missionary abroad from among my contemporaries. She remained resolute in Idi Amin's reign of terror even when soldiers at gunpoint invaded the hospital and began looting. During this Ugandan dictatorship another Christian who stood firm, although it cost him his life, was Archbishop Janani Luwum.

Janani was contemporary with Ray at theological college. His statue is numbered with nine other Christian martyrs directly over the west front of Westminster Abbey. These ten statues designed by Tim Crawley stand as a reminder in the final century of a millennium, a century that witnessed more Christian martyrs than any one previously. Dr George Carey, Archbishop of Canterbury, unveiled the statues on July 9th 1998.

In the new millennium year Maureen was awarded the MBE.

For me, however, my future took an unexpected turn and serving overseas would go on the back burner. The question I kept asking myself was, why had I been so clearly led into the Anglican Church? After all, the mission society I was interested in was inter-denominational. It didn't make sense, unless, of course, my future would be in that direction. This questioning occupied my thinking over the summer months of 1963. My meeting Ray at the Oxford Conference that autumn did not, at this stage, throw any light on my dilemma. He was not then part of the equation!

During the next year, my final at college, the missing pieces of the jigsaw began to fall into place in the overall picture. An apparent chance remark by a vicar's wife turned out to be one of those missing pieces.

'Gill, have you ever thought of being a Lady Worker?'

'What on earth is that?' was my immediate response. It sounded awfully old fashioned, at the very least Victorian!

She went on to explain that an alternative name was Parish Worker, which certainly sounded better! This title described a calling to join the ordained staff of a parish in a lay capacity. It was full-time and would be paid by the Church Commissioners on the same scale as a first year curate.

'To test that calling, there would be a process to go through. Perhaps the first step might be to go on a special weekend with like minded people, also testing their calling,' she said, and then continued, 'There's one coming up soon, run by CPAS' (Church Pastoral Aid Society.) 'These special weekends are called "You and the Ministry" weekends.'

I went. The 'like minded people' were both men and women. The men were looking towards possible future ordination: the door to women's ordination was still firmly shut in the sixties. (This door swung open for me, thirty years later, when Bishop David Sheppard ordained me to the priesthood in Liverpool Cathedral on Trinity Sunday, 1995.)

Another piece of the jigsaw came some months later when I went before a Selection Board. To my initial consternation, later amusement, it was to be held at Grey Ladies, Blackheath! This only served to add to the feeling of such a bygone era. Would I be letting myself become fossilised in some museum of Anglican antiquity, with the passing of the years? In the event, although the surroundings were rather austere, the interviewing panel did try to put me at ease, in spite of the very, very long bare wooden table coming between interviewers and interviewee.

The most significant and totally unexpected outcome was that instead of having to do a further year's training at an Anglican theological college, as had been thought, I could take the remaining exams while working in the Parish. The gap in the jigsaw between the exploratory weekend and the Selection Board had been filled by an invitation from John Delight, vicar of St Christopher, Leicester (where I would worship during vacations at home) to join his staff team. This, of course, would depend on my acceptance by the Board, the Bishop of Leicester's approval and a positive response by the churchwardens and Church Council.

With both the College Diploma and the examinations of the University of London satisfactorily passed and successful interviews completed, I was licensed as Parish Worker to St Christopher, Leicester, September 1964.

Chapter 5
G.M.T. ... but not Greenwich

After two years in what was a somewhat sheltered environment, it was good to be back in a more normal setting. The challenge now was to apply the teaching and practical experience learnt at college in the nitty-gritty of every day life in the area the parish of St Christopher served. I shall always be grateful for my training as both nurse and midwife. Again and again over the years it has opened doors to people's inner lives that might have remained closed otherwise.

The original church building was a very simple construction, ideally suited to its surrounding environment. Later, with a new church building this then became the Church Hall. Today the church has been relocated a short distance away. An ultra-modern church building has been incorporated in the brand new Academy school – the first to do so in the country. For a parish church, serving its wider community, to be part and parcel of a school is an innovative example of bridge-building across a perceived divide.

The parish itself in the sixties consisted of approximately 9000 inhabitants. It was compact and almost exclusively residential.

About three-quarters of the residents lived in council properties. The Saffron Lane Estate had a reputation of being a 'dumping ground' for 'problem families'. A good number of them had been re-housed from the Wharf Street area in inner-city Leicester. During the war and post-war years this area was referred to as the 'slums'. I knew it well, although superficially, because in my childhood my parents, Elaine and I would visit regularly from our corner-shop home in Frog Island, at least weekly and frequently more often. I would usually walk the distance with my father. We both loved walking. It would take us well over half an hour. A memory that remains vivid is the splash of pink that would brighten up what was at best a less than scenic route and at worst a drab, dull experience, excepting the company.

'Daddy, look at those lovely flowers! I must take some back to Mummy on the way home!'

The 'pink' was none other than Rosebay Willow Herb. To a child with a love of beauty and colour, the weeds were indeed beautiful flowers. Although my father found it hard to hide his smile at my enthusiasm, he didn't disillusion me as to the true nature of these. 'Beauty in the eyes of the beholder' proved to be true both for the giver and the receiver of the bouquet, a bouquet presented on more than one occasion!

The reason we made these frequent trips was that Carley Evangelical Church was situated in the heart of the Wharf Street area. Connections with 'Carley', as it was affectionately known, spanned many generations in our family. Both my grandparents, on my maternal side, and great grandparents worshipped there. My own parents met and were married at Carley and it was here that Gladys Aylward made her visit when I was eleven.

Unlike my father, who had a deprived childhood, my mother was from a secure and happy middle-class background.

Grandma and Grandpa Cave lived only a twenty-minute walk from our home. Many a happy time was spent with them. I loved Grandpa very much, but he died when I was only eight. He was a good-looking man with wavy grey hair. His matching coloured moustache, which in younger years he waxed at both ends, was twisted into what resembled the handlebars of a bicycle. With his horn-rimmed glasses, out of which shone twinkling eyes, he wasn't easily forgotten. I used to love sitting on his knee and often he would sing to me. The song most associated with these special moments was one often sung in Sunday school in those days.

'There is sunshine in my soul today ... when Jesus shows his smiling face there is sunshine in my soul.' His Christian faith certainly shone from within his own soul.

Grandma Cave on the other hand, although kindly, was a little austere and I don't remember ever being hugged by her. My own mother, who was the eldest daughter in the family, was very close to my Grandpa. She told me how much she would confide in her father and ask him endless questions. However, when it was her mother's turn to be on the receiving end of the questions, Mummy would be met invariably with the same answer, 'Eh, I don't know. I don't know,' said with a simultaneous shake of the head.

The family history on my father's side is sparse as far as my knowledge is concerned.

His mother lived around the corner from 'Carley' but never went to church. She did not possess a personal Christian faith. In fact, sadly, she was an inadequate mother, loving the bottle more than her family. I only knew her superficially. Sometimes I would visit her, with my father, after the morning service.

To a child she seemed a cute little old lady with her snowy white hair and bright rosy cheeks. She was very deaf and a two-way conversation was impossible. With a shawl draped around her shoulders, sitting in a rocking chair, she would nod her head, her face wreathed in smiles. She seemed a harmless enough lady.

It would be a few years later, when I was older, that my father disclosed a darker side to this 'quaint' old lady. What left an indelible impression on my mind was my father recounting the night she stood by the window with a bottle of what she claimed was poison, threatening to take it if the 'boys' didn't behave. My father and the brother he was sharing the bed with lay screaming for her not to do so.

My paternal grandfather, William Williamson, had died when my father and his brother Ernie, and sisters, Mabel and Dorothy, were still young. Having been widowed, he had remarried. One of father's half-brothers, Cyril, nineteen years older, became a favourite uncle of mine, almost a substitute grandpa for the one I never knew. My father together with the younger brothers and sisters was taken into care, my father staying in the Countesthorpe Cottage Homes.

Those childhood visits on Sundays to the Wharf Street slums would find another connection fourteen years later when I joined the staff team at St Christopher's Church.

Within the parish was the Working Men's Club. John Delight, as vicar, would visit on a regular basis. One day, soon after my arrival, he said he would like me to accompany him so that I could meet members of the community who, by and large, we would not meet in the life of the church. It was a Saturday evening. The wives or girlfriends accompanied many of the men for the evening's cabaret. John and I were ushered to the wings of the centre stage in the hall. The evening's entertainment of singers and dancers having been in full flow, it was now our turn. I was petrified.

'Ladies and gentlemen. I have much pleasure in presenting to you our Padre,' said the MC. John walked on the stage to resounding clapping. Then after a few minutes I did the same, very conscious of the footlights shedding their beams on me from the stage floor.

Would they light-up my blushing? How many would see my knees knocking? Facing me a few feet below was a sea of faces almost hidden by the large pints of beer capped in an inch of froth. I spoke of my roots being in Leicester and my working as a nurse at the Leicester General Hospital, what brought me to St Christopher's and finally what my Christian faith meant in my life. The clapping that followed at the end of my brief stint was every bit as warm as John's had been. With the ordeal now over the two of us mingled for a time among the members.

Through the crowded room, a tall young man about my own age made his way towards me, a big smile on his face. He was accompanied by a couple of friends. As he towered above me, to my utter astonishment, he said 'Gillian,' which in itself was unusual as I had long since discarded my full name for its diminutive. 'Do you remember me? It's Albert … we were in Sunday school together.'

Here was living proof of the links of Wharf Street with the

Saffron Lane Estate in the heart of the parish. What thrilled me was the warmth with which he acknowledged me in front of his 'mates'. Considering I had been the only grammar school child in that class I felt the social divide had begun to be crossed all those years ago. This encounter was a huge encouragement at the beginning of a new role, even though he didn't return the visit to my stamping ground!

The salaried full-time staff team consisted of Vicar, Curate and Lady Worker (how I hated that title!). These times were not only immensely enjoyable and instructive, but also humorous and prayerful. They provided a safe environment in which to share fears and uncertainties of how to proceed in tricky pastoral situations. I had nothing but tremendous respect for both my more experienced work colleagues. One member of the congregation said to me one day, 'The reason why St Christopher's is such a united church is that it reflects the unity of the staff team.' I firmly believe this was due to such wise, loving yet firm leadership from the top.

John Delight truly lived up to his name. He was a deeply spiritual man with a great love for people both inside and outside the church. His integrity was closely matched by a sense of humour. He had arrived in Leicester together with his wife Eileen and his family of small children, from Manchester. Having been involved in Christian ministry among students (what was then known as IVF, the Inter-Varsity Fellowship) the contrast with St Christopher's Church couldn't have been greater. Under John's leadership the spiritual life of the congregation deepened, leadership potential was released and with that an increasing reaching out into the community.

David Shacklock was the curate. He was a tall, dark-haired, incredibly handsome young man in his late twenties. David had had both a public school background and army officer training at Aldershot. He was also a Cambridge graduate. It didn't leave much to the imagination to realise here was a potential match-making between Curate and Lady Worker for some of the older women in the congregation to engage in! However, it was to come not so much from the older members but from the younger.

Perhaps because of this, David and I were somewhat wary of one another initially. Over time the reserve dropped and a genuine friendship developed. John and David, together with another friend, Tricia, from St Christopher days, would in fact become godparents to two of our own children several years later.

Pastoral visiting around the parish was a top priority among my responsibilities. Not owning a car, my means of transport was more often than not a bicycle. One day on my way to make a number of visits, I was happily cycling along, when from nowhere appeared a dog who decided to give chase. I speeded up. So did the dog, yapping furiously at my exposed ankles. Its barking alerted other canine friends and from all directions they came, varying shapes and sizes, and descended upon me.

All hell broke loose. By this time curious homeowners opened front doors to see this amazing sight. I was not amused. In fact I was absolutely terrified. The faster I cycled the faster the dogs were in hot pursuit. All I could think of was, 'I must find a home I know.'

I did. I jumped off my bike, opened the front gate and once safely inside shut the gate firmly. My friends weren't in so I sat on their front doorstep until the dogs had disappeared and I had recovered my composure.

On recounting this story I was advised that in the event of a recurrence the best thing was to dismount and walk, as it was the cycling that attracted the dogs. I never forgot this advice.

This event, reminded me of my favourite poem in my schooldays, 'The Pied Piper of Hamelin' by Robert Browning:

Into the street the Piper stept,
…Then, like a musical adept,
To blow the pipe his lips he wrinkled,
And green and blue his sharp eyes twinkled,
… And ere three shrill notes the pipe uttered,
You heard as if an army muttered;
And the muttering grew to a grumbling;
And the grumbling grew to a mighty rumbling;
And out of the houses the rats came tumbling;
Great rats, small rats, lean rats, brawny rats,

Brown rats, black rats, grey rats, tawny rats,
... Followed the piper for their lives.

John had encouraged me to get involved in an area of pastoral ministry with young mothers, many of whom were single parents. This resulted in a little weekday service called the Nursery Service. A handful of mothers pushing prams or pushchairs would cross the threshold of the church building for these occasions. Although not a mother myself, I felt being a midwife stood me in good stead. In addition, one project I had chosen at Mount Hermon, as another of my practical assignments, had been a weekly visit to a residential home for unmarried mothers. I witnessed the heartbreak of some of these single women, many of whom were teenagers, as they gave their babies up for adoption. It was to be good GMT for the days ahead.

David had, among his responsibilities, the oversight of the church youth. They were a lovely bunch of young people. But a new challenge confronted the congregation. How could the church reach out to the teenagers who hung around the streets bored to death? This boredom led a number of them into mindless acts of vandalism. The church windows being a favourite target!

It was decided to turn the church cellar into a coffee bar. David, Tricia, and I would work together, ably helped by the church young people. The only rules laid down were no alcohol and, because of fire risks in the cellar with only one exit, no smoking. In addition they were expected to stay for the closing three-minute talk on Christian teaching at the end of the evening. Little by little, the teenagers, a number of whom had already been in remand homes, came along on Friday nights.

Two brothers, one of whom was the gang leader, had both had police convictions and spent time on remand. Slowly bridges of friendship and confidence were built. These were not constructed without personal cost. David on one occasion ended up with a very black eye. The church young people, who were immensely committed, were often on the butt end of disparaging remarks.

Although Tricia and I were never physically threatened, there were times of verbal abuse.

On one occasion I felt very intimidated. One of the lads deliberately lighted a cigarette in full view of me, when he knew David wasn't around.

'Pete, put your cigarette out please.'

Silence.

'Pete, put your cigarette out please.' More silence accompanied by a long, deliberate, inhaling of the cigarette while a long eye-to-eye contact between the two of us ensued. I was anxious but determined to hold my authority. With a quick silent arrow prayer for protection and eye contact maintained throughout, my voice sounding to me as if detached from my body, I heard myself say emphatically, 'I said put it out.' Slowly he withdrew the cigarette from his mouth. I waited for the blow to follow. It never did. He quietly climbed the steps from the cellar and there was no further problem and he still continued to come.

I recall John telling us how difficult he found it to go to the Working Men's Club. He felt he was going into 'alien' territory. This was hard to believe given his warm, easy manner, but he firmly believed the mandate of Christ to go where people were to be found with the good news of the love of God. The crossing into so-called 'alien' territory was of course true in reverse. How 'alien' church culture is for those not accustomed to going, every bit as formidable. With the staff and those involved in such outreach modelling, the congregation slowly began to adjust its own thinking towards accepting the more challenging members of the community.

One memorable Sunday this was to be put to the test. John was about a third of the way into his evening sermon. Suddenly our attention was diverted. Down the centre aisle of the church marched seven or eight teenagers. Yes. The 'coffee bar kids' had arrived and had crossed into the 'alien' territory of a worship service! They went to the very front row, took out cigarettes, but didn't actually light them. John carried on as if nothing unusual was taking place. After no more than three or four minutes, at a given signal from their leader, they stood up as one man and marched right down the aisle and out of the church doors.

Although in the comparatively short time I was at St Christopher's, I don't remember them ever coming to a Sunday service again, although they did start coming to a Sunday evening for youth after the evening service.

There was one particular blond curly-haired lad called Colin Tudge, known as 'Tudgy'. He and I related well to one another, so much so that I would visit him occasionally in his own home. Away from peer pressure, sometimes he would ask me questions relating to the Christian faith. I was highly amused when one day he told me what his father had said about me.

'I like Miss Williamson 'cos she's proper cultivated!' I didn't put him right.

How very sad I felt, when a few years later a letter arrived for me, when I was married and living in the East End of London. It was from John in which he told me that 'Tudgy' had been killed in a motorbike accident. Enclosed was a newspaper cutting and staring up at me was the face of a teenager who had occupied a very special place in my heart.

Inevitably a gang of girls were in tow of the lads. We had no trouble with their behaviour. They would come round to my bed-sit and we would chat. On one occasion I was talking to them about the dangers of drugs, although in the early sixties we didn't encounter drug taking on the scale it is today. Suddenly, Kathy's eyes began to fill with tears. When questioned as to why I might have upset her, she answered, 'I'm not upset, Miss Williamson. You must really care about us to warn us of the dangers.' It was now my eyes that began to fill with tears.

Was the work among these, in many ways deprived, young people a success? If we were to look for tangible results of radically changed lives at the time, we would have had to admit it didn't appear so. Only time and even more importantly eternity would reveal just how successful it had been.

All too often in this deprived area, a legacy of inadequate parental role modelling, handed down would often be repeated in ensuing generations.

A television programme released in 2001 indicated that there were few lasting positive results. It was entitled 'Lifters' – based on the 'Saff', the Saffron Lane Estate. It was about a gang of shoplifters operating like a mafia, all over the country. The greater success was what the challenge of bringing Christ to those easily marginalized, both by society in general and the church in particular, did for those of us involved, especially our own church young people.

By far the most significant event for me in these years was my marriage. Ray was by now at theological college and the friendship begun on the occasions we bumped into one another at different conferences had developed into love. We were only to meet on average monthly due to our commitments. When visiting me in Leicester he would stay with my friend Tricia and they would sit together in church, invariably tongues began to wag.

Most people thought, quite naturally, that there was a new man in Tricia's life. We didn't enlighten them, for a time. The young people were let into the secret on the understanding that they kept it under wraps.

One weekend, while away on a youth weekend with David, they decided to write a little poem. The instigator was a very mischievous, young woman named Barbara. It would be some time later before I knew of this poem.

Our Lady Worker's quite a rave.
We tried to palm her off with Dave.
Dave got frit [sic] and ran away
So now she's going out with …?

Evidently they refrained from saying the naturally rhyming 'Ray' as they were sworn to secrecy!

When subsequently my engagement to Ray was announced, a regular member of the Young Wives Group wasn't in church that Sunday. A couple of days later, having heard on the grapevine that I was engaged, she came up to me.

'Gill. Congratulations. I always knew you and David would make a wonderful couple.'

'Oh,' I replied, 'I'm not engaged to David.'

Her face was a picture. 'Well, whom are you engaged to?'
I told her.

My mother and father were absolutely delighted with our news as they had become very fond of Ray in the comparatively short time they had known him. This was to be not only the first wedding in our immediate family, but in fact the only one as Elaine never married.

On the morning of Saturday, March 26th 1966 I woke up to a thin film of snow on the ground. It was my Wedding Day. St Christopher's Church was packed. John and David took the Marriage Ceremony between them. A longstanding Christian leader in the Boy Covenanter movement, 'Skipper' Pinchback gave the address. Mingling among the crowd of friends and relatives were a dozen or so unconventionally dressed young folk, every bit as welcome!

From this memorable day onwards my story would become our story as we began to respond to our calling together.

Our early months of married life proved to be quite challenging. There was still so much we didn't know about each other. We had, in fact, only met in person about a dozen times since the January 1965 conference in London, including our engagement in September of the same year and our marriage in the following spring. Ray was, by now, thirty-five and had lived a bachelor's life of considerable independence, although there had been quite a number of girlfriends over these years! I was just three weeks short of my twenty-seventh birthday the day we were married, with a track record of a few young men in my life: not so many boyfriends as he had had girlfriends, given his earlier start! So many adjustments, that other couples make pre-marriage, had to be faced and conquered in those early days, with varying degrees of both success and failure.

The first time I tackled washing Ray's socks was a total disaster and he wasn't amused! Not realising the majority of them were more woollen than synthetic, I threw them into the washing machine. At the end of the cycle out came eight or nine pairs of socks more suited to the patter of tiny feet that would appear from the next year onwards!

I remember our first row! It happened in the early weeks of our engagement. I don't recall what it was about, but what I do remember was the ensuing argument. It centred round the fact that Ray felt we should be of one mind on this particular matter and try as I would I didn't agree. He wanted to be able to use the 'royal we' and I felt unable to do so. It ended with me saying rather heatedly. 'I don't agree and in any case you can't swamp my personality in yours,' or words to that effect.

We have recently celebrated thirty-six years of married life with its attendant joys and sorrows, laughter and tears, hurts and reconciliations, strengths and weaknesses, health and sickness, romance and non-romance, working together and working apart; in fact all the various ingredients which make up a realistic married life. Underpinning our life together has been our joint belief in a God who said right at the beginning of human existence, 'It is not good for man to be alone. I will make a helper suitable for him.'[1]

Straight after our marriage we moved into rented accommodation in Little Chalfont, Buckinghamshire, while Ray finished his theological training at LCD. Our honeymoon had been deferred until the following July. It was spent with more than twenty young men and a handful of women! With a mischievous glint in my eye, I would share this fact with friends who knew me well.

Ray had given me a choice prior to our wedding. 'Gill, what would you prefer? We have the opportunity of going to Israel and Jordan with students from College. One of the tutors will accompany us together with fiancées and girlfriends. However, if we go it will mean there won't be any extra money for some needed furniture.' Given such a choice there was no hesitation on my part. It was to be the travel and proved to be an unforgettable experience. It was a year before the historic Seven-Day War.

In 1966 to travel to both Israel and neighbouring Jordan two passports were needed. The one for Israel only had to be handed in before leaving for Jordan. Israel was not recognised by her Arab neighbour and Jerusalem was still a divided city.

---

[1] The Bible: Genesis chapter 2 verse 18

Walking through the Mandelbaum Gate and then into no-man's land before reaching the Jordanian border was an eerie feeling. It comprised a stretch of barren, uncultivated land about thirty metres in length, quite narrow in width, and surrounded by barbed wire. Border guards with machine guns patrolled either end.

This trip was not only memorable for its, current recent history, but even more for bringing its ancient history to life. Eminent experts in their field, linking Biblical truth with archaeological discoveries, gave lectures. We visited many of these sites.

Our visit to Israel was even more memorable for us as it was here that our first child was conceived.

Naomi Grace made her entrance into the world April 25th the following year. Naomi is a Hebrew name and means 'a delight' and she still is!

As soon as we returned from our belated honeymoon in Israel and the grand finale to Ray's theological training, it was time to pack up home and move. The problem was that, unlike Ray's contemporaries, he didn't have a post to go to immediately. So we moved in with the in-laws, in Loughton, Essex. We couldn't afford to pay for removals so decided that Ray would make a couple of journeys between Loughton and Little Chalfont with a car full. As the house in Little Chalfont was rented fully furnished this wasn't so formidable. The problem confronting us was, 'What shall we do with my bike?' Being a cyclist all my life and having clocked up on occasions up to seventy miles in a day, I decided to cycle it over.

Philip Ward, a contemporary of Ray's who lived nearby, was also helping with the transporting of household goods. When he arrived at our rented home to load up and discovered I had left on my bike, he immediately came in search of me. I had only gone a few miles when he caught up with me. Not accepting my protestations he put my bicycle into his van and with me at his side drove me to the in-laws. I was both grateful and relieved, as I was very tired and unbeknown to me then, was in fact pregnant.

According to most experts on marriage, living with the in-laws was not to be recommended! We were to prove them wrong. Initially, however, I did have natural misgivings not really knowing them very well.

The rest of Ray's siblings with the exception of his younger sister, Chris, were by now not only married but already parents.

Would his mother prove to be possessive of her eldest son? What about his father? I knew, as a greatly respected GP and leading figure within the Gospel Chapel in Woodford, Essex, he had high standards for a suitable match for his eldest son.

Would he accept me, warts and all?

I needn't have worried on either score. They took me to their hearts and into their home with great generosity of spirit.

It seemed there was an aura surrounding Doctor Smith, affectionately referred to as 'Doc' by those who knew him well. He was a man with great integrity, strong Christian faith and a servant heart, and I loved him dearly. However, there was a tendency by family, friends and acquaintances to put him on a pedestal. The understanding shown to his patients on their visits to the surgery at times evaporated when a family member was unwell! He could be quite dismissive of sickness within the family.

Many a time he and I would walk out together, my arm linked through his, wrapped in deep conversation. This habit of soul-to-soul conversation would be continued through the years when on home leave from Chile and right up to his final years. Ray's mother was to remark one day some years later when Ray and I were visiting them, 'I don't know what it is, Gill, but as soon as you arrive David wants to go out for a walk with you!'

Our conversations would range from theology and medicine, to family and current world affairs. The discussions with my father-in-law were what I was unable to do with my own father, although I did with my mother. No doubt this same inclination to avoid the trivia in conversation was why he and my mother also got on so very well. I remember him saying to me one day, 'You know, Gill, there are very few people I can talk to on Biblical truth like I can with your mother.'

Only once do I recall we had a sharp disagreement and I challenged him. He became angry. I don't remember what it was about, but his anger on the rare occasions he displayed it, was in itself most awesome!

The generosity of spirit of Ray's parents showed itself in a remarkable way in those early months of married life. Furniture Ray had as a child was given a face-lift as I set to transforming it from its green paint, to an agreed primrose yellow and white. This was to be in readiness for our first baby. It was late autumn and my mother-in-law graciously handed over part of the large kitchen to be used as a paint workshop! Something I could never have done! Two Lloyd-loom wicker chairs, a wardrobe and a kidney-shaped dressing table as well as a chest of drawers took it in turns to stand on the layers of newspaper spread out across the floor.

The transformation was completed well in time for Christmas preparations and before we moved to London's East End in February two months before Naomi's birth.

Mother Smith was never happier than when working in the kitchen. We had a good arrangement. I would prepare breakfast, which was a cooked one, and dinner three or four evenings a week, while Ray's mother was responsible for daily lunch and the remaining dinners. This worked very well until it came to the washing up. There was no such luxury as a dishwasher. I'd already heard from Ray about the mountain of washing-up he would do, when living at home, ably helped by his father. The price of being the eldest! Now it was my turn to face this incredible phenomenon! There was no doubt in my mind that although the cooking and cleaning were fairly distributed, in this other respect I had the lion's share!

How on earth did she manage to produce so much? While busy on the furniture, sneaking glances to the far side of the kitchen over the weeks provided me with some of the answer.

In my peripheral vision I observed a short, plump woman, hair up in a bun with a rosy complexion, humming happily as she weighed this ingredient and that. Then came the stage of mixing them together. It was during this process I found the clue to discovering the answer to my question. As she put the spoon, with which she was mixing, down, it alighted on a plate. The plate was clean. A little time later another spoon, not the original one, went through the same procedure and landed on another unused plate. The spoon then found its way into a clean bowl. This was repeated a number of times and inwardly I groaned as once again I faced the reality of father-in-law and myself walking out of the kitchen, after our marathon, at around three-thirty.

Having demolished 'the mountain' we would move into the lounge, in company with the two cats, Mitzy and Pepys, and would snatch a much-deserved rest before father-in-law left for his afternoon surgery. It was during such a rest time, with feet propped up on a stool that I felt for the first time the 'fluttering' of our first baby. Something I'll never forget.

Perhaps it was the time we would spend together over the kitchen sink that provided the catalyst for Ray's father and my many and varied conversations.

The most difficult part of the washing up, however, wasn't exclusively the quantity but the quality. Burnt saucepans were a fairly regular occurrence. I was intrigued to learn mother-in-law's tried and tested method of dealing with these. Into the bottom of the saucepan was placed scouring powder, Vim or Ajax, covered by a little water. The saucepan was then put on the gas ring on a low light and allowed to simmer for up to an hour. It certainly did make our later task a little easier. What puzzled me was that if the paste of water and powder responded to being simmered, why on earth was the cabbage, and it was invariably the cabbage, cooked at full blast of flame in the first place? But then lunchtime washing up was not mother-in-law's part of the deal!

An even larger heart superseded Ray's mother's large frame. Like my own mother both were known for their wonderful cooking and generous hospitality.

Like my own parents too, my in-laws' Christian faith was an integral part of their everyday life. It was a privilege to spend those six months in their home and to discover that the inevitable minor irritations were more than compensated for by the genuine love experienced.

Chapter 6
Living among the Cockneys

Every child of our generation knew the nursery rhyme 'Oranges and Lemons', based on the bells of the various churches in London's East End. We moved into 10, Hoxton Square, Shoreditch in February 1967. Ray would be ordained at St Paul's Cathedral the following June and would serve his curacy in a parish of both fame, and as we would later discover, infamy. It was none other than the church of 'When I grow rich say the bells of Shoreditch.' We're still waiting for these prophetic words to come true!

St Leonard's Church was founded in the tenth century and later became known as 'The Actors' Church'. Shoreditch boasts of being home to the first permanent playhouse of London, known as 'The Theatre'. It was here that Shakespeare spent many of the most impressionable years of his life; years in which he worked out his apprenticeship in the 'drama' against a background of the contrasts of an Elizabethan city. In a brief 'History of Shoreditch', written for the church, those former days were described as ones of 'violent contrasts, of magnificence and squalor, of intellectual grandeur and extraordinary cruelty'. These were influences that would be enacted out again and again in his plays.

The present building of St Leonard dates from 1740 AD. Its architect was George Dance senior, a pupil of Sir Christopher Wren, better known for his design of the Mansion House. The church stands prominently at the junction where four main roads of East London meet – Shoreditch High Street, Old Street, Kingsland Road and Hackney Road.

Hoxton Square was tucked away, just around the corner from

Old Street. Our flat was on the top floor of what had been, in the second half of the nineteenth century, a fashionable home.

James Parkinson, who first described the disease later to bear his name, was born at 1 Hoxton Square on April 11th 1755. He practised here for forty years and was a regular worshipper at St Leonard's Church. After his death in December 1824, he was buried in the churchyard.

In the 1960s office workers and carpenters occupied most of the buildings in the Square by day. There were few permanent residents: the pub owners, the Roman Catholic priests in the presbytery on the adjacent side to where we were living, the Vicar of St Leonard's and his house full of young professional men and women. These, a number of whom were medical students at St Bartholomew's Hospital, became a willing and available source of babysitters for us over the next few years.

Furniture making, with expert French polishing, was the chief trade undertaken by our daytime neighbours including our immediate ones. As a result fire was an occupational hazard. We had two during our time in Shoreditch. The less serious one was next door: the other was between the pub and the presbytery and completely gutted the building. On both occasions Ray wasn't at home. Fortunately both happened in the day and not at night.

There was a single staircase in the whole of our building. We lived fifty-six stairs up, with only one exit door down to the floor below. On the landing at this lower level was an escape door leading to a flat roof. This was still an awfully long way from street level.

At times I would lie awake devising our means of escape. Without a coiled rope, as in the Cambridge College, I worked out how we might tie together enough sheets anchored somehow to our king-size bed and shin down to safety!

The fire station on Old Street was, thankfully, just around the corner, its activity incessant. Fire and police sirens took the place of birds in this part of London, except the former were heard by night as well as by day.

Other sounds by night were less expected, as one never-to-be-forgotten night within weeks of our arrival in the East End revealed. I was well advanced in my first pregnancy and was making my by now customary visit to the toilet. It was still dark. I had only been sitting on the loo seat a few seconds and was still half-asleep when a sound of banging reached my ears. In my semi-comatose state it took me a few seconds to realise that this was somewhat unusual at around two in the morning. It would have to take a very dedicated carpenter to come in to work at that time of night.

Standing on the lavatory seat, I peered out of the fanlight window. The half-light, radiating from a security light, revealed a man standing on the near side of the forecourt of a factory warehouse. He was facing the exit, which led into the Square, an alleyway separating the forecourt of this factory from our block of offices. Under the street light near our Catholic neighbours was another man. He was smoking, while frequently looking around. The two men were facing one another at a distance of several yards. No words appeared to pass between them.

Within seconds of the banging stopping, a third man emerged from the warehouse door, complete with gloves and crow bar in his right hand. He communicated briefly with the first man, who, in turn, gave the thumbs up to the smoker, then disappeared back inside. The banging recommenced.

In a loud whisper I hissed at Ray in the bedroom,'Ray, quick! Come here quickly!' Ray then joined me on the lavatory seat as we both looked through the fanlight window, a description that caused amusement when I later gave evidence in court. 'Something's not right,' said Ray, in the understatement of the year! 'I'm calling the police.' While he was dialling 999, I remained glued to the window.

Within an incredibly short time, a policeman on a 'noddy' bike (a motor scooter) shot down the alleyway and gave chase to the two men, both of whom, with the sound of police car sirens approaching, had made a dash for it.

Meantime the third man made a rapid exit from the forecourt of the warehouse, only slowing his pace on reaching the Square. A police car, blue lights flashing, siren wailing, swept into the Square from the opposite corner. I learned later in court that on being questioned as to what he was doing out at that time of morning had replied that he'd 'had a tiff with his girlfriend and was out taking the night air'!

I was the chief witness for the prosecution. Being unwilling to divulge my address in court, I had no problem in being known as 'Mrs Smith', assuming that with such a surname my anonymity would remain! They all received a custodial sentence.

The infamy referred to previously, was the work of a pair of notorious crooks. They headed up an East End 'mafia' and held immense power in London's underworld. They were wanted for murder.

On a dawn raid one morning, the police swooped on a home just around the corner from us and arrested Ronald and Reggie Kray! It seemed that on getting a tip off, the Kray twins had chosen a home in Shoreditch to go into hiding. We were, thankfully, quite oblivious to the presence of such famous, or rather, infamous near neighbours.

East Enders were very likeable people with their own unique culture. It wasn't long before we made friends and came to value immensely their genuine warmth and generosity. Their big heartedness would at times show itself in an extravagance that to many an onlooker new to 'Cockney Land' seemed flamboyant and over-the-top.

A funeral cortège, especially when the deceased was the mother, was an amazing sight. The mother in an East End family was very much the 'queen bee'. The black of mourning clothes was in sharp contrast to the over abundance of brightly coloured flowers making up the very many wreaths. Displayed through the back window of the passing hearse, in place of prominence, for all onlookers to see would be the largest wreath of all. Framed in the centre were the boldest and most colourful flowers spelling out the words 'Our Mum'. On one such funeral Ray was to take, he counted thirty-two wreaths.

One Cockney friend, Sandra (who had had a slight brush with the law), described her fellow Cockneys to me as 'open, if not always honest'! One day I happened to mention that Ray and I were looking to buy a second hand TV and like a flash,

Sandra responded, 'I'll get you one.' On seeing my immediate look of concern, she went on to say, 'Promise you, Gill, it won't be a nicked one!'

For Ray, living in Shoreditch was in many ways a 'home from home'. London's Cockneys had first endeared themselves to him while working in the London Hospital on Whitechapel Road, and sharing in the life of the Mayflower Centre in the Docklands.

Our three children were all born in our three and a half years in Hoxton Square. Only Andrew and Julian can claim to be true Cockneys as they were born at St Bartholomew's Hospital and came under 'the sound of Bow Bells'. Naomi was born at Edgware Hospital, where I had worked as a midwife.

The mixed blessing of joy and disappointments that family life can bring finds its counterpart in the Christian family. It was here that, for me in particular, God's call all those years back would be put to the test. It was the certainty that God had called a most reluctant follower that became the anchor that held me in the emotional turbulence that followed. This was to be GMT at the cutting edge and the 'cuts' hurt!

The long haul up the fifty-six stairs to the door of our flat was not conducive to a young woman facing three pregnancies and with 'piles' (haemorrhoids) thrown in for good measure on these occasions! Because of security, the front door on the street was more often than not kept locked. For the only other occupants, their office, being on the ground floor, this didn't present a problem. The intervening floors were not occupied when we first moved in.

Doorbells in the homes of both vicars and curates seem to ring endlessly, only overtaken by the more frequent ring of the telephone. Our bells were no exception. As the former usually rang when Ray was out on parish matters, concern for his often-pregnant wife having a daily marathon of climbing-training, meant that something had to be done. Between us we decided that it had to be a case of,

'If the hill [mountain] will not come to Mahomet,
Mahomet will go to the hill [mountain]'.[1]

---

[1] Francis Bacon: Essays (1625) 'Of Boldness'

When the doorbell at street level rang, I would go into the bedroom and open the sash-cord window. Remembering advice about the dangers of sash cords breaking, I would stick my head outside, and with one hand carefully supporting the window (not wishing to enact a scene from the French Revolution) would see who the caller was. If known to me, I would shout out, 'Watch out! I'm throwing the key down. Let yourself in. I'll open our front door.' If, however, it was a stranger, the marathon began. With a toddler in one hand and a baby cradled in my free arm, we would descend the fifty-six stairs only to climb them again a little later.

The answer to many a pregnant woman's prayer came during my pregnancy with Naomi. Mothercare, the first baby/child supermarket, had opened its door, but in the early years slings for carrying babies, strapped to their mother, were not in vogue. By the time Andrew was a toddler we did invest in a canvas seat on an aluminium frame carried on the back.

The climbing process was a regular occurrence until my third pregnancy, by which time we had exchanged the 'mountain top' lodging for a 'valley'. The process then was in reverse. Instead of starting off at street level ascending we actually began by descending. We had moved into the basement of the same building. Eight outside steps took us down from street level! 10A Hoxton Square had in its fairly recent history been used in part as a coal cellar!

One of our furniture making neighbours was horrified that such a young family was moving into the basement, even though it had been modernised. For us, however, our last year was by far our happiest, as we were now living in relative luxury. Upstairs we had been plagued with damp. On one wall in the children's bedroom were patches of dark green grey mould.

Sadly, the vicar, under whose leadership Ray was being trained, was less than sympathetic. He was still a bachelor in our first two years and had been an officer in the Dragoon Guards. This background prepared him well in developing strategy for growth in what was in many ways a pioneering situation in the church. Under his leadership we saw the congregation begin to increase. Today a number of those to be found in Christian ministry first responded to God's call while worshipping at St Leonard, Shoreditch. Nevertheless, for this young family, when after asking for the umpteenth time for something to be done about the damp, to be told, 'Well, when I was a curate in … I had rats running under the roof,' was small consolation. Nothing was done. In fact it was only the subsequent move downstairs that saw the resolution of the problem for us.

The pressures and difficulties of these living conditions in those first two years was GMT in the raw. Added to the sheer physical demands were the emotional and spiritual challenges of strained relationships. 'If my brother wrongs me,' said Peter, the disciple, to Jesus, 'how often should I forgive him? Seven times?' Then came the challenging answer of Jesus, 'Seventy times seven.' I didn't pass the test. That would be only towards the end of our three years.

Other questions came into my mind. What about God's call to us? Why was this happening? Had we got it all wrong? Alongside this we had to learn (and this lesson would regularly need to be re-applied) that with the call of God and the very many accompanying blessings, there was no guarantee that things would go smoothly. How often this phrase is used in prayer as if we have an automatic right to escape the pressures and difficulties of life. Like steel, faith is strengthened under pressure. Did we always have that quality of faith? No.

An even more important lesson to be learnt and one taking a lifetime to apply is that it didn't all depend on *our* faith but rather on a God who is faithful and can be trusted. What kept us on track was that in our heart of hearts we had an unshakeable belief that God had called us.

Out of loyalty it wasn't possible to share the depths of our problems with friends within the congregation but the vicar and his wife in the adjoining parish were a wonderful support. They provided not only a listening ear, but also very real practical help with the family. It was hard not having parents nearby. I had only passed my driving test shortly before marrying and didn't feel confident enough to drive through London without Ray, with a toddler, a baby and/or a pregnancy. The day Julian was born we actually had three children under three! The following day Naomi celebrated her third birthday.

Other listening ears were those of David and Grace Sheppard who were horrified at our living conditions, as was Canon Harry Sutton of SAMS (South American Mission Society), who said on a visit to us, 'Even the missionaries in the Chaco [the poorer regions of northern Argentina and Paraguay] live in better conditions.'

There were, however, both encouragements and lasting friendships. Notably among these were a young cockney couple, Dave and Janet. They were to be married. The doorbell rang one evening. Ray went down the long flight of stairs and there standing a few steps up from street level outside the front door was a hesitant, very nervous young couple. They had arrived for the initial interview. It took a cup of tea and general conversation before they began to relax.

Early on in the proceedings Dave was still very much on the defensive. Although they were requesting a church wedding, at Ray's suggestion that they attended the Sunday services before the wedding, like a shot Dave replied, 'You wouldn't find me dead going into that church!'

A short programme of preparation for the next two or three weeks was discussed with them. We spent more time just chatting before the evening came to an end. Just as they were on the way downstairs, Dave turned and said, 'What time did you say the service was?'

'Eleven o'clock.'

'We'll be there.' They were.

By crossing the busy junction where the imposing church building stood, they crossed an even bigger divide. The perceived prejudice that church going was only for the middle classes was crossed that first Sunday for Dave. Together they started coming regularly and so began for them their faith journey, which continues to this day. In time we were invited to be godparents to their first son. Dave and Janet still live in the East End.

For Ray and me a divide of another nature began to be crossed in our time in Shoreditch. This would have implications later, when living in Chile. It began as a protest to a remark made to Ray. He was making a hospital visit and as he and an Anglican colleague were approaching a staircase, a Roman Catholic priest was on his way down. The clergyman colleague turned to Ray and in a whisper said, 'Watch out here comes the enemy!' Ray was horrified, as was I, on his recounting the incident to me later. This became the catalyst for us going out of our way to befriend our Roman Catholic neighbours.

One day the priests invited us to the presbytery for lunch. Naomi and Andrew were with us. The furniture in the dining room was pretty basic. In a short time our kindly host showed us to our seats. After a blessing we sat down, a child on either side, the four or five priests occupying the remaining chairs. In the corner of the room, was what appeared to be a small, built-in cupboard, at waist level. Our host at the sound of a bell walked over to the 'cupboard' and on opening the doors put his hands inside. He then began to pull on a rope that was hanging inside the empty space behind the doors. Up came our lunch on a wooden lift!

On emptying the food containers on to the table the bell was rung again. With a small shudder the little wooden lift of two shelves, responded to a tug of the rope, operated from, the basement kitchen. Why, oh why hadn't we thought of getting a similar device installed in Number 10 but on a somewhat bigger scale?

The children were absolutely fascinated. This kept them entertained for a time in what turned out to be an extremely prolonged lunch. Soon, however, boredom began to set in. To help alleviate this, one priest produced a small ball, as a diversion. Andrew, who later proved to be very adept with a larger ball and with his feet, reached out with his hands and grabbed the ball. This was much more fun!

He then threw it across the table. All childhood training on how to behave at the table went out of the window, but not the ball, unfortunately! The game continued until Andrew, not yet two years scored his very first goal. The ball landed in a glass of water, shooting the contents all over the table! Once again Andrew scored.

The bell rang again and with the final course arriving, the match was over, before Andrew had a chance to score a hat-trick! The final score of the friendly game was two nil to the Protestants!

Chapter 7
South America on the Horizon

One day the telephone rang with an amazing request. It came quite out of the blue.

The voice at the other end was that of Canon Harry Sutton, the General Secretary of SAMS. 'Would you consider going out to the Chaco region of northern Argentina for up to a year?'

The purpose of this request was to enable Dr Michael Patterson and his family to take a much needed home leave. Our initial reaction was one of great enthusiasm. It was decided that he would come over to No.10 to talk over exactly what was on offer. It was on this visit that he remarked on our living conditions.

Harry Sutton was a real extrovert with a wonderful sense of humour. To say he exuded both optimism and enthusiasm would be an understatement. It simply poured out from him. He was a Liverpudlian, middle-aged, with thin white hair, and wore spectacles on his round, jovial face. In time he was warned, following a coronary heart attack, to slow down. That was the last thing he was prepared to do. He kept incredibly active until his death in 1993, at the age of seventy-seven.

As he began to recount the nature of the work involved, it became obvious to both of us that his enthusiasm had somewhat run away with him! Our combined medical qualifications were no replacement for a doctor.

We did approach him with the possibility of longer-term involvement with the Society in another role.

'How old are you, Ray?'

'Thirty-nine.'

'I'm afraid your age would be against you in the long term.'

In the sixties, mission personnel, it seemed, began their initiation and training in their twenties and early thirties.

Once again it seemed the door to overseas work was firmly shut and we reluctantly concluded that the remaining years of ministry would be in the UK. God had other things in store. No wonder he has been referred to as the 'God of Surprises'.

With South America now on the back burner, we busied ourselves with life in the parish, with the family and the move downstairs to No 10A. Then one day, just under a year later, a letter from Argentina awakened once again this now latent desire.

Jeanne Carter, who was a contemporary of mine at Mount Hermon, was working with SAMS in the north of that Republic. In her letter she said how the Society required new personnel to church plant in Brazil and she thought we might just be the couple needed to join a team! As we prayed about this, and recalled from our earlier biographies the men and women who hadn't taken 'no' for an answer, we decided to approach the Mission again.

Within six weeks of moving downstairs we had our formal interview with SAMS. We were subsequently accepted and Ray was by now forty! Harry Sutton suggested, however, that our particular gifts and experience would be better used in a pioneer work in the Argentinian City of Rosario.

Once Ray had finished his curacy, ahead of us lay a three-month orientation course at SAMS headquarters in Tunbridge Wells. Imagine our thoughts then, when within two weeks of acceptance, we discovered that our third child was due the following spring! Our 'little Mexican', as the midwives called Julian, was born on April 24th 1970 at 'Bart's'. He was so nicknamed due to his very dark hair, complete with sleek sideburns and due to a touch of neo-natal jaundice, his skin looked tanned. They had no idea of our interest in all things Latin American!

The summer was spent sorting out what we would sell, and what few things would go into store with family and friends. The rest would be packed for shipment to South America once we knew where we were going.

Our Morris Traveller car began a regular trip to a warehouse down by the Dagenham Docks. Into the back of our car, affectionately referred to as 'Fagoo' after its FGU registration, we first rolled, then lifted, two reconditioned oil drums. Each was about four feet high and came complete with a lid-locking device. Ray made four return journeys in all.

Plenty of help from willing parishioners followed. The challenge lay in packing, not the usual oblong case or trunk, although there were a number of these, but in filling up a four foot high cylinder! All innovative skills were mustered. A particular cockney friend, Betty, who was hardly five feet tall, had to stand on a small stool to reach the bottom of the drum. She nearly fell in head first! We had visions of her emerging, several months later, on the far-flung shores of the River Plate dividing Argentina and Uruguay!

Esme Russell offered to come over and help me pack up our breakables. A professional packer had taught her the method. Together with her husband, Paul, they were on home leave from Chile, where they were serving with SAMS. She proved invaluable and thanks to her expertise training, only two sundae glass dishes and a casserole pot were unpacked in pieces from their wooden crate, months later on the other side of the world. Before travelling up from Kent, Esme had telephoned to say I should put on old clothes, have plenty of Ray's large handkerchiefs at the ready, a stack of newspapers and a great deal of wood shavings. These latter proved very easy to come by. Our furniture-maker neighbours were more than willing to oblige! (The children had been palmed off with friends.)

Esme arrived mid-morning. My training began. The surface of the table was fast filling up. Wedding presents, which barely four years ago had been adorned in the 'riches' of beautiful wrapping paper, were now being dressed in the 'rags' of newsprint! Cinderella in reverse! Sheets and sheets of newspapers were folded two or three at a time in a particular way according to the diameter of the plate to be packed. The secret was to pack them so tightly they wouldn't be able to move. We stopped for a break before tackling the next and most demanding phase.

'We'll need to keep the kettle on the boil with a pile of tea bags handy. It's going to be thirsty work,' said Esme. 'Here, take one of Ray's large handkerchiefs and fold it diagonally.'

With that she picked up a second one, folded it, and tied it over her nose and mouth. 'That's to keep most of the dust of the wood shavings from being inhaled.'

We set to, placing each newspaper wrapped package of breakables as tightly as possible next to its neighbour in the wooden crate. Then taking a handful of wood shavings, we sprinkled these among the packages, pushing them into any tiny space that had been created. Ray arrived on the scene, sometime later, to discover two, dust-covered 'masked raiders'.

Esme was right: it was thirsty work. Despite the precautions taken, fine dust did get up our noses and down our throats. By early evening, with the task finished, we said goodbye to Esme, so appreciative of her sheer hard work and expertise.

Our friendship with Jeremy and Daphne, from St John, Hoxton, was such a support during these days. It expressed itself in many and varied practical ways, from invitations to their home and providing a listening ear to collecting Naomi and Andrew from my parents' home in Leicester when Ray was unable to make the journey. It wasn't all one-sided as in addition to calling for their daughter, Mary Clare, to take to pre-school with Naomi, I taught Daphne to bake bread. This was before the luxury of domestic bread-making machines – something she does to this day, and has also taught many others to do the same.

Ray prepared their elder son, Gregory, for confirmation. But it was for the practical skills of Jeremy's carpentry that we would remain forever grateful. Armed with hammer, saw and nails, he set to fixing lids on the crates and the tea chests containing other household goods. These were then put in store, in a brick out-house, under the pavement, to the right of the front door of our basement home, in readiness to be transported to Liverpool docks at a later date.

September 26th was the date we were to start our Orientation Course at Allen Gardiner House, named after the founder of the South American Mission Society. The 'Farewell Service' at

St Leonard, Shoreditch, took place on September 20th. Very many friends from all over the country, as well as family, came to support us, and wish us well. Canon Harry Sutton preached to a packed congregation.

On the 25th, with the last containers, designated in our minds to 'somewhere in South America', safely in store under the pavement and the remaining necessities for the following few months in the process of being packed and the three children tucked up for the night, we fell exhausted into our 'sold-awaiting-collection' bed.

We were up extra early the next morning to finish the remaining packing, and to clean right through No.10A. Once again help was on hand in looking after the children. The time of arrival at Allen Gardiner House for new recruits was early afternoon with tea at four. Our 'fagoo' was packed up to the roof with cases, bags, and carry cot, in which five month old Julian was sleeping peacefully (I would willingly have changed places with him, were that possible!), Naomi and Andrew clutching favourite toys and books in the back seat surrounded by more cases and bags. I clambered wearily into the passenger seat beside an equally weary husband.

We set off through the City, each with our own memories of the past three years; laughter and tears, fun and frustration, anger and reconciliation, faith tested and faith strengthened, help given and help received. We'd arrived in London's East End, as a couple. We were leaving as a family of five! The cockneys had endeared themselves to us and we felt enriched by sharing in their culture.

As we drove through the Blackwall Tunnel on our way south, the light at the end was a reminder that for us, on our faith journey into the unknown, light would also emerge.

An anxious look at our watches indicated we were running late. Leaving the Metropolis behind with its densely packed buildings, congested roads and overcrowded pavements, we drove out into the leafy suburbs. The nearer we approached our destination we couldn't fail to notice the marked contrast of what we had left behind with what we were now encountering.

Wide, tree-lined avenues were already changing a summer wardrobe of plain greens for an autumn one of greens flecked with gold, copper and bronze. Behind the trees were large, detached houses, each different from its neighbour, standing in beautifully manicured gardens.

No washing hanging from the windows here, or a housewife standing on the balcony of her tenement flat watching the world go by, exchanging local gossip with a neighbour. Instead of the familiar Black Cab, the red double-decker bus, the clapped-out Ford that had seen better days, we saw gleaming Jaguars, streamlined Vauxhalls and open-topped MGs.

No corner shop with its comings and goings, no appetising aroma of fish and chips, not even noisy laughing and shouting emanating from a pub were to be seen, smelt or heard along these quiet avenues of Tunbridge Wells.

And it was to be in this quiet, beautiful setting that we, together with fifteen other recruits, would start our induction into all things Latin American. It didn't take much imagination to realise that second to a Call of God there had to be the gift of adaptability for would-be missionary recruits.

Allen Gardiner House was situated in Pembury Road, on the outskirts of Tunbridge Wells. We turned into the driveway and there before us was a large mock Tudor house with a modern annexe attached. The moment we parked, Naomi, with ill-concealed excitement, scrambled out of the car, followed by her younger brother, anxious to explore her new surroundings. We had barely reached the front door when it was opened. There to greet us were the wardens, Ted Jenkin and his wife Marjorie, warm smiles on their faces. We were immediately made to feel at home. Within moments ready hands were helping us unload the car. We later discovered these belonged to Ray Perfect and Gordon Crawshaw.

One of the Jenkins' daughters helped with the little ones as we followed Marjorie to our rooms. Tea had been served at 4.00 pm. (By now it was 4.30 pm.) It was suggested we might like to go straight to the tea trolley where we would find the other recruits. Meanwhile Mary, Gordon's wife, would make some fresh tea.

Gathered around the trolley, every bit as different as the selection of biscuits and cakes on the plates was a group of young men and women, average age late twenties. The majority of them looked remarkably fresh and it seemed, from animated conversation, they were raring to go. Not surprising given that they were mostly single or newly married with no children, or as in one case with an only older child. However, to one side we spotted the Ellison family. We had been eagerly looking forward to meeting up with them again after more than three years since we had last met.

John and Judie smilingly made their way towards us the dark rings under their eyes a tell-tale reminder of our own. Like us they had arrived late and were every bit as weary. They introduced their little ones. Rosie was the same age as Naomi, and Richard a little younger than Andrew. Ray and John had been at theological college together, as had another recruit Glyn Jones. Glyn, his wife Jane, and two-year-old Timothy were occupying a room just across the corridor from us.

Derek Hawksbee, who had served with SAMS as an agriculturalist in the Chaco region of Paraguay, was responsible for our course programme. He later became ordained. By a strange coincidence his Aunt Lotty was a member of our congregation at St Leonard's Church. Derek welcomed us soon after our arrival, then handed us a programme of our first weekend. This initial two day programme remains a blur in my mind and it was only on discovering the outline in Ray's file that I realise it happened at all! After the exhausting past weeks I needed time to unwind before entering into the ongoing orientation programme.

The children, seven in all, ate their meals together, supervised usually by the mothers. This freed parents to maintain adult conversations with the other recruits over later meal times. Activities were run for the children during the mornings when the majority of the lectures took place. Rosie and Naomi became firm friends and Andrew, Richard and Timothy spent many a happy time playing together. Afternoons would see the children playing in the garden, in the autumn sunshine, crunching through the fallen leaves, and discovering the delights of acorns and 'conkers'. For Naomi and Andrew this was sheer luxury having such a wonderful garden right on their doorstep. A change of afternoon activity and one that Julian, in the limited way a five-month-old could enter into, were trips to the local park to feed the ducks.

Invariably there were limits to what I could attend having a baby to look after. However, I did manage to get to most of the morning lectures on the geography, history and religions of the South American Republics, the history of the Society and its Founder, the present work and new possibilities. All the information was given within the context of a God who was involved within his world and who cared passionately for the whole of his creation.

We looked at God's nature and mission as revealed in the Old Testament also the New Testament order for mission and ministry. There were very helpful sessions on relationships; with other missionaries, between the married and the single, husband and wife, parents and children, grandparents and parents back home. We were faced with the areas in these relationships where there would be legitimate sacrifices involved and also the pitfalls of neglecting some of those very relationships 'for the work'.

In the afternoons there were practical workshops; carpentry, car maintenance, dressmaking, hair cutting and even emergency dentistry! At this stage we didn't know where we would be assigned, although for us, Rosario was uppermost in our thinking, but we said nothing (wisely as it turned out). With that in mind, and the ever-present awareness of limited finances, I decided that to learn to cut four heads of hair in the years ahead would be a good investment! Ray meanwhile went to the car maintenance workshop.

Underpinning our communal life were the daily opportunities for prayer and worship. Most weekends the singles and the husbands would be out visiting churches promoting the work of the Society and sharing their own particular Call. The remaining wives and children became a support to one another.

It was December 10th 1970. We went down to breakfast. There was a buzz in the air with a palpable feeling of excitement. It was the day we had all been eagerly waiting for, the day when we would know where we were to be assigned. For the teachers, would it be St Andrew's School, Asunción, Paraguay or St Paul's School, Viña del Mar, Chile? For the agriculturalists, Peter and Frances, would it be the Chaco area of northern Argentina or Paraguay? For the ordained, which city and in which Republic?

With so much uncertainty there was one thing we all agreed on: the Society wouldn't send any family to Chile at this time! Chile now had a Marxist President. The Cold War was still a reality. The dangerous stand-off between Cuba with the United States in 1963 was still fresh in the memory. We were only too aware of the great divide between Communism and Christianity. Christians of all denominations were facing persecution in the Soviet Union, Eastern Europe, Cuba and China.

A timetable with all our names was put up on the notice board informing us of the time for our appointment with Major W. F. Batt, the Chairman of the Society.

Why are alphabetical lists never used in reverse? I read, only a few months before writing this chapter, an article in the *Daily Telegraph* about a theory put out by some psychologist on surnames. It seems that if yours falls in the second half of the alphabet you are not so likely to excel in life to the same extent of those in the first half! It then went on to list names of well-known high achievers, and surprise, surprise, their surnames all began with a letter between the range of A through to N. With that theory, I don't stand a chance.

From school days I was invariably either last on the list or second from last and according to this modern day psychologist I am doomed for non-achievement!

I have been known to say, 'I must have loved my husband to have exchanged a surname like Williamson (with its Scottish pedigree) for that of Smith.'

We were to discover very early on in South America that the *Latinos*, like their Spanish forefathers, have the best of both worlds. I would be known as Señora Gill Williamson de Smith (of Smith), my husband as Señor Ray Smith Medlock (this latter being his mother's maiden name). Naomi, Andrew and Julian were Smith Williamson. It all became somewhat confusing when in some cases we would encounter, for example, a Carolina López de López or a Rodrigo González González, this latter being the equivalent of Smith in its popularity in South America.

Our turn came, at last, late afternoon. 'Come in,' said a clear, commanding, cultured voice in answer to Ray's knock on the door where the interviews were taking place. We entered and rising from the chair behind a table facing the door, ready to greet us, was a very tall, erect man. He was bespectacled, had an enormous moustache, and was almost bald. It wasn't our first encounter with Major Batt. In fact he and his wife had entertained us to a meal in their home, Gresham Hall in Norfolk.

Ray had known Major Batt for a number of years, mainly through the Covenanter boys' camps in West Runton and summer mission outreach programmes. Major Batt, formerly in the Guards, was a much-respected evangelist and in big demand, both as a speaker and in leading university missions.

'Ray and Gill, please sit down,' indicating the two chairs strategically placed in front of the table. He returned to his side of the table, sat down and began to ask us how we'd found our time on the course. We chatted for five to ten minutes or so. Then, raising his head and looking directly at us both, he said, 'Now, I expect you're wanting to know where we as a Society believe your God-given gifts and ministry can best be used?'

'Rosario,' we thought. 'A foregone conclusion.'

'Chile. Yes, Chile. That's where we've assigned you to!'

We were dumbfounded. After what seemed an eternal silence, he said, 'Are there any questions you'd like to ask?'

Silence. Slowly I came to and heard myself reply, 'We're still recovering from the shock.'

Chapter 8
Frantic Frinton

The end of 1970 promised to bring some equilibrium to our lives. What better place to restore a measure of sanity than to spend the waiting-months in peaceful Frinton-on-Sea? There was the added bonus for our children of grandparents Smith living nearby. They had retired to Frinton during our second year in the East End, to be followed within a few years by grandparents Williamson from Leicester.

Frinton, well known as a retirement resort is on the East coast, not far from the large port of Harwich. Of interest to my American readers is that Harwich was home to Christopher Jones, Captain of the *Mayflower*. His house still stands in King's Head Street. Another resident of this Port was Christopher Newport, one of the founders of the colony in Virginia, thirteen years before the *Mayflower* carrying the Pilgrim Fathers left England in 1620.

We had taken a whirlwind trip to the continent with the two older children, a week or so before starting our Orientation Course. This was to combine some holiday with visiting family and friends to say goodbye. On Ray's side there were relatives in the South of France and French-speaking Switzerland. I had friends in Germany and German-speaking Switzerland.

We travelled in our tried and trusted 'fagoo', leaving from Dover to Calais and returning from the Hook of Holland to Harwich. Like all children experiencing their first ferry crossing, Naomi and Andrew were fascinated that we could actually drive on to a boat. Naomi was anxious to explore this 'house on the water'.

Meanwhile Andrew, with an early passion for cars, continuing right into adolescence, only to be replaced by an even greater passion for football, was reluctant to leave the parked car. Perhaps it was this trip, surrounded by cars, vans and lorries neatly parked in their respective rows, that was the origin of his favourite past time. Andrew and his Matchbox cars were inseparable. Over the next years he would spend hours lying on the floor or ground, lining up his cars bumper to bumper in extremely neat rows.

Not knowing what shopping in Chile would be like, we decided to stock up a little on clothes and other items that would see us through the next three years before home leave. This took us to Colchester, barely half-an-hour's car drive away. It was so named after 'Old King Cole', the ancient British chieftain Cunobelin who ruled much of southeast England. In AD 49-50 Claudius built a great Roman city on the site. Ten years later Boadicea, Queen of the Iceni, sacked it in a rising against the Romans. The Norman Conquest resulted in its castle and in 1648 Cromwell besieged the town, executing the two Royalist commanders of the defences. Colchester became a centre of weaving and famous for its oyster trade.

Frinton, by contrast, was a modern coastal resort, to which many people retired and had a reputation for being very select! There was no fish and chip shop, no pub, and no cinema. At the time of writing there is a fish and chip shop and to our amusement it advertises itself with large lettering stating 'Nice Fish and Chips'!

It was in 1976, while on our second home leave from Chile, that the average age of the residents was brought home to us very forcibly. While walking along the main high street, Julian, by now six, turned to me and said rather forlornly, 'Mummy, why are there no teenagers in England?'

We were later to find that the main avenue of Santiago, Chile's capital, Avenida Bernardo O'Higgins, (named after Chile's liberator from Spain, of Irish stock) also known as the Alameda, like most of South America's city streets, teemed with the under twenty fives, with hardly a grey head of hair in sight.

Connaught Avenue, Frinton-on-Sea couldn't have provided a greater contrast.

The main-line railway from Liverpool Street to Clacton-on-Sea separated at Thorpe-le-Soken, the branch line passing through Kirby Cross, Frinton and to its terminus at Walton-on-the-Naze. On the other side of the main road and railway line was an extension of the original resort of Frinton, with new housing estates and modern bungalows. The gates of the railway crossing provided the entrance to the resort.

The gates were not only a physical barrier to the town, there was also a social one. Some of the residents who lived 'within the gates' had the reputation of thinking themselves a cut above those who lived 'outside the gates'. This also was reflected in the disparity of the price of properties, houses and bungalows varying by several thousand pounds depending whether you lived 'within' or 'without the gates'. Not even buses were allowed, in the sixties and seventies, to enter the original Frinton.

Both sets of parents lived 'within the gates', mine in a small terraced house, Ray's in a more modern bungalow, but with hearts that extended outside. As a family we were to receive so much kindness, generosity and warm hospitality that, to this day, past memories and friends remain special.

The grass area stretching along the sea front was known as the 'greensward' and was the pride and joy of hotel owners and those fortunate enough to live in the large houses or luxurious flats overlooking it. In the seventies even picnics on the 'greensward' weren't allowed. It was so sacrosanct that you felt almost obliged to take off your shoes, as for a new carpet, before walking on it!

Thankfully, today this 'green carpet' is available for all to enjoy. It's a welcome sight to see young and old, families picnicking and playing ball and grandparents sitting on the wooden seats, quietly gazing out to sea. Eager yachts, their sails billowing in the fresh east wind, speed along past a slow moving red-sailed Thames barge, reflecting on the blue carpet of sea what is being acted out on the green carpet of land. This 'ancestral' sailing vessel makes its daily trip to and from Harwich and Brightlingsea. One future day when it is laid to rest, both sailor and onlooker alike will miss it, as a much-loved great grandparent.

The next home, in what was fast becoming a nomadic existence (a foretaste of what was to follow) was a sea-front flat. Number 14 Garden Court was a ground floor flat in a white painted block of no more than three storeys, belonging to friends of Ray. They wanted to be of help to us in our calling overseas and put their holiday home at our disposal, rent-free. This was particularly appreciated as our expected stay of around a month lengthened into three. The problem was the delay in our visas coming through. Although frustrated by the delay it did mean we could receive many friends. It also provided a base from which we, in turn, were able to travel to visit others who were unable to make the journey to us.

Reading diary extracts of these months of preparation leaves one breathless. All the to-ing and fro-ing was more like Clapham Junction than Frinton-on-Sea. There were various church meetings to talk at and other appointments to keep, and to have two punctures in transit in less than two weeks was and remains a record! We had been in London for several days and were driving to the Leicester grandparents. On the M1 we had a puncture. We pulled on to the hard shoulder and leaving the three children safely inside the car we began to unpack. This was our only contention with 'fagoo' Why oh why was the jack stored in such an inaccessible place? A lorry driver came to our rescue.

Our second puncture occurred only a few days later. It was a 'bad hair' day, literally, the moment we got up. We were leaving my parents, having had a hectic schedule, speaking at St Christopher's Church, 'Carley' Evangelical Church and saying our 'goodbyes' to a number of friends and relatives. With our customary early starts to the day as all parents of small children have in common, I opened the large suitcase, packed the night before, to hunt for my shampoo. It had leaked. With dishevelled hair and nice smelling but sticky clothes, we set out from Leicester.

This episode had delayed our departure for Cranfield University, Bedford (where my sister was Director of Computing) to have lunch. On the way back home we developed a slow puncture. The diary records that we stopped every twenty miles or so for air, limping back to Frinton for a very late tea and bed time for three very tired children and two stressed parents. At ten o'clock that evening our two overnight guests arrived!

Our guests were Christine Simons, a qualified nurse and Gloria Dean, a teacher, both of whom had been on our Orientation Course. Like us, they too were assigned to Chile. Bubbling with excitement, we heard from them that their visas had come through. My diary records that we stayed chatting until well past midnight. They left Frinton the next day and 'lifted off' on February 5th, the same day Apollo 14 landed safely on the moon. It would be over a month before our own visas arrived.

There were frequent trips to the Chilean Embassy and Consulate: the first time we were somewhat nonplussed to find they needed our fingerprints! We had yet to discover that, in common with all of South America, steering through the minefield of bureaucracy was almost as daunting as the real thing. The Spanish word for legal procedure involving so much form filling is *trámite*, but the Chileans on the receiving end would shrug their shoulders and say with resignation '*puro papel*' (Nothing but paper!)

When we weren't on the road, visiting friends, having the remaining required jabs, shopping in Colchester and Clacton, or taking yet another trip to the Capital we did manage to spend leisure time by the sea. For Naomi and Andrew the anticipated dream of magic moments with bucket and spade was dashed by the harsh reality of freezing cold east winds – it was full winter. Many visitors, with gentle persuasion, donning hats, scarf and gloves braced themselves to accompany the five of us on the prom. If the weather was a little milder, we encouraged them to walk on the 'wall' between the sea front and the golf links in the direction of Holland-on-Sea.

As if to send us on our way to sunnier climes with an unforgettable reminder of what we were leaving behind (just in case we were likely to forget), the snow fell and fell that winter of 1970.

We woke up on Boxing Day, in our sea-front flat, with shrieks of delight emanating from the children's bedroom. At the same time we became aware that it was incredibly light for a December morning. Almost half the windows were covered with snow that had banked up on the outside sills. About ten inches lay on the ground.

Today was going to be a very special day. It was a Smith family tradition for all the brothers and sisters and their families to get together on Boxing Day. As this would be for us the last time for a number of years, it was also to be a 'farewell' for us. My mother, father and Elaine joined us. A break from tradition was that we would celebrate in a hotel. Ray's father had booked the dining room for lunch and tea in a Tudor hotel in Suffolk. The Bull, situated on the High Street of Long Melford, dated from 1450 AD.

The question on our lips was, 'Will we all make the journey?' Added to the problem of travel from Leicester for my parents and Elaine, and from differing parts of Essex for the other members of Ray's family, was the fact that Ray had woken up with a temperature. Today of all days! He spent the best part of the morning in bed while I took Naomi and Andrew outside to play in the snow. Julian, wrapped up cosily, watched us from his pram. We were to arrive in time for lunch. Thankfully we all made it.

A festive scene greeted us, a real northern hemisphere Christmas card scene! (One we would savour when immersed in Christmas temperatures of well into the thirties in the next years.) The snow, still heavy on the ground, provided the ideal setting for our tastefully decorated Tudor hotel. Log fires threw out a welcoming heat, their characteristic smell of smoke mingling with the smell of roasting meat, a promise of good things to come. Fourteen adults and about half as many children sat down at the table, the remaining little ones either in highchairs or on willing knees. In all we were twenty-six.

After lunch, dining tables and chairs were cleared to the sides of the room and the eagerly awaited present opening ceremony began. I don't recall whether on this occasion we dispensed with the usual tradition of Grandpa Smith impersonating Father Christmas, but we did have our customary fun and games time. No Boxing Day would be complete without photos.

It was time to leave The Bull. Tea now over and the lights, both inside and outside that had shone and twinkled as they made their daily debut appearance at the first sign of approaching dusk, were now reaching their full glory as dusk gave way to an early December night.

The 'flu' virus Ray had contracted meant we arrived at the New Year SAMS Conference, at Whitelands College, Putney, a day late. My diary for the years we spent in Chile begins with this New Year.

We attended the Conference as day visitors to keep costs down, staying with David Shacklock, from St Christopher days. David was, by now, the vicar of St Mary, West Kensington. He had married Gillian, a member of the St Christopher's Church congregation. They were especially pleased to get to know their goddaughter, Naomi, a bit better. On the Sunday evening while Gillian baby-sat, I attended the Conference. Meantime Ray was out preaching in Finchley, representing the Mission and who should be in the congregation but Cliff Richard!

January 31st we left for Dagenham to pick up another steel drum and then on to Maldon to friends for tea, joined by Gloria and Chris (five days before they left for Chile). We had rather a sad task ahead of us. Gregory's garage had been recommended to us as doing good deals on selling and buying second hand cars. They made an acceptable offer for our tried and trusted friend. Needing to return to Frinton with the oil drum, we arranged to hand over the car the following day. We retraced our steps, Ray driving his father's car and me following in ours. We handed over 'fagoo' in exchange for £145!

Helped by Ray's mother we packed the recently bought steel drum and two trunks full of our purchases from the January sales, together with all the items not needed until we would land on Chilean soil. Father's car was broken into that evening when he was visiting us, but nothing of value taken.

The luggage was to be picked up and re-united with all the

packing cases and oil drums left in store in the bricked shed under the pavement outside 10A Hoxton Square. From here J. D. Hewett and Co. Ltd of Kingsway, London would collect them and deliver them to Liverpool docks. In total there were twenty-one items, comprising eight oil drums, five wooden crates, six tea chests and two wooden trunks – all packed by many willing hands of both family and friends!

Interspersed in the diary entries of hectic activity, countless trips back and forth to London, frustrating delays, bureaucracy, a postal strike, remaining vaccinations and very many speaking and preaching engagements, were entries of normal family life and quality time with very many friends. Outside of the capital there were 'farewell' visits to Eastbourne and Leicester. Snow wasn't confined to December 26th. The diary records we left Frinton March 6th in snow, bound for the south coast via Allen Gardiner House, Tunbridge Wells and encountered five blizzards en route!

In all the experiences in which following God's leading in our lives involved us, the children were very much a part. When, on the rare occasions, it wasn't advisable for them to accompany us, the support of grandparents and family was indispensable – a luxury denied us once we arrived in the land at 'the end of the earth'. This early exposure to travel stood them in good stead for the many adventures that lay ahead.

During these hectic weeks gems of their early 'conversations' and of their development are recorded in my diary when memories have long since faded.

"*Mummy, you won't die, will you?*"

"*Yes, Naomi, one day.*"

"*Will I?*"

"*Yes. Do you know where Mummy will go? She will go to live with Jesus because she loves him.*"

"*Will I?*"

"*Yes, if you love Jesus.*"

"*I do love Jesus and I want to live with him.*"

February 6th, '*Andrew woke us up with, "Daddy – tractor,*

lorry, car."' This was the first time he had strung together these words.

Four days later, with Ray having gone to London to collect our visas from the Chilean Consulate and from there to Shoreditch to oversee Hewett and Co picking up all the luggage, I remained in Garden Court. This was the day Naomi shut the front door locking Andrew and me out. There followed a mini lecture on the dangers of locking herself in. It must have had the desired effect because later that evening my diary records her words.

"If Naomi shuts the door, Naomi left on her own. I'm not big enough girl to get tea my own"

The same entry records, *'Andrew said "potatoes" today for the first time. Julian's third tooth through!'*

A phone call from Canon Bob Smith (SAMS staff) on March 11th informed us that all was clear now for us to fly out to Chile. He then told us we would be based in Quilpué, about two to three hours drive from the capital, Santiago. This would be a temporary location while we acclimatised and began our language study. To celebrate we invited mother and father Smith home to a special meal. While living with in-laws for those few months I had joined an evening class on cordon bleu cookery for one term. On this particular occasion tips learnt then came in useful, as I really pulled out the stops.

The menu reads as follows.

Aperitif: fresh grapefruit
Hors d'oeuvre: Aubergine casserole
Main dish: Maryland fried chicken with cream gravy, mushrooms, tomatoes, green peppers and roast potatoes
Dessert: Chocolate de crème with meringues and fresh cream
Coffee.

The eve of our departure for Chile was also the eve of our fifth Wedding Anniversary. A last visit was to the Frinton-based author George Pendle and his wife. As we left their home he gave us one of his books. *The Land and People of Chile* is one of my sources for this writing, and the inscription in the front reads 'Ray and Gill Smith with all good wishes for their time in Chile. George Pendle, Frinton 25/3/71.'

Lt. Grandpa Herbert Cave with my mother, Gt Grandpa Varney Cave with Winnie, Eddie, Grandma Alice with Margaret.

My Mother and Father.   *Myself and Elaine in our Scottish kilts.*

My childhood home. Courtesy of Leicester Mercury.

Me aged 11 years.

Far right: Me as a 3rd year student nurse - Leicester General Hospital.

Fellow students at Mt Hermon Missionary Training College - Margaret Morgan near left.

A 21st birthday photograph.

On the steps of St Paul's Cathedral - Ray's Ordination, 1967.

Andrew and Naomi in Basement Flat, Hoxton Square, Shoreditch.

Childhood happiness - outside Garden Court, Frinton, 1973.

Frinton family group. Standing Smith parents. Seated from left Ray with Julian, me with Naomi, Williamson parents with Andrew, Elaine.

Captain Allen Gardiner - Founder of the South American Missionary Society.

"The Little Woman" - Gladys Aylward

Naomi, Andrew and Julian. 14 Garden Court, Frinton-on-Sea, January 1971.

Family group outside A G H before leaving for Chile - October 1970.

Family group shortly after returning from Chile to the UK - February 1980.

Andes from the air.

Santiago.

Viña del Mar.

Valparaiso - Chile's main port.

Andrew and Naomi among the rubble
following earthquake - Quilpué.

Flowering cactus - Prickly pear.

'Huasitos'.

Chapter 9
Discoverers and Conquerors

In our school days, like all children, we had been taught and done projects on the great discoverers of distant lands: Magellan, Vasco da Gama, Marco Polo and, perhaps the most famous of them all, Christopher Columbus. I really enjoyed plotting their sea voyages across the pages of carefully drawn maps in my geography exercise books. Now in Frinton there was a little time to catch up on reading recommended on our course reminding us of the past history of the discovery of the Americas.

In the 15th century, the Portuguese were to the fore in their sea exploration and their Prince Henry, although no sailor himself was acknowledged as the leading light of his nation's legacy. This century marked the beginning of Portugal's Golden Age of discovery and subsequent trade. In a square in Lagos, Portugal, stands a bronze statue of Prince Henry, later known as Henry the Navigator, holding his sextant, gazing out to sea.

A young man, whose date of birth is as unknown as is his place of birth, has become synonymous with the discoveries of the Americas – Christopher Columbus. However, according to Pendle, the first Europeans to set foot on American northern shores, were, in fact, Scandinavian sailors.[1]

Christopher Columbus is acknowledged by historians to have been of Genoese origin. In a letter written by Columbus in 1502 he writes, 'In the city of Genoa I have my roots, and there I was born.'[2] According to his son, Ferdinand, in his biography, his father took to the sea at the age of fourteen.

On one of his early voyages, in a fleet of Genoese merchant

[1] George Pendle: *A History of Latin America.* Penguin p. 32
[2] Zvi Dor-Ner: *Columbus: and the Age of Discovery.* Harper Collins p. 46

vessels, he passed through the Strait of Gibraltar. Stretching ahead of him lay his first glimpse of the vast ocean that marked the boundary between a future of unparalleled opportunity and subsequent fame, and a past of relative safety and comparative obscurity. It was the future that beckoned him across this divide. But not before that sea to be conquered almost became his conqueror. French and Portuguese ships attacked the convoy just off the southern coast of Portugal, on August 13th 1476. The ship on which Columbus was sailing sank. The Atlantic of future dreams almost became the nightmare of his own watery grave. Desperately he clung to an oar and was washed up on the shores of the nation whose love of seafaring was closely entwined with his own.

Sadly his arrival at Lagos was too late to meet the pioneer of maritime navigation, Prince Henry having died sixteen years previously. In time the azure blue waters of the calmer Mediterranean increasingly faded into the background as Columbus contemplated the blue-grey Atlantic rollers crashing off the southwest tip of Europe. Beyond Cape St Vincent lay unknown continents yet to be discovered. It was here that his dream to sail west began to take shape. Failing to convince the Portuguese king, whose eyes were set on opening a sea route in the opposite direction, Columbus turned his attention to Spain.

On August 3rd 1492, having achieved sponsorship from Queen Isabella, Columbus set sail with a small fleet of three ships from the Spanish port of Palos. The *Niña*, *Pinta* and the flagship *Santa María* remain of legendary fame the world over. Columbus and his heirs were granted 'the title and office of Admiral in all the islands and continents of the ocean that he or they might discover'.[3]

On the first voyage, the first sighting of land, after thirty-three days at sea, was the most eastern island of the Bahamas. Once ashore, the now Admiral raised the Spanish flag, declared the island and its people as belonging to the Crown, and being a devoutly religious man, led his crew in a prayer of thanksgiving.

---

[3] George Pendle: *A History of Latin America*. Penguin p. 33

A cross was erected 'as a token of Jesus Christ our Lord', and the island named *San Salvador,* Holy Saviour.

Leaving the Island, on sailing along the north coast of Cuba, two weeks later, it was mistakenly thought that Japan or China had been reached. His return to the Spanish monarchs at court in Barcelona was greeted with both anticipation and great excitement. Ferdinand and Isabella thought 'that the East Indies were within their grasp'.[4] One can only imagine the look of incredulity at court on the presentation not only of fine ware, gold jewellery and green parrots, but also several Indians, incredulity on the faces of both hosts and 'guests' alike. With emotions running high at the belief that a way to the Orient was now open for Spain, the continuing threat of Portugal's discoveries had to be dealt with. Taking advantage of the current Pope, Alexander VI, being a Spaniard, the monarchs made their appeal.

The Treaty of Tordesillas was signed, in June 1494, between the two rival nations. After some renegotiation of the original Papal Bull a line passing from pole to pole, and 100 leagues to the west of Cape Verde, just over 300 miles west of the Azores, a new line of 370 leagues west was agreed. This gave all territories yet to be discovered west of the line to Spain and all land east of the line to Portugal. It was as a result of this re-alignment that Brazil, yet to be discovered, came to be included in Portugal's possession as well as the African continent.

The first voyage successfully completed, Columbus embarked on four more. His subsequent ones became not only a further quest to discover unknown lands, but, with royal mandate, to colonise them. On his final sea journey, 1502-1504, still searching for a passage-way that would lead into the Indian Ocean, he spent Christmas and New Year's Day 1503 just off the isthmus separating the Caribbean from the Pacific. By this time Vasco da Gama had been to India and back by way of the Cape of Good Hope. If Spain were not to be left behind in supplying her own court with eastern riches, it would have to be achieved via Columbus's transatlantic route. For the Portuguese, trade was

---

[4] Ibid: p. 34

the motivation behind their exploration. For the Spanish it was more a question of gaining territory.

The Indians of Central America had told the Spanish that they lived on a strip of land between two seas. However, Columbus sent no exploratory party to search for the opposite coast. It would be four centuries later in 1914 that a man-made way connecting these two seas was built. In 1973, we ourselves sailed through the Panama Canal, calling at the ports either end of the canal. My outstanding memory was not so much the amazing feat of engineering undertaken in carving out this connecting sea 'road', but rather the myriad of lime green butterflies that surrounded us as we stood on deck in the incredibly hot steamy atmosphere, the children somehow finding the energy to try and catch them.

The Pacific port of Balboa was named after the Spaniard Vasco Núñez de Balboa, who, unlike his predecessor, did listen to the Indians. As a result in 1513 he was the first European to set eyes on the Pacific from the recently discovered continent. The great explorer died in Spain in 1506, at the age of fifty-five, largely unacclaimed. It was to be three centuries before Christopher Columbus was rediscovered. At the opposite end, at the entrance to the Caribbean coast lie two ports. His name *Cristóbal* (Christopher) was given to the port lying north of the Atlantic entrance to the canal and *Colón* (Columbus) to the south. Ports and boats, towns and cities, streets and hills throughout Latin America would be named after its European discoverer. His statue is to be seen in many a *plaza* in the Latin American republics. Ironically though, the name of the continent itself would go to another.

Amerigo Vespucci, a well-to-do Florentine businessman had also turned to exploration. His first voyage in 1499, sailing along the coastlines of Venezuela and the Guianas, had been under the Spanish flag. In 1501, on his second, he sailed with the Portuguese, covering a great deal of the Brazilian coast. It was after his return, due to the speed and efficiency in which his well-documented reports circulated among the European mapmakers, that his fame overtook that of the Genoese.

In one of two letters (understood to be written by Vespucci), incorporated in an Italian collection of the 'discoveries', the title *Mundus Novus* was given to the transatlantic discovery. However it was 'America', Latinised in honour of Amerigo, that first appeared on a printed map of 1507, together with a portrait of the Italian. Columbus in his 'discovery' did not realise what he had found. 'Discovery must be given a meaning ... Columbus remains the Discoverer of America and Vespucci its Explainer'.[5]

Columbus engaged in slavery of the indigenous people in his earlier voyages shipping them back to Spain. However, Isabella, a zealous catholic, wanted converts rather than slaves and reasoned that, as her subjects, others could not own Indians. Instructions were issued to the Admiral that Indians were not to be sent to Spain. This became law.

History isn't always kind to the people and events it records. How many of us given hindsight would do things very differently were we to have that opportunity? Whatever our view of Columbus's role in the exploitation of 'the New World' which would continue for the following centuries, his legacy to that great continent has, undoubtedly, helped shape a civilisation as rich in its diversity as in its fascination.

The 500th anniversary of the 'discovery' of the Americas was celebrated throughout the Spanish-speaking world in 1992. We ourselves were working in Spain at the time. In a conversation with Naomi, now a young woman of twenty-five with a strong sense of justice, I happened to say how pleased we were to be living in Spain for the celebrations. 'But, Mum, what have the indigenous people got to celebrate?'

Her reply was both uncomfortable and challenging and was the catalyst for an initiative that we, as the English-speaking church, together with both the Spanish evangelical church and Roman Catholics, embarked on. (Who says we don't listen to our children?) The idea grew into a plan to put something back into Latin America.

We entitled the project 'Eat Simply so that Others may Simply

---

[5] Ibid: pps. 35, 36

Eat'. It consisted of a very basic meal, all provisions being donated, for which all participating would pay restaurant prices.

A couple from our congregation let us use their rustic country restaurant, free of charge. The Spanish father-in-law of a member of our congregation baked the bread and the local press gave media coverage. We raised just under £1400, of which we had no expenses whatever to claim. This money was split three ways between a Roman Catholic mission working in Central America, the Antioch Mission working among the street children of Brazil and SAMS towards their work among the Indians of the Chaco.

In 1521, the Portuguese navigator Magellan, under the Spanish flag, sailed through the southernmost strait, to be named after him, separating the vast landmass of South America from the island of Tierra del Fuego.

With the opening up of the continent to exploration came the opening up to increasing exploitation. Explorers gave way to conquerors. Gold and precious stones were plundered to furnish the royal courts of Europe and to adorn cathedrals and churches both in the home countries and also in the New World.

In Elizabethan England, with Spain and England at war, a young Devonshire man, Francis Drake, undertook a number of unofficial expeditions not only to the coastline of Spain itself but also to the New World, following in the steps of his Portuguese predecessor. His legacy, also, was a waterway named after him. Drake Passage lies south of the notorious Cape Horn. It wasn't for nothing that Drake's Spanish contemporaries called him 'Master Thief of the unknown world'.[6] Drake's piracy lay in ambushing Spanish vessels with their rich booty to present to the Queen.

Plundering of a different kind has continued down the centuries ever since. According to Andrews, both Magellan and Drake and their sailors killed a vast number of what are now known as the Magellanic penguins. In one day alone Drake's sailors killed over 3000 to stock up on food supplies, and wrote that their 'flesh is not unlike fat goose here in England'.[7] Unfortunately, while for these early sailors the slaughtering of

---

[6] Winston Churchill: *The Island Race* (abridged. Timothy Baker.) p. 133
[7] Michael Andrews: *The Flight of the Condor.* Collins p. 29

wildlife for food was out of necessity, a trend was started which led to increased exploitation. The oil from both penguins and sea lions became a much sought after commodity, threatening their very survival. Today, sadly, the practise continues with penguin meat being used as bait for the prized *centolla*, the southern king crab.

By 1550 the *conquistadores* had exported to the newly acquired territory a pattern of urbanisation familiar to their homeland. The gregarious nature of the southern Europeans meant they were more at home within a community. In the motherland they preferred living in towns and cities rather than the countryside. This Spanish love of urbanisation led to the founding of cities as soon as the explorers landed. In just twenty-seven years the major present day capital cities of Spanish America were founded: from Mexico City in 1521 to La Paz, Bolivia, the highest capital city in the world. Santiago de Chile was founded at the foot of a hill in 1541. Today Santa Lucia hill is a cultivated park with a garden, adorning the centre of the city. The Andes, when not obscured by the yellowish-grey cloud of smog hanging over the city, form the dramatic backdrop.

Names like Cortés, Pizarro, and Valdivia are legendary to all school children in South America. Our own three were no exception and in their early schooldays would know their history of Chile more than that of England. The dangers, adventures and incredible bravery of such men make childhood stories of the Three Musketeers fade into insignificance.

Chile by now had become our main topic of conversation. With an eagerness not anticipated prior to the shock of being assigned there we avidly soaked up all we could glean about the country soon to be adopted.

It fell to Pedro de Valdivia, while in Peru, but originally a native from Spain's harsh, arid region of Extremadura, to be commissioned to conquer Chile. He was one of the most courageous and intelligent of Pizarro's captains. Setting out from Cuzco, high in the Andes, Valdivia and his men marched south. They took about a year to cross the Atacama Desert, eventually reaching the fertile central region where he founded Santiago. He met with stiff resistance from the indigenous Indians, who had in the past resisted the attempted incursion of the Incas before the white man set foot in South America. A previous attempt by the *conquistadores* had failed. The Araucanian Indians had won for themselves the reputation of being the fiercest and most skilful warriors of all the Indians on the continent. According to Gunther in his book *Inside South America*, 'the Spaniards lost more men trying to subdue them than in all their campaigns elsewhere on the continent.'[8]

Over the next decade Pedro de Valdivia and his cavalry continued south, founding the cities of Concepción and Valdivia, facing constant skirmishes and danger from the Araucanians. It was at the River Bío-Bío that they fought their fiercest battle. We ourselves were 'introduced' on our arrival in Chile to the name of the leader of the Chilean Indians who defeated the *conquistadores*.

Lautaro, named after the famous historic Araucanian Indian, was the name of the road in which we lived for our first five months in Quilpué. He and his men captured the brave Spanish *conquistador* who was executed in 1553 'by being made to swallow molten gold. The legend has it that the Indians said, You come for gold – here it is.'[9]

The courage of the indigenous Indians is described in a classic poem, *La Araucana*. Chilean school children learn this poem written by Alonso de Ercilla, a 16th century Spanish officer.

In contrast to the most precious metal the Europeans coveted, the explorers also brought back the humble potato! It would, however, be some years later before it caught on in popularity in Europe. The original potatoes were cultivated by the Andean *campesinos* in the high plateau of the Andes straddling Bolivia and Peru and remain a staple diet of the Indians today. The original *'papas'* were smaller than our new potatoes and came in a variety of colours, before selective 'refining' produced our white version.

It is documented that in 1586, using potato plants probably

---

[8] John Gunther: *Inside South America*. Hamish Hamilton Ltd. p. 283
[9] Ibid. p. 283

brought back by Sir Francis Drake, the chef to Queen Elizabeth served her the cooked leaves, throwing away the potatoes. Not surprisingly she didn't request them again![10] According to Gunther the 'Irish' potato had its origin in Bolivia. Our recollection in Chile was the claim that the potato had its origin on the Island of Chiloé, in the south of the country with a climate like England, but no other source verifies this!

The influence of the Roman Catholic Church was by now extending far beyond Europe, the Explorers and *Conquistadores* inevitably importing not only their love of urbanisation but also their Roman Catholic faith. The Church for very many years held a tight grip on souls as well as on gold. The conquest was fought in the name of the Spanish Empire and in the name of the cross. Indians were baptised by the tens of thousands. There was no rival to the imported Catholicism as none was permitted.

The Church, by papal concession, was under the authority of the Spanish crown, its hierarchy working in conjunction with the secular authorities. According to Pendle, the earlier missionaries, especially the Jesuits, displayed zeal not characterised by the later clergy. The latter had become lax as a result of the increasing wealth of the Church.[11] With growing power and wealth it wasn't long before corruption and increasing exploitation increased. Those most vulnerable to exploitation were, of course, the indigenous peoples. Despite the effort of the Crown to safeguard their interests, Europe was too far away to effectively control the misuse of office and power of many of the *conquistadores* – both secular and religious.

The Andean Indians of Peru and Bolivia were put to work in the silver and tin mines of these countries. Thankfully, there were some Catholic clergy who, like their predecessors, the Old Testament prophets, took up the plight of the Indians. Notable among these was Bartolomé de Las Casas, a rich cleric, originally from Seville,who when faced with the deprivation and abusive treatment of the Indians, gave up all his possessions and devoted his life to serving them. With righteous anger against

---

[10] Zvi Dor-Ner: *Columbus and the Age of Discovery.* Harper Collins p. 266
[11] George Pendle: *A History of Latin America.* Penguin p. 59

their injustices he travelled to Spain to argue their case. 'He was largely responsible for securing the promulgation of the New Laws of the Indies in 1542.'[12]

An earlier champion of the oppressed was a Dominican friar. In a most uncomfortable sermon delivered to his congregation in 1510 in Santo Domingo, Anton Montecino, using a text from the prophet Isaiah: 'I am a voice crying in the wilderness,' thundered out. 'Your greed for gold is blind ... You are destroying an innocent people. They are God's people ... By what right do you make them die?' He went on to denounce the harsh conditions they were put to both in the mines and in the fields and the killing of them in the pursuit of colonisation. 'Are you not under God's command to love them as you love yourselves? Are you out of your souls, out of your minds?' He concluded his courageous speech by reminding his listeners that such action would bring damnation on them.[13]

Ray and I within the same continent centuries later would meet other Roman Catholic priests and nuns who shared a like passion for the poor and underprivileged in Chile.

---

[12] Ibid. p. 58

[13] Zvi Dor-Ner: *Columbus and the Age of Discovery.* Harper Collins pp. 315-316

Chapter 10
Captain Allen Gardiner: Pioneer

There was yet another later pioneer whose exploits remained an open secret to a few people. Those 'secrets' began to be shared with us on our Orientation Course and especially in the book *The Unquenchable Flame* by Phyllis Thompson. It was of particular significance to us as the story that began to unfold centred around the Patagonian regions of southern Chile and southern Argentina.

Allen Gardiner was born in 1794 into a home where the Christian faith was a reality. Like most children he had his heroes: his was Nelson. The young boy's favourite game was 'doing battle' against Napoleon and the French.

At the age of fourteen, he left home to enter Naval College at Portsmouth. For Gardiner his desire to engage the French on the high seas remained a dream played out in his imagination only. However, with the defeat of Napoleon at Trafalgar and the death of Nelson, three years before the teenager entered Naval College, the French continued to suffer reversals at the hands of the English. They no longer ruled the seas, the flying of the red, white and blue Tricolour, becoming a less frequent sight. In their place was seen increasingly the same three colours of the enemy's flag.

Allen Gardiner's first opportunity to sail with the fleet in HMS *Fortune* came in 1810, but it was while serving on another ship, HMS *Phoebe*, that Allen Gardiner first visited South America, calling in at Rio de Janeiro to re-stock on food and water before continuing into the south Atlantic, the beauty of its natural harbour in stark contrast to the squalor he would find in the city itself. Years later he would still remember the impact on him of seeing first-hand the shackled African slaves on sale in the market square. Their pitiful degradation was all the more marked against the backdrop of ornate Portuguese colonial cathedrals and churches, some of which were dripping with gold in their interiors.

The Falkland Islands would have been most probably the last port of call for provisions before rounding Cape Horn, and turning northwest into the Pacific. The reason for sailing into these waters was a result of an order from the Admiralty. This was to intercept and prevent a new threat; the English merchant ships were being attacked. It was in the waters of the Pacific in HMS *Phoebe*, that Gardiner was to experience his first taste of battle, not with the French but with the *Essex*, flying the 'Stars and Stripes'! They exchanged gunfire and when the *Essex* began to take in water, the Captain of HMS *Phoebe* gave the order for some of her crew to board and to capture the ship. Gardiner was among this boarding party. Men lay dying in agony, the half-hour attack leaving more than half her men killed or wounded. The Captain handed over his sword, the 'Stars and Stripes' flag was lowered and defeat acknowledged. For Allen Gardiner his first naval battle was now over.

This first encounter of death at close quarters was followed by a hazardous stormy Atlantic crossing in a badly damaged captured vessel. At last the safe haven of Portsmouth was reached. Gardiner was promoted to second lieutenant.

His own near brush with death on more than one occasion and witnessing the dying of others brought home to him the fragility of life itself and his own mortality. At such times he remembered the faith of his parents and the certainty they held of life beyond the grave.

After one such incident, while in Portsmouth, he decided to go into a shop to buy a Bible. 'Would the reading of this book unlock for him the answers to his own questions?'

'He made his purchase very surreptitiously. Walking casually up and down the street until sure that no one who knew him was within sight, he dived into a bookshop to obtain it, emerging rather shamefacedly with it hidden in his pocket. He did not want his fellow officers to know of his weakness …'[1]

Some months later he set sail for the Far East. When the eagerly anticipated mail arrived, there were two letters for him, one from his father, the other from Lady Grey, a family friend. They both brought totally unexpected news. His mother had died.

But it was the letter from Lady Grey that impacted him so profoundly. The writer, with deep compassion for her friends' son, recounted the last months of his mother's life. In the quiet night watches, with the ship heading for China, he recalled the many conversations Lady Grey had shared with him in her home, relating to her own personal faith in Jesus Christ. But 'it was not in the open sea, under the stars, that faith came, but in the dim recesses of a temple in China.' He had gone off exploring in one of the ports and contrasting the idolatry seen in the temple with the faith of his parents and Lady Grey convinced him of the Christian truth. 'The seed already sown in his heart seemed suddenly to come to life.'[2]

From this moment, instead of furtively hiding from his companions his interest in Christian things, he was known as an officer who read his Bible.

In the same year that Napoleon died, Allen Gardiner once again visited South America. HMS *Dauntless* followed up the Pacific coastline of the western Republics and berthed in ports of both Chile and its northern neighbour, Peru. It was on this visit that he encountered the indigenous Araucanians of Chile. The artisan skill and quality of work of these people, in both leather and woollen goods, impressed Gardiner and he felt keenly the injustices that exploited such craftsmanship. Given a fair price for work so skilfully worked, the Araucanians could be socially and economically viable. Instead they had become second-class citizens with few rights of their own. The killings and exploitations of the past, at the hands of the *conquistadores*,

---

[1] Phyllis Thompson: *An Unquenchable Flame.* Hodder and Stoughton. p. 25
[2] Ibid: p. 27

had caused them to move, fighting all the way, into the remote regions of the *campo* rather than submit to the enemy.

The Spanish Conquistadors in the wake of their military victories enforced their form of Christianity on those conquered by oppressive and threatening means rather than by persuasion and conviction. An exception to this had been the genuine concern for the indigenous people shown by the earlier Jesuit priests. They had combined the protection of the Indians with the basic teaching of the Christian faith. However, in time the Jesuits became too politically powerful in the eyes of the Spanish and Portuguese hierarchy and were expelled some sixty years before Gardiner landed there. As a result very few mission settlements remained and the tribes were scattered. These independent peoples were now largely ignored by successive generations of priests, who concentrated their attention on the majority. These were the peoples of mixed blood and the result of inter-breeding between various groupings, Spanish/Portuguese invaders, subsequent European settlers, tribeswomen and African slaves.[3]

As HMS *Dauntless* set sail, Allen Gardiner's concern was that the Great Commission of Jesus to make disciples of all nations should include the Indians of South America. In his homeward journey of 1821 little did he realise that he would be the one to spearhead that initiative.

A 'stop over' at the Pacific island of Tahiti was of deep significance in the formation of Gardiner's thinking. It happened to be a Sunday when HMS *Dauntless* docked in the port of this small Pacific island. The customary small boats that usually sailed out to meet an incoming ship and the eager traders congregating on the shoreline or rocky harbour wall were missing. As the ship set anchor he noticed a stillness and unusual quietness pervaded the land.

On reaching the sandy beach decked with palm trees, their fronds waving in rhythm to the gentle breezes, families of dark skinned people, brightly dressed, their faces wreathed in smiles waved their hands in welcome. The whole atmosphere was one

---

[3] Ibid: pps. 28, 29

of leisure and enjoyment. Rounding a corner Gardiner heard rousing singing coming from what was obviously a church building. Later that day, he discovered an enormous building able to hold around five thousand people, which the King had erected for Christian worship.

Christianity had reached Tahiti when seventeen missionaries, including a surgeon, skilled labourers and four clergymen and their wives, arrived in 1796, sent out by the London Missionary Society. At first they encountered opposition but by patience, friendship and the sharing of the truth of the Gospel lives were changed.

By 1821 when Gardiner arrived many of the inhabitants had embraced the Christian faith. Sunday worship was established, idols destroyed, and living conditions transformed. The contrast between what Christianity had done for the Tahitians and what still remained to be done in South America was glaringly obvious. In South America the power of the church had failed to bring such freedom to its people, and the gap between the privileged and the less privileged was wide. He was profoundly affected, so much so that soon after arriving home he visited the London Missionary Society headquarters with a suggestion.

Would they consider starting a new work among the indigenous peoples of South America, as they had done in Tahiti? He himself would be prepared to go at his own expense.

Then came the blow. The answer was 'No.' The Society was unable to take on new ventures. It was all it could do to continue supporting its existing work.

Another disappointment was to come when, at a later date the door to the ordained ministry closed. The interviewing Bishop gave him the advice to remain in his first calling.

Two doors had now closed for him, one to missionary work, the other to the Anglican ministry. He returned to the navy, subdued but not bitter. In time he would become the visionary leader whose courage and commitment to the God he served, would influence many in the years to come.

Allen Gardiner married Julia Reade and when not at sea, lived a settled life at Swanmore House, near Droxford in Hampshire.

He was promoted to naval Commander. The next years brought their share of sadness as well as joy. Two of the five children born to them died in infancy. In May 1834, kneeling at the bedside of his dying wife, 'in her presence, with her blessing, he dedicated his own remaining years to God, for the extension of His kingdom in those regions where Christ was not yet known.'[4]

Central to this prayer was the fanning into flame of the desire ignited so many years previously. This 'flame', to take the Christian Gospel to the remote people of the world, although in recent years had burning low, had never been reduced to ashes.

Space does not permit here, nor is it the subject of this book, to tell of this desire that led him to Africa, specifically to reach the fierce Zulus, nor of his part in the founding of a settlement in territory given to him by Dingarn, the ruthless ruler of the Zulus. The settlement, once built, became Durban.

In 1837 Queen Victoria replaced William IV on the throne of England and with the Victorian era came the expansion of British colonies. Like the Roman Empire in the first century AD the British Empire would be the catalyst for the spread of Christianity into previously unreached areas. It was in her reign that the Cambridge Seven and some of the other heroes and heroines left for India and Africa as well as China.

Sailing in HMS *Velocity*, on one of Gardiner's voyages home from the African continent, he called in at St Helena. It was here that Captain Allen Gardiner saw where Napoleon had been imprisoned and had later died. The western route the vessel took landed him on South American soil and on June 21st 1838 he reached the harbour of Rio de Janeiro once again.

Till his death thirteen years later, his calling took him to the mainly unexplored regions of Brazil, Argentina, Bolivia and Chile. In 1844 he founded the Patagonian Missionary Society, which in turn became the South American Society.

It was December 12th 1970 that had marked the end of the course for seventeen new recruits in the house named after the founder of the South American Mission Society. It also marked the end of his earthly course for our Warden, Ted Jenkin, the

---

[4] Ibid: p. 39

news of whose sudden death was broken to us, that morning. Like Allen Gardiner, he too had served his God as faithfully in his own particular calling. The baton was being passed on, not only to the seventeen, but also to at least two of the five children who shared in the Allen Gardiner House experience.

Chapter 11
Chile's Uniqueness

'Noche, nieve y arena hacen la forma
de mi delgada patria,
todo el silencio esta en su larga linea.'
Night, snow and sand make up the form
of my thin country,
all silence lies in its long line.
Pablo Neruda
From *Canto General: Descubridores de Chile* 1950

There is a unique quality about Chile. It has sometimes been called an island within a continent. The boundaries that separate its landmass from north to south and east to west are as diverse as they are protective. Each of the natural boundaries has over the centuries tested human endeavour to its limits. What has at first been seen as an insurmountable barrier has led to the innate desire to overcome and to conquer.

Sometimes referred to as 'the longest runner bean in the world', Chile in the whole of its 4200 kilometre length supports a rich variety of climatic zones, from the arid desert in the north, to the temperate rainforest in the south, and in between the Mediterranean-like central region. Even farther south are the fjords, glaciers and, at the extreme of 'where the land ends', separated by a formidable sea, lies the ice cap of the Chilean Antarctic.

The country's uniqueness also lies in its width in proportion to its length. Never more than approximately 350 kilometers at its widest and around 112 kilometers at its narrowest, it is possible, in theory, to ski in the Andes in the morning and swim in the Pacific in the evening.

The Atacama Desert stretches for around 1100 kilometers (approximately one third of Chile's length), from the border town of La Serena in the south to Arica on the border with Peru to the north. After La Serena the fertile central region gradually gives way to the desert. From here to Copiapó is known as *norte chico* and merges into *norte grande* the further and deeper one travels into the arid north. The Tropic of Capricorn runs through the desert about half way, just north of Antofagasta. It is the driest desert in the world. The area from Antofagasta to Arica is the territory annexed by Chile from both Bolivia and Peru in the War of the Pacific.

The High Plateau, *El Altiplano*, above 12,000 feet, is shared with both of these northern neighbours. It is also known as the *Puna* and is the largest tableland outside Tibet. It would be several years before we crossed this dry arid wasteland at ground level with its own unique yet stark beauty. First we saw it from the air – pockets of glistening white saucer-like depressions on the one hand, pristine white jagged peaks reaching upwards on the other, breaking up the seemingly endless sand-coloured canopy stretching out air mile upon air mile. The saucer-like depressions were the salt lakes, natural habitat of the flamingos, the jagged peaks the snow-covered volcanoes. Chile boasts over 2000 volcanoes, of which over 50 are still active.

Because of the lack of rain the naturally occurring minerals have been retained. Most lucrative in Chile's history were the nitrates, which were to fashion the country's socio-economic development. It was the British entrepreneurs at the end of the Victorian era that developed this industry, centred in Humberstone just east of Iquique. The nitrates heralded the industrial expansion transforming the labour movement.

The knock-on effect resulted in an export-dependent economy. Along with the nitrates came the necessary need for transportation. With their engineering experience the British built railways. Small metal plates engraved 'Made in Lancashire' or 'Cobb & Son, 1897' would leave no later passenger in any doubt as to the origin of these fine engines. Such was the engine, which pulled the train along the narrow gauge tracks we travelled in, as a family, across the desert all the way to Bolivia in the late 1970s.

According to BBC writer and photographer Michael Andrews in his book based on the documentary *The Flight of the Condor'* ... Chilean Nitrate was the hottest property on the London stock exchange. British capital owned it, British engineers built the railways that served it, British engineers staffed it.'[1]

The British influence can still be seen in the legacy of a clock, in a plaza in Arica, a town near the border of Chile and Peru, chiming out the familiar sounds of Big Ben.

The collapse of the nitrate industry with the complete closure of Humberstone in 1960 was due to two main factors. German scientists in the early years of the twentieth century began to manufacture synthetic nitrates resulting in a decline of Chile's natural commodity. In addition, the Depression of 1930 resulted in many British leaving Chile. The British influence, which left its mark on a nation referred to by many of its South American cousins as 'the little England', would be replaced by its largest cousin to the north of the great continent of the Americas. From then on Chile looked to the United States in most areas of life.

The percentage of true indigenous people in Chile is small compared to many of the other Republics – about five percent. They are mainly to be found in two opposite ends of the country. The rest have been absorbed through years of intermarriage resulting in the vast majority of Chileans being *mestizo*, of mixed race. The remaining thirty percent are white. Unlike Brazil, the black African slave trade never reached Chile.

It is generally thought that the ancient Aymará who pre-date the Incas are likely to have their origin in the Titicaca basin of Peru and Bolivia. From these ancient ancestors the pure indigenous people of the *norte grande* have descended. However, by far the majority today are to be found in Bolivia. Not a lot is known of their beginnings. They are short of stature with an enlarged thorax due to the expansion of their lungs because of

---

[1] Michael Andrews: *The Flight of the Condor* Collins p. 77

the lack of oxygen in the high altitudes. In common with other Indian peoples of this continent they have straight black hair, high cheekbones, and the usual facial expression is solemn and inscrutable, perhaps reflecting the harshness of their existence and their natural suspicion. Unlike the legacy handed down from the countries to the north of Chile right into Mexico (a legacy in ancient stone monuments reflecting advanced cultural civilisation), there are no architectural ruins in the Chilean desert. The only legacy they have in common is carved out of oppression, not only by hard to tame elements of nature, but also by past history of human oppressors seeking to tame them. Even the children seem to find it hard to smile.

In a somewhat macabre, yet fascinating way, the carved dour facial expression remains a handed down legacy. An expression etched in crinkling dark brown parchment-like skin remaining intact on a face or two of beautifully preserved mummies. These are to be found in the anthropological museum in San Pedro de Atacama near the border with Bolivia and about fifty miles north of the Tropic of Capricorn.

The founder of the museum and its first curator was a Belgian Jesuit priest Gustav Le Paige. We met him subsequently on a visit to the museum while holidaying in the desert region. Unlike the other indigenous people, in the south of Chile, the Mapuche, the Aymará were unable to resist the Spanish *conquistadores.*

Inseparable from the rural Aymará are their llamas and vicuñas. These related beasts of burden provide not only wool but also milk and meat. Llama meat is very high in protein and is completely cholesterol free.

Vicuña, a large village in the *norte chico,* is situated in an oasis of a green valley. It is known for two famous reasons – both unique.

Lucila Godoy Alcayaga, known by her pen name as Gabriela Mistral, was born in Vicuña. *'La Gabriela'* as the locals call her was among Chile's finest poets. Not only was she the country's first Nobel Prize winner, but also Latin America's first for Literature. Chile's other Nobel Prize winner was the poet and diplomat Pablo Neruda.

The other reason that Vicuña is of importance is for less artistic reasons yet equally considered with pride. Rather than the sensibility of the spirit being fed on a literary diet is the 'must-have' preceding a culinary diet fed by another spirit! The beautiful lush Elqui valley is home to a particular small white muscatel grape. From this is made *pisco,* about forty percent proof. The word *pisco* comes from the Peruvian Quechua word *pisku,* flying bird. There is a difference between the Peruvian *pisco* and the Chilean, each claiming their drink is the better of the two. The Chilean version, *pisco sour,* is made with the addition of lemon juice, sugar and egg white. Either way too much of this appetizer especially in the full sun and on an empty stomach and you really do feel that you're flying!

Before leaving the 'small north' there are impressive monuments, three in all, modern steel-designed dome-shaped structures set high on a desert hill. Located just a few miles south of Vicuña they lie sandwiched between the Pacific to the west and the Andes to the east. They stand sentinel on the foothills of the Andes, seen for miles around and surrounded by nothing but sand and overhead the deepest blue sky imaginable by day and the blackest myriad star-studded sky by night.

You could be forgiven for thinking that the white domes, glistening brightly in the daytime sun, were the centre of a modern day cult. In a sense you would be right. Scientists from all over the world descend on the Tololo observatory. El Tololo boasts the largest telescope in the southern hemisphere with a lens twelve feet in diameter. This, the largest of the three, can capture light that has been travelling for 14,000 million years. It has even taken pictures of the birth of a star.

Pounding the length of the western coast of the whole country are the Pacific waves. The Humboldt Current, about 100 miles wide, flows from Chilean Antarctica in the south to just short of Peru's border with Ecuador in the north. The water, as a result, is very cold, as we were to discover first hand. The coldness is not only due to the speed at which it flows, but also to the upsurge of the cold deep waters from the Chile-Peru trench.

The current as a result has a profound effect on the climate.

According to Andrews the temperature of the sea off Callao, Peru's main port, is three degrees centigrade cooler than that off Antofagasta, 900 miles farther south. The effect of this is such that 'along an immense distance of shoreline the climatic and physical conditions of the shore remain unchanged. It is as if from Norway to Gibraltar climate and fauna were constant – there is no other coast like it in the world.'[2]

In stark contrast to the poverty of both fauna and flora in the barren, inhospitable desert landscape, the ocean washing Chile's shoreline teems with a rich variety of marine life. Usually one associates penguins with snow and ice. Certainly the southern ocean has several varieties of these comic waiter-like birds. What a surprise it was for us one holiday, when we found one, swimming in the waters off Tongoy, just south of La Serena, on the edge of the *norte chico*. In fact there are large colonies of the Humboldt penguin, as well as sea lions, to be found so far north.

An abundance of sea lions, penguins and whales are amongst the mammals frequenting the southern waters. Sharing this vast space is the *centolla*, the giant king crab, a delicious delicacy. Without doubt, this delicacy has to achieve first place on the top-ten list of the *à la carte* menu of any up-market restaurant in the south.

Magical islands of childhood fame are to be found in these waters, although, with writer's licence, the author Daniel Defoe chose a more exotic tropical setting for his novel *Robinson Crusoe*. The Juan Fernández Islands, consisting of two, lie 400 miles off the port of Valparaiso. It was on the one '*Más a Tierra*' (Nearer Land) that the Scot, Alexander Selkirk, was abandoned by his captain after a quarrel. He was marooned there in isolation for five years, from 1704 until his rescue in 1709.

Another island belonging to Chile, which has been the inspiration of both writers and anthropologists, is to be found as far away as 2300 miles from the mainland. Easter Island, Rapa Nui, lies halfway between Chile and Polynesian Tahiti. This solitary, volcanic island has puzzled experts down the years. A

---

[2] Ibid: p. 82

Dutch explorer on his arrival in 1722 discovered islanders with large pegs inserted in their ear lobes. The various size pegs were being replaced one by one until the lobes had stretched almost to shoulder length. How the enormous carved statues of heads had been quarried, transported, and erected has been the subject of many debates.

I was fascinated to read, as a teenager, Thor Heyerdahl's book *Kon-Tiki*. He constructed a balsa wood raft and set sail to the Polynesian Islands. His theory was that the original inhabitants came from South America as opposed to Asia. The second book I read, *Aku-Aku*, centred on these mysterious statues so characteristic of Rapu Nui (Isla Pascua to Chileans).

It was thrilling to visit the Kon-Tiki Museum in Oslo almost a half-century later and see first hand the original balsa raft in which Heyerdahl undertook that first expedition. Although his theory that the inhabitants of Polynesia were originally from South America has been disproved, the museum full of artefacts from subsequent expeditions pays tribute to a man given Norway's highest honour. This award presented by Norway's king was given in recognition of all Thor Heyerdahl has contributed to the environment and for peace, in bringing together in his various crews men from nations formerly at war with one another.

Naomi, in her early twenties on a return to her childhood country, was able to fit in a trip to La Isla Pascua, staying with local families and friends of friends.

Another group of islands, separated from the southernmost point of the mainland of 'the long bean' by the Strait named after the Portuguese explorer Ferdinand Magellan, is Tierra del Fuego. This large archipelago, translated 'The Land of Fire', is jointly shared with Argentina in a mutually suspicious liaison. According to Pendle, Magellan named it thus because as the explorer sailed through the Straits he saw the smoke from the fires of the Indian inhabitants lining the shoreline of the largest island.[3] The explorer had referred to this island as 'Smokeland' but his patron Charles V of Spain preferred the name 'Land of Fire'.

---

[3] George Pendle: *The Land and People of Chile*. A. and C. Black Ltd. p. 81.

The archipelago, discovered by Drake to be in fact an archipelago, culminates in Cape Horn, a never-ending challenge to intrepid sailors, lone yachtsmen and women. Here the Atlantic Ocean meets the Pacific and frequently the clash of these two oceans, whipped up by gale force winds, results in gigantic waves. This most feared coast has been the graveyard of many a ship and its crew down the centuries. Unfortunately, Ray and I were aware of this when, during the writing of this book, we waved goodbye to our youngest family member from the shores of home.

Leaving from Portsmouth, as crewmember on an identical yacht to eleven others, Julian was racing around the world. The Global Challenge yacht race is reputed to be the toughest yacht race because, unlike others, these yachts sail the wrong way around the world – against the prevailing wind and currents. Due to medical emergencies *Stelmar*, the yacht in which Julian was sailing, ended up being the only one in the race to circumnavigate Cape Horn twice and to sail through the Beagle Channel, named after HMS *Beagle* in which Charles Darwin travelled.

Until that occasion Julian was the only one of our three who had not revisited Chile. However the visit was extremely short lived, just one hour to evacuate a crewmember at Puerto Williams, a naval and meteorological base, on Navarino Island in the Beagle Channel, before getting back into the race. Williams was made the capital of Chilean Antarctica even though it lay outside Antarctica.

Due to a second medical emergency, as a result of a freak wave, *Stelmar* had to return to land after 1000 nautical miles of sailing. This time they landed at the Argentinian town of Ushuaia on 'the Land of Fire'. According to John Gunther only 'a madman' would sail a ship in waters known to be 'among the most dangerous in the world.'[4]

There is a German fairy story that gives the origin of 'The Man in the Moon'. According to this fairy-tale the Man in the Moon is a navigator who was unable to circumnavigate Cape Horn. In frustration at his failure he swore, exclaiming: 'If I do not double

---

[4] John Gunther: *Inside South America.* Hamish Hamilton Ltd. p. 318

Cape Horn may I sit up in the moon for all eternity!' His ship was subsequently wrecked; and since then he has remained seated up in the moon. This is why sailors still say, 'See the Moon! There is the navigator who could not double Cape Horn!'[5]

Three small islands to the east of Navarino Island, were the centre of a dispute between Chile and Argentina in 1978 – a dispute so serious that the two republics were on the verge of war. Lennox, Picton and Nueva lie directly to the east of Navarino, all below the Argentinian half of Tierra del Fuego. The reason for the underlying tension was the rich deposits of oil.

Who were the original inhabitants that lived in such harsh conditions? Among the various tribes, the ones of significance are mainly three. The Ona lived on the larger landmass of Tierra del Fuego and are referred to by anthropologists as 'foot Indians' as contrasted with 'canoe Indians'. They were hunters, the main prey being the guanaco, a close relative of the llama and the alpaca.

When Charles Darwin was visiting these waters in the early 1830s he was unimpressed with these 'Fuegians', as the islanders inhabiting both land and sea in this southern area are generally referred to. He wrote in his diary, 'Viewing such men, one can hardly make oneself believe that they are fellow-creatures, and inhabitants of the same world.' Considering he lived in Dickensian times, when a so-called civilisation was sending children down coal mines, up chimneys and into mills, working until fit to drop, how would the Onas judge his own people?

The Yahgan were the nomadic 'canoe Indians' frequenting the waters off *Isla Navarino* to Cape Horn. I wonder what these sailors, from their ten-foot evergreen beech bark canoes, would have made of today's seventy-two-foot yacht with a ninety-foot mast calling in on their island? The last pure Yahgan, *abuela Rosa* (grandmother Rosa) died in 1982.

The third tribe, also nomadic and related to the Yahgan were the Alacalufe (westernised name for the *Kaweshkar* tribe).

---

[5] George Pendle: *The Land and Peoples: Chile.* Citing Agustín Edwards. A. and C. Black p. 87

They paddled their canoes further north and into the Magellan Straits.

Separating Cape Horn from Chilean Antarctica is a stretch of the southern ocean, Drake's Passage.

What of Antarctica itself? In the Antarctic there really aren't any frontiers – none is needed. Here in this icy wasteland differences are left to officialdom to thrash out in government buildings in the world's capitals. Chile and Argentina base their territorial claims to decrees and bulls inherited from Spain. Chile was one of the first signatories to the 1959 Antarctic Treaty, ratified by twelve nations in 1940. A handwritten note from Bernardo O'Higgins, Chile's liberator from Spanish dependence, was discovered in 1918 in the vaults of the British Foreign Office. In this note O'Higgins makes mention of Chilean territory in Antarctica. On this basis Chile made formal presentation to the international community in 1940 in order to certify its rights to this territory.

The 1959 Antarctic Treaty affirms that Antarctica shall continue forever to be used for peaceful purposes. To emphasis this aspect, among the buildings housing the few internationals who live and work there, are scientific research stations, a hospital and now the first Antarctic church.

A more worrying aspect of our modern world is the meteorological station, which, among other things, monitors the ozone layer. Each year the hole appears in the layer fifteen miles above the earth's surface.

The last boundary to encapsulate this 'island within a continent' is the mighty Andean range, the *Cordillera*. Curving down the west of South America, like the backbone of a giant dinosaur, the ever-present Andes Mountains form the spine of this vast continent. Following the curve through the length not only of 'the long bean' itself but travelling into the northern Republics is the mighty condor. Ugly in appearance yet beautiful in flight, this large vulture, utilising the air currents, glides over the mountain peaks. According to Andrews 'its wing area is nearly two square metres' and a bird can weigh upwards of twelve kilos: 'this gives it the low wing-loading necessary for slow soaring flight.'[6] This enables the giant bird to continue gliding for considerable time without flapping its wings. In 1834 Darwin describes such a phenomenon as he watched condors for over half an hour, in which 'they moved in large curves, sweeping in circles, descending and ascending without giving a single flap.'[7]

Although the Himalayas boast the highest peaks, this mountain chain, stretching from Central America to Cape Horn, is the longest in the world. The Andean peaks are as high as the depth of the Pacific as it suddenly plunges along Chile's coastline, to a depth of over 20,000 feet. The greatest 'vertebra' in this mountain 'spine' is Aconcagua. Lying just north of Santiago de Chile, it stands majestic at 23,034 feet, surpassed only by Himalayan peaks.

'No other continent possesses a north-south range which cuts straight through the tropics, bringing glaciers to the equator; no other range forms such a barrier dividing climate and species'.[8] It is all these natural barriers that have shaped and helped form both Chile's uniqueness physically and her identity as a people spiritually; barriers to be both respected and surmounted.

---

[6] Michael Andrews: *The Flight of the Condor* Collins p. 68
[7] George Pendle: *The Lands and Peoples: Chile.* A. and C. Black p. 43
[8] Michael Andrews: *The Flight of the Condor* Collins p. 17

Chapter 12
Chile: A Stressful Beginning

The day to leave Frinton for a country on the other side of the world had finally arrived – a country we had already read about. However, our first impressions on Saturday, March 27th were anything but favourable! There were valid reasons for this, not least because we were exhausted having experienced a gruelling journey out. Added to this was the disappointment of crossing the snow-covered Andes, dividing Chile from Argentina, in the middle of the night instead of the anticipated daylight. Our plane was twelve hours behind schedule!

The morning of Friday 26th began at 07:05 with the following entry in our diary: *'Children all awake and sense this is it.'* Followed by three-year old Naomi excitedly saying, *"Today we go in aeroplane."*

This was the day we had looked forward to, both with excitement and trepidation, the culmination of years of vision and preparation. *'09:15. Naomi goes off to play-school for the last time. Andrew to parents for the morning, great help for last minute packing, clearing and cleaning [sic].'*

Leaving Julian with Ray, I set off for the launderette with a last couple of loads of washing, mostly children's baby clothes and the inevitable nappies! The latter had been a continuous daily occurrence for the past three years without a break!

On arriving at the launderette, the only other visitor there was an elderly lady. She greeted me with a friendly smile. This encounter was to prove very significant, not only for the immediate future but also for the distant future and even the far distant future! Something I looked upon not so much as a co-incidence but rather as one of God's incidents.

We started to chat. Within a very short time my ill-concealed excitement came pouring out as I shared the why and the wherefore of what lay ahead for our little family. To my utter amazement, with a smile spreading across her face, she announced that she and her family had lived in Santiago, Chile. Her name? Elena Goodwin-Hudson. She was the wife of the Bishop who had preached at Ray's ordination at St Paul's Cathedral four years previously. Bishop Arthur Goodwin-Hudson had also preceded Canon Harry Sutton as General Secretary of SAMS. Before we parted she said they would be praying for us as we embarked on our new ministry.

After lunch Ray left Frinton in a borrowed Morris Traveller that had seen better days. The car was packed to its roof with our luggage and sagging with the weight of seven cases, one push chair, a guitar, two sleeping bags, a big bag with baby toiletries and the essential nappies. In addition Ray's hand luggage contained a reel-to-reel Telefunken tape recorder generously given by a church member for our work.

The rest of us were faced with a choice. If we wanted to travel together the only option open would be on the bonnet or the roof, the latter mode of transport we were to see from time to time in the years ahead! We decided it would be more prudent to follow behind in Papa's car.

A little later we set out in Father-in-law's car, Naomi and Andrew clutching their own precious hand luggage, a plastic bag containing a teddy bear and two much-loved Ladybird books in the one and a cuddly rabbit, a Matchbox car, and a Ladybird book in the other.

We were about ten to fifteen minutes' drive out of Frinton, when to our consternation we found Ray still at the garage where he had gone to re-fuel. The car wouldn't start! Visions of reaching Heathrow Airport on time were fast fading into the background. There were quick 'arrow prayers' all round. A mechanic arrived on the scene and to our great relief a very dirty carburettor was diagnosed. With grateful thanks to the mechanic and to God we set off again, this time in convoy.

We stopped off at Woodford where more of the family were waiting, for a very quick tea and toilet break. Car places were re-located and we said 'farewell' to the geriatric Morris with considerable relief! We arrived at Heathrow to find my parents and Elaine, friends and representatives of SAMS home staff, anxiously looking at their watches!

I will never forget the look of incredulity on the part of the staff at the check-in desk when we presented our entire luggage to be weighed! Fortunately the luggage for the hold was more bulk than overweight. (Our careful weighing on bathroom scales in Frinton had paid off.) However, the leather bag with the tape recorder pushed the weight up and we were asked to pay an excess of £32, which in the early seventies and to a missionary family was a lot of money.

We were hurriedly passed through security, which resulted in our 'farewells' at the barrier being much briefer than anticipated, and as a result less traumatic for us. For grandparents left behind however, it was understandably a painful parting. For my parents especially, it was difficult because they wouldn't see their only grandchildren for at least four years, when we would be due for home leave.

It was a great comfort discovering we were travelling with another SAMS family, Arthur and Helen Robinson and their two small daughters, Sarah and Susan. They were returning to Chile for a second term of service. We were all physically and emotionally too exhausted and drained to break into much conversation at this stage.

There would be many opportunities to make up for this, given my and Helen's reputation for being good talkers!

Soon we were airborne on a very full Air France Boeing 727 bound for Orly Airport, Paris, where we changed on to a Boeing 707. Naomi and Andrew were by now flagging and became irritable, having lived on bursts of extra adrenaline in their excitement. Julian, thankfully, was fast asleep. 'At last we can begin to relax and settle the children down and sort ourselves out for the long haul ahead,' we thought. But alas this was far from the case.

Barely had Naomi and Andrew dropped off to sleep when a voice from the cockpit said, 'This is your Captain. One of the engines has failed and we have to return to Orly Airport.'

After circling around for a further twenty minutes or so, we safely landed with three engines instead of four. We disembarked. Julian was carried in the arms of a stewardess, and Andrew fast asleep, was draped over Ray's left shoulder, Ray's right hand holding the leather bag with the costly tape recorder. Then came little Naomi, in a daze, following as best she could clutching her precious bag of toys as well as her younger brother's. I brought up the rear with the big bag of nappies etc. and the remaining hand luggage. This was the stuff nightmares are made of!

Andrew was in such a deep sleep that we had to spread-eagle him across the luggage on one of the trolleys. We wearily trundled down endless corridors to the waiting area we had left behind one and a half-hours earlier! We had had nothing to eat or drink since leaving Woodford, not even a drink on the flight from London to Paris.

All refreshment places at Orly were closed by now. I asked a stewardess for some water, she smilingly said she would see what she could do. Heels clicking down the corridor she faded into the distance and was soon out of sight. Ten to fifteen minutes later she reappeared with only one plastic mug of water. We hadn't even as yet left a so-called developed country for a so-called developing country – and this was all that the former could produce!

Together, with all the other passengers, we were left wondering whether the engine fault could be corrected in time to continue our flight or were we to have an overnight stop? It was the latter! A little after midnight we were driven in an airline coach to a hotel to have something to eat and to pass the rest of the night. The hotel was of a high standard and our diary records *'we had a lovely meal but too tired to enjoy it.'*

We went to bed around 02:00 hours but at 06:50, I was up feeding Julian. The remaining four of us eagerly devoured our continental breakfast. The one humorous comment I could muster was, 'Well, at least I can tell family and friends that you took me to a posh' (it was the Hilton) 'hotel in Paris for the weekend of our fifth Wedding Anniversary!' (Friday, March 26th.)

Duly fed and watered, hope began to soar. Perhaps the problems encountered so far were now a thing of the past. This was unfortunately not the case. After such a brief night's sleep on descending the staircase to our waiting coach we heard angry voices and shouting. An amazing scene greeted us. Could this be reality or were we watching a clip from a farcical film preview?

Two hotel staff complete in uniform stood with their backs to the closed doors of the hotel entrance, their arms outstretched, barring the exit; in front of them flight passengers shouted and gesticulated angrily. Above the din and commotion we could just about hear the broken English of one of the officials, 'Pleez no one leef dees otel weedowt peying!'

The Manager was sent for, who confirmed we all had to pay for our enforced over-night stop. We didn't have enough money to pay the full amount for our family but thankfully the Robinsons made up the difference. It was to be several months before Air France reimbursed us.

At 10.00 am we were again in the air. We had clear views of Gibraltar, Morocco and the Sahara Desert before continuing down the west coast of Africa. The plane touched down on the dry, dusty, deserted airfield of Dakar Airport, Senegal. Here we disembarked for a welcome stretch of legs.

Naomi and Andrew were fascinated to see the black faces of smartly dressed policeman on duty. Men and women, wearing a bright array of colourful national costumes, were selling an equally varied mix of wares; handicrafts of all shapes and sizes, beautifully carved wooden objects, beaded jewellery, not to mention a rich variety of edible fruit.

As we were returning to the aircraft we noticed some colourful and immaculately dressed bandsmen marching to the accompaniment of their music. Their instruments, mostly drums and bugles, made quite a cacophony of sound. To Ray's and my ears hardly melodious. However, the children were duly impressed! Accompanying the band were motor-cycle outriders in red capes. They were about to meet a delegation of Nigerian government officials.

Take-off was west across the Atlantic on the eight-hour journey to Buenos Aires. This was to be the most boring part of the flight with little to see from the windows. The attentive cabin crew came to our aid, with yet another diversion, when Naomi and Andrew became fractious. Colouring books and crayons, as well as all sorts of goodies were produced. Once the novelty began to wear off they later found their way into their own respective plastic bags. Julian, meanwhile, when not asleep, kept his parents well and truly distracted!

Mealtimes became the best distraction of all. Naomi in particular was fascinated with her little tray with the carefully packaged food and the novel containers. Andrew just enjoyed the food, as we did, once we had finished doing battle with all the fiddly wrappings for four and actually got to sample the food at the same time as keeping Julian's little fingers out. The whole experience of mealtimes became a juggling act in a greatly confined space.

As we flew over Brazil I noticed how dense the foliage was. The twisting and turning of the rivers broke up the green carpet of the Rain Forest, glistening in the sun, and, from our perspective, looking more like snail-trails across a large patch of lawn. As the plane began its descent for its next refuel, these glistening trails metamorphosed into giant anaconda-like rivers.

We approached Rio de Janeiro in the dusk and, with little light, were just able to pick out the Sugar-loaf Mountain and the Corcovado with the magnificent, floodlit statue of Christ the Redeemer. According to the Brazilians his arms were stretched out in blessing over the city. A joke we were later to hear in Chile was that the outstretched hands of the Christ were poised to give a big clap when the Brazilians returned to work! An actual visit to these impressive sights was reserved for a number of years in the future.

We continued to descend and suddenly all I could see was water, water and more water. Had we overshot the runway? I was certain we had. No sooner had fear taken hold than within seconds we felt the most-welcome bumps as the plane's wheels touched *terra firma*. On alighting we had to remain by the aircraft (safety and security less sophisticated in the early seventies), as the stop was so brief. The hot, humid air enveloped us.

Buenos Aires was reached in the darkness. The majority of passengers having reached the end of their journey disembarked. The last leg of the very long haul was, therefore, for us, in an emptier, lighter plane. We soared over the mighty Andes like a giant condor. It seemed that no sooner had we gained height than we began to descend. The rapid drop of height, as we neared our final destination, seemed to these weary travellers every bit as determined as the condor sweeping down to approach its prey. The anticipation of the goal achieved would be every bit as rewarding … or would it?

Exhausted, yet exhilarated, we arrived at the airport of Santiago, Chile, to begin a new life, but our stress was not yet over. The customary warmth for which Chileans are renowned was lost on us with the officialdom encountered at the *Aduana* (Customs.) With a smile on his face, perhaps more from an anticipated perk for his efficiency rather than a genuine welcome, our Customs man spotted the Telefunken tape-recorder sticking out of the top of Ray's leather cabin bag.

'*Señor, Señora*, there won't be much to pay for the items you're bringing in to Chile, just a little on this recorder.' The asking price of the 'little' turned out to be four times the retail price, not counting the £32 excess we had already paid thirty-six hours previously at Heathrow! Needless to say we could not pay this and sadly our much-desired and needed recorder remained in Customs. The next returning SAMS missionary would take it home. We didn't see it again for almost three years!

Chapter 13

First Impressions

Plans to go direct to our bungalow in Quilpué were changed, because of our delayed arrival in the early hours of a Sunday. As a result we were met at the airport, not by Bishop David Pytches and taken to the coast, but by a contingent of welcoming, smiling faces belonging to other mission personnel.

We were taken instead to the downtown Mission Centre in the heart of Santiago, and so to bed … but we hadn't reckoned with the long sleep the children had had towards the end of the plane journey, compounded by the time difference of four hours. The resultant effect was Andrew and Julian, as large as life, wanted to be entertained! Thankfully, with sleep patterns totally disrupted, we didn't even feel the earth tremor that rocked the central coastal region and was felt in the capital during our second night. We were told the next morning that there was currently a great deal of volcanic activity under the sea. The climax to this would be our own first-hand experience three months later.

Living out of suitcases was an unavoidable added pressure. Why is it that the necessary commodity is always at the bottom of the case? My diary records hunting high and low through the many suitcases to find little socks for little children!

Now we were in the metropolis, what about some limited sightseeing? The obvious choice was the Presidential Palace, known as the Moneda. This translated means money, coinage or small change, so named because it was originally the Mint. The Moneda, hardly known outside of Chile, would be seen on television screens across the world in just over two years from our first sighting of it.

To reach the building our outward travelling companions, Arthur and Helen, took us up and down a number of streets in the city centre. These were constructed on the block system and proved quite hazardous. The choice facing us was to risk tripping on the uneven pavements and being caught up in the sheer volume of pedestrian traffic pouring down the street, mostly under twenty-five years of age. The alternative was, in an attempt to avoid the many potholes in the pavement, to step into the road and be mowed down by the relentless surge of traffic; the latter resembled a stampeding herd of wildebeests! We chose the former.

The Palace itself, standing back from the Alameda, with an open asphalt forecourt, was an imposing rectangular building, not unlike a smaller version of Buckingham Palace. Proudly flying from the top of the building was Chile's national flag of red, white and blue with its characteristic white star occupying the upper blue rectangle nearest to the flagpole. The somewhat drab-looking beige walls of four feet thickness were constructed with function rather than fashion in mind.

Little did its architect imagine these walls would be put to the test of withstanding not only the onslaught of underground seismic forces on its foundations, but that one day, in the not too far distant future, attack would come from the air. That future, although we didn't know it then, for us lay just around the corner and would seal the fate of Chile's President.

On guard outside the Palace were the khaki clad *carabineros*, Chile's paramilitary police. Their very real presence on the streets on foot or on horseback, under whatever political party was in power, was either a comfort or a threat, depending on a person's political persuasion. For the common criminal it was always the latter. We were to learn in the months and years ahead just what part they would play in a country torn apart by division.

While we were living in Frinton, prior to leaving for Chile, our monetary system had changed to decimal currency. Having just made the adjustment, we were now faced with a currency dealing in units of hundreds and thousands rather than units of tens, all of which was very confusing. With an annual salary of

£300 per adult and allowances ranging from £70 to £40 for the children, depending on their ages, it was easy to be lured into a false sense of affluence. Within a few days of arrival our purses were bulging to overflowing with crumpled, dirty escudo notes, the value of many being just a few pence. By now we had moved from Santiago to our temporary home, in Quilpué, just fourteen kilometres from Viña del Mar.

The bus company, which linked Quilpué with Viña, was known as the 'Sol del Pacifico' (Pacific Sun). We soon discovered how aptly it was named. The roar of the Pacific waves would find their counterpart in the roar of the buses' engines as the drivers would try and outstrip one another down the summer sun-soaked tarmac roads, leaving a trail of scorching rubber as brakes were hastily applied! At the same time as these 'chariots of fire' were competing with one another, their foolhardy 'charioteers', one hand on the steering wheel, would somehow manage to take a fistful of crumpled notes and give not only the required ticket but also the correct change.

Hanging above the 'charioteer's' head would be a medley of mascots: a medallion of Saint Christopher, patron saint of travellers; a miniature statue of the Virgin Mary; a small bunch of cheap plastic flowers faded by the blazing sun through the windscreen etc. Most common of all was a cardboard or plastic plaque with the words *'Dios es mi copiloto'* (God is my co-driver). Many a time as we used these buses, together with our children, we would silently pray that in actual fact it would be God himself who would take the driver's seat! With road (and rail) transport so exceptionally cheap we couldn't, after all, expect a deluxe bus service. The cost of the fourteen-kilometre journey was one and a half escudos each and there were thirty-five escudos to the pound. (In today's terms, five pence!).

In the following years, when living in the capital, the three children would travel regularly by bus to their school seven to eight miles away. With hearts in our mouths and prayers on our lips, we would wave them off, having pushed them well down inside the bus past those cluttering the entrance and certainly past the few reckless hangers-on on the outside. Fortunately, given the Chilean's love of children, there were always ready and willing hands to assist in this. Not infrequently, a mother or grandmother fascinated by the blue-eyed, blond-haired children would offer an ample lap to the little *gringuitos* (an endearing term for a foreign child).

On our arrival in Quilpué, it had been suggested that, as we would need to purchase basic furniture at mission expense for the unfurnished bungalow, we would stay with the Skinner family next door. Little did we realise how very prudent this decision was. All thoughts of walking in to a fitted kitchen with an oven ready to function at the turn of a knob and hot water emanating from a turned on tap were soon to be dispelled.

The plumbing or rather lack of plumbing never ceased to both amaze and frustrate us. The minimum of three toilets in an average home, stretching to four or five in a wealthier one, seemed to us to be extravagant to say the least. That was until we discovered that, more often than not, more than one was not functioning! Plumbers were known by a mixing of the two languages. When we needed one, which proved to be frequently, the Church authorities would tell us to call for *'un gasfiter'* (pronounced 'oon gasfeeterr'). Famous among these were the Soto brothers (Soto being a surname).

One day they were called to repair a tiny hole and crack in the wash basin, near to the plughole, which left a small puddle of water on the tiled floor every time we turned on the taps. Never will I forget the look of utter astonishment on Ray's face as they set to work. Out from the trouser pocket of one came what looked like string, but in fact were fibres of hemp. This was then wrapped around the junction of the outlet pipe with the basin.

Intrigued, Ray waited to see what the next step in this Heath-Robinson approach would reveal. A putty type mixture was made and applied with an old knife over the hemp under the basin. The Soto brothers made their departure, once the work was completed, but not before the elder of the two, gesticulating and pointing to his watch, indicated how long we were to wait before we could use it.

Hot water was obtained from a gas ascot heater called a *'califont'*, connected to a portable gas cylinder. We learnt the hard way to keep a check on the amount of gas left in the cylinder and to have a replacement nearby. 'Ray, the gas has run out and I've a cake in the oven!' or 'Ray, the cylinder needs changing, the bath water is running cold!'

There were two sizes of cylinders used, the smaller for our portable fires, the larger for cooking and heating the water. When the empty cylinders needed replacing Ray, helped by Brian, would walk the half-mile to the depot with a wheelbarrow in which to transport the smaller variety, the larger were delivered by open truck. The luxury of piped gas to the home awaiting us in Santiago was as yet a dream unrealised. Living with such gas installations left us at times apprehensive. In a volcanic country we felt that living in our home was almost as hazardous as living at the foot of a dormant yet not extinct volcano!

Chile in 1971 was still classed as a developing country, yet more advanced than its bordering Republics. Certainly its population did not live within the safety limits that we were used to in coming from a developed nation.

We had arrived in Chile with only a smattering of the language, a few Spanish words strung together with no supporting grammatical structure. However, we were anxious to try these out. Unlike Europe, only the privileged would really have the opportunity to learn English, so it was no use at all to rely on using our own language. To survive one had to speak and understand Spanish. The sooner we got to work the better. 'What better opportunity to experiment than to take Gill out on her birthday,' thought Ray. He described this adventure in our second letter home.

As Chileans take afternoon siestas, shops remain open until late evening, so on this particular April evening:

' ... *we arrived down town at about 19:00 hrs. and spent the next three hours wandering around the various 'blocks' (streets) looking at buildings and people, window shopping, and actually going in three or four shops in an attempt to size up prices and buy Gill a present. We also investigated the cinemas only to find that the only decent film*

running was 'Scrooge' – on the following day only! – the English film
with Spanish captions.'

(I should add here that in the seventies, like T.V., cinemas
outside the capital, had an over abundance of American westerns
with dubbing, more often than not totally out of sync.)

'As we'd had a meal before leaving, we left a snack to about 21:30 and
thought we would try something really Chilean called "empanadas" –
a kind of Cornish pasty … We were dismayed when the mozo (waiter)
shook his head'. (Much later we discovered it was the custom to
eat *empanadas* at weekends and fiesta days.)

'He offered us no menu list, so we were completely stumped as to what
to ask for! So in desperation we glanced at the table … next to ours and
saw something which looked tasty …"churrascos", consisting of layers
of toast and grilled cheese and gammon or very thin slices of steak.'
We pointed to them and with gesticulations made it obvious we
would like the same. 'In fact they were delicious. For a drink we
tried to ask for a fruit juice – he came back with "Tuttifrutti" – a tasty
mixture of fruit juices including bananas – and most refreshing.'

Spanish lessons started within a week of our arrival, with
Gloria and Chris raring to go, having preceded us by several
weeks. Our language teacher, Señora Tagle, was the wife of a
high-ranking naval officer. It had been decided that lessons
would be on home ground because of our family needs. Naomi
was by now attending the mission school of St Paul in Viña del
Mar. Gill Skinner looked after Andrew and Julian next door to
enable me to attend classes, but also to be on hand.

Not surprisingly, our two single women coped far better than
we did, both in class and with the daily homework assignments.
Ray didn't find learning Spanish very easy, not being a linguist.
'No, Ray, it's not "de" but "dey". You must forget your French
pronunciation,' said Señora Tagle.

On one occasion we nearly brought the roof down with
laughter as a result of a noble attempt of guesswork by Ray. As
English and Spanish both have their language rooted in Latin,
many words are similar. There were times, therefore, when a
guess could prove to be near the mark. However, on this occasion
it totally backfired.

Wanting the correct vocabulary to describe an embarrassing moment, Ray said, '*Estoy embarazado!*'

'I don't think so,' replied our greatly amused *profesora*, for colloquially it meant, 'I am pregnant!'

To make matters worse we would later discover that the Latin American republics, while having a common language in Spanish, except for Portuguese-speaking Brazil, by no means share exclusively the same vocabulary, neither do they with the mother country of Spain. So an avocado, known in most of the Spanish-speaking countries as an *aguacate*, in Chile is a *palta*. An apricot, instead of an *albericoque* is a *damasco*.

All this when later travelling in the other republics proved to be a challenge at best and confusing at worst. But this wasn't our immediate problem. That in itself is an interesting statement, as we discovered one of the most used words in a Chilean's vocabulary was *un problema*. It seemed everyone had one and if they didn't, they would soon acquire one! It wasn't that these '*Latinos*' were always looking for difficulties; in fact they were an optimistic people by nature. In their desire to bend over backwards to help, their conversation would be punctuated every so often with '*no hay problema!*' (It's no trouble.)

The red tape was phenomenal. When making enquiries of officialdom, one would often be asked,'*Tiene un problema?*' (Do you have a problem?) Unfortunately, if the answer was in the negative it would only be a short matter of time before they created one! We learnt that often it was best not to ask a question in the first place!

We had to register with the authorities and acquire our temporary resident permits. The first question we were asked was if we were communists! We replied that we had no political affiliation in Chile, which as foreigners, and certainly as the following years' drama would unfold, proved to be the wisest answer. '*Apolitical*' was recorded on our documentation. In common with the other South American republics the subject of politics was introduced into conversation, as the English would comment on the weather.

We did have our fair share of problems those first weeks. These invariably consisted of equipment that didn't work efficiently. Given my temperament of high expectations, frustration was an ongoing battle I faced and the Chilean laid back temperament was a constant challenge for me to learn from them a little more *paciencia.*

The first meal I cooked on the gas cooker ended up all being placed in a saucepan on the only gas ring working. The washing machine was a basic twin tub shaped like a figure of eight with the washing section the larger of the two 'circles' and the spinner, the 'smaller'. On one particular occasion the problem was getting hot water in the first place as the *califont* wasn't working and had to be dismantled. Then when this had been fixed the washing machine pump failed. Ray and I had to wring out four sheets by hand.

Brian came to our rescue and discovered the problem was in fact simple to rectify. The fan belt had come off. All went well until the screw through the handle operating the rotary blade of the washtub snapped off. The following day Brian inserted a new screw but this involved a stripping down of the machine. Up early the next morning to put another load of washing on before the frenetic daily routine would start.

'Oh, no! It's happened again!' This time the water went straight through the wash tub onto the kitchen floor and the floods were out! Ray discovered the screw had worked loose. By now I was getting desperate for clean nappies for both Andrew and Julian. Disposable nappies were not to be had in 1971 in Quilpué and, added to this, Andrew had diarrhoea. We weren't sure whether this was due to the notorious Chile bug (known by the *'gringo'* community as *'chileitis')* that few escaped and was commonly contracted by foreigners soon after arrival (Ray had already had his fair share.) In Andrew's case the cause was more likely due to his wandering off into our garden unable to resist the tempting supply of grapes that would fall from the heavily laden vines! It was the height of the grape harvest.

With the screw tightened the washing machine was in working order once again but our problems were not yet over. The final straw came the following morning. The washing had been left out overnight and during the night the first of the autumnal rains had arrived. When they do, they come with a vengeance. (Later we would discover, at such times, it wasn't at all unusual for Chileans not to turn up for work or for children not to go to school.)

The added weight of the dripping-wet washing caused the line to break and there lying on the muddy ground were the essential nappies. I burst into tears. A husband to the rescue and a quick rinse and spin soon solved the immediate problem but the next was how to dry them? With all gas fires on at full blast and damp clothes strewn around the bungalow we survived that day; the routine of taking Naomi to school, the two boys to go next door and Spanish lessons to continue. Little wonder *'problema'* was heard on so many lips.

Fortunately among these times of frustrations were times of light relief and fascinating new discoveries. Never will I forget the excitement on seeing the first humming bird in our garden. These birds, aptly called *'picaflores'* (pecking flowers) are to be found throughout South America. The one I saw was the Green-Backed Firecrown, known in Spanish as *'Picaflor Chico'*, so named because of its small size and colour. It has green upper and under parts and iridescent feathers on the top of its head.

According to ornithologist Alfred Johnson, this particular humming-bird is among the smallest to be found in Chile and the most common. However, what it lacks in size is made up by being the species *'with the most extensive range'* covering the length of the country from Tierra del Fuego to the Atacama Desert. In addition it can be found to the west on the islands of Chiloé and the Juan Fernández and to the east reaching up to 7000 feet in the Andes.

These fascinating little birds hover while collecting nectar, their wings beating at a phenomenal rate. By contrast to the amazing energy they use by day, by night they hang inert and sleep. If the temperature drops to 7 degrees centigrade they enter into a 'state of torpor' that can vary from eight to fourteen hours.[1]

---

[1] A. W. Johnson: *The Birds of Chile.* Vol. 2. pp. 108, 109.

In addition to the plentiful supply of grapes in our garden were apple, pomegranate, fig and even a walnut tree. Most useful of all are the lemons. To walk out of the back door straight into an orchard area and pick fresh fruit was such luxury after the concrete jungle of London's East End.

Somehow I found time to make marmalade, lemon puddings and lemon curd, also our own mayonnaise. Lemon trees have the rare advantage of producing fruit on the tree at the same time as blossom. The aroma of both lemon and orange blossom is a smell to this day that I find simply heavenly!

Another fruit that we experimented with was to be found on a very large cactus. We had one in our garden. In Chile it was known as a '*tuna*', its prickles every bit as irritating as the bones of the fish bearing the same name, although in Spanish the latter was called '*atún.*' The cactus was the prickly pear. The tiny thorns were incredibly difficult to see, let alone remove, once they had penetrated the skin. To pick the fruit one had to wear gloves.

To present them on the table I had to resort to as much resourcefulness as could be mustered. Eventually we devised a technique. Taking a fork we stabbed it into the outside skin of the *tuna* and holding it over an ignited gas burner turned the fruit around in the flames, singeing off the prickles. It was then possible to hold and peel. The flesh was a straw-coloured green, succulent, but full of hard pips, not unlike a smallish pomegranate, though more pear-like in shape.

Food prices, with the exception of fresh fruit and vegetables, were generally more expensive than back home. It was the custom before price increases that certain commodities were withdrawn from the market, only to reappear later with a large percentage increase. The disappearance of some items from the shelves within the next two to three years would become the norm but on a much larger scale. Thankfully the difficult days ahead of economic chaos were hidden from us these early months.

Chickens, although somewhat scraggy in appearance, were plentiful and cheap. I had a shock awaiting me on cooking my first roast. I had extracted the giblets to make stock with cornflour (gravy powder was unobtainable). The following day the leftovers of the chicken were used. To my horror as the meat was cut off the carcass, protruding from inside, was a beak. I took the end in my fingers and out came the head followed by its two feet, all tied together! This custom of stuffing the extremities of the chicken inside its body would not be repeated once we moved, months later, to the capital and shopped at the supermarkets.

We were not the only ones to encounter strange food customs. Gloria recounted an experience she had in her early weeks. She was living with a Chilean family. Realising there were many cultural divides to cross and being by nature adventurous, she was willing to have a go at most things.

One mealtime, with the *entrada* (starter) already served on her plate, and not having any idea what it was, she took her cue from her host. Lying infront of her, on the plate, were several pink-orange segments of 'goodness-knows-what'. To the side of these was a brown-grey looking object and to the edge of the plate, a quarter lemon. She watched what the Señora did and proceeded to copy. Sticking the fork in the lemon, she turned its prongs into the flesh and out spurted the juice. To her consternation, the brown-grey object started to crawl, crab like, around her plate away from the small pool of lemon juice. Amazement soon turned to dismay as the Señora, with a smile of encouragement, took her own greyish object in her fingers and popped it into her mouth, signalling for Gloria to do the same. Not wishing to offend, she did.

The pink-orange segments ('*lenguas*' or 'tongues') of these sea urchins (for that's what they were) were usually served with chopped onions and parsley or coriander and lemon juice, minus the parasite. Naomi and I were the only members of our family to enjoy *erizos* which have a unique flavour. The presence of the live parasite was an indication that the urchins were fresh and, therefore, safe to eat.

It would be some few years later (when food shortages were a thing of the past), before I plucked up courage to eat (once only!), the live parasite that inhabited the *erizos* found off the coast of

Chile. The *desafío* (challenge) came from a teenage young man. I was at the local street market buying our week's supply of fruit and vegetables. I passed other similar stalls displaying their bright array of all kinds of fruit and vegetables: huge artichokes, red peppers, courgettes, figs, melons, spinach, peaches, apricots and *chirimoya* (custard fruit) and many other colourful varieties of fruit and vegetables to delight the palate.

With nylon string bags bulging at the seams with purchases (fortunately plastic bags then a rarity), I continued down the side of the road to the fresh fish stall. With its almost three thousand mile coast, fish was both varied and plentiful in Chile.

I placed my full-to-overflowing bags on the ground ready to select from the rich sea harvest that presented itself: swordfish, hake, tuna, *corvina* (a kind of sea-bass), among many other choices. *Merluza* (hake), being the cheapest, was the usual buy, but occasionally as a special treat I would purchase *corvina* steaks.

Next came my selection from the shellfish. (It was in Chile that Ray first began to like them.) Mussels were a firm favourite as were *machas*. These latter could be eaten raw but the most popular way to eat them, for both Chileans and *'gringos'* alike, was cooked. After opening the roughly shaped triangular shell, rounded on the longest edge of the triangle, any sand was removed. Leaving the mollusc in one half of its approximate two-inch shell, a small knob of butter followed by a sprinkle of cheese was added.

Fifteen or twenty would be sufficient for two people. Placing them in a baking tray they would be put under a grill, if the oven had one, or most commonly in a hot oven. Within a few minutes the flesh had turned a delicate pink and, with the melted cheese, *Machas a la parmesana* looked not only appetising, they tasted absolutely delicious.

Chile was not only a country of the *macha*, it also had, in common with the other republics a reputation for westerners of the *macho* culture. This Latin characteristic of exaggerated manly assertiveness showed itself in my encounter with a teenager that day. After choosing three large *erizos* and asking for them to be cleaned I started to chat to my challenger!

'What did the parasite taste like?' As quick as lightning, and with incredulity, he replied, 'Señora, haven't you ever tried?'

A shake of my head was the signal for the contest to begin! Throwing his head back, he tossed the small, wriggling, grey object from one of the three spiked urchins into his mouth. I watched with a combination of fascination and horror. Within a few seconds he spat out onto the ground a small mangled lump of shell. Eyes full of challenge he held out the parasite from the next *erizo* for me to try. Dark eyes meeting blue, the contest reached its climax.

Reaching out my hand, heart fluttering, but eyes holding eyes, I took the horrid little creature in my fingers and before I had time to change my mind put it into my mouth. I bit it immediately before it had time to, as much as, move even one of its tiny legs. However, I was totally unprepared for the strong iodine tasting juice that shot to the back of my throat. As quick as possible I discharged what remained into my cupped hand and threw it to the ground. The dark eyes were now smiling. This *'gringa'* had passed the test!

Another of our favourite shellfish was the albalone (colloquially known as *'locos'*). The flesh was white, firm and very meaty and would be served with lashings of mayonnaise. There was an art in cooking them.

First they had to be tenderised. This was achieved by beating them, but unlike steak, not with a wooden meat hammer or rolling pin. Instead they would be put inside a defunct rubber car tyre. Two men would then take hold of the tyre and with carefully practised rhythm would swing the tyre up into the air and bring it crashing down on to the pavement. This would be repeated a number of times. This phenomenon could be seen in any side street in any town.

The cooking process was also executed with great care. We were told only wooden utensils should be used. If a metal spoon were as much as inserted in the water in which the *locos* were cooking it would invariably result in their being inedible and tough. Months later I tried my hand at cooking them having been advised to add a cork or two to the water. Whether this latter addition was an old wives' tale, I never discovered, but the end result was successful. The sight we saw in the seventies of Chilean men beating *locos* in rubber tyres has become, sadly, a lost tradition today due to overfishing.

Chileans love to party and have the ability to make an occasion out of any situation. Their way of celebrating is more reminiscent of the East Enders for panache. Our first few weeks saw a number of family birthdays. In addition to mine there was Julian's first birthday and Naomi's fourth, one day apart. We celebrated by joining the Skinner family, exploring the rock pools on the coast near Viña.

We had left Quilpué in brilliant sunshine but by the time we reached the beach a sea mist had descended. Turning inland we found a delightful eucalyptus tree enclosure, ideal for our somewhat unusual picnic. Out of the basket came sandwiches, crisps, jellies and lemonade. Two birthday cakes resplendent with their respective candles marked this particular celebration *'… the first time any of us had birthday cake complete with lit candles in the open air.'*

If this had been a Chilean family birthday celebration, the middle class would celebrate with a veritable feast, in a plush restaurant or at home joined by a large group of friends and family. If at home it would be both prepared by and certainly served by the resident *empleada* (maid).

Chileans 'eat all the time'. So said Isabel Allende, popular novelist and related to the late President (but not his daughter, as is often assumed – that is another Isabel) in an interview with Lucie Young (*Telegraph* magazine June 2007). 'Even if a policeman raids your house, you offer tea.'

What really did amaze us was the way the poorer Chileans had a picnic. They usually arrived in the *campo* all piled in one or two or more large cars that had seen better days. If the family didn't own a car they were sure to have a *conocido* (a known contact) who owned a van or a truck that would oblige.

As we would sit eating our sandwiches we would observe

with amazement the make up of their picnic party. Out from the van tumbled excited children followed by parents, grandparents, friends and neighbours. Then with all hands on deck came a scrub topped wooden table, saucepans, kitchen knives and other utensils, even a gas cylinder, in fact everything but the kitchen sink!

Then followed the picnic itself. Nylon string bags out of which were taken potatoes, onions, tomatoes, several lettuces, all still to be prepared, several kilos of the indispensable bread and a number of large melons. While the women set to with food preparation the men offloaded the bottles of wine. Our eyes opened wider as with increasing incredulity we saw two men staggering under the weight of the carcass of a sheep! Firewood gathered, it wasn't long before the sheep was slowly rotating on a primitive spit over a fire. The combined smell of the eucalyptus wood and the roasting lamb stays with me to this day.

Another smell combined with eucalyptus that recalls happy days of walks with the family was mimosa, the trees in full bloom laden with their clusters of yellow flowers.

National holidays (*feriados*) figure large in South America. They usually commemorate a Saint, a battle won at the expense of another South American republic or most important of all a victory gaining their respective independence from the mother country of either Spain or Portugal. One such *feriado* occurred two months after our arrival.

May 21st commemorates the Battle of Iquique. In 1879 Chile was involved in a war with her northern neighbours, Peru and Bolivia. This was known as the 'War of the Pacific' or 'The Nitrate War' due to the rich deposits of nitrates found in the Atacama Desert. As Pendle comments, 'a dispute about manure started the greatest war which has been waged between Latin American nations'.[2] In a bid for the northern part of the desert Chilean troops occupied Antofagasta, which then belonged to Peru. Meanwhile Chilean warships sailed north to block the port of Iquique, which was then a Bolivian town. Chile was the victor and to this day Bolivia remains a land-locked country. Later these

---

[2] George Pendle: *The Land and People of Chile.* A. and C. Black. p. 41

natural fertilisers would attract business entrepreneurs from Britain to Chile. To harvest this natural wealth, British engineers laid the essential desert railway tracks.

To celebrate this particular *feriado,* we set off in our mission-owned Volkswagen van with children and picnic on board, to call for Paul and Esme Russell, now in their second tour of service and who lived in a housing estate about thirty minutes drive away from Quilpué. The small town was known as Villa Dulce (sweet village) and straggled rather haphazardly over the hills. It wasn't quite as picturesque as the name implied!

We headed to the coast and were struck as to how like Cornwall the rugged coastline was. Stopping at the fishing village of Horcón we watched the Pacific waves crashing on the large jagged rocks, the white spray flung high into the sky. Soaring above and avoiding the spray were a number of pelicans, so much more elegant in flight than their appearance on land. On another occasion, two of these ungainly beak-heavy birds caused us great amusement. They were engaged in a tug-of-war over fish thrown to them on land. With huge beaks grasping their respective end of a large piece of fish the struggle began. The contest lasted well over a minute or two before one conceded defeat. Back at Horcón, meanwhile, the cormorants preferring to play hide and seek, one moment were standing sentinel on their chosen rocks inviting capture by the relentless surge, the next diving out of sight only to reappear inviting another attempt.

On reaching the village of Puchuncaví we saw a group of *huasos,* the Chilean cowboys on horseback, decked out in their characteristic *ponchos.* There was to be a rodeo. What excitement! We couldn't believe our luck!

Chileans *huasos* like their neighbouring Argentinian *gauchos* are skilled horsemen but with the notable difference that the *gauchos* gallop across the pampas in pursuit of the rhea, skilfully swinging long leather straps attached at the ends to small hard leather covered balls (*bolitos*). With the leather straps and their *bolitos* swirling around his head like a lasso the *gaucho* gives chase, in an ever-increasing speed, to the fast running bird. Then as he draws alongside, with great dexterity he aims the straps and the *'bolitos'* at the rhea's feet and brings it to the ground.

We parked the van and following a growing number of villagers headed towards the entrance to the open air wooden amphitheatre, the *media-luna* (half-moon), so called because of its crescent shaped seating arrangement for the spectators. The judges and other dignitaries occupied the seating on the other part of the theatre.

Our rodeo was advertised to start at three o'clock. At four thirty the opening proceedings began with a speech of welcome. To our surprise at the end of the welcome Paul stood up and started to speak in loud Spanish. Still novices in language skills we made out something about visitors from *Inglaterra.* To large smiles and clapping hands delivered in our direction, we were duly acknowledged but if that wasn't enough a young *Chileno* of Irish descent gave a further speech in perfect English for these *'gringos'.*

The participating *huasos* entered the arena in pairs forming a procession. Having discarded the outer poncho, the brightly coloured striped *manta*, previously hidden was now revealed. The *manta* was a loose fitting square jacket with a wide slit for the head and was worn over the shirt. The black trousers were topped at the waist by a wide sash and the bottoms were tucked into leather boots resplendent with silver spurs. To complete their eye-catching appearance, they wore a wide flat brimmed straw hat. By now, thrice welcomed, the show was about to begin!

Chile did not and does not hold bullfights. In a rodeo steers were used. The purpose of the competition was for pairs of *huasos* to ram the particular steer against a designated, protected area of the wall of the theatre and to score points against the other competing pairs of cowboys. I must confess I never did grasp the rules and cheered all the participants regardless.

Living so far from family, photographs maintained an essential link with grandparents, uncles, aunts and cousins as well as many friends. In a letter Ray wrote to grandparents dated May 15th he stressed the importance of this.

'On Monday we received our May/June 'Sent' [SAMS bimonthly magazine]. *You should have seen Andrew's face when he flicked over the pages and came to page 9. His jaw visibly dropped, a broad smile broke out all over his face and he said "Like Daddy – Like Mummy!"* [The family photograph taken at Allen Gardiner House.] *We cannot underestimate the value of photos to the children. We have framed two of the Boxing Day ones ... Naomi and Andrew often study them with glee naming each person. Andrew can just about make all the names recognisable now.'*

Two days after our birthday picnic we heard the *Lebu* with its cargo had docked at Valparaiso. Ray left for the customs with Blanca, a Chilean administrator who worked for the Mission, to start the painstaking, time-consuming documentation. A return visit the following day revealed all twenty-four *bultos* (bulky packaged items) loaded in Liverpool had arrived and apparently in good condition.

Relief soon gave way to consternation. Lids were prized off oil drums, tea chests and crates, contents taken out and strewn on the ground. These were then shoved back unceremoniously, but not before a find of electrical goods was greeted with glee like a child excitedly opening a Christmas present. These treasured items were put to one side and we relived a repeat experience with the tape recorder, as on our arrival by plane a month earlier. It seemed electrical goods were like gold dust. One hundred and fifty percent duty on the small convector heater and four hundred percent on the vacuum cleaner was the asking price – a total of eighty pounds. We paid.

We *'left the Aduana at 12:40 pm, having spent over 3 hours there, most of it* standing *and* waiting' (my emphasis). These two words Ray wrote in the diary would prove to be both prophetic and some of the most used vocabulary in the not too distant future. The diary entry seven days later marked the beginning of a life-style that would test the commitment up to the hilt of our calling, the country of Chile and its people.

Señora Tagle informed us that toilet rolls and spaghetti were soon to disappear from the shops and that flour would become scarce. The same day Gloria had heard that in the north of Chile people were forming long queues to buy flour and sugar.

The following month storm clouds began to gather on the horizon. Not so much the clouds of winter rain but the dark clouds of political violence. June 13th we heard on the radio there had been a gun battle, politically motivated in which the Calderon brothers had been shot dead. This was followed three days later by the shooting of three detectives, two fatally, in the Police Headquarters in Santiago. The suicide bomber belonging to an extreme leftist group then blew himself up on leaving the building.

That evening President Allende called a public meeting in the main Plaza lasting over two hours. We were to discover that the Latinos are, by Anglo-Saxon standards, given to both hyperbole and an extravagance of vocabulary. This occurs not only in oratory speeches but also in conversation, journalism and literature.

The highly coloured language was an expression of a vibrant people with a *joie de vivre*. This love of life was to suffer a great blow in the months and years now stretching out as the country would be thrown into turmoil with Chilean rising against Chilean and families split down the middle politically. A deep divide was beginning to emerge leaving in its wake a devastation of pain, suspicion, and violence more destructive than the cracks that appeared during an earthquake.

Chapter 14

The Marxist Experiment

A country that had not made headline news prior to September 1970 found itself now the attention both of freedom loving countries and dictator-led ones alike. Chile had just democratically elected its first Marxist president and the eyes of the world were on this South American republic.

It was the fourth attempt of Salvador Allende Gossens for the presidency. In his first attempt in 1952, as candidate of Chile's Socialist party, he was also the favourite of the then outlawed Communists. He received only 6 percent of the Chilean vote. By his fourth attempt, almost twenty years later, this had increased to 36.3 percent. Although a democratic result it was hardly a landslide victory! The majority of the Radicals by now had joined the *Unidad Popular* (Popular Unity or UP), a leftist coalition, with Allende's candidature.

The National party pinned their hopes on Jorge Alessandri who had been president between 1958 and 1964 and was in turn succeeded by Eduardo Frei, of the Christian Democrats. Chile's Constitution did not allow for a serving president to be re-elected next time round. As a result the candidate put forward by the Christian Democratic party was Radomiro Tomic. He was sufficiently left of his party to sound alarm bells for a considerable number of the Christian Democratic electorate who threw in their vote with the Nationalists.

Alessandri obtained 35 percent and Tomic 27.8 percent. The margin of votes in favour of Allende over Alessandri was 39,000 out of three million.

On September 4th history was made, the Chilean people

having elected their first Marxist president. This result was greeted internationally on the one hand with grave concern and on the other with great acclaim.

Nathaniel Davis who became the United States' ambassador to Chile in 1971, wrote an authentic and unbiased book of the following most turbulent two years in Chile's history (*The Last Two Years of Salvador Allende*). His account of this time, through which we also lived, rings with a true authenticity. In his Preface he states his aim for objectivity; '… too much recent scholarship on Allende's Chile has been written by leftists shouting their case, by liberals who can see no bad in Allende and no good in his enemies, by conservatives who think the distinction between authoritarianism and totalitarianism justifies Pinochet [the army General under whose command the 1973 coup took place] and by rightists who see only the Red Menace.'

According to Davis, both President Richard Nixon and his Secretary for State, Henry Kissinger greeted the news of Allende's election with fury. Kissinger's comment on President Nixon's reaction was that Nixon was 'beside himself'.[1] A few years later in an interview between the former president and David Frost, the British radio and television presenter, Frost had been warned that Nixon had a 'short fuse'[2] on the subject of Chile.

A quotation in the *New York Times,* 20 September 1970, reporting on a briefing Kissinger gave to newspaper editors four days previously had this to say:

'I have yet to meet somebody who firmly believes that if Allende wins, there is likely to be another free election in Chile … There is a good chance that he will establish over a period of years some sort of Communist Government … in a major Latin American country … [and] joining … Argentina … Peru … and Bolivia … So I don't think we should delude ourselves that an Allende take-over … would not present massive problems for us, and for the democratic forces and pro-U.S. forces in … the whole Western Hemisphere.'

---

[1] Nathaniel Davis: *The Last Two Years of Salvador Allende.* I. B. Tauris & Co. Ltd. p. 6

[2] Ibid: p. 6

Meanwhile in Cuba, Fidel Castro was taking fresh hope that his country's days of isolation were coming to an end and a visit to Chile in the near future might favourably serve to raise his political profile.

During the election campaign, Allende had made clear he wanted to change the political institutions of the country. His aim was to substitute a single 'people's assembly' for the Chamber of Deputies and the Senate. There was only one way he could bring about such change legally. He would have to call for a national plebiscite in line with Article 109 of the Constitution. For this to be successful he would need to increase his plurality from just over a third of the electorate into 50.1 percent.

In the event he didn't call for it. In a speech two years later, January 20th 1973, he referred to this apparent missed opportunity at the height of the UP's popularity as one of his crucial mistakes. It would have been a risk-taking gamble and according to Davis a wiser move to have decided against it. 'I think Allende was right in 1971 and mistaken when he looked back on an apparent opportunity. It is one thing to have 50 percent for one's candidates; it is another to ask the Chilean electorate to dismantle its parliamentary institutions.'[3] In the unfolding drama over the next months Allende would return to the case of a plebiscite on more than one occasion.

In a few days before the September 4th elections the Christian Democrats had 'glimpsed the outlines of their strategy ... They felt little disposition to overturn the expressed preference of the Chilean electorate, but they were anxious to commit Allende to democratic guarantees that would protect Chile from a drift towards leftist dictatorship. They called publicly for such an agreement ... '.[4] By October 9th an agreement had been reached. But within a few months Allende encountered a shift in attitude of the Christian Democratic party. Economic troubles began to emerge.

Copper was Chile's chief export but by the end of 1971, with a decline in world demand, the price for this mineral was only

---

[3] Ibid: p. 18
[4] Ibid: p. 14

two-thirds of what it had been the previous year. In addition the government had spent most of its foreign-exchange reserves, moved to restrict imports and inflation was by now taking an upward turn.

A position of 'constructive' opposition was announced, by the Christian Democrats, which meant that Allende's UP government could count on their support 'in everything that contributed to the national interest'.[5]

The honeymoon period between the Christian Democrats and the government Marxist coalition parties was short lived. Eduardo Frei's Vice President, Edmundo Pérez Zújovic was assassinated on June 8th by extreme leftists. The propaganda machines began their claims and counter claims with much mud slinging and acrimonious verbal attacks. On September 22nd the former President accused the Communists of resorting to the very same tactics that had brought other countries into Communist bondage.

By the end of Allende's first year in office the relationship between government and opposition was turning sour. The bedfellows of politics and economics were not lying together comfortably.

Interspersed among the increasing chaos politically and economically was chaos of a different nature. At the height of winter, just two weeks after the murder of Zújovic, Santiago suffered the worst snowfall since 1855. In the port of Valparaiso 44 mm of rain fell in twenty-four hours. Two thousand vehicles with five thousand people were stranded in the sector of Angostura without food and adequate clothing. President Allende declared a 'state of emergency' and with characteristic Latin American exaggeration added 'almost as a war!' However for the majority of Chilean children it was an occurrence to celebrate. Not only were the schools closed but so very many children had never touched snow. Only those from privileged middle class and wealthy homes had experienced snow – on the ski slopes. The less privileged could only observe it from afar, on the white-capped peaks of the Andes.

---

[5] Ibid: p. 20

'Mummy, can we go out and play in the snow?'

Naomi and Andrew were so excited as all children are when seeing the large white flakes wafting down from the leaden sky and falling silently to the ground carpeting everything within reach in magical whiteness.

Wrapping the three of them in their winter woollies, the bright colours of hats, scarves, coats and gloves providing the dash of primary colours on the canvas of the white background, we went out to investigate the variety of snowmen in the neighbourhood gardens. It was late afternoon on what had been a clear sunny day. The deep azure sky was fading to a lighter blue and streaking across the horizon was an ever-changing kaleidoscope of colour. The orange red tones reflected in an awe-inspiring sight on the snow of the *cordillera* (mountain range).

By now we were living in the capital having moved there from Quilpué the previous autumn. Bishop David Pytches wanted us to pioneer a new work among the professional and middle-class people in what was known as the 'Barrio Alto'. The emphasis of the South American Missionary Society had been from its beginning on working among the poorer people first in the *campo* then in the towns and cities of the different Republics. This was in keeping with the vision of its founder Captain Allen Gardiner. In more recent years alongside the original vision emerged a strategy of pioneering in the major urban areas.

The early days of SAMS work in Chile had been in the south of the country in Chol-Chol near the city of Temuco. This was the centre of the southern indigenous people of Chile, the Araucanian Indians. In the 1960s mission personnel were assigned to the central coastal regions of Viña del Mar and Valparaiso. The headquarters of SAMS Chile was now in downtown Santiago. With our arrival in the Barrio Alto a new chapter was beginning for the Anglican Church but more about this later.

Dispute over land has been the single underlying cause of many a war. South American history is riddled with inequalities as far as land is concerned with so much of the land owned by the minority at the expense of the majority. This is more obvious in the Republics where there are higher percentages of indigenous people, and is the case where SAMS works in Peru, Bolivia, Paraguay and northern Argentina, whereas in Chile and Uruguay there is a larger proportion of European influence.

In 1971 the beginning of unrest in urban areas was overtaken by unrest in the countryside. The land reform policy previously pushed hard by the Christian Democrats and even harder by Allende, was increasingly being put into jeopardy. Agrarian reform under Frei directed that inefficiently managed agricultural land could be expropriated, as could property of any one farmer in excess of the permitted two hundred acres, with an agreed compensation package.

Under the new coalition government impatience at the slowness with which the reform had been implemented led to Allende's Cuban trained minister of agriculture, Jacques Chonchol, accelerating Frei's programme. Ultra-leftist groups, the most notorious being the MIR (*Movimiento de Izquierda Revolucionária*, the Revolutionary Left Movement) jumped on the bandwagon of a policy that on the surface promised a fairer distribution of agricultural wealth to be shared by both landowner and *campesino* alike. Take-overs of land, *tomas*, began to occur in rural areas beginning in the rich fertile land of southern Chile and extending into the central region.

Political activists, in small, armed groups, under cover of darkness, would descend on a pre-selected landowner's farm, hoist the red, white and blue Chilean flag and claim the land. But in this case there was no agreed compensation for the evicted owners. Not only did the UP turn a blind eye to the illegal seizures but these *tomas* were actually encouraged by the more radical left of government.

Long lists of *fundos* (farms) due for immediate 'reform' would appear every week in the press. Nothing could be done. Their acres of land were parcelled out among landless *campesinos*. If justification was needed for such action the extremists argued what better 'compensation' for the Mapuche Indians, whose land had been 'usurped' by the whites back in the 1880s.

As a result the peasant farmers, faced with a potential takeover stopped working their land. In addition cattle owners in the south of the country drove their livestock over to neighbouring Argentina, not so much out of concern of a *toma*, but for economic reasons. The government had control of the price of meat at an unrealistic low level; the neighbouring republic gave a much fairer price.

As Christians, SAMS mission personnel were called to respond to the injustices in another way. This was no less radical, yet in keeping with the life and teaching of Jesus: to provide a voice for the powerless, to take up the legal battle for lost land alongside the need to show the power of the gospel to forgive. Some years later indigenous Christians in a Declaration gave a moving tribute to this effect.

The first American Indian Congress of the Anglican Province of the Southern Cone was held in 1990. On the agenda was the 500th Anniversary of Columbus' discovery of the Americas (1492) to be celebrated throughout the Spanish-speaking world two years later. How would this best be achieved, given that the two cultures, Indigenous and European, viewed that historic event with differing emotional responses? After reflection the Christian Indians headed up by the indigenous people from the *Chaco* region of northern Argentina issued their Declaration:

1992 sees the 500th Anniversary of the arrival of Columbus in 1492. History tells us that when the Spanish arrived the Indian peoples received them with a lot of love. They thought that they were bringing love to the people.

Later, in 1500-1510, more Spaniards arrived, and forced the Indians to work for them. They robbed them of all the things they had, such as gold and silver, which they took to Europe. They took away everything the Indians had.

After that the Indian people became ill with the sicknesses brought by the Europeans, who also made them work hard, without giving them the food they needed. The colonists became owners of the Indians. They did not respect them as human beings.

Today it is almost the same for us. We suffer through laws we do not know much about. There are few jobs for indigenous people. They do not pay us what we should earn. Often we have to survive by selling a few goods. We live as we did before.

In 1992 there will be celebrations for the 500th anniversary of the arrival of the Europeans. Some people say we should celebrate. Others say we should not, ... There are many arguments against these celebrations, and many questions.

What should we say?

As native people of the Chaco, as the indigenous churches, our vision of these memories is that the past is the past. We hope that this conflict never happens again. We know that all this was because of the great ignorance and the mistakes of man.

We are now new people. We have new news, which is the holy Scriptures, the gospel of Jesus Christ. 'Peace I leave with you; my peace I give you. I do not give to you as the world gives. Do not let your hearts be troubled and do not be afraid' (John 14:27) 'I tell you the truth, you will weep and mourn while the world rejoices. You will grieve, but your grief will turn to joy' (John 16:20).

The prayer of Jesus Christ says forgive them, because they do not know what they are doing ... 'Make sure that nobody pays back wrong for wrong, but always try to be kind to each other and to everyone else' (1 Thessalonians 5:15)...

Dear brothers do not take vengeance into your own hands, but let God be the one who punishes... '.[6]

In 1971, while increasing countryside was lying fallow, the government's policy of nationalisation and expropriation of privately owned industry had brought in its wake a dearth of productivity to the towns and cities. Multi-national companies gradually began to pull out as further investment was seen to be too risky.

A thousand miles away from the farming problems of the southern province of Cautin were the problems of the mines. Copper was the pride and joy of Chile's exports and its bread and butter. The USA had invested heavily in Chilean copper, developing many of its mines. Included in these was the largest open-pit copper mine in the world, Chuquicamata, found in the Atacama Desert, over 1370 kilometres north of Santiago. A mere seven weeks after taking office, President Allende introduced an

---

[6] Article from magazine of Tearfund: *Tear Times*: '500 Years of Grief will turn to Joy'. p. 16

amendment to the constitution, nationalising all of Chile's large mines.

At this time much of the political intrigues were lost on this ordinary family who had come out to Chile in response not to a political mandate but to share the Christian message; the message that challenges the inner needy environment of the human heart as well as the outer physical and social environment, which, at first glance, may appear to be top priority.

To a young mother who had not been interested in politics I was soon to discover that to live in any Republic within South America, this lack of interest would need to be addressed if we wanted to understand the people we were living and working among. In fact political issues were thrust upon us whether we liked it or not.

My first encounter with a member of the Communist party was, of all places, in the dentist's chair. My dentist, having been recommended to me for her standard of work (which to this day has proved excellent), knew I was a missionary but was unaware that I knew that she was a militant Communist.

Why is it that dentists ask so many questions when, with mouth propped wide-open, answers can only be given by way of a grunt which can be interpreted equally as a 'yes' or a 'no'? Our initial dialogue was without doubt one-sided!

It felt a bit like the Spanish Inquisition as she bombarded me with questions. Where did we live? Did we own a car? What sort of a car was it? Which school did our children go to? Why were we in Chile? In the respite that eventually followed it was now my turn to ask the questions. I went for the jugular not with a question but with a statement of fact! It was just as well that being a professional her English was excellent!

'I understand you are a Communist!'

With all pretence stripped away we were able to have a serious conversation between two people both equally committed to their cause. It was apparent in the ensuing conversation though where the essential differences lay.

'We have a lot in common, you a Christian and me a Communist.'

'Well, inasmuch as we both want to see the problem of inequality and injustices addressed, yes. But there can never be agreement' I answered. 'You see' (and here I used a phrase a Communist in the seventies would be familiar with) 'we are diametrically opposed. You start from the premise "there is no God" and as a result I believe your understanding of human nature and its remedy is flawed. Changing social conditions alone will not change the human heart.'

Discussions between us continued over my next few visits, always cordial but with neither of us reaching agreement. Once work was completed I didn't see her again and two years later, together with her paediatric psychiatrist husband, I heard they had fled the country as political refugees, after the military coup.

Little did I know, nor could I have imagined, that before long we would make some very deep friendships with Marxists, one of whom we came to love as a younger brother; after all weren't they the enemy of the Christian Church? I had a lot to learn.

Two political events heralded the end of the year. The first was a visit to Chile of the Cuban President Fidel Castro. On November 11th the newspaper headlines of *El Mercurio* reported that there was an 'enthusiastic reception for him in Santiago' as he 'began a tour of Chile'. The contrast in physical appearance between the two Marxist presidents couldn't have been more marked. The small, suave, dapper, bespectacled, suit clad Chilean contrasting with the taller, heavily bearded, combat clad Cuban. Thinking back again to the potentially very dangerous stand-off between J. F. Kennedy and Fidel Castro in the sixties, which threatened world peace, it was quite a thought that for a few days the latter was a near neighbour! The invited guest was staying in the private residence of President Allende, only a few roads away from where we were living.

The other event that made a resounding impact, not only internationally, but even more telling on our ears, was 'The March of the Empty Saucepans'. This had taken place on Wednesday, December 1st, the day before Castro's farewell. Several thousand women marched through the streets of the capital banging empty saucepans, joined by militants from the ultra-right political groups as well as from the moderate Democratic opposition. According to Davis it was not so much a protest against food shortages, but rather a political protest against the Cuban visitor. Although the demonstration began in a peaceful way it began to turn ugly as stone throwing extremist youths began to target not only the escorts to the women but the women themselves.

This wasn't the only reason Castro returned to Cuba somewhat disappointed in his visit. In his farewell speech December 2nd 1971, to a less than full audience in the national stadium, he highlighted what he saw as 'weaknesses in the revolutionary processes' in Chile, and that he would '… return to Cuba more of a revolutionary than when I came … more of a radical … more of an extremist than when I came here!'[7]

At the end of Allende's first year in office, the majority of women that were involved in the march were hardly 'scraping the barrel' literally, as far as food supplies were concerned. Many of these women were middle-class professionals. Two Chilean sisters, whom we had recently befriended, were witnesses of this demonstration. They arrived at our house two hours later and told us tear gas had been used by the police to disperse both the women and the crowds. This would become in the months ahead a regular phenomenon.

At ten o'clock the next night our eardrums were suddenly bombarded by metallic clatters of sound. The quiet residential cul-de-sac in which we lived had its peace shattered as first one neighbour, followed by the next and the next joined in the 'Symphony on a Theme of Cymbals'! Patio doors and windows were thrown wide-open as the female members of the 'orchestra' picking up their kitchen instruments of saucepan lids, crashed them together in an ever-increasing crescendo. We went outside our house to investigate and discovered that the 'conductor' happened to be our immediate neighbour Gladys, married to an Air Force Group Captain.

It wasn't long, after our move to the capital, that we discovered our neighbours were all military personnel. To our left, occupying

---

[7] Davis: *The Last Two Years of Salvador Allende*. I. B. Tauris & Co. Ltd p. 44

the corner plot at the end of our cul-de-sac 'Los Almendros' (the Almond Trees), were Gladys and her family. Next to them, with the two gardens forming the horizontal bar of the T-shape *pasaje,* was the house of another Air Force Group Captain, Luis and his wife and two little girls. These young daughters became Naomi's first new friends and from them she began her Spanish lessons in earnest.

Immediately opposite us was a retired Air Vice-Marshal and his wife and by way of a change, to our right was an Army Major and family. The latter were always polite but we didn't really get to know them very well. The homes by English standards, especially for such high-ranking officers, were modest. All the properties were painted white, semi-detached, three bed-roomed with two of them opening onto a narrow balcony. The kitchen was very small, with a door leading to the lounge/diner. In addition there was another small reception room, which Ray used as a study. We soon became friends with the two Air Force families.

Two years later, when the country was on the point of economic and political collapse, surprisingly it was our Major neighbour who came to our rescue. With petrol in short supply, like every basic necessity in Chile in 1973, a general strike (*huelga*) had been called for August 8th. This was the day of our departure for home-leave. Panic buying of this already scarce commodity meant many pumps had exhausted their supplies and immense queues had formed at the remaining ones.

Although our lives had been dominated by queues for over two years, on this occasion, we simply didn't have the time to stand for hours on end in any *colas* (queues). Our hardly-known Major, totally out of the blue, as military personnel were able to have a limited supply of petrol and knowing we were leaving for the UK, said that he would give us enough to get us to the airport. I could have hugged him. This was yet another way we found God supplying our needs but more about these in another chapter.

What we didn't know on the eve of our departure was that we would be returning in three months' time to a country reflecting politically what happens all too frequently geologically. The economic chaos, the ever-increasing violence, the pressure from the opposition encouraged by outside forces reached a climax.

On September 11th 1973 the 'volcano' erupted. The bitterness, suffering, division and hatred that had been accumulating suddenly spewed out. The fallout of the 'molten lava' of opposing political interests could not be contained. Wherever it flowed it left in its wake two divided rivers; one of disillusionment of unfulfilled dreams, the other of renewed hope and stability. The Marxist experiment was over. Our neighbours had been called upon to play their part. How were we to cross the divide? What bridges did we need to build? That was the challenge we had to face.

Chapter 15
'Enemies' Become Friends

In an earlier chapter I mentioned the unfortunate attitude we had come across regarding Roman Catholics. It was in Chile that we met first hand priests and nuns with a heart for the underprivileged. Kevin, a Columban priest, was such a man. Living at the cutting edge brought many challenges and in his case a crisis of faith. When we first met him the 'attractiveness' of the newly elected Marxist government to bring in better conditions for the marginalized was very appealing. But how compatible is a political view, founded on atheism, with the Christian faith? This tension led him in his confusion to have special dispensation from his superiors to take time out in Ireland.

He returned to Chile a new man. Not only had he had a deeper encounter with Christ and a clearer focus of faith, but he also became a leading participant in the Renewal Movement which had taken the Anglican Church by storm in the early nineteen sixties. Underlying the Movement, by now gathering momentum in the mainline churches, was a rediscovery of the work of God's Holy Spirit to equip Christians to present a more rounded gospel message. Alongside preaching the good news of God's kingdom there needed to be evidences that God was still at work through his church. Bringing release to those bound by obsessive, unhealthy life-style habits, healing the sick, speaking a prophetic word and other 'kingdom' benefits, too long neglected, were to become an integral part of proclaiming the gospel.

Our own Bishop, David Pytches and his wife Mary were

sharing with the Anglican Church insights into the releasing of the gifts of the Spirit for a more effective ministry. It would be a few years later before we ourselves saw evidences of God at work in ways that for us, at the time, were quite remarkable.

Another Roman Catholic priest, in whose parish we lived when we first moved to Santiago, was Juan de Castro. Our meeting with Juan came as a result of a ski-ing accident. It was our day off and one bright winter morning we decided to go up into the Andes to a well-known ski resort – not that either of us could ski. The children were very excited as we packed a picnic, helped them pull on their Wellington boots, got together warm clothing, and clambered into our mission-lent blue Volkswagen microbus. Off we set for a day in the snow and mountains.

Farellones was just an hour or so drive out of the capital. Living in the northeast of Santiago, the area known as Las Condes, it wasn't long before we left the shops and houses behind and began to wind our way up a river valley. Eucalyptus, weeping willow and mimosa trees, interspersed with an occasional small shack, lined the banks of the small but fast flowing river. The water was incredibly muddy due to the melting snow gathering soil as it gained momentum in its downward journey. Tumbling and somersaulting over rocks and boulders in its relentless surge ever onward, it picked up branches and even small tree trunks before joining the Mapocho River, that runs through the capital. In a few months the river's bubbling-laughter's playtime would be cut short by the increasingly hot drying presence of the summer sun, leaving in its wake a dried-up bed.

As we continued to climb, trees gave way to shrubs and patches of grass to scree and within a short time we left the tree line behind altogether. Hairpin bends were to test both our driving skills as well as our stomachs as we gained altitude. If it was my turn at the wheel I chose the ascent rather than the descent. At last we saw the ski station and the ski lifts and within a few minutes drew to a halt in the mountain village. The remainder of the day was spent watching the skiers, playing in the snow and making the inevitable snowballs. Luxury holiday homes for the middle classes and the wealthy provided architectural interest.

By mid afternoon we decided it was time to make the homeward journey. Tired, from the invigorating mountain air, our three contented children, faces glowing, scrambled into the back of the bus. We were just passing the last of the holiday homes and reached the police check-point. A severe *carabinero* clad in his paramilitary khaki uniform, white webbing cross strap and belt holding both truncheon and revolver in hip holster, raised his hand in a command for us to stop.

'Ray, what do you think we've done? Are all our car documents in order? Oh, I think I've forgotten to bring my *carnet*.' (ID card)

'Señores, which part of Santiago are you returning to? There has been an accident and a young man needs to be taken home and on to hospital.' The young university student had broken his leg, which was expertly splinted. Our arrival with a suitably large vehicle for the leg to be supported horizontally was timely.

The young man, Fernando we discovered also lived in Las Condes, in fact only about ten minutes' walk from our home. The effect of the analgesia meant conversation in true Latin character flowed unabated with a mixture of both Spanish and English. Inevitably the question was asked why were we in Chile. He soon made it clear that he was a young Catholic with a very vibrant faith. We asked him if he knew about posters that had appeared all over our district, on the posts of streetlights and in the local shops. These posters in red, yellow and orange had a cross in the centre with the words '*Cristo la Respuesta*' (Christ the Answer). It had never occurred to us that the Catholic Church was responsible. We quite thought the strong evangelical Pentecostal Church would be behind such advertising. We didn't know then that the latter worked almost exclusively among the poorer Chileans in other parts of the city.

When Fernando saw our interest he went on to tell us of the weekend to be held in the near future, which the posters were advertising. He was going along with a number from his church. We decided to go on the Sunday afternoon to the '*Verbo Divino*' (Divine Word) Church where the special event was taking place. On entering the modern building we saw hanging from the ceiling lots of mobiles with large letters incorporating the seven 'I am' sayings of Jesus found in St John's Gospel. In the packed building, filled mainly by over four hundred teens and twenties, we spotted our friend – not difficult seeing his leg was in a plaster cast. He made his way towards us accompanied by a tall bespectacled man in his forties with thinning dark brown hair.

'*Hola.* I'm so glad you could make it. I really would like to introduce you to my parish priest who is also here for the day.' Juan de Castro, his face lighting up with a broad smile, reached out his hand to us both. We chatted for a time and when he knew that Ray was an Anglican minister, he put an arm around his shoulders and said '*Entonces somos colegas.*' (Then we are colleagues.)

While acknowledging the very real doctrinal differences that existed between us, a genuine friendship developed as we built on what we held in common rather than on what divided us. Later Juan drove us home and this Roman Catholic priest subsequently visited our home from time to time and enjoyed kicking a football in the garden with Andrew and Julian. Later he became involved at a high level in the reconciliation and healing process of the country after the military coup.

The following Pentecost Juan invited Ray to join him in con-celebrating Communion in his church, *Santo Toribio,* in the Plaza del Inca. This church had embraced the Renewal Movement. 'I won't tell my bishop if you don't tell yours!' said Juan grinning mischievously.

As the political situation deteriorated over the next months and into the following year there was a call from Cardinal Raúl Silva Henríquez and the Bishops for a National Day of Prayer. The day was Sunday, July 22nd 1973 and we decided to join with our Chilean friends in our local Catholic Church at this time of national crisis. My diary records that Juan preached from St Paul's letter to the Colossians pointing the congregation to Christ the creator and sustainer of all things. Parents had brought their children for baptism and were challenged that the most important thing was their own commitment to Christ as Saviour. During the service he evidently had spotted us for surprisingly he mentioned us by name as his 'Anglican friends, Ray and Gill and their family' and promptly prayed for us as 'they return to England for leave'.

Another Roman Catholic who became very special in my own journey of faith some two years later was a Peruvian nun. Sister Georgina looked every bit Peruvian with strong characteristics of her indigenous roots. She was squat in physique, with high cheekbones and almond-shaped brown eyes. Belonging to an open order she wore ordinary clothes and her short, straight, jet-black hair was free. Together with a priest, Carlos Aldunate, she led renewal retreats. Georgina had a remarkable ministry and was used to bring God's healing to many people damaged emotionally from deep hurts in life.

It was on a retreat, which she was co-leading, that God used her to bring inner healing into my own life. Not conscious of any particular pressing need as such, I went, however, to her one afternoon and asked if she would pray with me. She prayed that the Holy Spirit would reveal anything needing healing. We spent a short time in silence and then she said to speak out anything that God showed me.

It wasn't long before with deep sobs seemingly coming from the pit of my stomach I had a picture of myself as a small child of around four. In this picture I was running upstairs to my bedroom having just come in from school. I flung open the door and stopped suddenly as sitting on the bed was Jesus. He was smiling in welcome holding out his arms to me. I rushed into them laughing and chattering non-stop as I poured out all I had been doing at school. We laughed together.

Then he scooped me up in his arms and sat me on his knee and I nestled into his left arm, my head resting on his chest. I stopped talking savouring the closeness and felt so loved and secure. After a short time the bedroom door opened a couple of feet or so and in the half-open doorway stood my father. He hesitated, not sure whether to come in further. As I looked across the room at him, Jesus gently lifted me off his lap and whispered in my ear: 'I want you to go up to your father and tell him that you forgive him for not being there when you needed him'.

I was born six months before the outbreak of the Second World War, and when Elaine was six and I was two, my father was called up to serve his country in North Africa and Italy. We didn't see him again until the War was over. Childhood memories subsequently were of a father who was fun to be with, to enjoy doing the physical things – swimming, walking and playing games – with but not one with whom I felt able to share my inner self; this was always with my mother. On coming into the shop after school my first words would be, 'Daddy, where's Mummy?'

I was in my mid-thirties the day I prayed with Georgina. Now as an adult and parent myself, I realised the hurt was two-way. My father, too, had his pain at the forced separation that war brings and the subsequent shutting him out only added to it. I had no idea how deep the sense of abandonment had gone even though the reason for father's absence was understandable. I had a lot to learn about the need and the power to give and receive forgiveness – lessons still being learnt!

That occasion with this humble Peruvian instrument of God was incredibly powerful and the very first time I had come across anything like it, either in the lives of any known to me or in the Christian Church generally. Since then we have experienced extraordinary situations in both our lives and ministry and in the lives of others where God breaks through in ways that leave us with a deep sense of humility and wonderment.

I asked Georgina what I should do with what God had shown me. She wisely advised nothing in the immediate future. Apart from sharing with Ray I told no one for many years and in fact it was to be over ten years before I told my father. But from that moment with Georgina my relationship with him changed and over the ensuing years we enjoyed a greater closeness. It was in the mid-eighties and by now we were living in Cambridge. On one of our regular visits to parents in Frinton I sensed it was the right time to tell him what had happened all those years back in Chile. We had just finished the washing up and were on our own in the kitchen. My father, like mother, had a strong Christian faith but I wasn't at all sure how he would react to my somewhat unorthodox story. He was very moved. I was so glad I'd shared it with him. He died in September 1987 at the age of eighty-two.

God is a God of both detail and surprises. In 1988, we returned to Chile for three months. On our first Sunday back in the Santiago Community Church, a North American nun we had known in the seventies excitedly rushed up to me in welcome. She belonged to the Maryknoll Sisters. Some of them would worship in this International Protestant Church from time to time.

'It's lovely to see you both back. Did you know Sister Georgina is in Chile from Bolivia? She'll be in Santiago for just one night on her way to Viña del Mar where she's helping lead a Retreat.' I was excited as Georgina, like us, was no longer living in Chile and we had lost touch over the years. 'Would there be any chance of meeting her on this one night in Santiago?' A couple of 'phone calls later, it was all arranged. This was my opportunity to share with this lovely nun what God had done in my relationship with father. She was delighted and asked me if she could share publicly 'my story' on the Retreat. I was happy to say 'yes'.

Not only did Ray and I learn to leave behind us the prejudice against Roman Catholics, a leaving behind which had begun in the East End of London, but we were now to be confronted with another kind of challenge and a further divide to cross.

Coming to Chile brought us face to face with a new 'enemy'. This was a political one. For its whole history, right from the early church of New Testament times, Christianity has faced persecution. In our generation this had often come through Communism. The Church was forced to go underground in China and in the former Soviet Bloc countries as well as in other parts of the world. Missionaries had to leave these countries often with little notice; some were imprisoned and others killed. Those returning to Churches across the free world shared stories of such happenings. Accounts were documented of the suffering of the national believers left behind. Not surprisingly then, with this background in the early seventies, we arrived in Marxist Chile somewhat apprehensive about what we would encounter.

Nicolás when we first met him reminded me of pictures I'd seen of 'Che' Guevara, except he didn't wear the beret. A handsome, twenty-one-year-old, he was tall, slim, and wore his dark wavy hair the same length as his Argentinian icon. Ernesto 'Che' Guevara had chosen the pathway of guerrilla warfare. His territorial arena was in Bolivia, where he was finally captured and executed. Like many martyrs who died young he had captured the imagination of the young. Left wing idealistic university students in Latin America looked to this role model encouraging revolution as a means of bringing liberation to the oppressed. Such was Nicolás.

It was Lydia (not her real name), ironically daughter of a high-ranking diplomat in the US Embassy, who introduced us to this fine-looking geology student. We had met Lydia, a seventeen-year-old, at a request from her parents who were concerned about her. She had become caught up in new age philosophy, especially astrology and also in the drug culture. Like many, her search for deeper meaning in life and a sense of purpose had led her into blind alleyways. Our meeting with her was clearly God's timing.

On her first visit to our home after a long conversation held in our bedroom for privacy, she prayed asking God for forgiveness, handing her life over to Jesus as Saviour and Lord. Ray had been looking after the children downstairs but after what seemed to them a long time the search began for 'Mummy and her friend'. Naomi and Andrew burst into the room as we were kneeling by the bed praying. Prayer was momentarily interrupted, but there was no way that I was going to shoo them away. Somewhat unceremoniously I pulled each child down to join us saying as I did, 'This is a very important time in Lydia's life.' Explanations followed later! Lydia never looked back from that decision and now lives in the States with her husband and family.

Nicolás, accompanying Lydia, now became a frequent visitor to our home, or rather, our front door! He was always polite but declined our invitation to come in. After all we represented in his thinking, an 'institution' (the Church) that had, at times in its history, become corrupt and had wielded power over the disenfranchised.

Lydia a few months later returned to the USA for higher education. Nicolás' visits to our front door inevitably stopped, but we didn't give up on him. Friends and prayer partners in the UK as well as SAMS friends in Argentina and other Republics began to pray for this earnest and extremely likeable young man.

One day, months later, Ray returning from the centre, suddenly heard his name being spoken from inside the bus. The voice belonging to another passenger was that of Nicolás. '*Hola*, Ray! How are you? How are Gill and the children?' (The customary enquiry after the family before the main conversation takes place) 'I would like to visit you in your home.' This was the break-through we had been praying for.

From that bus journey onwards, Nicolás visited us on a frequent and regular basis. It wasn't at all unusual for him just to turn up and often eat with us. The children loved him. It wasn't long before we were using the diminutive of his name, 'Nico'.

Nico lived a ten-minute walk from our home in Los Almendros. He was the oldest of four, the three others all girls. He was raised in a middle-class, Catholic home. His paternal grandparents were Catholic, as was his maternal grandmother. His maternal grandfather, a physician committed to the poor, worked within the Public Health System.

This grandfather was a Communist, as were Nicolás' favourite uncles. We would listen respectfully to his views trying to understand where he and so many were coming from in this new era for Chile. At the same time we gently shared our firm view that politics were not the answer to the condition of the human heart. Let me continue in Nico's own words in a recent letter filling in for me those earlier years.

'*I used to spend my vacations in my great grandmother's farm in the south of Chile, since I was little. I used to play with 'campesinos' children' and share with them their homes, food and friendship. That was my contact with a different world, a world of discrimination, for I was forbidden to share with them by some relatives living there, but fortunately not from my parents. A world of poverty just around the corner, that later on I thought I could help to improve.*'

In 1969, two years before our arrival, he had started his studies in geology at *La Universidad de Chile*. It wasn't long before he started to get involved politically with others who shared his leftist views. To their delight, in a mere two years with the election of Salvador Allende, it looked as if their cherished dreams for a bright new future were opening up, to these young idealists a future that would promise a fairer world for the majority. Let Nicolás speak for himself.

'I started ... supporting the first Marxist democratic elected president in Chile. But that kind of politics was not enough for me. By that time I was ... studying Marxist theory ... It matches so perfectly with my scientific background that I was thrilled by such approach [sic]. *And I understood that to speed up the process I have to participate with the idea of creating the right conditions for a change, and this change had to be, unfortunately, violent, mainly for the retaliation* [sic] *from the ones in power, to that attempt. So I agreed with the inevitable process of taking ... weapons to generate, defend and maintain a new kind of order that I thought was going to be more fair, less violent at the end and with opportunities for all, regardless* [of] *the social condition.'*

This was where Nicolás was at when we first met him. Our conversations were deep and very often took place over a mug of coffee, but more memorably over the washing up. Nico, like the majority of firstborn Chilean males, especially in middle-class homes, was spoilt. A live-in *empleada* would do everything from making their beds to all the household chores and acting as a nanny to the children. The Señora either went out to work or lived life to the full socially and was always immaculately turned out!

We will never forget his look of amazement the first time he saw Ray either washing up or with tea towel in his hand to do the drying up. It made a huge impact on him and, in time, he himself would help with the drying up. Being a busy mother and not initially having the luxury of any outside help in the home (I did later) life had to go on and conversations had to continue while chores were undertaken or interrupted as children were attended to – especially as he would turn up often unexpectedly.

Other 'enemies' were Omar and his wife Lía. They were communists and with the political situation in Chile now reversed, (but that story will be told in another chapter) they were leaving Chile as political refugees. How we first met was as a result of a hair appointment that in fact we came to see later as a divine appointment.

It was January 1974 and we were back in Santiago from home-leave. This was my first visit to this particular hairdresser. We were now living in another part of the capital, as Ray was now in another appointment – more about this later. I arrived at the hairdresser's and was met by a dark-haired receptionist. She, unlike many of her country counterparts with dark hair, didn't have the olive-skinned complexion but rather fairer skin and rosy cheeks.

She greeted me with a smile and asked me if I was English. When I replied in the affirmative she followed by asking if I taught English. I said 'no'. I noticed she looked disappointed and I asked her why she wanted English lessons.

'My husband and I, together with our two small sons, will be moving to Canada next month.'

'I'm very sorry, but I don't.'

Supporting a fresh coiffure, I went home and recounted my conversation in the hairdresser's to Ray. 'Why don't you?' he replied. 'There's not a lot to do in the Church until the holidays are over and most things start up again in March anyway.'

'Not a lot to do,' and with the three little ones on school holidays and the temperatures in full summer reaching well into the thirties! Anyway I listened to husbandly advice (not always!) and decided to go back to the hairdresser's.

On arriving the next day and enquiring for the receptionist I was told she had left.

'Yesterday was her last day.'

'Oh! She asked if I gave English classes and I said no. I've since thought about it and would be willing to.'

'I'll give you her telephone number.'

'*Gracias. Muy amable,*' I replied.

Later that week, Omar, a scientist in his early forties and his wife, a twenty-seven-year-old, found themselves in the home not only of Christians, but also that their English teacher was a pastor's wife, although they didn't know that then!

Life is full of reversals. Chile was on the sharp edge of political reversals between our first meeting with Nicolás and our later meeting with Omar and Lía. Those considered enemies by the political persuasion in power in November 1970 would find in three years that they were now the top dog.

In these political reversals, the former hunted would become the hunter. Our military neighbours and friends in *Los Almendros*, were certainly the enemies in the eyes of Nico, Omar and Lía, together with millions inside and outside Chile.

Against this background what as Christians was our calling? Our mandate had not changed. We were called to show them Christ's love too.

Christ was and is still calling people to become his disciples whatever their political, social, or educational background. After all didn't he choose within his inner circle of twelve disciples such a contrasting mix of men? Simon, known as Simon the Zealot, when he was first called belonged to a radical political party. The Zealots were highly nationalistic and resorted to violence in their attempt to oust the occupying Roman force. Meanwhile, Matthew, writer of the Gospel bearing his name, collaborated with the enemy by collecting taxes from his fellow Jews.

This challenge for us came into sharper focus as the political temperature heated-up and the country became increasingly polarised.

Chapter 16
Strategy

Building bridges was what the *conquistadores* were adept at, along with all those who find themselves in new, uncharted territory. As in the natural, so we ourselves would have to learn ways of 'building bridges' as we pioneered a new work for the Mission among the professional middle classes of the capital. Past experiences cross-culturally in our own country had prepared us a little. Our time in Quilpué gave us somewhat of a crash course into the Chilean way of life but it was only a short introduction. There was so much to learn. The fledgling Anglican Church in Quilpué, Villa Dulce and other small congregations as well as Viña itself had shown us some model. For us though, we were to be breaking fresh ground in Santiago with an entirely new approach.

Having recently arrived in the capital, my diary records that on September 23rd 1971 we had our first unexpected visitors at the front door, Jehovah's Witnesses! What a challenge! But how were we even to start when we had no congregation, no church building, no other Protestant churches or ministers in the whole of the Barrio Alto? This area stretched to approximately a third of the square mileage of the city. It contained about a quarter of Santiago's eleven million inhabitants.

A question some have asked over the years is, 'Why go as missionaries to a country that is Christian, that is Roman Catholic?' In some people's thinking this was little more than a case of 'marketing one's own brand of religion'. For us, personally, our first priority was not so much a case of establishing an Anglican Church (this would follow some years later!), but rather forming meaningful relationships out of which it would became natural to share the Christian faith. This in time would, in some friendships, enable them in their own search of faith to enter into a meaningful relationship with Christ and to become his disciples. This was the same priority as we had in the UK. If it meant such people, after discovering a personal relationship, would find their ongoing journey of faith best served within the Catholic Church, then who were we to persuade them otherwise?

This was the case with two Chilean women. They were both named Julia. One lived about a ten-minute walk away, the other was the Chilean wife of Richard Collingwood-Selby, the children's English headmaster. Both of them had deep faith but their Biblical understanding was limited. The first Julia met with me regularly for Bible study, as she wasn't getting this in her own church. I later linked her with *Padre Juan*.

A point of growth in faith and in friendship with Julia, the Headmaster's wife, was when she was ill with stomach ulcers and I visited her. Like many Chileans, Julia was a heavy smoker. We talked about the need to give up smoking and I prayed with her. Not only were the ulcers healed but also the desire to smoke disappeared.

The beginning of our friendship with Richard and Julia was with the choice of school for Naomi. When later all three were pupils, their youngest child, Benjamin, became Julian's best school friend. According to what Julia told me several years later, their daughter, Elizabeth, who was in the same class as Andrew, would chase him round the playground wanting to steal *un besito*, a kiss. Andrew had never breathed a word!

Redland school in 1971 was a fledgling school, consisting of only a few classes of primary schoolchildren. The secondary aged pupils came at a later time. It was situated on the northeastern outskirts of Santiago, in Las Condes. It was a beautiful spot with the Andes forming the backdrop and, at that time, was above the blanket of smog that lay over the city. There was even a cow grazing on the grass verge at the side of the road. From our home in Los Almendros, the school was barely a ten-minute drive away. One Wednesday in early October, it was arranged that Naomi, four years old, would join some other prospective candidates for a test the following Friday.

The big day arrived. Feeling more nervous than Naomi, we set out. We had been advised that the bus marked *'Los Dominicos'* would pass the school. What we hadn't been told was that there were two buses to Los Dominicos, one carrying a white disc on its front, the other a red. We took the wrong one! When we eventually arrived late (not the best way to make a favourable impression!), the Headmaster, Richard Collingwood-Selby, was already testing two children. The epitome of the English gentleman, he was a tall, slim man, in his late thirties or early forties, with receding hair, a cultured voice and carried himself with dignity. He was an Oxford graduate and had come to Chile as a young man to teach at the well-known English school, The Grange. Richard remained in Chile, married Julia and some years later they were now setting up their own school from modest beginnings. They were both incredibly dedicated to staff, pupils and parents alike. Julia supported her husband one hundred percent.

Naomi was asked to join the other prospective pupils and I was allowed in with her. Her first task was to do a drawing. Paper and a lead pencil were supplied. I don't remember what her drawing was but after a short time, not content with only a grey pencil, she asked for some coloured crayons! After this there were puzzles and a jigsaw and a few questions to answer. A sheet of paper was introduced with four shapes to copy. She managed only one. 'You'll be hearing from me, in due course,' said Señor Collingwood-Selby.

One evening, eleven days later, the front doorbell rang. Ray up on the stepladder; drill in one hand, rawlplug in the other, shouted out 'Can you answer the door?' I carefully put down the paintbrush I was holding and went to the front door. It was Gladys, wife of our Air Force neighbour. She told us that Ray was wanted on the telephone (we weren't as yet connected up to our own 'phone). It was the Headmaster. Naomi had been accepted to start at Redland School in March, the beginning of the new school year. It was 9.30 pm! When Ray returned with the news of Naomi's acceptance, he followed by saying, 'Forget an early night.'

'Why?' I replied.

The evening being quite early for *los Chilenos,* Gladys had promptly invited us to meet her husband and *hablar castellano.* Fortunately we had a resident babysitter, as Jean Llewellyn, a SAMS dentist was living with us at the time. I had to do a quick change from working clothes. We arrived next door at 10.00 pm and got back at midnight. Not the best time of the day – or night – to get one's head around vocabulary and verb tenses!

The Chilean approach to timing was a big adjustment for the English to make and we were just beginning to learn this. Take, for example, the entertaining of Chileans for a meal. We would invite recent friends around for dinner. A convenient time for us was around 7.30 pm, once the children were bathed, had a story read and were settling down for the night. Eight o'clock would come and go, still no guests. Another half an hour later, disappearing into the kitchen for the third or fourth time, I would adjust yet again, the temperature of the gas oven.

By nine o'clock both of us had resigned ourselves to the fact our guests were not coming. Just as I would begin to serve the meal for a desperately hungry and disappointed husband and wife, the doorbell would ring. There on our doorstep, dressed immaculately, beaming broadly above a large bouquet of flowers were our friends!

This late arrival was by no means an occasional occurrence, as we would soon discover. Neither was the time at which they left. It wasn't at all unusual for guests to leave in the early hours of the next morning. Many a time Ray and I would be washing the dishes between 2.00 am and 3.00 am! But if this *mañana* attitude would take some getting used to, what about the occasions when we would be caught out again? Some of our invited guests would in deference to their English hosts keep '*la hora inglesa*' (English time). The problem was we never knew in advance which it would be! Other problems were that we had neither any domestic help initially, let alone such a luxury as today's dishwasher.

Sophisticated kitchen appliances to benefit housewives weren't in place in the Chile of the 1970s. No wonder we soon began to appreciate why '*un problema*' became part of everyday conversation. The day did come, however, when against natural inclinations, we decided to employ domestic help. Many a woman desperately needed employment and to work for '*una gringa*' rather than a Chilean was attractive and more lucrative. For us, it was a huge financial sacrifice, but worth it, especially with the worsening political and economic situation. So much time would be spent over the next two years in an effort to bring some measure of normality to life.

The first *empleada* was Néli. We decided on very clear boundaries of responsibilities. She was there to help me with the chores. Unlike the majority of professional Chileans the responsibility of bringing up the children would be ours and ours alone. Néli came from a *población* a short bus ride away or a walk of about twenty minutes. The estate in which she lived was a step up from a shantytown, but only just, by our definition. She was in her early twenties, an attractive young woman who always took a pride in her appearance. She had a very friendly disposition and we got on very well together. Later, I was to hear from a professional Chilean woman, 'You know, you can never make a friend of your *empleada*.'

'I disagree,' I replied. 'I believe you can be friends while maintaining the respect between employer and employee.'

Building bridges of friendship tested our ingenuity. Entertaining was a very large part and a rather more obvious way of making friends, as we could still be sitting at the dinner table two or more hours into the meal. Ray, however resorted to a more devious way! Within a few days of our arrival, one afternoon he heard the sound of a mower in the garden of a neighbour.

'Gill, I'm just going out into the garden to cut the grass.'

'But the grass doesn't need cutting yet,' was my reply.

'Well, our next door neighbour is cutting his and I might

have an opportunity to begin to get to know him.' So began the friendship with Gladys and Renato.

For Ray, it was particularly difficult not having a work schedule that meant leaving the house at the same time each morning and returning at the end of a working day. Being asked what your job was and replying, 'I'm an Anglican pastor,' but with no congregation or church building was at best a bit disconcerting.

Seeing the genuine need to have a positive contribution to make to Chile, he decided to explore the possibility of using his professional background on a voluntary basis. An interview with Dr Rubenstein, the Director of the José Joaquín Aguirre, the main teaching hospital, led to Ray working in the Blood Bank each morning – just three weeks after arriving in Santiago.

To work in the teaching, medical and nursing professions required the necessity of revalidating your qualifications. However, you could work in a voluntary capacity under supervision. My nursing training came in useful in an advisory role. Such a situation happened a day before our move from Quilpué. The church under Brian Skinner's leadership had put on a *despedida* (farewell) meal for us.

News came of a boy who was very ill. The date was Sunday, September 19th when the whole of Chile was celebrating its independence during the weekend of *dieciocho* September 18th. The chance of getting a doctor to visit was thought to be impossible. When Brian and I arrived at the home we found a very sick boy who valiantly tried to smile. I found his pulse to be 136, temperature 100 °F and his respirations were 52 a minute. Under his olive skin was pallor tinged with cyanosis (blueness). We got him to hospital where he was diagnosed with bronchopneumonia.

On arriving in Santiago and word spreading that I was a nurse, it wasn't long before requests began to come from both SAMS personnel and neighbours to give injections. I was allowed to do this, and saved them the fees of '*practicantes*' (people especially trained in the art of giving injections). However, to have to give your own children a shot of penicillin, when necessary, wasn't quite so easy.

Even more difficult was when Ray needed a course of antibiotics when ill with paratyphoid compounded by acute tonsillitis. He was improving sufficiently to hop around the bedroom hand on buttock moaning 'Ouch! Ouch!' It has been my experience that his reaction was in keeping with the majority of male patients I have nursed. When really ill they face it with true manly stoicism, but with minor illnesses, at times you would think they were about to draw their last breath! 'Ray, if I was your nurse and not your wife you wouldn't react like that! You're making me nervous.' He grinned by way of reply.

Ray has a very patient and placid temperament, most of the time, and is generally very laid back. However, he has been known to react in some situations with exaggeration. I readily concede very few people like their bodies being a pincushion, and I'm sure Ray had every right to find the experience disagreeable, but over the many years of giving injections I have been told again and again what a light touch I have. One justifiable exception was giving Andrew a particular form of penicillin. This meant only one dose, as it was long acting. Unfortunately though, the liquid was particularly thick in consistency, horrible for the one administering the substance, but even worse for the recipient.

Early in the New Year, we were sad to say farewell to Gladys and Renato. He had been posted south to Puerto Montt. We were sorry to see them go. Their house was let to an American Peace Corps family, the only other foreigners in Los Almendros.

One day, the wife told me they had to take their cat to the vet. The diagnosis was acute hepatitis. The cat had been prescribed a course of injections and they asked whether I could give the injections! As it was pretty likely the cat wouldn't live I decided I had nothing to lose.

Nursing training had shown where not to inject within the buttocks of two-legged mammals, in order to avoid the sciatic nerve. I wasn't at all sure exactly where the sciatic nerve ran in a four-legged creature, or even if it had one! The cat survived! Its owners more than grateful, we now had other friends to add to our expanding collection.

Before I leave the fascinating subject of injections, I must add we saved on extortionate vets' fees when in the future I gave the necessary vaccinations to our pet dogs, even the anti-rabies.

Several years later, it was the turn to try my hand at minor cosmetic surgery! This came about as a result of a specific request. Would I pierce the ears of two teenage Americans from the Santiago Community Church? 'We don't mind if you don't,' was the answer from both of them, when my misgivings were shared. The technique stretched my improvisational skills to the limit. Due to the success, I pierced Naomi's ears at her request. 'Why not mine?' I thought. This wasn't so easy as the process was mirror-imaged. The only person who lost a drop of blood was 'yours truly'!

In such a variety of ways, both orthodox and less orthodox, our circle of friends became wider and wider. There was always the 'friend of a friend' to look up. Mario and Bernadita were such a couple. We had been given the name of Manuel Manríquez and set off to track him down. We arrived at 527, Waterloo only to find no Manríquez family lived there. We turned into a cul-de-sac and stopped a couple loading things into their car to enquire if they knew a Manríquez family. They didn't. But they did invite us into their home and on looking up our contact in the telephone directory discovered the house number was 571. Two hours later we emerged from the home of Mario and Bernadita! The visiting of Manuel and his family would have to wait for another day.

Reading my diary over the spring months from our arrival until the summer holidays following on after Christmas I am amazed at the amount of hospitality we not only gave but also received. The Chileans are an exceptionally hospitable people. Many of our friends wanted to practise their English as well as to help us learn Spanish.

In time we began to think and plan for opportunities to explore the Bible together with our new friends, sometimes in their homes and sometimes in ours. Careful preparation was spent in studying the Spanish text and even more the careful working out of questions in our very limited Spanish. But there was a huge problem we weren't ready for. Having read the biblical text together and asked the appropriate questions to set us off on a discussion we were left high and dry in a fog of confusion.

We couldn't understand the answers to the questions! How could we have a really meaningful discussion? Frustration wasn't easy to cope with. A great deal of patience was needed. We had a lot to learn about pioneering a new work. These were very early days. All the adjustments to another culture and language were against a background of mounting political tension with increasing shortages of food. This also meant our patience and frustration, at seemingly wasted time spent on simply trying to live a normal existence in a far from normal situation, were tested to the limit.

Queues became part of everyday life. Everything from meat to toilet rolls began to become scarce. It was easy to cope with the latter. The airmail edition of the *Guardian Weekly* was torn into appropriate strips and put at the side of the toilets! Wherever you travelled on foot, by bus, or in a car you would see queues outside all the shops selling essential commodities. Gradually and relentlessly the infrastructure of Allende's Chile was breaking down, and with attendant chaos.

Days at school for the children were at times disrupted as an increasing number of demonstrations took place and buses were requisitioned to transport protesters to the rallies. This was really only the beginning of difficulties and stress. Worse was to follow. Our friend Nicolás was still a frequent visitor to our home, the relationship becoming stronger all the time. For his part there were many conversations about his Marxist dream of Utopia for his country. For our part there were increasing opportunities to share what faith in Christ meant. Each listened with respect to the other's passion but without reaching any compromise.

Julian and Andrew on the balcony of 'Los Almendros'.

Our Air Force neighbours - Gladys and Renato.

Andrew in his 'delantales'.

Nicolás with Naomi.

Neli.

A visit to Nana's home.

Shanty homes.

'Carabinero' - Policeman.

President Allende with Fidel Castro.
Courtesy of PA Photos.

President Allende with Gen. Pinochet
on the latter being sworn in as C-in-C.
Courtesy of PA Photos.

Protester against Pinochet outside his rented house
on his arrest in the UK, January 2000.
Courtesy of Insnews.

The Moneda Palace.

An illegal takeover of land.

Anti-American graffiti.
(Youth together with their Government against "Yankee" aggression.)

Dustmen's Strike.

Chilean naval submarine -
Valparaiso Bay.

Independence Day Parade - mounted cavalry with Andes in background.

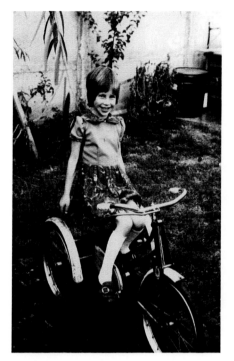

Naomi.

Julian with 'Patsy'.

Andrew in favourite pose.

Julian.

Supermarket 'Almac' with queue forming.

Redland School.

*Headmaster Richard
Collingwood-Selby.*

Naomi in school uniform.

Los Dominicos - where Andrew and Julian went to playschool.

Kevin 'Miguel' O'Boyle far right.

Ray with Monseñor (formerly 'Padre') Juan de Castro, 1988.

Me with Sister Georgina during a return visit in 1988.

Together with Richard and Julia, October 2000 - outside Pablo Neruda's home at Isla Negra.

Chapter 17

The Worsening Economic Situation

A new arrival in our family was a rabbit. Patsy was not only lovely to look at – a soft, large lump of lovely white fur – but she would become indispensable to us. With the worsening food shortages we jumped at the gift offered to us. The bonus was that Patsy was pregnant. The children simply adored their new pet. How to tell them that, in acquiring Patsy, we had other more devious plans in store, was the challenge confronting us. But honesty as always was the better approach.

'Patsy is going to have some babies. You can choose one to keep as a pet as well as Patsy. Mummy and Daddy are finding it hard to get enough food so we will have to look after the other baby rabbits and when they are big we will have to eat them. Then later Patsy will have more babies and so we will have enough to eat again.'

In due course Patsy delivered eight little balls of 'fluff' to the delight not only of three excited children but a very satisfied midwife who had taken a 'professional interest' in the whole ante-natal care and labour! The post-natal care would have to be somewhat more detached! At least this was the plan. But the best-laid plans do backfire at times.

Bread, which used to be baked fresh every day, by now was hard to get and was only available every three days or so and after the first day was beginning to go stale. We had to learn a number of ingenious tricks as far as food was concerned during these months of food shortages. When vegetarian recipes were not the vogue in Chile, how do you serve lentils more than three days running, without the family becoming completely bored?

Friends gave me a tip of doctoring up stale bread. 'Sprinkle water straight over the rolls and put in a hot oven for a few moments.' It worked.

On this particular morning, Ray had left home before seven to get some bread. Just before getting the children up and dressed he arrived back. I'll never forget his look as he climbed the stairs, shoulders drooping, head down – a picture of abject misery.

'What's wrong? Wasn't there any bread?'

'Yes. I've managed to get bread. It's the rabbits. They're all dead.'

I rushed downstairs and out into the garden, followed by Ray, and what a sorry sight met our eyes. It was complete carnage. Eight little fluffy bodies were strewn over the lawn and among them a larger ninth. It seemed a dog had got into the garden and pulled the wire netting off the front of the hutch. Patsy was the only rabbit that had any blood on her, no doubt trying to defend the little ones. They possibly died from shock trauma.

'We can't let the children see them like this.'

Ray quickly set to and buried the baby rabbits. I picked Patsy up and placed her on a scrubbed-top table, which we kept outside. We had, by now, made the decision that we would have to salvage some meat from this unexpected turn of events and, of course, it would have to be Patsy. We went upstairs to break the news as gently as possible to the children. Once tears were dried and cuddles over, it was time to get ready for breakfast and the school run, but not before they went into the garden to see where the baby rabbits were buried.

Later that morning, with heavy hearts we turned our attention to Patsy. How on earth were we to skin a rabbit? The only time I had seen fresh livestock being prepared for the table was while living next door to the Skinner family. We had watched Brian kill two cockerels, one of which became ours, and under his instructions helped pluck and dress them. However, a cockerel was not a rabbit – and a pet one at that! Reluctantly we set to work. Ray managed to skin her while it fell to me, with a greater knowledge of anatomy and physiology, to engage in the cleaning process.

With Patsy now dressed and in the pyrex 'coffin' and entombed in the oven, I drove to collect Naomi from Redland school picking up Andrew and Julian en route from their playgroup at Los Dominicos.

Los Dominicos was the name given to a former Dominican monastery, now a church, built on Spanish colonial-style architecture. The church of Los Dominicos, in the seventies, stood in a commanding position where the main Apoquindo road finished. The building was made of adobe, covered in plaster and painted an off white, the paint peeling and giving a very rustic look. Copper domes capped the imposing twin towers.

I always found it a particularly impressive sight in the autumn sunshine as the church stood out against the backdrop of the changing colours of the trees. Leaving the tarmac road where buses and taxis pulled in, a short drive up the very wide dirt track led to the main wooden door and into a large courtyard. Here, unless the weather was inclement, I would hand over the two boys to the welcoming staff. This particular *jardín infantil* (kindergarten) was only the second government-sponsored place of its kind in the whole of the city. The members of staff were university trained and the children were from a social cross-section.

It was run on lines similar to Save the Children Fund. We were extremely fortunate to get them in as the private playschools were beyond us financially. Their days were well structured with educational and creative activities, interspersed by playtime in the courtyard. After lunch, out would come each child's blanket and they would have a sleep and the staff a well-earned siesta, until early afternoon when the little ones were picked up.

Andrew started at playgroup when he was almost four. It wasn't long before Julian pleaded and pleaded to go. 'Me go to playgroup with Andoo,' was the persistent refrain until, against our natural inclinations (he wasn't yet three), we caved in and registered him on a trial basis. We needn't have worried. He loved it and stole the hearts of all, as did Andrew, their blue eyes and blond hair enabling them almost to get away with murder!

Having collected both the boys I continued up the hill to

Redland School. To my dismay the first thing Naomi asked when she came out of her class was 'Mummy, where's Patsy?'

'Let's get in the car. Have you had a happy day at school?' I stalled.

'Mummy, where's Patsy?'

Quickly trying to collect my thoughts I replied, 'Naomi. You saw Patsy on the table outside. You know she's dead.'

'I know, Mummy, but where is she now?' I should say here that, around this time, both she and Andrew had taxed us with many questions about what happens after death.

Swallowing hard, with both hands on the steering wheel of our minibus and eyes straight ahead, I answered, 'She's in the oven.' That seemed to satisfy her because there were no more questions. Our dilemma, however, was how would they react when teatime came and we sat down to consume a casserole of Patsy!

We sat down later at the table. The dreaded moment had arrived. Naomi started her meal without any hesitation and the two boys taking their cue from big sister did the same. Conversation continued as normal except I was struggling to cope with my dinner. With four empty or near empty plates, it was Naomi who suddenly said, 'Daddy, Mummy, doesn't Patsy taste nice? Can I have another helping?' Ah well, nothing like children to blow away all pretence and speak honestly from the heart.

As the older two had been asking many questions relating to what happens after death, diary extracts at this time were reminders not only of the transience of this life but also where as Christians our true roots are to be found. It is both challenging and humbling to allow our children to teach us things that in our more complex and sophisticated thought patterns and life styles we all too easily forget.

It was our custom to follow breakfast with a short time of reading from a child-friendly Bible storybook followed by prayer. On September 7th the diary records that both Andrew and Naomi prayed and Andrew in his prayers mentioned the food he liked '*red jam and honey*' and that we needed milk. His prayer continued on the subject of heaven and that we couldn't get to heaven on our own *''cos the sky is too high but God would come for us.'* Three days later again at breakfast his thoughts still on deep theological matters he said, *' we can't all join hands to get to heaven 'cos its too high and only God can take us there.'*

Around this time Ray and I were to be faced with a situation that would bring the whole question of the uncertainty of life itself and the very real fact of heaven much closer than either of us could have imagined.

Naomi had been born with a birthmark on the back of her neck, its diameter about the size of a small pea. As I was bathing her I noticed the character of this mole-like mark had changed and in the centre were tiny nodules. We contacted an American Methodist missionary doctor who had been recommended to us. When Dr Moore later examined the 'mole', she looked concerned and said we would need to see a skin specialist immediately for a biopsy to be taken. The waiting days were naturally anxious ones, compounded by the children's current fascination with dying and heaven!

In between Andrew's profound theological statements on those two occasions, my diary records a conversation I had with Naomi about a holiday back in England one day, to which she replied, 'Heaven is our home.' While waiting for the biopsy results, one morning at breakfast Naomi announced that she was going to live with Jesus in heaven.

I remember leaving the table and going into Ray's study where I started to cry convinced that we were going to lose Naomi. A few moments later, with the pressing need to take Andrew and Naomi to their respective kindergarten and school, I washed my face and we left the house. When I returned home Ray and I sat down together in the sitting room. We needed to speak out what was in both our minds.

'What is God trying to tell us?' was the question we were both thinking, yet not daring to face.

'Is he preparing us for her death?'

It seemed just too much of a coincidence all this talk of heaven at the same time as we were facing an uncertain outcome of her skin lesion. That morning we had to learn in a deeper way than ever before that all we are and have come from God. Our children are given to us in trust and we need to hold them on the open palm of the hand.

I recalled then, as I have had to do so many times in life, something I had read in my early twenties of one of those earlier 'heroines'. It was in a book written by a missionary to the Far East. Isobel Kuhn had spoken of the need to hold lightly to the things of this life. If we clutch on tightly to any object of our affection then we would be hurt even more if God had to prise open our fingers to remove the object. Better to hold it on the open palm. Sounds so easy but in reality the art of relinquishment is one we have to constantly learn and re-apply.

We were now faced with a choice. Was our trust in God big enough to hand over to him our precious daughter should that be necessary? With tears streaming down both our faces we relinquished Naomi.

Three o'clock in the afternoon and it was time again for the school run. Being more composed I said to Naomi on driving home, 'Naomi, that was a funny thing you said at breakfast about going to live with Jesus soon.'

'I am, Mummy.'

'How do you know you are?' I replied.

'He's told me.'

'How has he told you?' There was no answer.

The following Monday we went with Naomi to the El Salvador Hospital to see the skin specialist. To our immense relief the nodules were diagnosed as non-malignant and a form of acid and a dressing were applied. We returned home light hearted and full of thankfulness. Two years later when they re-appeared we were home on leave and had a biopsy taken and surgery to remove them completely.

Before the month was out another incident during prayers at breakfast caused much needed light relief from the intensity of recent days. We were no longer on the subject of heaven. Instead it was the story of the Apostle Paul's conversion on the road to Damascus. When Ray asked who was it that spoke to Paul, like a flash Andrew replied, 'Two little dickie birds. One named Peter one named Paul!'

When his table manners on one occasion caused a sharp reprimand from Ray: 'Andrew, you're eating just like a pig.'

Without hesitation our three-year-old replied, 'But, Daddy, pigs don't have spoons!'

Another howler came one lunch time when on seeing a dragonfly hovering over the patio, he was heard to say, 'Look! There goes a helicopter!'

Intense days, however, would be on the increase as the politically worsening situation gathered momentum. How grateful we were for such light relief our children brought us.

Although we were living in far from normal days, family life continued with its ups and downs, the laughter and the tears, the humdrum and the surprises, the quarrels and the making up, the punishments and the forgiveness, the going without but also the treats. One early treat was going to the cinema. *The Railway Children* was the first film they ever saw, in Chile.

Not having a television stretched our ingenuity in providing sufficient activities and entertainment for the children, especially in the wet winter months and during school holidays. I taught all three to read in English before they each had to tackle reading in another language. Ladybird reading books were my most tried and trusted method. In spite of what today's educationalists may say, it worked!

We also tried never to mix the two languages in conversation. We had observed other compatriots introducing the odd Spanish word into an English sentence in talking with their children and found it led to some confusion. As a result, we found when our three were completely bilingual, they knew exactly who to speak in Spanish to and who in English. It was interesting to see that they would naturally lapse into Spanish with one another as their play language.

However, some cultural confusion in the mind of Julian was evident in a conversation he was having in Spanish with the *empleada* when he was around three years old.

'I'm Chilean,' he proudly announced.

'No, Julian, you're English.'

'*Soy chileno,*' the fair-skinned blond determinedly answered.

'*No, tú eres ingles,*' was the just as insistent reply.

'I'm Chilean.'

'Julian, why do you say you're Chilean?'

Then came the reply that caused us such laughter, on being told of this conversation.

'Because I have blue eyes!'

These were some of the many lighter moments interspersed among the very real frustrations and tears. The never ending scenario of broken-down washing machines, the lack of mod cons, the relentless heat in the summer months, the relentless rain in the winter, time wasted in endless queuing for food and the increasingly dangerous situation all began to take their toll.

'What is our role?' I found myself wondering one day. There hanging up on the wall was the answer to my question. The Apostle Paul in the New Testament and his other missionary companions were trying to enter a different province in Turkey but were prevented, by none other than God's Spirit.[1] The comments at the side of this verse on the pad on the calendar read as follows:

'Remember that the Spirit has not only a service of work, but a service of waiting. Inspire me with the knowledge that a man may be called at times to do his duty by doing nothing …'.

I, we, had so much to learn.

Another area of GMT when patience was tried had to do with communication or rather lack of it.

It's hard to imagine nowadays with e-mails, mobile 'phones in addition to landlines that we were actually without our own telephone for over six months. This wasn't because Santiago was less developed than London. (although in the seventies it was), but rather because of the usual red tape that accompanied any transaction. Every thing took so much longer than back home.

This lack of communication caused us many headaches and added to the stress of our lives. A message would be got to us via next door's telephone to say a missionary from the south

---

[1] The Bible. Acts chapter 16 verse 7

would be visiting the capital for some important documentation that needed doing. Could we please provide a bed for the night or nights and a meal or meals depending on how long it would take? Plans were rearranged and bed and meals got ready. No one turned up. Something had cropped up and they were unable to contact us.

On one occasion we well remember, being woken up to the sound of tapping on the bedroom window. Climbing out of bed and going to the window, Ray discovered Gordon, a young bachelor teacher from the Mission school in Viña, was throwing small stones at our upstairs window. 'Have you got a bed for the night?' came the request. It was around midnight!

Being a family of five we had the largest mission vehicle for our use. Ray, therefore, was often called upon to help transfer personnel and luggage from the coach station and also to help missionaries move house. Often the coach would be late and with no telephone Ray would be unable to let me know when he and the expected guests would arrive.

A letter written home January 29th 1972 explains the frustration we were feeling and the urgent request for prayer that the 'phone situation would be resolved. The same letter recounts our need for a holiday (we hadn't had one since leaving the UK more than fifteen months previously), the rising summer temperatures of 31-32 °C, and all three children going down one after another with diarrhoea and high temperatures.

In Naomi's case the rapid rise in temperature brought on two convulsions, the day after a strong earth tremor had rocked our beds during the night. We called a doctor and were advised to wrap her in cold wet towels while the doctor was on his way. Within twenty-four hours and starting a course of antibiotics she made a rapid recovery only to be followed by both Andrew and Julian starting another round of diarrhoea, in Julian's case provoked by cutting more teeth and accompanying fretfulness. '… *the last two months have been very difficult and we've both found our patience sorely tried …*'.

The letter goes on to say that in spite of praying for patience I end up '*almost losing my temper with them*' feeling defeated and left with a sense of failure. Conscious of the spiritual battle we were in, in pioneering a new work, we were able to recognise the attack of the enemy capitalising on our weaknesses. I quote '... *left to ourselves we are failures, he* [the enemy] *then goes on to attack our faith so that the thought comes that God can change others and give them victory but not me.'*

Time spent in queuing for food and other basic commodities was increasing from one week to the next. In addition prices were going up and the scarcity of some items meant that when they were available the price was high. One example I mentioned in a letter to parents in April was that I had paid the equivalent of eight shillings for six plain navy buttons for a school cardigan I had just finished knitting for Naomi.

Our local supermarket was called Almac, not unlike a smaller version of Tesco, modern and initially well stocked, but as the months went by it became increasingly depleted. We had become friendly with one of the senior cashiers, named Doris. This friendship would prove to be a two-way advantage. For Doris, it was an opportunity to practise her English and for us, a 'phone call (once we were connected!) informing us when certain food supplies had arrived.

'Ray, Doris has just 'phoned. Sugar and oil have arrived in Almac. Are you able to go or will you look after Julian' (the other two being at school) 'while I go?' This refrain, or similar, would be repeated over and over again in the passing months, with the substitution of meat, milk, toilet rolls or batteries, in fact anything but the kitchen sink!

By the time one of us arrived at the supermarket, it was evident the grapevine had been at work. People were converging on Almac from all directions.

By 1972 the queue cult was a daily occurrence. One day I automatically joined one. After about twenty minutes I turned to the lady in front.

'*Para qué la cola?'* (Colloquially 'What's the queue for?')
'*Cigarrillos!'*
To think we had wasted twenty minutes of precious time!
Not so humorous were the occasions when we got caught up

in a stampede. For me, this happened twice, that I recall. The car park, for some months no longer used for its intended purpose but for accommodating the growing numbers of hopeful shoppers, was teeming with around four hundred people already waiting. When the signal came that the supermarket was open the mass of people moved forward as one man. It was a frightening experience as over four hundred people surged forward. I went home empty handed.

Confrontation between the government and the opposition was becoming uglier by the day. October 1972 was a particularly difficult month. The following accounts from my diary sum up the next two weeks of our living. It all started with a march on the 10th by the main opposition party, the Christian Democrats. Two days later was a public holiday. *'El Día de la Raza'* was an important day for the whole of Latin America, a day commemorating Christopher Columbus discovering the Americas. On this very day a National Strike was called. We queued for fifty-five minutes to get petrol.

The following day I record a *'tense situation in the country due to the strike of the 'dueños de los camiones'* [lorry owners].' The supermarkets closed and remained so until Monday. Disturbances in the centre were met with the customary tear gas. However, a lovely surprise came later that day in the form of a present of a fresh trout. Tom, our American Peace Corps neighbour had returned from a trip to the South of the country and had been fishing. He was one of the privileged who had access to a ready supply of petrol!

A week from the day of the Opposition march, we went to Almac but the margarine ran out before we could get any. That afternoon, having picked up Andrew and Julian from Los Dominicos playgroup, and continuing the school run to fetch Naomi, the car packed up on me. As it was on a gentle hill I managed to do a U-turn to park it on the wider verge on the other side of the road. With the minibus safely off the road I was faced with a dilemma.

We were still over a mile short of Redland School. The two boys were tired. There was nothing for it but to thumb a lift!

It worked. This wouldn't be the last time we resorted to this method. Once Naomi was in tow we had to travel the three to four miles home. Fortunately some buses were still on the road. This depended on whether they were private or government owned.

That night the government announced a *toque de queda*. The curfew was to run from midnight until six the next morning until further notice.

On Wednesday the doctors and dentists threw in their lot with the other strikers and the next day lawyers joined in. Schools were now closed. A few small food shops, sympathetic to Allende's government, were still opening their doors. Armed forces were stationed to guard them and to patrol the streets.

The 'phone rang. It was Mimi, an American friend married to Carlos. 'Gill, some of us are going to the Mercado Central' (the main Market in downtown Santiago). 'would you like to come?' Several *gringas* piled into her car

We decided, as the anti-American feelings were increasingly surfacing, that we would only converse in Spanish when in public. Over these troubled months, Ray and I were greatly amused to be taken as Germans, Americans and even Russians – for some unknown reason that we might be English was not the first question of identity that surfaced.

This particular visit was especially memorable. For the very first time I bought whale meat – unthinkable now. It tasted like steak.

The day before, the Sunday of the second week, an '*army major was shot dead*' during the curfew. The worsening situation was spreading right through Chile with '*twenty zones* [counties] *in a state of emergency and at least four with curfews.*'

On the last day of this really difficult two weeks, the Opposition party, not short of innovative ideas, came up with the idea of '*el día del silencio*' – *a call to all members of the Opposition to remain in their homes as a protest.*' More about this critical month of October and its political fall-out is reserved for another chapter.

For the past three days, we had been only able to get water between midnight and 9.00 am. We filled up as many containers as we could to see us through the day. It meant, however, that for hot showers and baths, the whole family had to take these early in the morning before the water was cut off – not the best time for little ones who hadn't had time, as yet, to get dirty from playing. Ten days later the water was back on during the day, but with insufficient pressure to work the *califont.* So still no hot water. The restricted supply of water was to continue throughout the next six months over the hot spring and summer. We took to filling up containers with water and leaving them in the sun to warm up for bath time! The very same containers had been used to collect snow during the exceptional snowfall of the previous winter!

Water, so easily wasted in our previous lifestyle, could no longer be taken for granted. Three very real but distinct reasons for this greater appreciation of a major life-giving source had been thrust upon us in our first eighteen months in Chile. The earthquake followed by the snowfall and now the 'wind' of severe political unrest.

As well as the children's schooling being disrupted, Ray was unable to get to his voluntary work at the hospital. No postal service added to our sense of isolation.

Hard times bring out both the best and also the worst in people. A neighbour stopped me as I walked by her house and gave me a large piece of pumpkin and two roses. Another sold me four packets of butter. This was the happier climax to an emotionally demanding fortnight that October. Worse was yet to come in the unfolding of Chile's economic and political power struggle.

Amazingly we found both the time and the energy to continue with the work we came out to do although inevitably adaptability had to be a priority. Lydia and Nico continued to visit. For Lydia our home was like a second home. It would be some time before Nico would see it in this way. One day Lydia arrived with the news that he had given her an ultimatum. The choice facing her was Christ or Nico!

'Christ,' was her answer.

He wasn't really prepared for that. Although their relationship didn't finish at this time, with Lydia's departure to college in the

States we inevitably saw less of him until the encounter with Ray on the bus. Gradually Nico's initial wariness of us decreased and with the passing weeks he would quite spontaneously drop in and eat with us.

There were two incidents that stand out in my memory where my attitude to the shortages was put to the test – I didn't come out with flying colours, initially, in either of these. The first that ushered in a massive 'U-turn' in this convinced Marxist's relationship with us centred round saccharins!

As shortages intensified we asked parents to pop into their letters to us items like pepper – no warning sign on the envelope saying 'Opener, beware!' which if a censor had resorted to opening …?! Sweeteners were another.

This particular day in question, Ray had said Nico had 'phoned to say he would be calling. Our stocks of sugar were almost out. In rather a piqued tone I said to Ray, 'I'm a bit fed up with Nico depleting our stocks. After all he's the Marxist! Well, he's going to have to go without his customary sugar in his coffee and have saccharins.' (Like many Chilean men he did pile into his coffee several teaspoons full of this, by now, precious commodity.)

He arrived. I brought in the tray with three mugs of coffee on it. Also on the tray was a saucer with the sweeteners. A surprised look crossed his handsome face. 'Don't you have any sugar, Gill?'

'Yes, but what sugar I have I'm keeping for the children. You'll have to do what the rest of us do, manage without.'

Scarcely hiding his puzzlement his next question came. 'How do you shop?'

Now it was our turn to look puzzled. Wasn't it obvious?

'Like everyone else, in the *colas.*'

His puzzlement gave way to incredulity.

'Don't you shop on the black-market?'

'No!'

'Why's that?'

'As Christians we don't think it's right,' was our reply.

We'll never forget his reply to that simple statement. It marked a full acceptance of us. It also gave us the opening and the right to share our Christian faith in the months ahead.

'You're more socialist than Allende himself! I'm now prepared to listen to you.' This was the catalyst that in the future would open up a whole new work among Chileans but not before many more bridges had to be crossed politically.

The second incident took place some months earlier. Ray had been invited by David Pytches to preach at St Peter's Church in Viña. 'Do come to lunch.' This meant lunch for a combined 'family' of eleven!

During the hunting for food that all too easily was beginning to take over our lives, Mary had recently made the decision that her time was too precious for this. She would trust God to provide for the needs of her family.

We were to travel down from Santiago to the Coast very early on the Sunday itself. What were we to take to Mary as our contribution? There were two packets of precious meat in the top freezer of the 'fridge. These had represented hours of queuing over a period of four weeks or so. They were being kept for when our protein supplies had depleted sufficiently to warrant their use. An inner voice said, 'Take one of the two packets!'

I thought, 'Why should I? Mary has made her decision not to queue and we don't know when next we'll be able to get any more meat.' The following seconds were spent tussling between my conscience and my sense of justice. God, the Source of that inner voice, persisted. The gauntlet was now thrown down! I capitulated. With shame I said, 'I'm sorry, Lord. How can I be so selfish? Of course I'll take Mary one of the packets.'

The following Wednesday, there was a telephone call from a Canadian Embassy diplomat. Agatha Morey worshipped at the same international English-speaking church we went to. The congregations consisted of members of St Andrew's Anglican Church, serving mainly English expats, and the Union Church, mostly Americans. How these two congregations came to unite was a direct result of the economic and political situation. Our involvement in the ongoing process of this 'arranged marriage of convenience' is the subject of another chapter.

'Gill, would you come round to my apartment?' was the surprising invitation. At this time we didn't know Agatha very well. She gave me directions and off I set.

On arriving, she showed me into the lounge. We chatted for a few moments in which she told me she had been in Cuba as one of her postings. While there she had seen the effects of economic shortages. A few minutes later, leaving me sitting on the sofa, she disappeared into the kitchen, later to emerge with her arms full of packaged items.

'We are fortunate in the Embassy. We have an allocation of food provided. The Lord has told me I'm to give these to you.' So saying, she handed me three family-sized packets of meat. I could have wept. I recounted the story of the previous weekend. We hugged one another as we marvelled at God's working in both our lives.

In this far from normal lifestyle some semblance of normality had to be carved out. Our work and calling had to go on.

There was a series of films relating science and the Christian faith, which Ray and I in our young adult years had seen. The series was known as 'The Fact and Faith films'. Coincidentally, before we had even met, we both had facilitated the showing of one in our respective hospitals.

Red River of Life was on the wonders of the human circulatory system. In both instances hospital personnel from nurses and doctors to technical and ancillary staff came. Matron herself as well as the two Sister Tutors were present at the showing in Leicester. One senior tutor had even given the student nurses (currently in their intensive study period in the Teaching Unit) the afternoon off. This was on the condition they attended the Nurses' Christian Fellowship for the showing of the film. It was after this occasion that she said to me, 'Nurse Williamson, I can see you would make an excellent minister's wife.' Prophetic? – at least the statement of becoming a Vicar's wife!

Over ten years later and the other side of the world this same film would equally impress its audience. Not having a hall in which to show it we had to use innovative means to accommodate the twenty-five Chileans who came. Being spring, we used the garden and projected the film on to the side of the house, the walls of which were white – at least in theory. The peeling paint and decidedly off-white walls with patches of grey undercoat didn't in any way detract from the enthusiastic response. Richard Collingwood-Selby was so impressed with the well-researched scientific facts of the film that he asked about the possibility of showing it at school.

The next day, Saturday, there was another showing, this time for teenagers, mostly students. My diary records forty-five young people came for the film and barbecue. We ate *vienesas* (sausages) and *empanadas.* I had spent a considerable amount of time and energy in a lengthy walk on the Friday in order to find the sausages. With success!

At the end of the showing of the film a dark-haired, olive skinned young man gave a word of appreciation. This was none other than Fernando, the university student who had had the skiing accident. This young man with a deep faith had invited many of his friends. It was the following day that we went to the Verbo Divino church for the Youth Congress and met Juan, our priest friend.

By early 1973 political forces, each with their own particular agenda, were now at work capitalising on the vulnerability of the populace. Open-backed trucks, full of people, were being ferried in from the outskirts of the city. The new arrivals were from the poorer areas and often consisted of families of at least three generations. Many of them did not live in our sector at all.

When it came to commodities being handed out these were given to each person. Those with a large family of older children and extended family had a decided advantage and could, between them, go home with eight or more packets of meat (when meat was in stock), flour, sugar, margarine etc. It was hardly suitable for Julian at two years old to join his parents in a queue. With no other family members to help, it meant usually only one of us was able to spend our time in this way and this meant only one commodity of 'whatever' for a family of five. This took, more often than not, anything from one hour to three.

Some help, however, did become available, when a SAMS doctor, Thea Coates lived with us as part of the extended family. Thea would be another source of food income as well as being good company and an adopted *Tia* (Aunt) for the children.

One day she and Ray went to Almac as we heard meat had arrived. In a letter to our friends and supporting churches, Ray described what happened.

'It's our day off [March 31st 1973] *and I'm in the meat queue outside our local supermarket. It's 07:30, 1½ hours before opening time, and there are 520 people in front of me. Some have been here all night, huddled on the pavement beside rubbish fires. I can see Dr. Thea Coates ahead reading her medical journals. I might as well use the time to write this letter, because, judging from previous occasions, I shall be here at least another three hours ... I'm now at the head of the queue, it's 11:00, and there are as many people behind me as there were in front ... I've just been handed one packet of meat (no choice) and there will be no more for 2 or 3 weeks.'*

'So began a recent Saturday. Gill, with gastric 'flu, had to get up and look after our three lively youngsters until Ray returned. We always used to take them shopping, but its not easy queuing with them running everywhere! These police invigilated queues take their toll of our time and health too (leg veins and haemorrhoids). At what point do we say, We can't do what we're here for?'

He goes on to recount the price increases, some doubling overnight:

'The cost of living in the last 12 months increased by 195%, creating a world record.'

'No problems? ... Not to write about them would be less than honest ...'

'If we don't share our problems (as well as 'praise points') with you and you with us, how can we intelligently and effectively pray for one another?'

'No, we refuse to withold the complaints so as to appear to be idealists; to dwell on past failure and be pessimists; to be concerned with the present rumours and be alarmists, or to think of the future only and be optimists; we want to be realists!'

On another unforgettable day for Ray, he eventually got

through the doors and to the meat counter, to find only a few packets were left. These were then thrown into the air for any one to catch. 'What have we come to?' Ray said on his return empty handed. 'It was just like feeding animals at the zoo.' Those prepared to push and shove in an effort to grab the tossed meat did have their reward – or did they?

The worst experience of the futility of queuing happened on the day before my thirty-fourth birthday. We woke up on a Saturday morning to discover via the grapevine that a supermarket a bit further on from Almac had supplies in. We hurriedly finished breakfast and getting the three children ready drove up to Sani. It was 9.15 am when the five of us joined the *cola*. My diary records that over five hours later, we returned with a scrappy, fatty piece of meat, only suitable for soup, and some vinegar.

We well remember that we were so emotionally exhausted we packed the tired, fractious and bored children off to bed.

'I want to go home,' I said to Ray in despair.

'So do I,' was his reply. 'We can't do what we came out to do.'

'Let's get the next aeroplane back. We don't have to live here. It isn't our country anyway. Its problems are not of our making.'

We went to bed too! We had hit rock bottom.

As we've learnt so many times in our journey of faith, this is where we can encounter God in a new way. God didn't give up on Elijah or Job when they hit an all-time low of despair and depression. God meets us when we cry out to him in our vulnerability and dependence. He still had work for us to do in our adopted country and among our adopted people. A very special birthday gift would come the next day, the 'unwrapping' of which would occur over the next months, layer by layer.

Nico turned up in the afternoon to show us his 'new' second-hand motorbike. When it was time for him to leave, he said, trying to sound casual 'Oh, by the way, I want to start reading the bible with you.' As he left with a roar down the cul-de–sac, Ray and I hugged one another.

'This is what we came out to do. That queue was worth every minute!'

Chapter 18

Some Welcome Respite: Going South

'Work hard, play hard' was what my mother often said to Elaine and me. This was advice we've tried to follow most of our lives. Although life was far from normal for us now, we tried to build this 'playing hard' into our family life.

There was so much of this beautiful country of Chile we wanted to explore. We were determined not to let the tensions and 'wasted' time spent on living rob us of making the most of what free time was available. It was important to keep a regular day off and to take our holidays as well as enjoy the many *feriados* Chileans celebrated. A good laugh was also good medicine when it would have been all too easy to succumb to a prevailing climate of increasing *problemas*.

Two events seemed to us to be unbelievably funny. One occurred on my way home with the children from school. As I drove down the hill towards Los Dominicos, an incredible sight met our eyes. A taxi had pulled into the dried muddy area where the buses turned round at the junction of the then unmade road with the main road. The back doors of the taxi were open and a reluctant passenger was being unceremoniously coerced in. The unwilling passenger was a black and white calf!

The taxi driver arms gesticulating wildly seemed to be as unwilling as his potential passenger. The owner of the animal, not to be daunted in his attempts to transport his precious cargo, apparently struck some sort of a deal. With a shrug of his shoulders and further conversation the taxi driver gave in. I sincerely hoped that the stressed-out calf didn't resort to nature's way of coping, on the journey, by leaving a 'present' for his accommodating driver!

On the other occasion, this too had to do with an animal. In our own country we do sometimes see a dog being exercised with its owner riding a bicycle, dog in tow. In these cases both owner and dog get their exercise. However, what I witnessed in this second incident meant only one of the parties having a workout! It wasn't a dog in tow but a horse. The rider wasn't on a bicycle but leading the way on a motor scooter!

We have learnt over the years in ministry that the only way to really get away from it all is to be out of the house on our days off and holidays. Never more so than when three years later we found ourselves living next door to the Santiago Community Church where Ray was Chaplain, with his office and one of the church halls at the bottom of the small garden – a see-through wooden fence an inadequate attempt to give some privacy.

Holidays! How we've loved them and made the most of them. These were our opportunities to discover both the south and the north of the 'long narrow bean' in its stunning natural beauty and its immense diversity.

January and February are the months when there is a mass exodus from the capital for the summer holidays. Paul and Esme had invited us to meet up with them in the south and to spend some of our holiday together. They booked the seven of us in a small wooden hotel in a small lakeside town, a distance of over 1000 kilometres (just under 630 miles). We would take the opportunity of visiting other SAMS personnel and seeing something of the work in the south. It would now be our turn to be on the receiving end of hospitality.

With great excitement we set off in our Volkswagen in the early hours of one mid-February morning. The farther we headed south the farther we left behind the heat of Santiago and the central region. The cloudless blue skies gave way to a mixture of blue sky interspersed with billowy white clouds. With the passing of both time and distance the white clouds were replaced by grey, the sun playing hide and seek, leaving in its wake shafts of sunlight dodging the sheets of rain.

Our journey was mainly driving on the Pan American Highway. This was the road we would spend hours and hours travelling in the years to come, sometimes driving, sometimes being driven and once being towed. Stretching longitudinally down the two American continents, it provides a vital means of communication. The only interruption to this 'aortic' artery is to be found in the Darien jungles of Colombia and Panama.

As far as Chile was concerned, when we lived there, the Highway finished just beyond Puerto Montt, south of which lay fjords, glaciers, myriads of uninhabited islands culminating in Cape Horn. Because of this terrain, local residents would have to travel by air, sea or through neighbouring Argentina to reach north of Puerto Montt.

Since those days an amazing engineering project has seen the construction, over many years of the Camino Austral. This road stretches around 600 kilometres farther south from Puerto Montt, and reaching over half-way between it and Puerto Natales, provides links with towns such as Puerto Aisen, Coyhaique and Cochrane – the last named after Lord Cochrane, a British naval officer. He sailed into Chile in 1819. Before long recognising his expertise he was given command of the navy 'and at once began a series of daring and brilliantly successful operations against the Spanish'.[1]

We aimed to get as far as the city of Temuco, by late afternoon, a journey of over 670 kilometres, where we would spend a couple of nights at the mission centre. A welcome lengthy stop, after a short toilet and nappy change, was for lunch. I had packed a picnic. The recommended place was Salto del Laja ('Leap of Laja'), just north of Los Angeles, about two thirds of our southward journey. The waterfalls in this idyllic picnic place fascinated the children.

I digress here to recount an incident that took place at these waterfalls a few years later. Elaine had come out to visit us over Christmas of 1975. We wanted to show her the beauty of the southern region of lakes and volcanoes. She had been duly warned that January was the worst month of the year for the

---

[1] George Pendle: *The Land and People of Chile*. A. and C. Black Ltd p. 31

flying insect, the *Colihuacho* (pronounced Collywacho). This is a flying dark, beetle-like insect, about the size of a very large bumble-bee, but with a larger wingspan and the capacity to inflict a nasty sting. It is found only in the south of the country where there is a large surface area of water. The *Colihuacho* emits a high-pitched buzzing sound, is attracted to blue and will follow its target relentlessly. I can't remember what Elaine was wearing but she was stung.

Our first encounter with the winged nuisance was on another trip we made down south between our first visit in 1972 and Elaine's holiday with us. On that occasion we had been kindly lent the holiday home of Alfred and Elsie Johnson. Alfred Johnson was an eminent ornithologist. He had been awarded the MBE for his definitive work of listing, for the very first time, all the birds of Chile. For our tenth Wedding Anniversary they gave us the two volumes of *The Birds of Chile*, which he compiled and which were beautifully illustrated by his companion on the field, Jack Goodall. (Ray took the funeral of both Alfred and Elsie in subsequent years.)

We arrived at the wooden cottage nestling among trees by a lake. Lago Ranco, only superseded by Lago Llanquihue in size, was a large lake right in the middle of the Lake and Volcano region. It lay to the south east of Valdívia, the capital of the region, a three-hour drive or so from Temuco. The holiday was memorable for three things.

On a lovely sunny morning we decided to go for a walk along the lakeside shore. Suddenly from several directions came high-pitched sounds. The dreaded *Colihuachos* had arrived – and I was wearing blue! Without doubt I was their main target, fortunate for the children and Ray, unfortunate for me. I've always remained calm and collected on encountering wasps and bees back home and even known to stroke the back of wasps on their settling at the edge of a plate, which appears to mesmerise them; this was different, an unknown enemy.

Arms flaying wildly in the air trying to beat them off and running at full speed along the lakeside edge I must have looked a comical sight. A title of music most fitting the phenomenon of being chased by these persecuting winged creatures, as they relentlessly bore down on me, would have to be Wagner's 'Ride of the Valkyries'! Amazingly I wasn't stung.

The second incident was one of three outstanding fishing events. But whereas two of the three were successful, as you will read later, this one was a disastrous failure. We knew the lakes were abundant with trout. In the cottage was a medley of fishing rods complete with 'flies'. So why not try our hand? Ray was more than keen – food shortages did govern much of our thinking, even on holiday! Togged out with our wellington boots we made our way to one of several riverbeds (which river it was escapes my memory), leaving the three children safely on the bank. Standing knee high in the shallow waters he cast his line. Very many fish of all sizes were jumping up out of the water, all around him, in the most spectacular acrobatic show imaginable. As I watched anticipating the mouth-watering menu for the evening, joyful expectation gave way to mounting disbelief. Amongst such a rich picking, Ray was unable to land one!

The last memory of our Lago Ranco holiday was the spotting of the *'chucao'*. This bird, heard much more often than seen, inhabits the forested southern regions. According to Johnson the species ranges from the Bío-Bío River at Concepción as far south as the Magellan Straits and into Argentinian Patagonia. It has also been sighted farther north in smaller numbers.

'To nature-lovers in this country the Chucao and the temperate rain-forest are synonymous.'[2]

The *Chucao* like its close relative the *Huet-Huet* is difficult to see, its greyish-brown head and back blending in with the wet environment of its normal environment. Its throat and upper breast is a rusty red colour. A telltale feature, apart from its sound as of a bubbling stream descending in scale, is its tail. According to Michael Andrews the tails of both the *Chucao* and the *Huet-Huet* are at such an erect angle that they incline towards the head. The local name for this bird is *'tapaculo'*, a bird that evidently Charles Darwin translated as 'cover your posterior'.

---

[2] Alfred Johnson: *The Birds of Chile. Vol. 2* p. 213

Johnson's research shows that the *Chucao* has featured in Araucanian folklore for very many years. In the mind of the indigenous Indians the call of the bird can be a good or a bad omen, depending on which side it comes when riding through the forest. There is a second call of the bird, high pitched 'suggestive of the neighing of a young horse' and even a third like 'the croaking of a frog'. If the cry is that of the neighing horse and comes from the left (it doesn't matter if it proceeds from the right), then 'it is a very bad omen indeed and the rider turns his horse's head and returns home'.[3]

I return to our holiday of 1972. Temuco was reached on schedule. Five weary and cramped passengers were relieved to find their legs, three little pairs being put to good use in a fraction of time! We had arrived at the Anglican Centre – the home of Ian and Marion Morrison. This was only to be an overnight stop on the way down. On our return we would meet up with other SAMS personnel and visit the mission hospital at Maquehue.

With a plateful of porridge inside us, we set off the following morning to continue our journey south. We left in cloud, but as we saw our first glimpse of Villarrica volcano the sun had broken through. From a distance the summit of the volcano was veiled in its own grey shroud, a timely reminder of the tragic events that had occurred at the end of the previous year – just six weeks earlier. The first we knew of those events was a report in the national newspaper *El Mercurio* on December 31st 1971.

It reported that the volcano had erupted. Four were dead (later this became fifteen), fifty missing and roads and bridges destroyed. Skiers had first reported a build-up of activity the previous October. Violent rumblings and explosions from the crater above where they were staying had woken them up. A steady spiral column of steam, accompanied by black acrid smoke, rose in the air. Although Volcán Villarrica was active, it had remained dormant for over a year.

In November hot, molten lava overflowed from the crater forming a channel, of up to thirty metres deep in its ice cap and 600 metres in length, down the cone. Inside, over the next few

---

[3] Ibid. p. 214

days, the pressure was mounting as first a red-hot, followed by a white-hot cone was forming. At 11.45 pm on December 29th 1971 the lid was off! The summit had split open. A crack of about four kilometres resulted. Out of the fiery inferno spewed white-hot lava.

The knock-on effect was to melt the snow and ice, which in turn provoked avalanches of mud. Down the sides of the volcano six torrents of lava and mud poured at neck-breaking speed, picking up rocks and small trees that happened to be in their way, tossing them wildly around as relentlessly the journey of destruction continued. The mad route of devastation followed existing river valleys. Three of these reached Lake Villarrica where two main towns were situated. Both lay on its southern shore, Villarrica to the west and Pucón to the east. Although the towns themselves were spared, holidaymakers camping on the shores of the lake weren't so fortunate.

The Lake and Volcano region of Chile comprises some of the most beautiful scenery in the world. On sunny days the paler turquoise blue of sky is reflected in deep lakes set in emerald forests, changing them from turquoise to sapphire blue. The white clouds and pristine ice caps of volcanoes, together with the light shimmering on the surface of the lakes, glisten as if a treasure box of jewels was open.

We visited the lakeside just six weeks later from the post-Christmas pillaging of the 'jewel chest'.

Keeping Volcán Villarrica in view, grey smoke still spiralling into the air, we left the Panamericano driving on to a roughly paved B road skirting the lake. We were unable to reach Pucón as the road had been cut and a bridge partially swept away by the flow of lava. As we looked at the shore, covered in a grey mixture of silt and lava, we were poignantly reminded of the campers whose all too brief holiday had been so suddenly cut short.

Continuing south, we encountered breathtaking scenery at every twist and turn of the road. Nine of the lakes in this region closely follow the north-south line of the Andean 'vertebral column' in the 'lumbar' region. These pockets of 'spinal fluid' are replaced further south in the 'sacrum', by narrow, open channels, fjords and sounds, to the Pacific. The 'bones' becoming very much smaller in dimension as the 'spine' continues its southerly curvature. The 'column' bending inwards from west to east ends in the 'coccyx' of Tierra del Fuego. Here the land ends.

It would be several years later before we were able to visit both the 'sacrum' and 'coccyx' of the huge landmass that constitutes the 'body' of South America. These areas have held a fascination for centuries for many brave and foolhardy travellers. Many of these have left little mark on history but an exception to the former is, of course, Charles Darwin in his famous voyage on HMS *Beagle*.

South of Valdívia, we stopped by a lake for our picnic lunch and who should turn up but the Skinner family heading back north after their holiday! The children were delighted to see their friends.

From Temuco onwards the scenery became increasingly rural. To these city dwellers it seemed we were back in time by almost a century. We spotted an ox-drawn cart with completely closed-in large wooden wheels. The two oxen were pulling in tandem, a large wooden yoke straddling their necks. Such a yoke from Chile has adorned several of the homes we have lived in, in subsequent years. 'El Yugo' (the Yoke) was the name of our Cambridge home – a reminder of our marriage, and joint ministry under the Yoke of Christ as Jesus reminds us in Matthew's Gospel.[4] But sometimes in our vulnerability like oxen we can be stubborn and not always pull together and chafing occurs.

Our destination for one week of the holiday was the Bella Vista Hotel where we were to meet up with Paul and Esme. The description of 'hotel' was rather an overstatement. It was a wooden construction, very simple and not unlike a Swiss chalet in its design. The most beautiful part of it was its position. Overlooking the largest of the lakes, Lago Llanquihue, the Bella Vista commanded an excellent site in the small town of Puerto Varas. Although pretty basic we were well content. It suited not

---

4 The Bible. Matthew chapter 11 verses 27-29

only our pockets but also our family needs. There were no lush carpets or sumptuous furniture that small children could spoil. The bare wooden floors were in keeping with the rather austere first generation German owners.

There was, and still is today, a large colony of Chilean-Germans in Chile's south. Originally the majority of these had left Nazi Germany before World War Two but conversely South America has also been a haven for those implicated in Nazi war crimes. Paraguay, Brazil and Argentina headed the league table, as these Republics had a much longer history of military governments.

The German influence was seen not only in the surnames and the architecture of the buildings but also in the high standards of cleanliness and the lack of the '*mañana*' way of life which characterised the more laid back, gregarious, characters of the southern Europeans who too had adopted the country, centuries previously.

To my utter delight, as well as the rest of the family, there was another legacy attributed to our Caucasian cousins – a legacy I made full use of on my several trips to Germany before I was married; the famous German *kuchen* and *torte*. These delicacies, to delight both eye and even more palate, were to be found in every café and *pâtisserie*. We indulged ourselves on a couple of afternoons. To watch three little faces, eyes shining, smiles wreathed in cream and chocolate, mouths bulging to overflowing with a mixture of sponge and raspberries or strawberries, was as much a treat for the parents as for the three owners of those very happy and contented faces. We also enjoyed our treat but with a more refined way of demonstrating our pleasure!

Leaving Puerto Varas, we headed due south to the port and capital town of the region, Puerto Montt. We passed through the town of Alerce so named after the tree. The *alerce* (*Fitzroya cupressoides*) is related to the California giant sequoia. The tree, now partially protected due to excessive logging, produces incredibly hard and durable timber, hence its desirability and suitability for the inclement weather of the south. Many of the buildings, more so in the past, were constructed of its timber.

The tree, an evergreen, can reach a height of forty metres and live for up to two thousand years. It is incredibly slow growing and according to Michael Andrews attains 'a diameter of ten centimetres after sixty years, and only sets its seed after several centuries'.[5]

Our route took us off a paved road and on to a bone-shaking '*ripio*' track. Such tracks, often wide enough for two cars to pass easily, are to be found all over Chile. The surfaces of these tracks, over which small stones appeared to be indiscriminately scattered, were indented with potholes of varying shapes and sizes. These holes, unfortunately, were not confined to the stone-decorated dirt track *ripio* roads, as we would discover on a future trip south when the big end of the car went!

Another tree, distinctive and indigenous to Chile's Araucanian forests, is the monkey-puzzle tree. Although there are groves of these Araucaria pines, the tree can often be seen standing tall and solitary on the slopes of the South Andean mountainsides, the high, slender trunk culminating in the branches and foliage looking like an upturned umbrella. The 'spokes' are ringed and packed tightly together and along these are the dark green spiny leaves. Its seeds, released more frequently by far than the alerce, were, at one time, important in the diet of the Indians living nearby.

How this species of pine came to England, proving so popular to many homeowners is interesting to recount. According to George Pendle the first monkey-puzzles arrived in England in 1795 in the form of five tiny seedlings. A surgeon, Archibald Menzies, sailing with Captain George Vancouver's expedition to survey the Pacific, kept some of the pine nuts served up for dessert. Once back on board from exploring the land, he sowed the kernels under a glass frame. This had been set up specifically to cultivate any unusual botanical specimens they came across. Five seedlings survived the return voyage and were presented to Kew Gardens where they grew successfully. Later, in Victorian England, they were to become very fashionable.[6]

---

[5] Michael Andrews: *The Flight of the Condor.* William Collins Sons and Co. Ltd p. 63

[6] George Pendle: *Lands and Peoples of Chile.* A. and C. Black Ltd pp. 75-76

We had now reached our destination. Puerto Montt lying on the coast to the north of the Gulf of Ancud was effectively the end of the road. Beyond here lay approximately 1400 kilometres of interlocking waterways, both fresh and seawaters, also frozen glaciers culminating in where the Atlantic and Pacific oceans meet off Cape Horn.

A suburb of the port of Puerto Montt was Angelmo, noted for its lovely cane furniture, baskets, and wooden bowls, hand knitted woollen sweaters and socks. The wares displayed outside the shops straddled what was hardly a pavement. I still have a pair of socks used with my walking boots bought here on either this first occasion or when we went back when Elaine was with us! Here was an abundance of fish restaurants. It seemed that food shortages were more acute in the central part of the country, at this time, than in the south.

The culinary highlight began when Paul and Esme suggested that we join them for the famous *'curanto'*, for which the South is noted. This famed dish was enjoyed on special communal events and festivals in this region. At the height of the summer tourist season, December to early March, it would provide a steady income.

A *curanto*, like its New Zealand counterpart (*'hangi'*) is cooked in the ground. However, it wasn't at Angelmo itself that we enjoyed our culinary treat, the memory of which remains vivid to this day. We had booked our *curanto* in a rather special location, the tiny island of Tenglo. At Angelmo the seven of us piled into a small rowing boat to cross the narrow stretch of water. The simple rustic restaurant chosen was aptly named 'Miramar' (Sea View) as we were surrounded by water on all sides.

With great excitement and anticipation we joined other tourists to watch the preparation of 'the hole-in-the-ground' meal as we described it to the children. They, like us, were absolutely spellbound. We stood around the perimeter of the outdoor 'kitchen' covered over by a rough wooden beam roof (in case of a sudden downpour) the four sides open between the downward supports. The diameter of the hole was approximately a metre and a half. In the centre were the white-hot ashes from the wood that had been burned earlier under which was an assortment of large round stones, by now piping hot.

To the side, on a scrubbed top table, was a medley of fish of various kinds including the shell varieties in which Chile's long coastline excels. There was also meat and some round whitish things we couldn't identify, as well as jacket potatoes. Towards one side, standing on its own in the open air, was the clay oven, a characteristic feature of life in the *campo*. From it wafted the wonderful smell of *pan amasado*, loaves of bread baked in this type of oven.

The 'chef' helped by his assistant began to arrange the food. Light cloths were placed over layers of a rich variety of fish, both steaks and shell. Then came the meat, lamb, pork, chicken and sausages and the potatoes, each layer in a pre-determined order. More cloths followed. Last to go on were the whitish objects, which we discovered on eating were a form of dumpling. Finally, several large sacks were carefully placed over the growing mountain. The side table was now empty save for the many bottles of wine and carafes of *chicha* (strong fermented country-brewed drink produced on festivities). We were told to return in an hour, as the food would take that time to slowly steam through.

After filling in the time we arrived back and found scrubbed top tables simply laid in keeping with the rustic atmosphere. We sat down, the children catching the excitement of anticipation, fuelled by the delicious smell emanating from the steaming miniature 'volcano'. Ray's entry in the diary catches something of the youngest two-year-old's full involvement.

'Julian in his element, cracking open the mussels and squeezing lemon-juice on, adult- like [sic]*.'*

Many of the shellfish were still an unproven commodity to our palates but we were prepared to have a go. The *picorocos* proved the most challenging. They looked absolutely disgusting! Protruding from the opening in the large barnacle-like shell was a hard beak. When alive this would open and close and although fascinating to watch on the fish stalls in the market giving an assurance of its freshness, well, it was quite another thing to eat!

I was the only one prepared to give it a try. Even Naomi with her mother and grandmother's willingness to try new cuisine balked at the suggestion.

My mother had on one occasion put her own culinary curiosity to the test. Sometimes she would shop at an up-market delicatessen in Leicester, Simpkin and James. On this occasion she came home with two tins of supposedly great specialities. One was of chocolate-covered ants – presumably not of the English garden variety! She enjoyed those! The other contained fried grasshoppers. When she opened the tin and saw the little creatures looking exactly as you would expect, before the edible processing had begun, she was unable to bring herself to sample even one. The tin ended in the dustbin, disguised. It was some time later before she confessed to my father her wasted extravagance!

'How do I eat the *picoroco*?' I asked turning to Paul and Esme.

'Just grab it by the beak and pull.'

I did just that. Dangling from its beak was a pale, succulent, but firm fleshy body. With mouth wide open I positioned the hanging mass over my mouth and aimed it in, in one go, to a round of applause. It tasted delicious, as did the rest of the meal. To this day we recall our *curanto* as probably the best meal we've ever had.

Puerto Montt was where our original Air Force neighbours in Los Almendros, the Valenzuelas, were now living. After arriving at their house and greetings over we drove in convoy to Frutillar, a delightful resort on Lake Llanquihue. After a swim in the lake, we sat down to a wonderful barbecue of beef steaks, followed by watermelon and *Apfel kuchen* – the famous German apple flan.

The rest of our holiday was spent picnicking by the lakeside, throwing in pebbles with the children and watching the ripples in ever widening circles (an illustration of what we trusted our ministry under God might become), and enjoying many lovely walks. On these occasions other SAMS workers, including Australian co-workers in Argentina, the Blaxlands, joined us. There were so many lovely panoramic scenes to explore; waterfalls and other lakes and volcanoes to visit.

Ray, taking Naomi and Andrew (I stayed behind with Julian for a quieter day) joined by Paul, Esme and Sheila also on holiday from Santiago, went for a drive around Lake Llanquihue. To circumnavigate it took four hours. They picnicked at Enseñada by the lakeside. On another occasion we returned and visited the beautiful waterfalls of Petrohue between Enseñada and Lago Todos Los Santos (All Saints Lake). The Emerald Lake as it was also known for its colour, lay on a popular tourist route to San Carlos de Bariloche in Argentina. This was a trip we longed to do but could never afford.

Our desire was fulfilled in the Millennium when, to celebrate Ray's 70th birthday, we returned for the second time to Chile. This was the occasion we saw icebergs for the first time close at hand. Our four-day cruise had taken us into the waterways south of Coyhaique (now on the map for many English as Prince William chose this area of Chilean Patagonia for his gap year).

We had heard of the San Rafael glacier, a well-known tourist attraction. The glacier then (sadly receding year by year now), was an impressive four kilometres wide, and around sixty metres high. It stretched back inland about twenty-five kilometres towards the mountains. The glacier ended in the lagoon named after it. Laguna San Rafael was tidal yet almost land-locked and around ten kilometres at its widest.

In the late seventies the BBC television crew filming the documentary 'The Flight of the Condor' visited Chile, including a visit to our home in Santiago for dinner. Michael Andrews recounts in his book, based on that film, the danger they encountered from a huge piece of the San Rafael glacier breaking away as their small boat approached it for filming.

They were 'awed' on hearing parts of the ice breaking away from the glacier 'almost like shots'. When a considerable sized piece of ice breaks off it can be heard as far away as ten miles.[7]

Andrews and the cameraman in their small rubber boat were

---

[7] Michael Andrews: *The Flight of the Condor*. William Collins Sons and Co. Ltd p. 46

about 100 metres from the glacier when some of the ice began to break away. As the cameraman got into position suddenly '… a cube the size of a four-storey house thundered into the water, the glass-blue sliding into a white ring of spray from which a shower of ice was fired out sideways like an explosion.' Andrews describes the phenomenon as he slowly continued to drive the boat nearer '… until I saw a five-foot high breaking wave heading for us. I held course for what I thought was another second to let Hugh finish the shot …'. They then sped away, glad that their boat had a powerful engine. 'Both of us were very excited to have got such a good shot, and could not stop laughing with relief at our narrow escape.'[8]

It was in the Laguna San Rafael that the small group of passengers we were travelling with, in November 2000, transferred into an iron boat to get close to the icebergs; so close we could reach out and touch them! The various shades of blue differed from one 'berg to another; from a pale ice blue to a deeper blue and from aqua to a deeper turquoise – a spectacular and beautiful sight.

As we drew alongside one, a crewmember reached over the side of the boat and with a small pickaxe chipped off a quantity of ice. Each of us were then served with a brandy 'on the rocks'! The age of the 'berg we were told was around 30,000 years!

With cameras well in position we took photographs of the glacier but at a much safer distance than the BBC television crew. After an hour or so our captain turned the iron boat back towards the 'cruise boat'. We were steadily chugging along when suddenly, one of our Colombian passengers shouted, '*Mira! Mira!*' As we turned to look in the direction from which we came we saw and heard a huge piece of the glacier break and fall into the water. I managed to capture this amazing sight on to our camcorder. Unfortunately for Andrews and crew, of all the filming they took in the Laguna, the only shot that was damaged was the one of the falling ice from the glacier.

The ice collected by our crew was used to restock the freezer on board the boat. An idea started to form in my mind. 'Please

---

[8] Ibid. p. 47

can I have some of the ice?' Once the pieces had melted I filled our two plastic water bottles. These two items accompanied Ray and me all the way back to the UK two weeks later. On arriving home I boiled the contents of the two bottles and, once cool, poured the water into two ice cube trays. Each guest at Ray's celebration party was served a glass of champagne with a cube of ice! What are seventy years when compared with 30,000?

Whenever the sky was clear, the one thing that was a constant companion around the vicinity of Lago Llanquihue was the ever present Volcano Osorno. It dominated the skyline. Our aim, during this our first holiday in the south, was to ascend Osorno. We started the ascent in the minibus, but before long the steep gradient and loose gravel caused the wheels to spin round. Abandoning the vehicle the five of us took to our feet. The memory of that occasion was outstanding. With no pollution, the sky was the deepest blue imaginable. The thick blanket of snow draped over the top was pristine white, the trees on the lower slopes spring green and the intense silence broken only by the hum of insects. The children, too, caught the magic of this moment and were exceptionally quiet for a brief interval.

It was time to leave the Lake region and begin our return journey to Santiago but not before visiting colleagues working in the South.

Kath Clark lived in a lovely little wooden cottage in Carahue. As she would be away on leave she had invited us to make use of her home in her absence. Carahue, in the countryside, was near to Quepe, a small town to the south of Temuco. Maquehue Hospital situated just outside Quepe was where the medical and nursing staff belonging to the Mission worked. Kath's cottage was at the back of the home belonging to Dr Bill Maxwell, the medical director, and his wife Agnes. With true Maxwell hospitality we found Kath's home well lit, warm and with hot water bottles in the beds. A welcome meal was waiting for us in the larger home of Bill and Agnes. Our lives would cross many years later when they replaced us in the English-speaking church on the Spanish Island of Ibiza.

The next day we piled into Bill's Land Rover to have a

conducted tour of the hospital, meeting staff and Mapuche patients, many suffering from tuberculosis.

Rural life wasn't without its challenges. For me this came in the form of a most unwelcome occurrence. Sleep had been interrupted with sounds of scampering and scratching up and down the wood panelled walls just the other side of our pillows. It seemed the rats were having a mid-night gig. I was to meet the star performer in a head on encounter the next day. Turning a right-angled corner in the small, dark passageway, my eyes were drawn by a slight movement. There was the biggest rat imaginable on a small horizontal ledge straddling the corner just above eye level. I stopped dead in my tracks. The creature, now as still as a statue, glared at me with two bright, beady, baleful eyes. Neither of us moved for a few seconds as we weighed one another up. I recalled past advice, 'Never corner a rat because it might jump in your face in self defence.' What was I to do? After a few more seconds I slowly turned the corner, closely hugging the wall nearest to me. Then, running as fast as I could, I reached the safety of the sitting room.

Another day we set off with Bill and Agnes in their jeep to Lake Budi to the west of the town of Nueva Imperial and very near to Chile's coast. Their medical launch was moored here. Bill had served in the navy and his love of sailing was put to good use in Chile. He and his team would visit outlying villages and hamlets attending the sick, taking medical supplies and bringing emergency patients to Maquehue Hospital. On this particular occasion it was a day off, for this hard working doctor with a pastoral heart, as he took us on a sailing trip. It was on this trip that we had our first glimpse of the national flower of Chile.

The *Copihue* is to be found only in the south of the country. They come in a variety of colours, mainly bright red, but also white and pink. Attached to the stem of large bushes, the bell-like flowers hang down, often in pairs, forming clusters. About two and a half inches in length they have a waxy texture with bright shiny leaves not unlike a laurel leaf.

In a letter home, Ray wrote to our parents of the Sunday afternoon when he drove the Maxwell family, Naomi and Andrew to one of the outlying Mapuche churches. Bill was on duty and I stayed at base as we felt it was too long an afternoon for Julian to be cooped up. The congregation consisted of a handful of locals, two less than the six visitors and, true to custom, started more than half an hour late. During a lengthy prayer by one of the Indians, Andrew, in an attempt to speed up the process, interrupted by bursting into a praise song in Spanish!

On the way back they called in on another church, again in an outlying location. Unlike the former which had met in a brick building, the local Mapuches here *'met in a wooden hut, about the size of a large English garden shed, next door to a "ruca".'* Ray goes on to describe this traditional home of the Araucanian Indians.

'A ruca, 'is a one room family dwelling, usually round, with a central fire on the floor. The roof is covered with long thatch, which hangs over the eaves, like a shaggy dog.' The pastor and his family lived here *'a very simple life, with the chickens running in and out. We went in to meet the family – quite an experience – whilst the children then went off to play on a haystack.'*

No holiday is complete without shopping for presents. Monday found us in the Indian market of Temuco where so many arts and crafts were on display – souvenirs at such a reasonable price. The presents were to keep for our home leave in England, two years later, and were mementoes of a fascinating holiday for us. We still have two wooden dishes, for fruit or bread rolls, with brightly coloured dyed raffia inset in the rims. Also a large basket wall plate with a wooden centre on which is an oil painting of an ox-cart with a snow-capped volcano in the background. What fascinated Naomi were the artefacts made of horsehair, dyed different colours – bookmarks, brooches, small dressing table dishes among other items.

The alarm broke into our deep sleep at 3.30 am three days later. We left Carahue bound again for Temuco. Two extra passengers would accompany us for the return journey to Santiago – one a missionary, the other a national pastor who had a sick relative he wanted to visit near the capital. True to most journeys in the Chile of the seventies, this was not without its *problemas.* An enforced stop at The Angels (Los Angeles) – not a pub but a garage in the town of that name – meant a delay of an hour and a half. A vibration had occurred in the steering; maybe, just maybe, angelic beings, were, in their attempt to act as co-pilots (as with our Quilpué bus driver), a little too enthusiastic to wrest the steering wheel from our hands! We arrived home to our welcome beds at around 9.00 pm.

Chapter 19
The Political Temperature Heats Up

Alongside the ever-increasing queues, tension was mounting throughout the country boiling over into demonstrations and counter demonstrations. These became more and more violent. On June 29th 1972 a bomb exploded outside the Medical College in the city centre destroying part of the façade. Also down town police and people were facing one another in ugly confrontation. Jets of water and tear gas were in constant use to break up crowds getting out of hand. Ray got caught up in one in the centre returning home eventually with his eyes and throat still smarting from the effect – not a pleasant experience.

The spring strikes of 1972 culminating in the influential Lorry Owners' strike almost toppled Allende's government. A few weeks prior to this, economic conditions were so dire that the President felt compelled to dismiss Pedro Vuskovic, his Minister of Economy. However, the political extremists were an increasing force, which Allende seemed either unwilling or unable to curb. The Cubans were shipping in arms and agents. Paramilitary forces and rural agitators were springing up from among the shanty towns and in the *campo.* Among young academia the MUI (Movement of the University Leftists) and the MIR (Movement of Revolutionary Leftists) had been gaining ground. They were highly political agitators jumping on the bandwagon of discontent among industrial workers, shanty town squatters and farm workers. For them, change could be achieved not through the ballot box but only by revolution and violence.

The Communist party had little sympathy for the ultra-left movements. The latter, for their part, had greater shared interests with the more extreme socialist party in which their roots were to be found. The communist Volodia Teitelboim described the *Miristas* in a September interview as 'these individuals [who] flow out of the people's party like excrement ...'. In the same interview he also criticised the MIR-occupied farms for stripping 'the governments expropriation plan of legality.'[1]

These two extreme movements were not the only ones giving Allende's government headaches. There was VOP (the Vanguard Organisation of the People) that had split off from MIR in 1969. Left of centre political parties, which had started out moderate, drifted increasingly to the left. Such was MAPU (Movement for Unified Popular Action). In 1971 it declared itself Marxist. Both the Christian Left and the MAPU had ties with the *Miristas.* Within these political parties factions began to emerge with increasing infighting. Perhaps it was just as well that the extreme element had formed such splinter groups as united they would have brought the country to a blood bath.

According to Davis 'in July 1972 Chilean military intelligence uncovered what it said was an extreme leftist plot to attack the president's residence on Tomás Moro Avenue' (this you will remember was not far from where we were living) 'and identified the plotters as the July 16th Command of the National Liberation Army.'[2]

On the other hand extreme right-wing groups were flexing their muscles. The most influential of these was the nationalistic party '*Patria and Libertad*' (Country and Freedom).

With a country deeply divided against itself what was one to believe? Such were the rumours of blame and counter blame in the attending confusion: blame, which would arise time and time again over the following months and indeed years. Wild accusations were banded about from people out to put their own political sympathies in the best possible light, each out to show how their side had been wrongly victimised. To try and remain

---

[1] Nathaniel Davis. *The Last Two Years of Salvador Allende.* I. B. Tauris & Co. Ltd. p. 85
[2] Ibid. pp. 87 and 88

impartial when feelings were running high was as difficult in Allende's Chile as later in Pinochet's Chile.

We were reminded of the words of Jesus in the gospels, 'If a house is divided against itself, that house cannot stand.'[3] When a country is divided against itself, rather than uniting to fight a common enemy, the roots of bitterness run very deep indeed.

Allende was finding himself leader of a country that was becoming increasingly polarised with both right and left elements resorting to ever more extreme measures to champion their own cause. He himself was facing mounting opposition. The moderate Christian Democrats who had been previously in power were becoming increasingly concerned about the worsening economic situation and accompanying violence. Foreign investment was being withdrawn, as companies were naturally reluctant to invest in such an uncertain climate. Farmers in the south were driving their livestock over into neighbouring Argentina. Fields were neglected and left fallow. Outside influences were also at work guarding their own interests. It has been documented that the CIA and FBI had bugged the Chilean Embassy in Washington, Spring of 1971 and into 1972. These were later removed.[4]

Orlando Letelier was the Chilean ambassador at the time, who subsequently was assassinated under President Pinochet's military junta.

In the current climate of polarisation, interested parties were becoming highly organised. There were the establishments of the *focos,* the *campamentos,* and the *cordones.* According to Davis the first of these were outposts of political centres in the isolated countryside – not dissimilar to the Viet Cong's control of the Vietnam countryside. The most famous being the densely wooded stretch of land near to the Argentinian border about 800 kilometres south of Santiago 'where *"Comandante Pepe"* held sway and where *"carabineros"* did not dare venture.'[5]

The *campamentos* were shanty-towns, some of which sprang up almost overnight. The extreme left were responsible for

---

[3] The Bible. Mark chapter 3 verse 25

[4] Nathaniel Davis: *The Last Two Years of Salvador Allende.* I. B. Tauris & Co. Ltd pp. 94 and 95

[5] Ibid. p. 88, *New York Times,* 21 September 1973, p. 12

these militarised hamlets of poorer families which were placed strategically among the affluent. One was named Campamento Fidel-Ernesto.

The third to be set up, the *cordones*, were also highly organised. These worker-controlled industrial belts operated in various areas of the capital, targeting the still privately owned firms. The one aim of the disciplined worker leaders and their vigilantes was to mobilise sympathetic workers into 'People's Power'.

But in all the uncertainties, increasing violence, rampant inflation and the never-ending queuing, life had to go on. The cost of living increased by 24.9 percent in the first few months of the year alone. Adaptation became the order of the day. In this we kept company, although in a somewhat uneasy companionship, with the President himself. He too was forced to adapt in ways he may not have initially wished for.

The scapegoat dismissal of Vuskovic in June 1972 was an apparent attempt to appease both Opposition demands for a modification of the nationalisation programme and also ironically the Communists. This party had become increasingly concerned about the speed of the economic programme Vuskovic was pursuing. It preferred a consolidation of changes already in place and not to provoke unnecessarily 'the enemy'.

However, Allende was not letting go of his plans for drastic political change. In an effort to placate those from his own party, pushing for faster and more sweeping reforms, he appointed Carlos Matus, a Socialist, as Vuskovic's replacement. Matus was in full sympathy, not only with his predecessor but also with those pressing for a less cautious approach, notably Carlos Altamirano. For his part, Altamirano would increasingly become a thorn in Allende's side.

The attendant reshuffle of the all-civilian Cabinet took place on June 17th 1972. Before long it became abundantly clear that the new economic leadership was failing to find an effective solution to the country's problems. Increased prices in August followed by wage adjustments added to the inflationary spiral.

Unrest in the South added fuel to the fire. A shopkeeper in Punta Arenas died of a heart attack as a result of the authorities forcing him to open up his store. He had closed it in protest at government policy. The 125,000 members of the national Confederation of Shopkeepers throughout the country called for a one-day strike on August 21st as their response to this event. This strike escalated to the capital. The government sent in inspectors to force shops to open. Riot police armed with tear gas canisters were out on the streets as were opposing youths. These set fire to barricades along Providencia Avenue in the prosperous sector and the ensuing violence between baton wielding, shield covering *carabineros* and brick-throwing youths resulted in a state of emergency being declared.

Meanwhile the University of Concepción, over 500 kilometres to the south, became a focal point of violent confrontation between right and left students. A policeman was killed, which led to a state of emergency being declared in this province too.

All this escalating unrest led to the October Lorry Owners' strike joined within days by the professionals; doctors, medical workers, bankers and even lawyers. The strikers had the support of the powerful opposition Christian Democrat party who had been more favourably inclined to offer support, albeit with some hesitation, to Allende when he first assumed office. Rumours of impending civil war now began to surface – rumours flatly denied by Allende.

He addressed the nation. All privately owned radio stations were required to carry the President's message. In his broadcast he admitted the country faced grave difficulties and pinned the blame politically on his Opposition and economically on the blocking of credit lines by the United States. Undoubtedly Allende's government was facing not only opposition within the country but a network of opposition from abroad.

Frank Taylor, correspondent in Buenos Aires for the *Daily Telegraph*, reported part of President Allende's October broadcast:

'We are living in an abnormal period which could culminate in a civil confrontation. I reject this, roundly and categorically. I believe that my Government is the best guarantee of peace. Here there are elections and freedom. Ninety per cent of Chileans do not want armed confrontation.'

In an attempt to allay fears from moderates on both sides of the widening political divide he went on to say that he would not allow the setting up of 'People's Militia': 'There will be no armed forces here other than those stipulated by the Constitution – the Army, the Navy and the Air Force. I shall eliminate any others if they appear.'

On October 17th a '*toque de queda*' – a curfew – was imposed from midnight until 6.00 am. This was the first of many to come. The one good thing was that late night party revellers would no longer disturb our sleep. Armed forces, both military and the police, were out patrolling the streets and during the day guarding shops that defied the Opposition and remained open. In some streets of the capital they outnumbered the pedestrians. The President himself flanked on either side in front and behind by bodyguards, made a walking tour of the business area in open defiance of opposing forces.

As the spring weather hotted up, matching the political climate, it became increasingly clear that the President was finding himself in a tight corner. Before long there was talk of Allende bringing the military into the Cabinet. It seemed this decision had more to do with convincing the Opposition that he was reining in his extreme party members more than he wanted to.

Tighter control of the media led to the closure of three of the Opposition radio stations for almost a week. The closure was for infringing emergency regulations by broadcasting anti-Government programmes. Subsequently the government assumed control of all forty of the nation's radio stations with official statements, government-prepared news and music. One of the radio stations '*Minería*' decided to break the enforced '*cadena*' (chain) of government controlled transmission. Political rivals stepped in to try and prevent this station transmitting its own propaganda. As the station went off the air it was followed by a total blackout in that section of the city. We were with a number of friends at church in Providencia, enjoying a bring-and-share meal.

Riot police and jeep-loads of troops continued to patrol the streets of Santiago. On October 24th thousands of Chileans stayed at home for a 'Day of Silence'. The instigating five Opposition parties described this act of protest at government policies, as 'civil resistance'. Two days previously an Army major had been shot dead during the curfew. My diary records that on that *'Día del Silencio'*, a Tuesday, the three children were all bathed before breakfast and before Naomi went to school. There was no playschool operating for Andrew. Since the previous Saturday we had had no water between 9.00 am and midnight on each of those days. Then came a ray of hope and encouragement in all the political mêlée. '[I] *passed by a neighbour's house on* [the] *corner and she gave me 2 roses and a large piece of zapallo* [pumpkin].' In ways like this the goodwill of so many people rose to the surface.

The next crisis facing the President was the entire resignation of his Cabinet on November 1st. This was to give Allende a free hand to form a new Cabinet in response to serious signs of a split in the Marxist-Socialist Coalition Government. Rumours were now circulating of bringing in military representation. These rumours were well founded and on November 2nd senior military officers were brought into the Cabinet. This move was reluctantly accepted by the Communist party but rejected by the Socialists.

Central to this strategic decision was the appointment of General Carlos Prats, Commander in Chief of the Army, as the new Interior Minister. In this appointment he became constitutionally the Vice President. Two other high ranking military men were brought into the Cabinet, representing the Air Force and the Chilean Navy. I believe it to be important for the reader to understand that the military were involved politically before the later events that resulted in a military dictatorship.

General Prats, of medium height and stocky in build, vowed to end the strikes that were crippling the country, and opened up talks with the syndicate strike leaders that had reached stalemate. He was, according to Davis, 'crisp, self-confident, and straightforward' and his political manoeuvre was 'to offer substantive conciliation to the strike leaders in private talks, while publicly threatening drastic action if the strikes did not end'.[6] Prats went on to promise that transport would not be nationalised, the leaders not prosecuted and that there would be legislation to protect small businesses. Allende supported his Minister of the Interior. Carlos Altamirano did not. On November 5th after more than three weeks of economic paralysis some normality was restored – at least in the short term.

During this respite Allende felt able to leave Chile for a tour abroad. Included in this tour was a visit not only to Moscow, Cuba and Algiers, countries sympathetic to the Marxist experiment in Chile, but also to the United States. In New York, according to Davis, he outspokenly condemned American imperialism, describing it as 'insidious, bland-faced, financial aggression'.[7]

Such public rhetoric disguised the fact that Chile remained dependent on economic help from capitalist as well as socialist world governments. The Communist countries' assistance, especially the Soviet Union's was not as bountiful as Allende desired. They were afraid of becoming dependent like Cuba. In addition they were not impressed with a Marxism that included 'red wine and meat pies', nor one that did not demand of its government and citizens a costly allegiance, such as their own history had experienced. [8]

The inclusion of the military into the Cabinet did not solve Allende's problems. Not only were the extremists still hard to rein in, but initiatives emanating from such groups were introduced and became policies before the government had time to properly evaluate them. Two of these that rocked the boat were the 'rationing' of food on the one hand and proposed educational reform on the other. Both initiatives had as their goal a tighter control by Allende's leftist government.

The distribution of food would be channelled through the existing Councils of Supply and Prices (JAPS). This proposal sent alarm bells to the Opposition as it was seen as being based on a Cuban model.

---

[6] Ibid. pp. 114, 115
[7] Ibid. pp. 114, 115
[8] Ibid. pp. 114, 115

Jorge Tapia, a member of the anticlerical Radical party and Minister of Education, took control of the second initiative. The plan announced on January 30th 1973 was to create a unified national school (ENU). This was to bring Marxist teaching into the schools through the back door. A clear objective was laid down. According to the government the plan would bring in 'values of socialist humanism' and achieve a 'harmonious development of young people's personalities'.[9]

The reaction from the Roman Catholic Church as well as the Christian Democrats was both swift and strong. The voice of the Church hierarchy thundered out in opposition, as did an influential segment of the military. Parents concerned about the indoctrination of their children spent anxious weeks weighing up any options they may have. Richard Collingwood-Selby called an urgent meeting of parents and teachers at Redland School. Ray and I went along. The only schools in the capital that would be exempt were the two English-speaking international schools, one the 'Nido de Aguilas' (Eagle's Nest) to which many children of embassy personnel went and another recently opened Protestant Christian school.

Our friends and colleagues, Helen and Arthur, had decided to withdraw their two daughters from their school and to put them in the second of the international schools. What were we to do? After praying and talking together we decided that we would keep them at Redland no matter what. We liked Richard and his wife, Julia, and wanted to continue to support them in the difficult times we were all facing. Our reasoning was also based on the fact that we lived in the real world and we could not shelter our children from all adversity and problems. We believed that with God's protection and Christian teaching in the home we would be equipped to deal with the possible fallout from any opposing influence. Risky? Yes, but that was what faith was about.

According to Davis in a stormy session between Tapia and a contingent of high-ranking military leaders, Tapia admitted that his educational plan had been based on a pattern from East

---

[9] Ibid p. 135

Germany. Tapia was forced to back down in a public letter to Chile's most senior Roman Catholic cleric, Cardinal Raúl Silva Henríquez on April 12th. In it he stated that the ENU would be postponed. In fact it never did happen.

After the summer recess of January and February in which there is a mass exodus from the capital for the long holidays – one just prays (for those remaining at home) that illness in these months doesn't require a doctor – March brings a return to school and work. March 4th of this year 1973 brought congressional elections. Amazingly they passed off relatively peacefully.

The Opposition parties had a clear majority of 56 percent but this, to their disappointment, did not change the political balance. It failed to reach the two-thirds majority, which would have resulted in the impeachment and removal of Allende.

The threatened Government resorted to questionable tactics to improve their ratings.

Official vehicles were used to transport likely sympathetic voters to rallies. Food supplies especially in the poorer areas magically increased. There were possibly two or three contributing factors in better than predicted results for the UP. The first was a demographic factor. Since the last nationwide elections the age for voting had been lowered from twenty-one to eighteen. These younger voters were presumably more left in persuasion, as were the illiterates who now also had the vote.

The second factor, as always, had to do with the question of fraud. Davis in his book clearly documents the reasoning behind this allegation, but concludes that although there was fraud, it was less than Jaime del Valle, dean of the law school at the Catholic University of Santiago, had suggested 'and not enough to make a significant difference'.[10] The third factor was the enfranchisement of illiterates. In his opinion it was the demographic reasons that were the most influential.

Following on from the election the class struggle in Chile intensified. Within Latin American politics, Chile, together with Uruguay, led the way with a larger politically aware middle-class. The hard core of workers and peasants did not constitute

---

[10] Ibid: p. 144

the majority and from among these, women particularly had a middle-class mentality. Although the government could count on support in the *campo*, in the cities the artisans and shopkeepers had become increasingly disillusioned. Their growing antipathy to nationalisation had been underlined by the October 1972 strike. The opposing political ideologies had become more entrenched.

The election had solved nothing. The noose was tightening around the President's neck – a noose that would be pulled even tighter before many more months expired. He was becoming increasingly estranged from the militant Socialists in the government and their call to violent means to bring about revolutionary change, but he stopped short of forcing a showdown with the 'lunatic fringe'.

Changes were made in the leadership but he didn't sideline the 'thorn in his side', Carlos Altamirano. What he did do was to induce 'Clodomiro Almeyda to leave the Foreign Ministry in order to devote his efforts to the Socialist party, the consolidation of Unidad Popular, and domestic policy. It was a sensible step, but it came too late. Had Allende made the move a year or two earlier, the history of Unidad Popular might have been different.'[11]

As it was, on March 27th, the military leadership left the Cabinet, much to the delight of Altamirano who hailed it as a victory.

Eduardo Frei of the Christian Democrat party and President before Allende, was elected in 1973 as President of the Senate. Many in the Opposition saw his re-emergence as a light at the end of a tunnel. For eight years after the military rule that followed from the final tightening of the noose around Allende's neck, Frei lived quietly in the suburbs of Santiago. In Davis' opinion had not Frei died at the age of 71 on January 22nd 1982 'changing circumstances might have given him a role in helping to restore democracy in Chile'.[12] As it was, when democracy

---

[11] Ibid: p. 145 Alexander p. 272
[12] Ibid: p. 148

finally returned, Frei's son, also called Eduardo, was elected President in 1993.

Much of what I've written in this chapter of the inside of political manoeuvring was unknown at the time to those of us ordinary citizens living in those critical days. We had to get on with our lives and work as best we could, and still try and build in some quality time. Newspaper articles from both inside and outside the country, as always, would reflect not an entirely objective viewpoint. My main source in Nathaniel Davis has been acclaimed from both sides of the political spectrum as both authentic and unbiased.

It was in all the mounting turmoil of these critical spring months of 1972 that we had our own particular stresses and frustrations. We had discovered the small nodule on Naomi's neck written about previously.

The morning of September 15th, the day we had a clinic appointment for Naomi, had started with pouring rain. When it rains it rains! A few days earlier Ray and Andrew had both developed temperatures and chest coughs. So early, leaving the two invalids at home, I set off for the local supermarket with Naomi and Julian in tow. At 8.30 am on that September morning we were in a queue for one hour – remember Julian was only two years old – and managed to get a small packet of meat and a chicken.

On returning to the minibus I managed to lock the keys inside, but fortunately not the children. Abandoning the bus in the car park we set off on the ten-minute walk home to collect the spare set of keys. Retracing our steps to Almac, we picked up the vehicle arriving in time to keep Naomi's appointment.

In the afternoon I returned to the supermarket, this time alone, queuing for another two hours. My purchases consisted of a large tin of powdered milk and a smaller tin of Nestlés condensed milk. My childhood craving for this tempting treat was now shared by the next generation! We had learnt that the best way to enjoy this was to place it in its tin in a large saucepan of boiling water and heat for up to two hours. The end result was a soft light brown toffee-like mixture. This was absolutely delicious, spread on bread or sandwiched between two layers of sponge cake.

With so many frustrations and pressures, we determined with God's help, and the support of friends and colleagues as well as letters from home, not to give in to despondency and self-pity. At times we were sorely tempted to do so. On rare occasions we did succumb. The most notable time had been the queue surpassing all others in duration on the eve of my birthday. This led to a revolution but this time not of a political nature. We had both hit rock bottom, but more about this revolution in another chapter.

Having already visited the south of the country, we decided a much-needed holiday should be taken in the north. Camping was our only option. With spring temperatures in the central region still variable and rain all too frequent, we decided what we needed was guaranteed sun and dry weather. So what better thing to do than to exchange, at least for a short time, the mounting political heat of the capital for the increased heat at the edge of the Atacama Desert.

Chapter 20

Some Welcome Respite: Going North

The north of Chile is as distinct from the south as chalk is from cheese. Our first visit was to be a camping holiday as soon as the children broke up from school for the very long summer holidays. Two tents had been bought second hand and had seen better days.

The days before leaving were packed full of pressure and unexpected hassles. The diary records me using my Singer sewing machine in an effort to machine netting into the tents, a far from easy task handling such bulk, and generally fixing patches here and there. In addition to getting ready for holiday, there was the standing in queues (one of 2¼ hours duration for cooking oil) for supplies to take away, a sick child and an overnight guest. A letter Ray wrote home six weeks earlier told how food prices were '*again accelerating*' and the '*cost of living has increased 99.8%* [sic] *between January and October.*'

For some reason, that neither my diary nor my memory recalls, Ray had to leave for Talca at 7.00 am on the Monday calling for John Jacklin, a colleague. Talca lay 255 kilometres on the Pan American highway south of Santiago. Whatever the reason for the trip they didn't arrive back until 2.00 am the next day, having had to abandon John's car 80 kilometres outside Santiago. The 'electrics' had seized up. Now with daylight Ray was back again on the road to take John to retrieve the car and bring it back to the capital to get the faulty wiring sorted.

A penicillin injection was prescribed for Naomi's sore throat, high temperature and swollen glands. It was the very first time

I actually did the administering on one of our children – an unenviable experience for us both.

Two days later than we had anticipated, we set out, with the minibus packed full of children, toys, luggage, tents and the essential food provisions. We didn't know what food shortages we would find in the north. With a very long journey, made longer because of necessary detours, it would be wiser to travel at night when it was cooler and the children would hopefully sleep for most of the journey. First we had to call at the Robinsons to borrow extra sleeping bags. Continuing through the capital, still buzzing with life at midnight, we headed to Viña (a detour northwest) to drop our house-guest, Bishop David, back home. The detour that should have taken no more than a couple of hours or so in fact took over three hours. We were slowly getting accustomed to the unexpected twists and turns of life in Chile. We arrived at the Pytches home just after 3.00 am!

The reason for the extra delay was *los perigrinos*. In the planning of the holiday dates we had failed to realise that, in common with all of Latin America and Iberia, December 8th was celebrated as '*El día de la Virgen*'. Pilgrims had come from all the surrounding countryside on foot (some bare-foot), others not so energetic by bicycle, on horseback, and one even on a child's scooter! Mothers with babes in arms, fathers carrying toddlers, boys and girls in tow, teenagers, young and old alike all headed in one direction to honour the Virgin Mary. There were hundreds and hundreds of them. Just over half way between the capital and the coast, the shrine of '*Lo Vásquez*', was their ultimate destination. The strain on Ray's driving, in an effort to avoid the many pedestrians in the dark, was somewhat alleviated, when police diverted us on to a *ripio* road. However, even here the pilgrims flocked. What impressed us was the high percentage of teenagers among the crowd.

Leaving David at his home, followed by a quick toilet break, we continued north joining the Panamericano at La Calera. The one disappointing fact of travelling through the night for our first trip up north was that we couldn't admire the daylight scenery. That would come later on other occasions.

A further seven hours travelling time later, we pulled into our campsite at Guanaqueros, the boys having slept through most of the night. Naomi had, for a number of years, a fixation on the moon and was subsequently entertained with the delights of the night sky. The more miles we covered, the more populated countryside receded and with it the lighter sky reflected back the lights of small towns and hamlets. The nearer we approached the edge of the desert, so the velvety mantle of the night sky increased in its darkness – the full richness to be appreciated on other trips. Peeping between the 'folds of the mantle' were sequin-like stars and planets. For now we had to be satisfied with the decorated 'hemline.' The jewelled display of 'diamonds' on the rich, dark 'bodice' would be a treat to be indulged in on future visits, when we would explore further into the desert.

'Right, children here we are. Naomi! Andrew! Please can you help Daddy and Mummy unpack a few things from the Volkswagen?' Willing little hands responded at once. What excitement! It was to be their first thrill of sleeping in a tent.

'Please keep an eye on Julian. We must all make sure he doesn't wander off.' Our third was known for being like 'quicksilver'. There was no fear of this now. He was only too willing to help!

One day, back in Los Almendros, he had gone missing. I was on my own at the time and feverishly searched every nook and cranny but couldn't find him. In desperation I went next door for help from the resident maid who was very fond of him – a mutual fondness.

'Carmen. Have you seen Julian?'

'No, Señora.'

Just then we heard a faint noise from upstairs.

'*Un momento, Señora. Me voy a ver.*' (I'm going to see.) '*Ven por aquí, Señora!*'

I responded to her call to join her. What a sight met our eyes! There he was putting polish on the beautiful parquet floors of our Peace Corps American neighbours. The problem was it was black polish! We burst out laughing. But then followed my concern as to whether it would permanently stain the lovely floor.

I needn't have worried. Carmen came to the rescue and

taking wire wool used a tried and tested method Chileans used on wooden flooring. Placing her foot on the large wad, with leg swinging from the hip and foot remaining on the pad, she vigorously moved her leg forwards and backwards. The rogue polish was removed from the surface and the rogue child removed from further mischief! The right colour polish was then applied, followed by the machine, and the floor was returned to its former glory. I found this art of treating parquet floors to be an excellent way to trim up the hips, if a bit too energetic when the whole floor needed covering.

Guanagueros was a small picturesque Pacific bay and lay to the south of Coquimbo, which in turn, was a very short distance south from La Serena, a lovely coastal town. We had to pass Tongoy, a popular holiday resort, just before arriving at our holiday destination. On another occasion some years later we revisited here. On that particular visit we saw our first penguin, swimming just close to the quayside. It was a first hand witness of what Michael Andrews wrote in his book as to how far north these birds are to be found. The reason for this was due to the Humboldt Current maintaining the coldness of the northern waters.

'Children. The first thing we must do is to put up our tents.' So saying, Ray chose a position half way between the sea and the site office to pitch the two small tents: so small we could hardly kneel in them let alone stand. Ray and I could just about crawl into our tent to sleep. The three children all shared the other. A letter home described how we used our vehicle to get dressed and undressed in as well as a storeroom-cum-kitchen. We decided to stay on just one site rather than moving and taking down and putting up our tents. It took a day or two for the children to settle, Andrew especially kept asking for our home back in Santiago, but by the third day they were really enjoying life.

The campsite was basic, showers with only cold water, primitive toilets, a simple and a communal brick structure over an open fire in the centre for cooking purposes. The beauty of the place and the certainty of sun made up for the minimalist life style. Other campers in true Chilean friendliness soon made our acquaintance. One couple offered the use of their Calor gas cooker in their caravan while we were sorting ourselves out – our *rubio* children once again unlocking the key to these warm hearted nationals. The impression that all *gringos* from the developed West were well off must surely have been dispelled on this occasion when our possessions received a greater scrutiny. Our children's fan club included a number of teenagers.

Resourcefulness in the 'kitchen' was certainly put to the test for me cooking on an open fire and for Ray with the unenviable task of cleaning blackened saucepans and kettle. There was no such thing as barbecue charcoal – we had to do with finding our own fuel. Children to the rescue! Ray enlisted their help, even two-year-old 'quicksilver'. Off they would go into the *bosque* to scavenge for fallen branches from the many trees, while 'the chef' started food preparations taking advantage of their absence. With Daddy tying up small pine and eucalyptus branches into suitably sized bundles, the children, hand on their rope, would drag their own precious firewood behind them, or together would help Ray drag a larger bundle.

Finding food was still a challenge but surely there would be plenty of fish? The local fishermen, however, didn't always have spare fish for us to buy direct. This meant a trip into Coquimbo to see what we could find. '[We] *bought some very large sausages, [5] – nearly died at* [the] *price E 175.'* There were 112 escudos to the pound at that time, so these five sausages cost us at today's rate approximately £10. Surprisingly, it worked out cheaper to eat in a restaurant. We introduced the children to their first taste of Chinese cuisine.

The next day my diary records going to the quay to see if there were any crabs to buy, but there were none. Not to be daunted I saw some between the rocks right by the steps leading into the water. Some local women came to my rescue and helped me in my attempt, in Spanish, to persuade one of *los pescadores* to catch one (many were dead). This local fisherman obliged and caught three live ones. *'He wouldn't take any money. A cheap tea!'*

Later that day the second of my fishing exploits, referred to in a previous chapter, happened. Ray was taking his afternoon siesta and the rest of us were on the beach, not far from the water's edge, making sandcastles. Suddenly a movement in the sea caught my attention. About ten metres out to sea was a fish leaping in and out of the water parallel to the beach.

Like a shot, without further thought, but obviously conditioned by the quest for food, which had become a way of living, I ran into the sea. Just what I intended to do was anyone's guess, not least my own. Running through the calm waves I headed towards my prey, leaving three bemused children wondering what on earth Mummy was up to. She didn't even have her swimsuit on.

Somehow I must deprive the fish from its life-giving source, was my only thought. The most logical way was to get between it and the open sea and somehow try and get it onto the beach.

But how? I had no fishing tackle, no bait. What I did have was determination. There was no earthly point trying to catch the slippery fish in my hands but I could still use them. So thinking, I scooped both hands behind the fish and with a wafting movement managed to land it!

Then what?

Seeing the fish writhing on the beach and with all bravery fading fast I did the cowardly thing and walked away. Even if there had been a stone nearby I wouldn't have had the stomach to use it to put it out of its misery. After a sufficient interval for its demise to have occurred, I returned to collect the unidentified spoil. Later we discovered it was a young *corvina* (sea bass).

Once we'd settled the children in bed after their supper, Ray and I enjoyed a lovely meal of barbecued fish – there was only enough for two. We well remember my cleaning and filleting this wonderful provision by the light of a full moon, as we had no light, only a tiny torch.

Trips to the harbour with the children to buy fish straight from the boats became an early morning or late afternoon excursion, with varying degrees of success. My diary records one early evening we bought a *corvina* weighing 3 kilos (7 lbs) for only E 40 a kilo.

The campsite began to empty, the *feriado* long weekend now over. Fewer weekenders arrived the following Friday, as the main Chilean holiday season wasn't until the months of January and February.

Our second Sunday saw us taking Sunday School, with our three, as we had done the previous Sunday. What better story to recount on the first occasion than the disciples leaving their boats and nets to follow Jesus? One week later it was the turn of the foolish man who built his house on the sand and the wise man choosing the solid foundation of rock for his.

Another trip to Tongoy succeeded in buying a kilo of *machas* for only E 15 – a true bargain considering they were already shelled! This time we ate them for the first time raw as there was no such luxury of either a grill or parmesan cheese! However, we weren't disappointed. They tasted delicious. A small rivulet of shallow seawater provided great enjoyment for the children. Even more importantly it was safe from the Pacific rollers and the tendency of Chile's beaches to shelve steeply and abruptly. A youth of fourteen had almost drowned the previous Saturday and, in joining to help the father drag him out of the water and turn him onto his side, we got to know this man and his two sons. The youth, after initial shock, fortunately was none the worse for his experience. The father later told us he worked in the customs at Pudahuel and offered future help – if only that help could have been forthcoming on our arrival in the country we almost certainly would still have had our fated tape recorder to put to good use.

All good things come to an end. With our holiday over, it was time to take down the tents, pack the VW, bid 'adios' to our friends, especially the *jovenes* (teenagers) ready to return to Santiago, but not before returning to the harbour to stock up on fish. We were disappointed. There were none. A restaurant meal at Los Socos (noted for its thermal waters, of which there are very many in this land) was conveniently placed just off the Pan-American south west of Ovalle – with time for a quick swim. The three-course meal of fish and chicken followed by coffee was amazingly cheap, E 120 plus service charge. An order for two was more than enough to feed a family of five.

All Chilean meals are served with a generous basket of bread.

Over the years, given our economic constraints, we became used to taking doggy bags with us. Many a time, a lunchtime meal would stretch in providing for the rest of the day, or so much bread at breakfast added to by a couple of tins of sardines or tuna, bananas or cheese would be sufficient for lunch.

The vast majority of our holidays were self-catering. On future occasions, when we had to use restaurants or modest hotels, this thrifty method meant that as a family we could often accompany Ray when there was a later change in his ministry.

Antofagasta was the future destination for Ray to make two visits a year. The purpose was to take Communion services and to see to any pressing pastoral needs of the Anglo-Chilean community. The resident lay pastor, Philip Monypenny, who was also the British Vice-Consul was licensed to take regular services including funerals, but not to officiate at the Holy Communion service.

Antofagasta, a coastal town, lies directly to the west at the widest point of the country, 900 kilometres north of La Serena, well into the Atacama Desert. It was 1370 kilometres from the capital yet still south of the border with Peru by over 700 kilometres. Santiago, for all practical descriptions, was approximately halfway between Chile's northern frontier and the southern archipelago of 'Where the Land Ends'.

After a few winters in Santiago, when all too often the city was awash with heavy rain and temporary bridges were placed over the gullies to enable pedestrians to cross the roads, it seemed sensible to escape the city for a respite. School winter holidays during the last two weeks of July provided us with the excuse needed. What better destination than the 'Costa del Desierto' (my description). The small Anglican community then, were only too happy to have 'the Padre' visit. By this time we had changed from an exclusive work among Chilean nationals to a new emphasis in ministry. How this came about is the subject of my next chapter. Expenses consisting of the equivalent of the return airfare for Ray and his hotel accommodation were sufficient for a family of five to travel overland.

Colleagues would transport us plus luggage to the coach

station in downtown Santiago. Fortunately we didn't need any rainwear but a sweater each was essential because the temperatures dropped considerably at night. The children were very excited at travelling on a double-decker bus. Overland travel by coach was very advanced in the mid 1970s. Chile had acquired several Mercedes Benz double-decker coaches. These were certainly luxurious to us. Although we were not able to recline completely in the horizontal there was ample legroom. We needed this for a journey that would take around twenty-four hours.

There was one interruption impossible to avoid in all the relaxation of such luxury travel, which took us by surprise on our first visit. When this interruption occurred at night, especially in the very early hours of the morning, it was particularly annoying.

Chañaral is a coastal town a little more than half way between La Serena and Antofagasta, a distance of approximately 970 kilometres from Santiago. The Pan American highway passes through it. Just outside the town the bus stops at a small wooden building where a barrier extends across the road. It's always an enforced stop and a policeman boards the bus.

'Everybody out. You are required to bring all luggage with you.'

'Whatever contraband are they searching for?' I ask Ray.

'Do you have any fruit?' asked a gruff voice.

They began a search through our luggage. Simultaneously with our search other officials were emptying a medley of cases, bags and cardboard boxes on wooden table-tops. Cosmetics, clothes, books, nappies, towels began to pile up.

'Ahh!' With a triumphant flourish the official pulled out an orange from among a couple of magazines and a toilet bag. It wasn't long before a very small quantity of oranges, apples and bananas were collected.

Were these custom men so hard up for desserts?

It turned out that it wasn't the innocent fruit in itself that was such contraband but the fruit fly that may have been attempting to move district!

The financial provision from the Anglican Ex-Pat Church meant all five of us could have B & B in a modest hotel. It was this sort of occasion in which the doggy bags came in useful.

The Anglo-Chilean Community was absolutely delighted that we had chosen to visit as a complete family and, in turn, we received so much kindness and hospitality. Our somewhat frugal meals were amply supplemented by invitations out over the duration of the official part of the venture. Phil Monypenny and his Scottish wife Liz became great friends over the years. On one of a number of occasions they took us to a restaurant. This was several years later when they had moved to Santiago and food was again in plentiful supply. We chose the albalone (*locos*) to begin with. It wasn't our first taste of *locos* but what a plateful! There were three on each plate dressed with lashings of mayonnaise covering their tops, completed by a garnish of lettuce. I wasn't able to eat all of mine and this was only the starter!

Once the official bit of the official visit to the Anglo-Chilean community was over it was holiday time and a return to thriftiness once again. Over many years right up to the time of writing we have often combined ministry with holiday. Antofagasta several times became the base from which we travelled further afield.

Arica, you will remember famous for its clock, directly north of this town, lay on the border with neighbouring Peru some 2050 kilometres from Santiago. This town fought over and won by Chile from its neighbours would provide a much-needed port for landlocked Bolivia. This concession, to this day, comes at considerable cost to the poorest republic of South America in the tax levies imposed.

Our exploration further into the heart of the wild, arid desert to the northeast came on later visits. Notable among these visits were two train journeys of a lifetime taking us across the divides separating one South American republic from another. One took us across the desert right into La Paz, Bolivia, the other from Cuzco to Macchu-Picchu, in Peru, the heart of Inca civilisation. These trips subsequently were brought into everyone's living room through Michael Palin's popular television series.

Chapter 21
Change of Direction

You will remember that the mandate we had been given from Bishop David Pytches was to church plant in the professional area of the capital. As there was no other national Protestant church in the Barrio Alto we went as a family to the English-speaking church situated in Avenida Holanda in the 'West End' (Providencia).

The Santiago Community Church (SCC) consisted of expatriates and Anglo-Chileans, some second generation or more whose forebears had, in some cases, come out with shipping companies, the railway and nitrate industry. Included in the congregation were also a number of disaffected Roman Catholic Chileans wanting to improve their English!

As it was at this time the only Protestant Church for English-speaking people in Santiago, it had a very international appeal. It served the various embassies where the English language was the language in common. This meant that the South Korean and Swedish embassies were recognised alongside the more obvious Canadian, New Zealand, Australian, American and South Africa. Those from their home countries on business contracts of varying lengths of time, as well as the permanent residents, together with the various diplomatic personnel compromised much of the congregation. Some of the companies and organisations represented within the congregation were: the British Tobacco Company, the United Nations, the American Peace Corps, the Pacific Steam Navigation Company, Price Waterhouse, Coates' Thread and British Caledonian.

There was, from time to time, a sprinkling of passers-through:

representatives from the UK or USA based firms out to visit their Chilean subsidiaries, friends and family members of others and only a few tourists. The reason few tourists visited was not so much because of the political climate but rather because Chile, for most visitors to South America, was the end of the road and distances prohibitive for those on tight budgets. One tourist whose enforced stay in the capital brought him into our lives was a New Zealander. His story you will read later in this book.

The Community Church had come about through the merger of the Anglican Cathedral Church of St Andrew with the Union Church. The Union Church catered primarily for those of a Free Church background: Methodists, Baptists and Presbyterians whereas St Andrew's attracted those with Anglican and Episcopalian affiliation. The joining together of congregations evolved through economic reasons, reflecting the nature of the changing country, rather than an overwhelming desire for church unity. However, in the following years the 'arranged marriage' of these two worship centres brought a rich diversity of various threads of worship, enriching the lives of so many down the subsequent years. It meant respecting the different church traditions, and involved each participating denomination being prepared to give and take on some of their cherished forms of doing things.

Our first impression of the church was very mixed. It was decidedly middle-class but then we ourselves were living and working among the Chilean middle-class. More concerning for us was that it smacked of a somewhat social club with a greater emphasis on merely social events. Outreach for the gospel in mission was virtually non-existent. The only outreach, important though this was, was a 'Nearly New' shop ('*Casi Nuevo*'), which sold good quality second hand clothes. The funds from this enterprise helped finance a retirement home for elderly expatriates. Other fund raising and church giving, almost exclusively, was used to keep the church afloat. It would be a visit from the then Archbishop of Canterbury, together with the subsequent appointment of the next minister, which would serve as a catalyst to help change this inward looking tendency.

One Sunday after we had returned home from the morning service, we received a telephone call from Canon Graham Jack, the minister, to ask if Ray could take a dying woman back to her home near Melipilla?

Melipilla was a small town in the *campo* just under 70 kilometres south west of Santiago about halfway between the capital and the coast. The Chilean woman was the sister-in-law of Enrique, the church caretaker. We made up a bed in the Volkswagen flattening the back seats and laying a mattress on top. I managed to get an analgesic injection prescribed and after administering it we set out. Our three children were left with Rosa, Enrique's wife, and her two little ones, Luis and Guigo. Her husband accompanied the very ill woman as well as one of her children and her brother-in-law.

We made a good journey until we reached Melipilla, but to reach their home we had another 30 kilometres to drive. This last part of the journey was taken very slowly. The paved road had been left behind and Ray was now driving on a *ripio* road. He drove as carefully as possible avoiding most of the potholes. The woman was sleeping as a result of the analgesia. While Ray was concentrating on the driving I was left conversing with the relatives.

Once we arrived at the humble dwelling the woman woke up but was still free from pain. I made her as comfortable as possible and talked briefly with her of the love of Jesus. It was so much more natural to speak of Christian belief with the average Chilean than with our own people, as the majority were less secular. Leaving the family with a copy of a modern version of the New Testament in Spanish we made our departure. She died four weeks later.

Four months after this trip, in February 1973, the post to succeed Graham Jack was advertised in church periodicals in most English-speaking countries of the world. Among the forty applicants were our names! How did this come about?

Having found our camping holiday just before Christmas had not refreshed us as much as we had hoped and February being the main holiday month, we were able to take another week away. We were badly in need of this because since Christmas all three children had gone down with chickenpox. The boys only had a few spots each but Naomi was really poorly. She was covered from head to toe, including scalp, eyes, ears, and even inside her nose and mouth.

For almost three days she just lay in bed totally lethargic, no smile, no appetite and no interest in anything. As her throat was so affected she could only take liquids and puréed food. In a letter home I described how I gave her egg beaten up in milk and puréed apple. Jelly was unobtainable now but fortunately I had four packets in stock but I had to pay 30 shillings (over £15 today) for two kilos of apples. The letter goes on to say how I gave her a *'tiny disposable enema for children'*, advised by our resident paediatrician Dr Thea!

Naomi, of course, had lost weight and once again Thea came to the rescue in recommending a good tonic, *'one that really helps to put on weight'*. In fact Ray and I had lost weight but not Andrew or Julian. In the same letter home I wrote how I was down to my pre-marriage weight of just over nine stone. To lose weight in the hot summer was not *'unusual … but this time I've lost more and all in the last four weeks. Living here is a strain, yet we have never gone hungry and only last Fri. we were able to buy chicken at a good price and I only queued for 1¼ hrs. We take collapsible chairs and a book, so that if we don't get involved in conversation we can read.'*

So another holiday was a welcome break. We couldn't afford to go far or afford the luxury of a hotel. What better opportunity than to house sit for colleagues taking their holiday? What better place than 'the Vineyard by the Sea'? Peter Woods and his wife Evelyn lived in Viña. Peter was chaplain of St Peter's Church.

The journey itself in this central region of the country took us through once pretty scenery now sadly beginning to show signs of neglect. We left behind the backdrop of the huge peaks of the Andes and passing through Lo Prado tunnel entered a potentially fertile plain. This lay between the jagged superior peaks and the lesser more rounded hills hugging the coastline.

Rain is always in short supply, as the dry season, normally with no rain at all, extends from October to March. Crops and fruit are dependent on artificial irrigation. The melted snow from the summer sun fills the streams flowing down the mountains. These empty into the valleys and find their way into the canals channelled out by the *campesinos*. The land gently slopes in a westerly direction as the Andes continue pushing it seawards. Some of the irrigation channels, therefore, are able to use gravity to disperse their life giving contents on thirsty crops.

Among those harvested were other overgrown fields full of knee high weeds, brown and scorched by the searing sun, fields that had no longer been sown for fear of an illegal *toma*. Normally the route would be littered with little stalls selling fruit and vegetables, eager boys, girls and women risking their lives in their attempt to flag down passing motorists. There were one or two. We managed to buy some fruit of the season: melons, watermelons and tomatoes.

The holiday week itself was a good combination of family time on the various beaches of this beautiful coastline and visiting colleagues. Our favourite beach was Reñaca, reminiscent of the rugged Cornish coast. The sea wasn't conducive for venturing out very far other than getting our feet wet, because of the steep shelving, huge rollers and the cold temperatures. The children though were more than happy. By now Naomi was beginning to brighten up.

On one subsequent holiday I did decide to brave the cold water but the force of a large wave followed by another Pacific roller so scared me I never tried again. The first had knocked me right off my feet and before I had time to get up the next followed, relentlessly crashing down on me. The undercurrent was so strong my swimming hat was wrenched off and taken out to sea but at least I was left behind – safe but badly frightened. As the combination of waves tossed me around like a rag doll I twisted my spine and spent the rest of that holiday resting.

We took a boat trip out with Gloria around the harbour of Valparaiso and were most impressed with the modern naval vessels including a large submarine. However, no photography was allowed. Later in the week we met up with our friends from Santiago, Mario and Bernadita, also on holiday in Viña.

Unfortunately we weren't able to see the Skinner family as they too were away on holiday. The children had to make do with playing with one another. For the boys this was no problem as they got on so well at this age. It was a bit lonely for Naomi but without her usual energy she was more than happy to play on the beach and enjoy the trips out.

Our time on the coast proved to be more meaningful than we could have envisaged initially. Ray, readily admitting that his struggle with the language had left him feeling hampered from exercising a fuller ministry, was at times feeling frustrated. On the Sunday of our holiday we were invited to tea at the Pytches. In the course of conversation Ray happened to share with his Bishop something of the sense of inadequacy he was feeling with the language and the attendant limitation in ministry. Somehow the conversation got around to the concern we both felt at the lack of mission outreach from the Santiago Community Church within the community the church was serving. The congregation knew that Graham Jack was coming to the end of his present contract and would not be renewing it, as did our Bishop, of course, but Ray was not prepared for David's next question.

'Ray, why don't you apply for the post? I would certainly back up your application.'

I was less than enthusiastic. The Great Commission of Jesus (to make disciples of all nations), that had influenced our lives over the years was as binding within the affluent business and diplomatic worlds of those whose language we shared, as with those of the country we had adopted. Certainly many nations were represented in this Church. Yet I wasn't convinced. Hadn't we left home and family to serve Chileans? Would moving into the English-speaking world be a denial in some way of the calling to South America? I struggled with these questions. On the one hand it was obvious Ray was not really fulfilled, yet my heart was truly among the Spanish-speaking people. After a few more days we reached a consensus. As we prayed about it, we decided to 'try the door' believing that God would open or shut it.

This possible big change of direction wasn't shared even with our parents until we discussed it with Canon Harry Sutton, who was visiting mission personnel in Chile following on a visit to Peru. His reaction was favourable. 'If you were to be successful we would want to keep you as associates of SAMS.'

Successful? The next few weeks and even months left us thinking that humanly speaking we didn't stand a chance. To the amazement of the interviewing body there were over forty applicants from all over the English-speaking world. It seemed that a number were politically motivated by this new Marxist experiment.

Ray wrote home: '*A duplicated information sheet was sent to all 40 applicants about the church, its activities and the sort of man required for the job. From this 25 people approx, were on the list* [sic]*. They then prepared another sheet outlining the problems and difficulties in order to put people off! Now the short list is down to 7 or 8 of those who are being considered as having a reasonable chance of success. Several of these are in the U.S.A. and others in the UK.*'

He went on to mention that interviewing would take place in these two countries over the following two or three weeks '*on behalf of the Selection Committee here.*' It was expected that the results would be known by mid July. Our interview took place on home ground, as we were the only applicants from inside Chile itself.

Letters home indicated I was feeling somewhat ambivalent about remaining in Chile. On the one hand there was the encouragement that Nico was now reading St Mark's Gospel and visiting us every week to ask questions arising out of his reading. On the other hand life was becoming increasingly difficult to cope with.

'*On Fri. I had another downcast day when I just wanted to pack up and come home. Our gas cylinders had run out and there are none to replace them! Production is only at 50% and, as this is our means of cooking, heating water and heating the house (mainly, although we have a small electric heater and a paraffin heater, both of which are not effective enough for heating adequately) you can imagine how I felt with the prospect of winter so near* [sic]*!*'

I went on to say that in spite of a rush on buying alternative means for cooking we had managed to procure two small electric rings. This meant all cooking would be done on these. One of the single missionaries, Sheila, kindly gave us a gas cylinder *'which we'll use only for real necessities, occasional baths and baking bread in the oven. Bread is getting scarce and rumours have it there will be almost no bread at all next month. ... The gas shortage will hit all except those who have piped gas.'*

This letter was written on the Sunday, following the Friday when the sermon in church had been just what we needed. The verse that became both the encouragement and the challenge to remain focussed on our calling was from John chapter 9 verse 4. Jesus was speaking to his disciples:

'As long as it is day, we must do the work of him who sent me. Night is coming, when no-one can work.'

I continued with my letter: *'... the sermon this morning made us realise we have to work while it is day and after it I told the Lord I was willing to stay here as long or as short as He wants* [sic].' Yet another example of how God meets us at the point of our deep needs.

A week later in another letter home I mentioned that *'our letters will have to be more guarded in the future as the "authorities" have stopped all airlines accepting letters direct.'* Up until this point we had been able to take letters down to the British Caledonian Airline's office duly stamped with English stamps sent out by friends and relatives. This ensured the letters arriving so much quicker. However, this was now no longer possible. The reasoning behind the decision was thought to be to maintain a control and possible censorship of news to the outside world. In addition *'our postage rates have gone up alarmingly – 400% so we shall include as many notes in your letters ... for you to forward to the appropriate people please.'* A friend commented on receiving a letter from us his absolute amazement on finding 17 Chilean stamps on the envelope – a tangible sign of the increasing devaluation of the escudo. The net was closing in.

The day of interview came. After the church service on June 10th, Bob Ely, a director of the British Tobacco Company and Chairman of the Board of Trustees of the Community Church and of the Selection Committee, approached Ray. 'Ray, I'm going to the UK at the end of the week and would like to arrange an interview for you and Gill with the Selection Committee. Can you make it this evening?' As Nico and Lydia (visiting her parents) were coming to tea they were more than willing to hold the fort with the children.

We met in the home of Willie Reid, a Scot, who together with his elder brother, James, was director of the family business Cameron Reid. Willie's wife, Gertrude, was Danish. The Committee consisted of four, two representing the two churches that had merged. Jeff MacDonald, another Scot, and Willie Reid were from the Union Church. Bob Ely and Captain Graham Balfour, the churchwarden of St Andrew and a relative of the former Prime Minister, represented the Anglicans. They made us feel very welcome and relaxed. The interview lasted over one and half-hours.

Ray wrote: '*We felt that there was a real care and concern for the needs of the minister and his family, the congregation and the English-speaking community. I felt perhaps for the first time, that if we were invited to consider it seriously, I could go ahead seeking the Lord's final confirmation quite happily, and Gill feels this too now. We had had various qualms, particularly about the social life of the congregation, but we see that we would need to make a positive contribution using our own gifts and preach a biblical ministry with a pastoral concern. However, all along we have committed it to the Lord and he will guide them and us as to the outcome.*'

The contract was for an initial three years followed by a second term of three years. Graham Jack was due to leave in November of the current year 1973. The church council did not want a long interregnum. For us that would mean, if successful, six years without home leave. We had already raised this with both our Bishop and also SAMS chairman. Now we brought this to their attention during the interview. It was agreed that if Ray were appointed we could take home leave from August to November. The letter continues: '*However, we have to wait at least until the beginning of July … because of the others to be interviewed in the UK and USA. That is the snag because if we are accepted, we're only going to have 3 weeks or so to pack up and get all our documents in order.*

However, we're not assuming that we're going to be successful, because there are strong competitors.'

One of these strong competitors seemed to have so much more going for him than we could offer. Before ordination he had been a businessman, was widely travelled and his wife had been brought up in Chile. Not only was she an Anglo-Chilean she happened to be the daughter of the church treasurer!

My comments home gave the reason why we hadn't shared more with our parents. Not only did we feel that *'humanly speaking we didn't stand a chance.'* We hadn't wanted to raise their hopes about the possibility of our coming home so soon. *'... in fact up until a few days I had put the possibility right out of my mind. It certainly is a challenge, yet full of opportunities for the Lord, eg. take 'Lydia's' case (conversion of a diplomat's daughter.) I don't suppose one could find a situation so different from working in the East End of London ... However, the Lord knows where he wants us and where he can best use us. He just wants of us availability and learning to be all things to all men – but in order to win them for Christ even if it means having to go to Embassy functions [and] cocktail parties at times [sic]!'*

The Sunday following our interview, Grace, our consul's wife, told me that Graham had told her husband that it had been reported back to him how well the interview had gone.

Between these two Sundays my diary records a week of the amazing variety that these days in Chile were bringing; a house-guest Derek Hawksbee (our director on the Allen Gardiner orientation course), two showings of another film from the Moody Bible Institute *Dust and Destiny* in our home, a parents' meeting at the boys' pre-school, a visit from our priest friend Padre Juan, Naomi with an ear infection, a Bible study Group in the home of Argentinian friends, two visits from Nico and Lydia, and more political disturbances and of course, the never ending queues.

A frightening incident happened to one of our SAMS colleagues. Felicity Houghton was caught up in a disturbance. About 5,000 *trabajadores* from the copper mine of El Teniente converged on the capital in protest. This mine lay 90 kilometres south of Santiago and east of Rancagua into the Andes.

A consortium of companies, the Braden Copper Company, the Guggenheims, and the Kennecott Copper Corporation had developed it. Together with Chuquicamata, way in the north, it also held a world record. Both were the largest copper mines in the world but whereas Chuqui (popularly referred to) was an open mine, El Teniente held the record as the greatest tunnelled mine.

According to Davis the issue with these miners was one of bread and butter. The government had renegaded on a previously agreed wage increase. On April 19th they stopped work. In El Teniente alone loss of production cost Chile a million dollars a day. [1]

Felicity was travelling by train from the south in the unexpected company with many of the miners. Near to Buin, just over half way between Rancagua and Santiago, police confronted the miners. She was occupying the next carriage to two that had been set on fire by incendiary devices.

By July the remaining interviews had eliminated a further three or four candidates, leaving only Ray and the son-in-law of the church treasurer. But before we could know the final outcome the rumblings of tanks down the streets of the city would leave all of the country, for a time, wondering what its impending destiny would be.

---

[1] Nathaniel Davis: *The Last Two Years of Salvador Allende*. I. B. Tauris & Co. Ltd.
    p. 150

Chapter 22

Radio Rumblings of a Political Tremor

In my opening chapter I described when an earth tremor became an earthquake and how it moved along the Richter scale to reach an intensity of 7.0 or more. I also described the rumbling noise as of a fast approaching train. Within just over two years from that awesome event the 'train' of politics was gathering in both speed and intensity. Before the political 'earthquake' of September 11th 1973 shook the nation to its core, lesser tremors of varying magnitude acted as warnings of an approaching crisis.

A letter home from Ray describes some of those events:

'We've just had the BBC Overseas Service News on (8pm here, midnight GMT) and not surprisingly Santiago headed the news items. We've had quite an eventful day here-the nearest yet to the feeling of civil war or a military coup. It followed the strange incident that happened on Wed. General Carlos Prats was being driven down the road on the southern side of the Mapocho river called the Costanera ... when a woman driver drew alongside his vehicle and stuck her tongue out at him! He reacted by giving chase and firing at her vehicle ... We gather that he got out and demanded an apology whilst other motorists stopped and crowded round. Indignant bystanders let his four tyres down and he had to hail a taxi that took him to report to the President. As a result a state of emergency in Stgo. [sic] was proclaimed, which reduced the whole thing to the level of a pathetic joke.'

It was the morning of June 29th 1973. The telephone rang and I recognised the voice at the other end of our Argentinian friend, Marisa. 'Quick, Gill, put the radio on, it looks as though we're having a military coup!'

I switched on the radio, calling Ray who had just returned from taking the children to school and was about to leave for the centre. With our still somewhat limited Spanish, as far as the radio was concerned, we were totally confused as to what was going on. However, what was certainly coming over the radio waves loud and clear was gunfire. Even Marisa, with no language barrier, couldn't make out what was happening. She was still on the 'phone to us as we remained tuned in to our respective radios. Our primary concern was to collect the children from school and bring them home.

Ray continued:

'Today it was no joke. I was just about to leave for the centre, having just returned from taking the children to school ... A 'phone call advised us to switch on the radio urgently. We gathered that the President's Palace – the Moneda – was under attack and we could hear a background of gunfire. Reports were very confusing and we were under the impression that there had been a military takeover. The obvious thing was to go and collect the children and keep well away from the centre. As I passed the road in which the President lives, Tomás Moro, I noticed that it was sealed off by police armoured cars (like small tanks), but otherwise came across nothing abnormal, except long queues at petrol stations.'

After depositing our three back, Ray then had to make a round trip of over eight miles to El Arrayan to safely deliver two other small passengers. Our American friend, Mimi, married to a Chilean, had her two small sons in the same pre-school at Los Dominicos as Andrew and Julian. Their car was off the road. Before Ray left we decided to pull the large shutters across the windows as extra protection. You will remember all our neighbours were military.

Ray joined a queue at a petrol station and filled up *'... in case we had to travel somewhere at short notice. We had the radio on all morning and the children were obviously a bit bewildered, Naomi especially so ... It seemed that one part of the army was fighting against another part, with the carabineros – the police – strongly supporting the President. By this afternoon it was clear that everything was under* control, the whole country was declared to be in a state of emergency and a strict curfew has been imposed from 23:00hrs to 06:30.'

Later that day all the government supporters were called to a mass meeting of solidarity outside the Presidential Palace. Allende addressed the nation. We listened on the radio. He thanked the armed forces for their loyal support, especially mentioning General Prats who had now become something of a national hero, but only to government sympathisers. As on previous occasions, and therefore not the least unexpected, the radio was now under its obligatory *cadena* transmitting only music and government controlled information.

My diary records that the government wanted the State of Emergency (*Estado de Sitio*) to continue for ninety days but that the opposition in Congress opposed this.

'We were so tired from the strain of uncertainty and possible danger that we all went to bed for an hour after lunch. We still feel drained so we're going to have an early night and then we'll continue the letter in the morning, when, perhaps, the newspaper will give us a bit more information on what has been happening around us.'

The next day in need of company we invited Marisa and Alfredo, committed Christians with leftist sympathies, together with Lydia (in Chile for holidays) and Nico to supper. We wanted Nico to meet them as they could relate so well to him. If we had to leave the country because of the worsening situation Nico would need others to fire his many questions at. You can imagine the main topic of conversation over the supper table, at least initially. However, before long Nico, full of questions as usual about the Christian faith, changed the conversation around from politics. With other supporting input coming from our Argentinian friends, as well as Lydia, a lively and meaningful conversation took us just short of curfew time. At least much earlier nights were now guaranteed when entertaining.

On a beautiful afternoon, the first Sunday in July and two days after Friday's events, with a vivid blue sky overhead, we felt the need to get out into the lovely sunshine. The sun in winter was a delight and ideal for climbing the small hill of Lo Curro. The lower hills were mantled in soft green from the winter rains with a fresh fall of snow covering the higher mountains and the ever-present majestic Andes in the background. The smell of eucalyptus cones fallen from the trees, the smoke from the wood burning in local dwellings and the sweet smell of mimosa in full bloom helped to lift our mood.

Even as I'm writing this current chapter in southern Spain, many years later, I have, in a tangible way, a reminder of those earlier memories. On the table is a large vase full of yellow mimosa. Margarita had arrived at the chaplaincy town house last Saturday. '*Un recuerdo de Chile,*' she said, as she handed me a large bunch of freshly picked mimosa. And what a reminder it was as the unique fragrance wafted up my nostrils.

The mimosa, however, wasn't the only reminder of past times, as an amazing 'God-incident' had occurred the previous year, 2005. We only discovered Margarita and her husband, Lorenzo, last year, when we were covering the same locum as now, in Andalucía. Imagine the surprise, followed by overwhelming joy, when we set eyes on this recognizable face in the congregation. It was the same Margarita who had been a member of our Sunday night, mainly student, group of *Chilenos*, in Santiago twenty-eight years previously! That Sunday morning, leading the service in Sotogrande, Spain, I had a sudden flash back to those years in the church hall in Avenida Holanda, and saw her with her hands raised in praise and worship.

Behind the large bunch of fragrant yellow flowers and smiling face of Margarita last Saturday, were three other beaming faces. Margarita and Lorenzo, together with another Chilean husband and wife, had arrived for lunch. The four *Chilenos* were now living in Spain.

There was much noisy conversation around the lunch table and plenty of laughter. Chileans like Spaniards are known for being very vocal and speaking loudly. Like Margarita, Lorenzo was from a Chilean-German background. Both had come from Christian families. Lorenzo, a rotund, blue-eyed, blond jovial man, with a big heart, had the warmest of personalities. They both were extremely generous with an open home. They had adopted a Chilean boy and a girl – now teenagers.

With a gap in the light-hearted conversation I turned to Margarita: 'Margarita, what are your memories of those days in Chile?' I asked having no idea where her political loyalties lay.

'You must remember, Geel, I was young then and not fully aware of all that was going on. My parents with memories of what communism had done in Germany, were so worried that in Allende's time my father bought a one-way ticket to Germany for all the family.'

For Margarita's family the military coup meant those tickets were not used but many in the early 1970s, of course, did leave. Among that number were our American Peace Corps neighbours due to leave on Monday. My diary records, how together with their *empleada* Carmen, they joined the five of us for lunch; it also records my feeling depressed and wishing we were the ones who were leaving.

On our trip out to Cerro Lo Curro that first Sunday in July of 1973, still not knowing whether Ray had been accepted as the new chaplain, we met a German family. The wife, Irene, had been on a previous Spanish course with Ray and had told him of this lovely place for walking. We were able to buy two loaves of bread from them. That morning before the morning service Ray had gone out at 7.00 am to buy bread but there hadn't been any available. In the same letter home, Ray had written of the solution to our liquid gas shortage as the tankers had arrived and we had been able to renew the cylinders.

He continued his letter home: '*By now we have more information about Friday's event* [June 29th], *and as the picture becomes more clear, there is a growing suspicion that it was a put-up job by the Govt, but who are we to judge. No.2 Tank Regiment was led from its barracks not far from the Moneda by a Col. for whom it was his last day in the Army (so from the point of view of his career he had nothing to lose). Some of the 10 tanks surrounded the Moneda and some the Ministry of Defence in Plaza Bulnes, not far away. They held their positions for nearly 3 hours during which their canons were trained on the main doorways, there was quite a bit of firing, windows (70 odd) were broken in the Moneda and about 15 people killed (7 of them soldiers)* [sic].'

The following day, Saturday, Ray had to go to Plaza Bulnes

and saw all the shell scars around the doorway of the Ministry of Defence. Apart from the inevitable sightseers, everything had apparently returned to normal, at least on the surface after only twenty-four hours. Another letter of mine written on July 4th recounts there were twenty-two deaths and that it was 'Patria y Libertad' that supported the rebel unit, five of whose leaders entered the Ecuadorian Embassy seeking political asylum.

More information both corroborating, but also adding to our own knowledge of these events are to be found in the writings of Nathaniel Davis. He confirms there were reportedly twenty-two, mainly civilians, killed on June 29th He also gives more background information both leading up to that morning and what actually lay behind the assault on the Presidential Palace.

The involvement of the extreme right-wing 'Fatherland and Liberty' party had been becoming increasingly visible and violent. Mario Aguilar of *'Patria y Libertad'* had been killed in a violent demonstration in the city centre, on May 4th. Two days later at his funeral, Pablo Rodriguez Grez, head of the movement, called for a new government. Over in Mendoza, Argentina, news broke that Roberto Thieme, second in command of this extreme right-wing organisation and thought to be dead, was in fact alive. He, together with another fellow militant, had flown over the Andes to the neighbouring country in a private aeroplane. It was said at the time of the staged 'accident' that he had been plotting a coup that had been discovered. Later accounts reported that *'Patria y Libertad'* in the early months of 1973 had opened up a clandestine northern route of arms from Argentina to Chile. It seemed that military personnel from the Atacama district, a retired army major who had taken refuge in Bolivia (after having plotted against both Frei and Allende) and Brazilian anti-communists were all involved.[1]

On June 4th arrests had been made in Valparaiso of leading figures in the movement. A couple of weeks later, in the capital, bombs were going off in various government-favoured key places. This was reputedly the work of the right-wing extremists.

---

[1] Nathaniel Davis: *The Last Two Years of Salvador Allende*: I. B.Tauris & Co.Ltd.
    p. 154

Hot on the tail were extreme reactionary left-wing bombings. We were almost caught up in one of these bombings.

On June 28th, the night before the so-called attempted coup, we had gone into town. We'd been invited out to hear a friend, Mina Dresser, give a recital at the Chilean German Institute but under the auspices of the British Council.

Mina was English and had a beautiful rich contralto voice. Her husband was a British diplomat. They lived not far from us. It's quite ironical that having had an invitation to dinner from the 'Dressers' on a previous occasion I found to my acute embarrassment to have got my dress for the occasion completely wrong! The first and only time ever. As Mina herself was not fashion conscious in any way and not realising it was to be a formal occasion with many other guests, I turned up wearing a corduroy daytime dress. All the other ladies without exception, including Mina herself, turned out in elegant long dress evening wear. In the early 1970s and in Chile there wasn't the freedom in fashion as there is today.

Anyway, after the concert we had decided to go for a meal and discovered a nearby Chinese restaurant. We ended up sharing a bowl of soup and one dish of chop suey between the two of us, as it was so expensive. Ray continues in his letter home:

'We walked down the very street which 12 hours later was to have tanks clattering down it. We got back to the car ... 35 mins. later a bomb was thrown into the entrance of the 'Colegio Medico' (equivalent of the HQ of the General Medical Council) by some extremists, causing damage but no casualties.' We had stopped to look at the modern architecture and the lovely plants in the foyer of the Medical College, only two doors away from the Institute where the concert was held. *'We very rarely go into the Centre these days at all let alone in the evenings. So we praise the Lord for further protection.'*

After the incident of General Prats, the day before (Wednesday, June 27th), his reputation was sorely damaged. The Chilean public were not going to forget such a humiliating incident. Referring to General Prats, Davis wrote, 'Allende's strongest supporting oak in the Chilean military establishment had been struck by lightning. It still stood, but not as before.'[2] Being better aware of the full facts of what happened on that June morning, he describes the build up. Military officers of the Second-Armoured Regiment, impatient and restive with the way Allende was governing entered into a pact with Patria y Libertad. The idea was either to stage a coup or to kidnap the President on June 27th. The plot was leaked. A Fatherland and Liberty leader, learning of the leak of information, warned one of the officers in the Regiment of the plan's discovery. The coup attempt was cancelled. 'Military intelligence was not deterred from reporting the plot up the chain of command in the evening of 26th June, however, and the wheels of military justice began to turn.'[3]

The prime target for arrest was Captain Sergio Rocha Aros of the Second Armoured Regiment. He was imprisoned in the basement of the Ministry of Defence, lying diagonally across Morande Street from the Presidential Palace. Under interrogation Rocha, so it was reported, implicated his regimental commander, Lt Col Roberto Souper. Others denied Souper was involved. Either way, Souper was relieved of his command. Before the army's generals had their way, Souper and his supporting officers at the regiment decided to take matters into their own hands.

Shortly after 8.30 am on the morning of June 29th the events we described from our letters home and my diary took place. What we didn't know at the time was a situation that Davis describes as having its comic aspect. The rebel unit, comprising of three tanks, and armoured cars and around a hundred troops, stopped at all the traffic lights on its way rumbling down the main streets and one even stopped to fill up with fuel!

Allende was not in the Moneda at the time but in his Tomás Moro residence near to us. This was why Ray found the road sealed and the mounted police on guard when he went to collect the children from school.

In his radio speech the President called on the industrial workers to mobilize. 'I call upon the workers of the industrial belt to take over the industries, all the firms, to be alert, to pour

---

[2] Ibid: p. 155
[3] Ibid: p. 171

into the centre of the city, but not to become victims; the people should come out into the streets, but not to be machine-gunned; to do it with prudence, using whatever resources may be at hand. If the hour comes, the people will have arms.'

General Prats and the rest of the armed service chiefs pledged their support for the President. The senior generals communicated with the commanders of key military installations to prevent the rebellion spreading. Among them was General Pinochet who went to the Buin Regiment.

Prats at the scene of battle, submachine gun in hand, strode up and down the plaza outside the Moneda, demanding authoritatively, that the rebels surrender. They did. By 11.30 am the last of the rebels had done so. General Prats had won the day.

Three weeks later, Nico came to visit, but this time on his own. He looked serious, his face pale. He wanted to talk. 'There's going to be civil war.' This comment didn't surprise us, as it was the talk among the majority by now.

'I shall take to the streets and fight because I believe in my cause. But since I've known you two I can't take up arms. I'll fight with my bare hands and I'll be killed.'

I remember my reply vividly.

'Nico. Yes, you might get killed, but what is more important is that if you are, are you ready to face God?'

'No,' was his reply.

Chapter 23
Last Three Weeks in Allende's Chile

Our letters home weren't all about politics and food shortages, although fall-out from these did take up much of both time and energy. Our ministry in building up friendships, entertaining and running small group discussions on the Christian faith continued. We were always looking for innovative ways within the obvious constraints of language skills, family needs and the never-ending queues for essential commodities. Through the kindness of Derek and Grace Fernyhough, we were able on one occasion to use the 'Diplomatic bag'. This meant we could have a few items sent out via the Embassy without the risk of them being tampered with. My own letter home on July 4th 1973 refers to this occasion:

'The shortages of food etc. are becoming more serious each week but we praise the Lord we haven't gone without anything essential for our health. Clothes & shoes are getting scarcer & very expensive. We were so thrilled to receive the parcel via the DB! What a treat to find so much chocolate & the packet of biscuits ... The boys of course were thrilled with their [Matchbox] *cars ,& Naomi with her doll.'*

Our letters and my diary entries of the month of July 1973 give a good summary of how we were living our lives in fulfilling our God-given call against the backcloth of the final year of Allende's Chile.

The Sunday we went for our first walk up Cerro Lo Curro Ray had asked a member of the Vacancy Appointment Committee how the interviews had been going. In the same letter home describing the political events Ray wrote of our continuing uncertainty as to what the future held for us as a family as we continued to await the outcome of the Church's decision.

There was to be a meeting of the Board of Deacons (remember it was an interdenominational community church) on the next day, Monday, July 2nd. Their recommendations would then be put before the Board of Trustees who would be meeting one week later. The Selection Committee would then assess the joint findings and combined recommendations, the following week. Finally the proposal would be put before the whole church for approval.

'So if we are accepted your maths and ours indicate that we couldn't possibly know in time for us to travel on the "Verdi" on the 21st July.'

As the Italian Line wanted confirmation of the preliminary booking by the next day we had to cancel. The next boat, the *Rossini*, was due to leave Valparaiso on August 13th arriving in Barcelona September 8th.

One of the main considerations – one we could understand, humanly speaking, given the economic and political uncertainty of these days – was the financial aspect: *'... because it would be considerably cheaper to bring a man to Chile with no family than one with three children, and to maintain him. So the real prayer focus is that spiritual values will supersede financial in their considerations and an act of faith may be made and expressed publicly about future finances ...'*

We felt also that the other chief contender, as mentioned before, had the edge on us. The uncertainty surrounding these days is clearly seen in our letters. It was so hard to plan anything without the proviso 'if we're still here then ...' or 'if we're going home then ...'.

If we were going home we planned to pick up the boat at the Peruvian port of Callao after sight seeing in Bolivia and Peru – a lot to work out with three little ones, accommodation with colleagues en route – and the possibility all the plans would have to be cancelled.

Meanwhile Ray, with a return to relative normality in the country following the 'after shocks' of the political tremor of June 29th, was able to go back to his volunteer work at the Blood

Bank. On one of the three afternoons he worked, I took all three children 'to see where Daddy works'. Julian was convinced that Daddy owned an ambulance! What wasn't so thrilling for him and Andrew was that they both ended up with injections to bring them up to date ready for traveling abroad if this was to be the case.

Pomaire is a little village off the main road, a short distance south from Santiago towards the coastal town of San Antonio. We visited the village one Saturday during this waiting time. It was famous for its ceramics. The whole village was given over to making pottery from the local clay. Lining the road into the village and filling the streets outside the houses were all manner of shaped pots. Displayed on rough wooden tables or stacked on to tarpaulins covering the ground were pots, pots and more pots.

By far the majority of them were unglazed, retaining their natural warm terracotta colour. Some were decorative and more elaborate but most were simple and beautiful in their simplicity. Casserole dishes, some open, others with lids were completely oven proof. Somehow food cooked in them tasted so much better. I bought several. They were very cheap as well as being rustically attractive. The shortages hadn't affected this village of its constant supply of earthy material! The challenge lay more in finding a constant supply to fill the dishes!

We had, of course been introduced to these cooking containers when visiting friends.

'Be sure to render it non-porous before cooking in it for the first time,' was the advice given.

'How?'

'Put in some milk, bring to the boil and let it simmer for some time. This will act as a seal.'

It worked. Haricot beans were particularly good cooked in these dishes. While living in Chile we were unable to buy baked beans as such. An American friend gave me a recipe for making my own. First the beans were soaked overnight, followed by very slow cooking in the oven. They were cooked in juices consisting of water, tomato and Worcester sauces, mustard powder, salt and pepper. Added to these were pieces of bacon fat. They tasted as good as, in fact better than, the tinned variety.

The large pots were ideal for serving rice or pasta to a large crowd when entertaining and looked most attractive on the dinner table. I still have several of the original that have by now travelled to various destinations and remain intact.

What particularly fascinated not only Naomi but also her mum was the miniature stoves complete with their little pots 'cooking' on the top – a little girl's ideal gift for playing mum. We bought one. The Chileans are so very creative in their artisan crafts. Another ingenious way of using these little rustic pots was for them to be hung at various intervals on plaited fine string. These were used as wall decorations or if the string was extra fine, together with smaller pots, made into necklaces.

One very wet and cold Sunday, very much wishing we were sitting in front of a good old English log-fire we tried to light one in the open hearth of the lounge. It was a disaster. Houses in Chile, like so many countries, including Spain, with very many months of the year enjoying hours and hours of hot, sunny weather, are not built for the cooler winter days. Having recently had the chimney swept we anticipated a nice, cosy afternoon in, reading and playing games with the children. We had no television and didn't in any way miss one. Before long, clouds of grey smoke drifted down the chimney and into the room. We gave up after a number of abortive attempts. Later we were informed that the opening to the chimneystack needed completely reconstructing.

One day Richard and Julia Collingwood-Selby and their three children came to tea (Richard, you will remember, was the Headmaster of Redland School). It was bedlam as six excited children, who got on so well together, made conversation between the parents, once tea was over, a virtual impossibility. Ray continued: '*Gill's scones were a favourite*' (a tried and trusted recipe of my mother's which had always brought favourable comments – a recipe that Andrew, in particular, took pride in as a child when he learnt to make them, with great success) '*as also her fruit cake.*' Such niceties were now considered a luxury.

The main reason we were able to enjoy both cake and scones

was that for some reason the local shops and supermarkets were inundated with supplies of cooking margarine and sugar. Having not seen any for a number of weeks we ended up buying eight packets of margarine and five kilos of sugar over two days! In the first week of July between us, we had already bought nine slabs of margarine and a five-kilo bag of sugar! To think only weeks and months before we had been eating bread without any butter or margarine and making do with saccharines. What a strange lifestyle we were living.

Entertaining and being entertained have always figured largely in our ministry over the many years of our lives together. Friends out with ODA (Overseas Development and Aid) invited us to dinner. The curfew had been lifted only the day before so it turned out to be a nice, long evening. The meal was a veritable feast for us in these days of stringent living: soup, followed by fried steak, potatoes, mushrooms and peas and for dessert a choice of apple pie, or lemon sponge with cream. Our friends were able to get food through the Embassy.

In the evening of the following day we started a new venture in our home. Instead of a film we invited Arthur Robinson, who, together with Helen, had shared our initial plane journey to Chile, to speak to a group of sixteen including ourselves. The group included Nico and a friend, three of my women friends, the wife of an Air Force neighbour, and the teenage daughters and son of our friends the Manríquez family.

Arthur, of course, had Spanish at his fingertips but we were still fairly limited, especially in deep discussions. His theme was 'Is contact possible with the beyond?' He opened with the universal desire that exists to communicate, using the illustration of a telephone. This was followed by the need in the human heart to contact God, which led on to how this is possible in God coming to us in Christ. He also spoke about the dangers of trying to make contact with other spirits that were not from God. The forty-minute talk was followed by one and a half hours of discussion.

'Almost everyone joined in the discussion, which was sustained the whole time. Several bought books afterwards. The questions and *contributions revealed a very deep spiritual interest on the part of many. We were only sorry that Mario and Bernadita were unable to come. If we are staying here for another eighteen months, then we would certainly consider repeating this type of home meeting at monthly intervals with various Christian professionals taking a theme relevant to their "line".'*

One day I went to collect Andrew and Julian from Los Dominicos playschool only to find no children were there! '*Señora*, you'll find them at *el supermercado*, Almac.' Being our most frequented supermarket I didn't have to search long to find the missing boys. They had been on a learning project about fruit and vegetables. They were able to look and carefully feel the various exhibits.

When I arrived it was the climax of the afternoon. Among the thirty or so olive skinned, dark-haired three and four year olds all dressed in their '*delantales*' (beige-coloured overalls, like boiler suits) were two little rosy-cheeked *rubios*. Incredibly there was no excited shouting to be heard. In fact hardly a sound emanated from them at all. They were all busily engrossed eating biscuits and ice cream! What a treat.

Two days later, a Thursday, was marked by a couple of events. First, Ray fell off a stepladder in the front garden. He had been climbing up to fix the young mimosa tree we had planted to the upstairs veranda to encourage it to grow straight. As he took one step down the ladder broke under him. He fell backwards on to the lawn, first landing on his spine then hitting his head, just missing the rockery. Thursdays were one of the three days he did his voluntary work at the Blood Bank. He didn't go. Instead he went to bed with a thumping head and feeling naturally shaken. When he returned the following Tuesday, his colleagues insisted he saw a neurosurgeon, but thankfully all was well.

The second event was Naomi returning home with her school report. The winter school holidays were to begin. Having got off to a chequered start at Redland, especially in her reluctance to speak Spanish, she had now turned the corner. Great improvement was shown in ten '*buenos*', six '*suficientes*', and no '*deficientes*'. In Spanish dictation she had made only one mistake.

Unfortunately, she returned home not only with her school report, but also with an acute ear infection and a temperature. She also went to bed with a dose of penicillin and missed the last day of the term.

Chilean school terms were known as '*semestres*'. The year was divided into two main holiday sections. The long summer one from just before Christmas until the first week in March and the winter break which was two weeks in July. The rest of the year's academic programme would be punctuated by the inevitable *feriados* commemorating some national battle or hero.

During Easter Ray had introduced an Easter Sunrise Service for the international church in 1972, which was repeated the next year, with the encouragement of chaplain Graham Jack. To see the sun rising was guaranteed providing no man-made obstacle got in the way. The built up area of Providencia, however, wasn't the best of places. Richard Collingwood-Selby gave his permission for the use of Redland School and came along. It was the ideal venue. Ray had to go up several times in the preceding week to accurately time the rising of the sun.

During the service on Easter Sunday at the exact moment the sun began to rise over Cerro Calan, Ray led those present in the triumphant and pivotal fact of the Christian faith:

'Christ is risen.'

Our response was, 'He is risen indeed.'

Over fifty came to that first service.

Involvement in the schools of the children meant that one Saturday in July Ray went to Los Dominicos armed with a shovel and pickaxe. Andrew and Julian wanted to go too. The staff had organized a work-party of parents in the creating of a garden area. This gave me a free morning to do more baking with the surplus Banda Azul (Blue Band) cooking margarine as we were expecting visitors. Doris, the cashier, had telephoned a few days earlier to say there was sugar in Almac. This was the visit that I returned home with five kilos, two more packets of margarine, a large tin of powdered milk, a box of Omo washing detergent and even toilet rolls. What a successful shopping spree!

Our visitors were Chilean Jews. My American friend, Mimi,

had introduced me to the wife, Eugenia. After tea we showed them slides of Israel from our honeymoon trip seven years previously. Eugenia joined in a number of our home group discussions. After they left Nico turned up, unexpectedly, as he frequently did. It was on this occasion that he shared with us his concern about getting killed on the streets of Santiago.

Nico was anxious that we should get to know his parents. We had already met them but only briefly. Nico had three sisters, two younger than he. Juanita, the elder of the two was about eighteen or nineteen with the long dark, slightly wavy hair. Like the majority of Chilean teens and young women, close fitting denim jeans and tee shirts were the dress code of the day (Little has changed in over thirty years!) Her clothes hugged a slender proportionate figure. Chilean women are very beautiful and have often come in the finalists of the Miss World Contest. Monica was about fifteen or sixteen and was shorter in stature with a more athletic build, more like her mother in looks.

Nico's father, Rafael, was very tall, for a Chilean, with dark thick wavy hair and a warm, ready smile. His wife, Juana, was slimly built and with small facial features. Juanita baby-sat for us, while we went to their home, a short distance from us.

'They have an architect-designed, chalet-type house with an open plan downstairs, modern parquet flooring, ... indoor plants with large glossy leaves made the open stairs look very attractive. They are such nice people.'

This Sunday was particularly memorable because in the morning Ray preached 'with a view' – a view to being appointed or not depending on how the sermon goes down! This practice, familiar in Free Churches is not one the Anglican Church adopts. It can be rather an artificial way of judging a person's suitability even granted it's not the only criteria. Decision time was now fast approaching.

My Roman Catholic friend (the other Julia from the Headmaster's wife), whose adult daughter had severe learning disabilities and was severely handicapped, invited me to go with her to a charismatic prayer and worship group. I went. It was held at Las Monjas Inglesas (The English Nuns) but it was all in Spanish. There were about sixty present, including our very dear priest friend Juan de Castro. I felt very much at home in the worship: singing, prayer, bible reading and the sharing of testimonies. The presence of the Lord was very evident.

My diary records that it was '*a real privilege to be there.*' I had already introduced Julia to '*Padre*' Juan as she was unhappy in her own Roman Catholic Church and I felt the fellowship at Santo Toribio Church, of which he was priest, might be more helpful for her. This was the same church that we went to for the Sunday morning service, as a result of the Archbishop and Bishops calling for a National Day of Prayer.

Ray sent a translation of the prayer in his next letter home.

'*Father of Mercy, behold us meeting in the Name of Jesus Christ, Your Son, with the grief over our country. Forgive us for every time we have been violent with our brother. Free us from hate, selfishness and bitterness. Lord ... give us your Holy Spirit in order to illumine our consciences and give us the strength to construct with truthfulness, justice and love a great nation of brothers. Amen.*'

The whole month of July 1973 seemed to be a never ending round of visitors: Argentinian, American, Chilean and English including a number of our mission colleagues, our Anglican Bishop, David and also '*Padre*' Juan. This was just a foretaste of what our developing ministry would become over the next years, with one huge difference that, in the years to come, the queues were not part of it. A count of people in my diary shows that fifty-nine people came to our home either for meals or just coffee and biscuits, some invited and others just turned up. Among the latter was the Skinner family of seven but thankfully they brought their tea with them! We also had several invitations out. Such was the climate of generosity and friendships. No political disturbances and hard times were going to rob us of being human. In fact, it was out of hard times that friendships were cemented.

There were of course sadder moments. An empty gas cylinder was stolen. We discovered it was missing early one morning towards the end of the month. We had noticed the front gate was ajar when we returned home early evening the previous day but thought nothing of it. Two days later, during the night, the regulator valve together with its tubing had been cut off the cylinder in use. Not only were they very expensive to replace but almost impossible to find in the current climate.

Neli, a good friend, as well as a help in the home in the past, had just returned to give me some hours of work in readiness for a quick exit if Ray was appointed. The day before she happened to say that she and her husband had moved into their own place. She mentioned that they hadn't had any gas since Monday. Ray writes they *'were having to cook their meals at husband's parents' place … because they had been unable to get gas cylinders … So when the regulator disappeared, we faced her with it on Friday morning. She appeared to be innocent, but broke down and called her husband here. She was going to go back home, but decided to see the morning out. We weren't entirely satisfied with her husband's story* [he was known physically to abuse her] *but it's so difficult trying to cross-question someone in another language.'* I really did believe Neli to be free of blame and we remained good friends.

We were also saddened by the demise of Patsy and the eight baby rabbits, but these weren't the only deaths that month. Ray writes:

'Thurs. saw the beginning of another lorry owners' strike, which has included petrol. Then during the night [July 27th] *the naval aide-de-camp of President Allende was assassinated at his home, just off Providencia by extremists. Both sides had a slanging match blaming each other … they have a suspect and it looks as though govt. supporters are responsible … there is no petrol available. If we have to pack up and transport things in the next few days, we shall need another miracle.'*

This high-ranking naval officer was Captain Arturo Araya, who was killed when he went out on to the veranda of his home to investigate an explosion. Originally it was thought to be the work of *'Patria y Libertad'* but in fact it came from the left. As a result Allende agreed to meet Patricio Aylwin, President of the Christian Democrats for a dialogue in an effort to resolve some of the nation's problems.

All the events of this chapter (just a summary) took place in just over three weeks. The first week of August was even more frantic. We were going home. Jean Marshall, a SAMS teacher, was at our home on the last day of the month, enjoying the results of Banda Azul used in yet another bake when the telephone rang. It was 8.45 pm.

'Ray, we are delighted to invite you to be chaplain of the Community Church … We look forward to you, Gill and the family being among us.'

It had been a unanimous decision. We knew our suspense would be over either that day or the next as the church council met that evening. I had written in my diary on waiting for the results how I had *experienced tremendous peace all day … a peace passing all understanding and not my own.'*

A telephone call on Wednesday August 1st assured us that the berth on the *Rossini* was still available, even though they had said they would only keep the reservation until the Monday. It was now all systems go. We had only eight days to do all the required documentation, pack up house and transfer items to 'the Manse', pack suitcases for five, and with the country in chaos and no petrol available – what a challenge!

But then we have a God who responds to challenges. We were also blest with many friends who magnificently came on board with so many offers of help.

It was with this news that Ray closed what was to be his last letter home before we arrived, but not before four-year-old Andrew, sitting on Daddy's knee at the typewriter, added his own secret note to his grandparents – *'ytyiopiu df65'*. We were never good at deciphering cryptic code!

Chapter 24
Going Home

The sun broke through the early morning clouds. Winter was slowly giving way to spring. Would the 'sun' ever break through with its warmth and healing bringing hope to a country caught in the tightening grip of the 'winter' of its current political life? The cry that was being heard increasingly from many lips was for the military to act and deliver the country from an inevitable fast approaching civil war. For this family of five, needing to 'thaw out' from a very long 'winter' the sun was beginning to shine and to shine brightly.

Always up early with our three never failing alarm clocks, we got up even earlier one morning this busy month of July. There was so much to do.

'We're going to England.'

'Soon we'll see Grandma and Grandpa, Grandma and Papa.'

'Going on a plane,' piped up the youngest, not that he really knew what this meant. He was, after all, only eleven months old on his first and only flying experience, two years previously. Such excitement. Naomi, Andrew and Julian could hardly contain themselves.

We were up just after 6.00 am. Neli arrived after breakfast to help me begin sorting and packing. Two cabin trunks had to be packed ready for dispatch to Chile's main port. Here they would be loaded on to the *Rossini* ready for us to connect with them, in less than two weeks, at the port of Callao, Peru. Friends returning to England and booked on the same boat had offered to look after them until we boarded. David Pytches, in Santiago, for a couple of nights was to pick them on his way home to Valparaiso.

Meanwhile Ray left for the centre to begin the dreaded *tramites* – not knowing what he'd find. Every trip down town was becoming fraught with the unexpected and at times dangerous.

So very many friends rallied round to help us with the pressure of these last few days. Willing homes were opened to have the children, freeing Ray to do the documentation and me to pack, willing hands to fetch and carry, even with a petrol shortage, willing hearts generously sought out *despedida* (goodbye) presents. One of these was a pair of leather bound wooden bookends.

General Andersen, a tall white-haired and fair-skinned gentleman, lived opposite us. He was retired and, by nature, retiring. Very likely, with such a surname and colouring, he had a Scandinavian pedigree. We never did find out. The General was one of our military neighbours and, in fact among them all, the one we knew least. Imagine our surprise then when he came across the *pasaje* from his house, and knocked on our front door with an invitation to dinner. We weren't the only guests. The husband of the other couple was a pilot of Lan-Chile (Chile's national airline). He knew English and in fact was *encantado* (delighted) with a chance to practise the language.

Our military neighbours were fantastic and pulled out the stops in a number of ways. The Air Force husband of my friend, María Diaz, who lived two doors away, got us some petrol to make the several trips with household goods to what was to become our next home. Comandante Luis Valdéz, who lived in the corner house and whose little girl I had given an injection to, got us petrol when our final morning came. Without this provision we could never have left. Another general strike was arranged for Thursday, August 9th. There was also a demonstration of government supporters planned on the day we were leaving for La Paz, Bolivia en route home. There was no petrol at the pumps, taxis were off the road and we had to get to the other side of the city to Pudahuel airport.

Nico was ever ready to help Ray with the boxes and boxes

of crockery, saucepans, our books, children's books and toys, rocking horse, tricycles etc. He and Ray made two trips with a full vehicle to the suburbs of Providencia, about four miles from Las Condes. We were moving from The Almond Trees to The Violets. What remained familiar were the ever-present Andes, although more obscured by housing than in our present home. While Nico was helping Ray, Lydia, still in Chile on holiday, was a great help to me sorting and cleaning out cupboards.

The Manse was a large solid looking four bedroom detached house situated in Las Violetas and was just over a mile away from the Community Church. It was the home of the minister belonging to the Union Church before the merger. Unlike our beginnings in Los Almendros, where there were no trees when we first arrived, 'Las Violetas' as we came to refer to it, was surrounded on three sides by gardens. There was both a front, back and side garden with a number of mature bushes and trees. Three stand out in my memory from the days we lived there.

A huge incredibly productive fig tree was at the bottom of the garden. At the right season the plump, blue-purple figs, just ripe for picking, were delicious. The only problem was that there were so many that a good few would fall with a plop to the ground, burst open and leave a very dark stain on the paving stone paths. This was the same fig tree that in the months to come Andrew and Julian would climb into and converse with the nuns next door. Nestling in the tree was a simply constructed tree house just waiting to be explored.

The persimmon tree always looked at its best when denuded of its leaves, the ripe orange-ball fruit stood out on the bare brown branches like Christmas decorations. Humming birds found the red flowers of the large poinsettia bush too good to resist. As this bush was framed against the wall of the house, overhanging the open entrance leading from the garden to the enclosed terraced area, we could easily watch these fascinating birds.

The garden was huge and gave the children plenty of scope to let off their boundless energy – a far cry from humble beginnings in the East End of London. The open-sided tiled terraced area was on a corner of the house. It was furnished with cane furniture, relaxing chairs, as well as a large wooden table and chairs. The only disadvantage of this patio area was that it made the open-plan interior dining room and lounge dark. The kitchen was also big, with two open entrances and between the two, against the wall, was a very big freezer.

Each working day morning during these last eight days Ray would continue in the city centre getting our documentation in order. Help was on hand to get all this through in record time including the necessary paper work for our trip to both Bolivia and Peru before picking up the *Rossini*. Our consul, Derek and his wife, Grace, had shown us so much kindness in a number of ways. They became firm friends for many years to come.

Just three days to go before departure, Andrew went down with a temperature and cough. The following day, two days before the announced General Strike, all transport went on strike, as a protest of the petrol situation. For these drivers this shortage was crucial to their existence. In this case, Lydia's father, in the US diplomatic service, came to the rescue and took Ray to the centre in his car. We knew Lydia's parents well, having been at their home a number of times, including Thanksgiving. What we didn't know then was that her father allegedly worked for the CIA!

This was the irony of our situation in Chile. On the one hand, our friendly neighbours were military and in only a matter of weeks would be aligned against the left-wing government, making international headlines, and on the other hand a number of our friends were Marxists, supporting the government. Also among our increasing international friends were both protestant and catholic, rich and poor. These divides were man made. As far as God was concerned his love reached to all regardless. We were called to cross these divides.

On Thursday, August 9th at 4.30 am, while it was still dark, we stumbled out of bed, weary but excited. Two of our SAMS colleagues came to the airport as well as our dear Nico to see us off. Considering the early hour, the scarcity of petrol and the tense situation with the country coming to a standstill and both protestors and supporters gathering ready for confrontation, the farewells of our friends meant so much.

In no time we were up in the air. Unlike our first plane journey into Chile when we crossed over the dividing line of the Andes separating Chile from Argentina, we now had the snow covered 'spine' on our right as we headed north crossing the dividing line of the desert separating Chile from Bolivia. From the plane we had a wonderful view. I looked down and saw pushing up among the seemingly endless canopy of saffron, caramel and cinnamon colours, what appeared to be inverted ice cream cones. Out of the inverted top and spilling over the sides the 'ice cream' was frozen in its flow. The two most impressive inverted cones, each with their white tops vividly standing out from their desert surroundings, were the twin volcanoes of Saint Peter and Saint Paul.

There were very few passengers on the flight. The present climate in Chile was not conducive for travel unless you were leaving the country for greater stability. Bolivia, certainly, would not have been on most people's itinerary. Potentially this could well be a case of 'out of the frying pan and into the fire'. The cabin crew was very attentive to our needs, pointing out sights of interest. Our three were the only children and one hostess was totally besotted by our three-year-old *'rubiosito'* (little blond).

What were my thoughts as we left Chile? Relief that so much time spent queuing for food could, at least for a time, be forgotten. But what of the country? What was going to happen? Would any of our friends get killed in a civil war? Only one person known to us had committed her life to Christ as a direct result of our ministry. There were no big success stories of a church being planted to share with our supporting churches back home. How would our two and a half years as missionaries in Chile be judged? What did God think? Had we failed? With so many questions milling around in my head only time would tell but, even more importantly, only eternity would give the final answer to these questions. One thing we knew for certain was that we would never be the same again. The testings and trials had had their refining purpose.

We had been warned that once we arrived in La Paz we should take it very, very gently because of the high altitude. The plane touched down and with this in mind we slowly walked from it carrying our hand luggage. We took a taxi to the Methodist guesthouse where we were staying for two nights. On the way from the airport we saw a bus run out of control. It careered down an incline embedding itself in the wall of an *adobe* house. Some of the Indian passengers jumped from the emergency exits. In the few moments it took to slow down and circumnavigate the area no one was badly hurt, as far as we could tell.

What really struck us, apart from feeling just a little breathless as we breathed in the rarified air and began our slow walk, was the complete contrast from the Chilean capital. There was hardly a European looking *Latino* in sight. As we entered La Paz itself, the streets were no longer filled with mostly olive or fair skinned, comparatively well-heeled, men and women; grey suited-businessmen, smartly dressed women in subdued colours and denim clad *jovenes*. The streets of La Paz, by contrast, were vibrant with such a kaleidoscope of colour.

Interspersed among the westernized dressed Bolivian, were Aymará women in their amazingly brightly coloured voluminous skirts. Higher up and draped around the chest, falling down the back in a pouch, was material of various striped colours. In this pouch was either the day's shopping or a toddler peeping out over the folds. Even higher up and at a jaunty angle perched on the head was a bowler hat.

This was our first introduction to the Bolivian Aymará Indian woman. It was quite amazing to see a hat, that for us represented the smart London banker in Threadneedle Street (in our former days in Shoreditch), being sported by Indian women the other side of the world! The paler olive skin was replaced among the pure Aymará by a much darker shade and the hair instead of flowing freely or immaculately 'coiffured' was worn in two pigtails.

After a good night's sleep we set out to do a bit of exploring, our lungs and the rate of our heart beat reminded us in no uncertain terms of the need to take it slowly.

La Paz itself, surrounded by mountains, is at a height of over 12,000 feet. The scenery was beautiful in its starkness and the constant changing colours of the rocks was a never-to-be-forgotten sight. The colours changed from a light yellow sandstone first thing in the early morning sun through to light terracotta and on to a rich deeper red terracotta as the sun went down. The August sky in daytime was at its brightest winter blue and at night became a star studded inky blue.

San Francisco cathedral was our first stop. It was four hundred and fifty years old and built in characteristic Spanish colonial style. What really upset us was to see such an ornate interior with so much gold decoration and a poor Aymará woman with bare feet begging outside.

I left Ray resting on some seats in the plaza with the children while I went on my own to the Indian market. The brightly coloured woven materials, the beautifully carved wooden and silver ware showed an artistic skill handed down from generation to generation. We met up again, bought some provisions for lunch and supper and made our way back to the guesthouse. With so much travel to fit in we didn't want to risk tummy upsets, so we restricted our meals to fruit we could peel and tinned fish. We drank filtered water at the guesthouse and bought bottled water when out and about. By late morning we were tired, hungry and feeling the effects of the altitude – increasing breathlessness, a racing heart, weak legs and the occasional stomach cramps. The thumping headache would come later, but first we had to get back to the Methodist hostel. The problem we faced was this involved a steep walk up from the plaza.

So many plazas in South America have, as their central focus, large statues of their historical heroes. Plaza del Sucre was such. Antonio José de Sucre was General to Simon Bolívar, the great liberator of much of South America and from whom Bolivia had taken its name. The two made a formidable pair on their campaigns of liberation from Spanish rule. In December 1824, the strategic battle of Ayacucho, in lower Peru, won by Sucre for Bolívar, finished Spanish rule on the continent. This was followed by the liberation of Bolivia with the creation of a government and the distribution of some land for the Indians.

'After a dramatic attack on his life, he left public office in 1830, turning over the presidency of Colombia to Sucre. Since Sucre had previously been president of Bolivia he takes rank as one of the few men in history ever to have been a chief executive of two countries.'[1]

Ray was ahead with Naomi and Andrew and I followed behind hand in hand with Julian. We hadn't gone far when a little voice whimpered, 'I'm tired, Mummy. My legs hurt.'

'So am I, Julian. Let's rest a bit,' I replied.

My heart was beating fast, my breath coming out in gasps. The altitude was really kicking in. We collapsed on the front door step of what I seem to recall was a house or perhaps a closed front door of a shop to get our breath back before continuing.

Once back we all had a good rest before tackling any lunch.

In the afternoon we took a taxi to the Valley of the Moon. Struggling with the effects of altitude finding a bus meant too much exertion. Taxis were frequent and cheap anyway. The landscape of this valley, resembling a moonscape rather than a landscape, was stark and spectacular; jagged pinnacles of rock formed by the erosion of the yellow sandstone, changing colour as the sun continued its daily circuit. Silhouetted high on a pinnacle stood a lone figure clad in a poncho, a haunting melody emanating from his direction. '*Altiplano*' music is breathtakingly beautiful, at times vibrant at times melancholy. The main instruments are the *caña* (made from bamboo), the ten-stringed *charango* (similar to a tiny guitar) and the *zampoña* (panpipes).

It was hard to imagine we'd only been in Bolivia for two days and yet managed, with the children, to see so much. We were anxious to see Lake Titicaca and would love to have taken a boat to visit the Island of the Sun and the Island of the Moon but it wasn't possible, given the tight schedule we had. Thirty-one years later I revisited Lake Titicaca and even sailed on it. Andrew and his four children, Daniel, Iloni, Joelle and Angelina

---

[1] John Gunther: *Inside South America*. Hamish Hamilton Ltd. p. 117

took their grandmother, 'Nana', by boat on the Lake to visit La Isla del Sol.

Lake Titicaca is huge, measuring over 300 kilometres by approximately 150 kilometres. It is at a height of over 3810 metres and reaches 370 metres in depth and is shared with Bolivia's neighbour, Peru. Rushes grow in abundance at the lakeside edge. These are used to make the famous reed boats and balsa rafts – the former more as a tourist attraction now than a functional means for fishing or transport. Motorized boats bring the indigenous people into more modern living. As Bolivia is land-locked, the vast Lake, serves as the base for the country's navy.

Saturday we left for Peru and set off by taxi from La Paz bound for Puno. We paid the handsome sum of ninety US dollars, a lot of money for us in 1973. With infrequent and slow buses, mindful of a culture when the unexpected can all too easily happen, a taxi was more prudent. We had too many memories of buses liable to break down and crossing the *altiplano* might leave us stranded for many an hour. The plan was to take a train to Cuzco as our sights were set on visiting Macchu Picchu. From Cuzco a flight had been booked to Lima, the capital and from here to board the *Rossini*.

The taxi driver was a fine example of indigenous Aymará, with his short thickset stature, dark caramel skin and high cheekbones. Almond shaped eyes, with finely etched creases in the corners, corresponded to even deeper 'crevasses' in his forehead, topped by a thatch of straight ink black hair. His expression gave nothing away as to what he was thinking or feeling. Even the three poncho-clad, blond, blue-eyed children didn't draw from him the same enthusiastic response that a Chilean taxi driver would have displayed.

Our journey took us across the high plateau for the very first time, but by no means our last. The bleak desert landscape, with its inhospitable *altiplano*, held a fascination to be explored on future occasions.

The Tiahuanaco ruins were our first stop. Preceding the Inca civilization, the growth of viable centres of culture of the

Waru indigenous peoples first in Cuzco and also at Tiahuanaco represented a major development in Bolivian history. This centre from 100 AD advanced in pottery and metal, alloy, tin, bronze and later silver. Agriculture formed an important part of the shared indigenous cultures of both Peru and Bolivia, the domestication of all the known plants and animals. Five hundred years later it had spread its influence beyond its local site. Its importance in Andean history owes itself to its dominance within the whole highland region from the seventh century until the thirteenth century AD. The square or rectangular platforms surrounded by sandstone and basalt blocks are characteristic of the religious centers of Tiahuanaco culture.[2]

Leaving the famous ruins we skirted the edge of Lake Titicaca shimmering in the bright morning sunlight. As we left Bolivian territory to enter Peruvian, we found an abundance of cattle, sheep, llamas, alpacas and pigs.

At Puno, to our dismay but not entirely surprised, we discovered there was no train to Cuzco until Tuesday, four days later. We needed to get there if we were to make Macchu Picchu. It seemed our plans were well and truly thwarted. But these Chilean groomed *'gringitos'* had been learning some hard lessons. We were not giving up that easily. There yet could be a way around this latest hiccup. After all what would we do for three full days in Puno? A few more enquiries to several officials (we had learned never to take just one person's answer) and we found the solution to our *problema*. If we took a train to Juliaca, from there we could catch a train to Cuzco on the Monday. This extra day meant all the difference.

Installed in Juliaca, the five of us slept in two single beds, the three children lying side by side horizontally and Kay and I occupying the other. There was a shower out in a courtyard, with four walls making a square but completely open to the sky. At an already high altitude it was freezing!

My diary records that we met a Seventh Day Adventist nurse who invited us to the hospital for supper and that the following

---

[2] Herbert Klein: *Bolivia: The Evolution of a Multi-Ethnic Society.* Oxford University Press. pp. 13, 14

day, Sunday, we had all meals at the hospital. Neither of us can recall how this came about but then it is almost thirty-three years ago! What I did write was that Naomi was still feeling the effects of the altitude, that we tried to find the Baptist Church without success, bought some small gifts from the Indian market and spent the rest of the day quietly.

Monday morning we were up at the crack of dawn ready to catch the train to Cuzco. The platform was fast filling up with locals and tourists. To our surprise we had noticed that the backpacker tourists had bought first class tickets. We bought the most economical, but when the train arrived on the platform it was already well filled.

'Gill, you try one door and I'll try another so whoever gets there first can save seats for all five of us.'

Holding hands with Naomi and Julian, leaving Ray with Andrew and the luggage, I spotted though the compartment window of our third-class section of the train empty seats facing us (the wooden-slatted seats ran the full length of the compartment, the centre ones back to back and the outer two running the length of the windows on either side). I shouted to Ray that I would aim for these seats in the centre that would easily seat all five of us.

As I made my way down the compartment an Aymará woman touched my arm '*Señora, es muy sucia.*' It really was dirty, as someone hadn't made it to the toilet in time.

'Quick, Ray, the opposite direction!' I shouted.

We managed to get seats together, three of us on one side and the other two opposite. We shared our compartment with colourful characters, both in their dress and their bundles of market produce. There was a Peruvian man dressed in rathera shabby western-style suit, sitting opposite me and next to Ray. He was very affable and engaged us in conversation. I noticed that he was chewing what I took to be chewing gum. In fact he was chewing coca leaves, used to combat the effects of altitude sickness. Unfortunately, a regular clearing of the throat, followed by spitting, punctuated the conversation. The coca contents were deposited inches from my feet. After a couple of hours and with little floor space left, I said to Ray, 'If he doesn't stop soon I'll have to say something! He may even have TB.' Fortunately he got off the train before this became necessary.

A young Indigenous woman fascinated us all. She was probably no more than eighteen or twenty. With full regalia of voluminous coloured skirt and bowler hat perched on her head and carrying her weekly shop in her *aguayo* (the multi-coloured wrap slung over her back) she marched down the train. She looked immensely strong, a veritable Amazon, and was evidently known to a number of the passengers. Eyes flashing in her high-cheek boned face, and in no uncertain way, she made claim to available space both for her wares as well as herself. I was glad that we had not met her earlier in our search for vacant seats. I was certainly no match for this Peruvian Queen Bee.

The scenery was magnificent. The snow capped mountains of the Peruvian Andes becoming gradually higher the further our slow, very slow, train took us. I seem to recall in the earlier hours of travel there was so much green, with an abundance of trees and also grass mountain slopes, unlike the high plateau of Bolivia. The sheer beauty helped make up for the less savoury aspects our senses recorded of that particular journey. Naomi still remembers that journey as both fascinating and enjoyable.

Once in Cuzco we had to find accommodation for our scheduled three nights.

'*Lo siento mucho señor, no hay habitaciones.*'

Not just once, but several times we were to receive the same negative answer on enquiring for an available room. It seemed every hotel and hostel was full. Eventually we found one. It was rated third class, which in comparison to English standards would be off the numerical scale! To our surprise there was an English woman with a North American husband also booked in. Like us they too had drawn blank in their enquiries. They advised us what to see in the one day we each had in the city itself, due to our pre-planned decision to visit Macchu-Picchu separately.

Our next *problema* was trying to exchange our US dollars. A man who had lived for thirty years in Chile was able to help us.

He took us to the Hotel Cuzco where we managed to get some local currency and were each able to buy our tickets for the next two days visit to the famous Inca ruins.

The day Ray went to the most visited of Peru's ancient past, I took the three children sightseeing in the city centre. Here archaeological remnants of highly cultured former days, belonging to the original inhabitants, were found alongside impressive monuments of a culture bent on conquering and colonizing. One street, lined on either side by large stonewalls consisting of large rectangular stone slabs, is famous for one special stone. This very large stone has twelve angles. The walls, which were built by the Incas, contrast vividly in their plainness to the ornate interiors of the cathedral and churches. My diary refers to the cloisters and the various paintings of the church of La Merced. It also mentions the church being so ornate and a very telling entry as I describe the gory blood stained burial statue of Christ dressed in a red velvet sequined loincloth as '*repulsive*' We visited the Archaeological museum in Tigre Street, fascinated by the burial posture of the well-preserved Indian mummies. As in the Atacama Desert of north Chile, the position adopted by the mummies was that of a squatting posture.

With so much to see and limited time it was only possible to make very brief diary notes – and of course even more importantly three wonderful little ones to look after! You may be surprised we attempted so much. It was always our policy to do things together as a family wherever possible. Not surprisingly they have all enjoyed travel and look back to their childhood days as happy and adventurous.

Like all parents we have made many mistakes and certainly would have done some things differently, with hindsight, but a comment from our daughter-in-law stands out in my memory. One of the things that impressed her when she and Andrew first met was how he said that he couldn't have had a happier childhood.

Not all the memories of travel in Peru were such good ones for him, however. It was in the airport of Lima (he insists it was Lima although I thought it was in La Paz) on our arrival from Cuzco, that he left behind his much loved cuddly rabbit, Ladybird book and a Matchbox car.

Our hosts in Lima were SAMS colleagues. Bill Flagg was the Anglican bishop of Bolivia and Peru – a much loved and respected man. His wife, Marjorie, made us so very welcome when we arrived by taxi to their home at Miraflores. After a week of 'roughing it' this was sheer luxury. I managed to get all the washing up to date and in the afternoon took the children plus two Flagg children to the beach.

The next morning was another treat for our two boys. (Naomi preferred to stay behind and play with the Flagg girls.) In the Plaza San Martín was yet another military band. It seems from our original flight to Chile when we saw the military band in Sierra Leone, that military bands had featured large in so many ports of call on our varying journeys.

Lima's Cathedral, in the Plaza de Armas, was not as elaborate as that in Cuzco. The brief diary entry records that we didn't see the remains of *conquistador* Pizarro because we '*didn't know they were there!*' Relics feature large in the cathedrals of Latin America as in very many Roman Catholic and Orthodox churches.

We woke on Saturday morning, after our final night's sleep on the *terra firma* of South America as first-term SAMS missionaries. We would return in another capacity. We took a taxi to the port of Callao to board the *Rossini* which had been hugging the Pacific coast of the 'Long Bean' from half way down, or more accurately half way up. Hopefully somewhere tucked away in a safe place were two cabin trunks. Also aboard the ship were English friends. It meant we had some company and the children some friends for the next three weeks.

The Ayton family whom we had met in Chile but didn't know well had been approached by David Pytches to look after our trunks. Philip and Dorothy Miller, also SAMS personnel from Argentina, had travelled over to Callao to pick up the *Rossini*.

Sailing in the ship was the part of the journey home I had been most looking forward to. It wasn't only the interesting ports of call on the way to Europe, including the Panama Canal, but for this weary worn wife and mother the rest it promised to provide. The stress of queuing for food, stretching the mind to think of innovative ways of meal planning was going to be a thing of the past – at least for a time.

We had no idea what kind of a Chile we would be returning to early in December. Meanwhile, to sit down to a meal in the ship's dining saloon and even have a choice of menu, let alone having it put in front of you, three times a day for the next three weeks was pure luxury. No more threat, at least for us, of civil war, assassinations and bombs, would give us time to be refreshed. Hopefully we would begin to put on some of the weight we had lost before meeting up with family. However, we hadn't yet left the waters of South America.

My letter home from the ship as we were approaching the Ecuadorian port of Guayaquil had an all too familiar ring,

'We've heard a rumour that there's been a revolution in Ecuador so that we may not be able to get off the boat in Guayaquil. I'm just going to find out. Returned! The Purser couldn't really inform us but said there was unrest but he didn't know if a revolution had actually taken place, and we shall be advised accordingly when we arrive [sic].'

It was once again a case of *'así es la vida'* (such is life) – a phrase usually said with a resigned shrug of the shoulders and about as common on Chilean lips as *'tengo un problema'*.

The same day we crossed the Equator, we heard news from Chile that the strike was still on and unrest in the Fuerza Aire de Chile (FaCh), due to the resignation of General César Ruiz from the cabinet. As a result Allende had asked him to resign from his role as head of the Air Force. On our return from Buenaventura in Colombia where we disembarked to buy coffee beans we heard there was fighting between right and left extremists outside the Chilean Congress and the burning of the Trade Union headquarters.

A day later we were sailing through the Panama Canal. It took all day with so much shipping and having to wait our turn to pass through the various locks. Once we arrived on the Caribbean side of the canal Ray went down with 'flu. Running a high temperature in such a steamy place anyway only added to his misery. At the same time we began to notice the sea was becoming increasingly rough.

Cartagena on the Caribbean coast of Colombia was the first city liberated from the Spaniards by Símon Bolívar in their fight for independence. I disembarked with the three children and other passengers whom we had befriended and did some sightseeing.

The old part of the city was very colonial in architecture with winding narrow cobbled streets. The Spaniards built the fortress and adjoining walls, as a defence against the French and English. Three museums were housed in a building that was formerly where the Inquisition took place. I bought two sets of maracas for half a dollar. Julian then decided he wanted to go to the toilet. Fortunately we hadn't left the museum site so there was a WC on hand. Suddenly I heard Julian shouting with fright. In the next WC were five parrots their raucous shrieking giving him such a scare. Why they were there I had no idea. We were still in Latin America: '*así es la vida!*'

That night the seas were very rough again and in the morning few passengers turned up in the dining saloon for breakfast.

Curaçao was our next stop. Sunday while still on board we held our own Service with our friends. Ray led and Philip preached while I provided Sunday school for our three and the Ayton children.

The next morning, Monday, we disembarked at La Guaira, theVenezuelan port. Here we caught a local bus to the capital, Caracas, seventeen kilometres away. Caracas was the birthplace of Símon Bolívar, the country's hero. Bolívar was the liberator from the Spanish for a number of South American republics, Peru, Ecuador, Nueva Granada and Bolivia.

On board the ship was one passenger I'll never forget. She was around fifty, quite tall for a *Latina*, and with a full curvaceous figure. She wore her dark hair sleekly drawn back into a bun. She wasn't particularly beautiful in appearance but was striking to say the least. She carried herself with great poise and I referred to her as 'the Queen'. She was travelling alone and dined alone. Her arrival at mealtimes always caught our attention as her table was near to ours. What fascinated me were her painted lips. It was the first time I had seen such purple lipstick and what made the lips stand out even more against the dark olive skin was an even darker blue/purple outline. Her cabin was also near to ours and we noticed the door was left open late at night on occasions with a few comings and goings of the crew!

Due to the rough seas there was an increasing scarcity of passengers to be seen, but within a couple of days the near-empty dining room began to fill again but only for a short time. One by one passengers were going down like flies as a number of infections began to spread, sore throats, swollen glands, high temperatures and tummy bugs. Julian and his parents all succumbed. 'The Queen' also failed to make an appearance.

King Neptune and his slaves made their appearance on Thursday, August 30th when we crossed the Tropic of Cancer. I'm not sure so many years later why we didn't have the celebration on crossing the Equator but my diary clearly refers to this celebration on this date, when many of us ended up in the swimming pool in various costumes and painted faces. It was in *Rossini*'s pool that Naomi swam for the first time on her own.

We now left behind us land that would no longer be a feature for days to come as we headed into the vast expanse of sea. Activities on board gained in momentum, together with feature films, deck games, competitions and a full children's programme. There were fancy dress balls, the Ayton girls winning first prize. Ray and I went as king and court jester.

Eight days later we landed at Santa Cruz, Tenerife, head and limbs still aching from the virus that had been going round. The next day Philip and Dorothy went down with the bug and I went to bed with a high fever, followed by Naomi (Julian was still unwell).

Two items of news gave us something to talk about. A cholera outbreak had spread to Genoa and a letter from my parents mentioned hurricane 'Batenda' had done a lot of damage in Mexico. Ray took Andrew on to the Bridge and, on mentioning the rough seas we had on 24th and 25th to the Captain, learnt that we had experienced the effects of the hurricane. We also learnt we would be sailing through the Strait of Gibraltar at night. Not to miss this we decided to stay up in the hopes of seeing the Rock. We stood out on deck and could just manage to see its outline and twinkling lights dotted about. Our first view was so unlike the view I have today as I write this current chapter. Thirty-three years after that first faint silhouette of the Rock, today we're able to walk out onto the balcony of the Chaplain's house in Estepona, where we've been for the past six weeks covering the locum, and see the Rock in all its grandeur.

On arrival in Barcelona we took a 'plane for our final journey home. Unexpectedly we were allocated the only seats available, first class! And so we arrived back in the homeland in style and to a wonderful reunion with parents.

Three days later in the afternoon Ray's father called us urgently to the television set,

'Ray, Gill, come quickly, something's happening in Chile!'

We dropped what we were doing and ran into the lounge. There on the screen in front of us was the Moneda Palace in Santiago with plumes of smoke billowing from within. Overhead, planes zoomed, dropping carefully targeted bombs on the Presidential suite.

It was the first media spotlighted September 11th. Another would occur a year into the new Millennium. Our arrival in Chile was under Allende. Our return would be under Pinochet.

Lake Llanquihue with Volcano Osorno in background.

Osorno Volcano.

Upturned tree following eruption of Volcano Llaima.

Andrew enjoying mud bath in
thermal waters high in the Andes near border with Argentina.

Statue of Christ of the Andes - on the border of Chile with Argentina.

'Los Cuernos' - Paine National Park.

Me eating a 'picaroco' during our 'curanto' meal - Tenglo Island.

Mapuche church - Ray and my father right of back row, Naomi, kneeling third from left.

Icebergs in the lagoon of San Rafael, October 2000.

Left: Grave of Pringle Stokes - Captain of HMS Beagle.

Aqui. yacen los restos del
C.C. Pringles Stokes, R.N Comandante
y activo hidrógrapo del BSM."BEAGLE"
Permaneció dos años levantando nuestras
costas desde el Estrecho de Magallanes
hasta el Golpo de Penas.
Agotado por las penurias de su expedición,
los malos tiempos y las constantes
situaciones peligrosas, falleció el
12 de Agosto de 1828.

Plaque commemorating his two-year arduous sailing in the southern waters of Chile culminating in his death, 12 August 1828.

Monument to Gabriela Mistral.

Fertile Elqui Valley - near Vicuña.

Avocado tree - Elqui Valley.

Ray at the Pisco Distilley - Vicuña.

*Collecting firewood - camping holiday
at Guanaqueros.*

Inca ruins at Machu Picchu, Peru.

*Andrew and Julian at Tiahuanaco
Ruins, Bolivia.*

Andrew at Tiahuanaco.

Lake Titicaca - Island of the Sun in the background.

'Altiplano' - The High Plateau of Bolivia. Photo Andrew Smith.

Llamas.

*Andrew with street children from
Alalay Home - La Paz.*

Valley of the Moon - La Paz.

Carol's home help - Flora with José.

*Carol and Andrew with their family -
from left Joelle, Daniel, Iloni
and Angelina.*

299

The Iguassú Falls - 1988.

The boat in which we sailed down the Amazon.

A fishing success - one of the three piranhas caught.

Our shared meal on board including piranhas on the menu.

Chapter 25
Catching Breath and Catching Up

The next day's media coverage left open the question as to whether President Allende's death was an assassination or suicide. Each person's answer to that question would depend upon his political persuasion, until much later when the facts came to light. Today few would opt for the assassination view, but in those turbulent and suspicious years wild rumours based on high running emotion circulated both nationally and internationally.

Nathaniel Davis quotes at length the script of Allende's last address to the nation. This was at 9.30 am and was broadcast by Radio Magallanes, the pro-government station. I quote from part of the broadcast.

'Surely this will be my last opportunity to address you ... My words are not spoken in bitterness, but in disappointment. They will be a moral judgement on those who have betrayed the oath they took as soldiers of Chile, as legitimately designated commanders-in-chief ....

'I shall pay with my life for the loyalty of the people ... They have the might and they can enslave us, but they cannot halt the world's social processes, not with crimes, nor with guns ...

'Surely radio Magallenes will soon be silenced ... it does not matter. You will continue to hear me ... My legacy will remain that of a worthy man who was loyal to his country ....

'The people should defend themselves, but not sacrifice themselves. The people should not let themselves be riddled with bullets nor cut down, but they should not let themselves be humiliated either ....

'May you go forward in the knowledge that, sooner rather than later,

the great avenues will open once again along which free citizens will march in order to build a better society ….

'*Long live Chile! Long live the People! Long live the Workers!*

'*These are my last words, and I am sure that my sacrifice will not be in vain …'.*

According to Davis, Allende's military aides wanted to talk with the President on his own but Allende's personal guards took much firm persuasion to acquiesce with their President's willingness for this to happen. In a brief dialogue lasting less than ten minutes the aides failed to persuade him of the 'futility of resistance and urged surrender as the only way of saving the President's life'. This Allende declined to do under the conditions they laid down although he was willing to talk with the Junta members if they were willing to come to the Moneda.

'Finally Allende declared: "I shall defend myself to the end, and the last bullet of this submachine gun [given by Fidel Castro] I shall shoot here"; and the President indicated his own jaw.'[1]

Back in England we were glued to the news over the next few days in between normal family life continuing.

It was reported on the BBC that gun battles were continuing and that the President's wife, Hortensia, had been killed when their home in the suburbs was bombed. On September 14th she was said to be alive, having taken refuge, in the Mexican Embassy. A plane from Mexico was to take her and her family into exile. The military Junta, consisting of four, representing the three Armed Forces and the Police, constituted itself by 4.00 pm on the day of the coup. Later that evening, the members of the Junta took their oaths of office. The Generals Merino, Leigh and Mendoza, the navy, airforce and *carabineros* respectively, formed the new government headed up by General Augusto Pinochet.

Known Allende sympathisers thought to be a threat were rounded up and herded into the Football Stadium. Sadly but inevitably in the prevailing war situation some were killed without even a trial.

Others, who gave themselves up, especially those occupying positions of influence in government, health and education

---

[1] Nathaniel Davis: *The Last Two Years of Salvador Allende*. I. B. Tauris p. 255

were offered *'salvo conductos'* (safe exit from Chile but with a permanent loss of citizenship). Otherwise they were arrested and tried. A number of hardcore leftists in the UP government had in fact arranged for their own personal safety and managed to get out of the country. Others less fortunate were imprisoned on bleak Dawson Island far down in the south of the country immediately to the west of Chilean Tierra del Fuego.

But for us in safe, secure Frinton, these events would not begin to unfold for many months and years to come. All we could do for the present was to pray for the country and its people so dear to our hearts. What of Nico? Our friends Marisa and Alfredo? Was my Communist dentist under arrest?

We decided to write a letter to Lydia's father in the US embassy enquiring about Nico's well being. The problem was that letters in and out of the country were liable to censorship.

We drafted out a general letter about what we were doing and asking how *'Lydia's friend is. Is his health good?'* or words to that effect. With the uncertainty of the situation regarding communication in and out of the country it would be several days before we would know the answer to our letter.

The relentless queues involving so much time standing had well and truly taken their toll and my haemorrhoids needed surgery. Naomi too was to undergo an operation for the removal and biopsy of the 'mole' on her neck that had reappeared. We were both booked in for medicals at Mildmay Hospital. This hospital, with a Christian foundation, was just a few minutes walk away from where we used to live in Hoxton Square, Shoreditch.

Three days later I was admitted and Naomi a couple of days later. An enforced rest provided time to catch up with many friends and I was thoroughly spoilt. Local friends visited me including our very good friends Jeremy and Daphne who were still at St John's Church, Hoxton. One of my Cockney friends brought me ... Can you guess? None other than whipped cream walnuts, without even knowing of my childhood misdemeanour! SAMS home staff visited too and brought the news that the university son of one missionary couple in Chile had been imprisoned for two days but was now released. Ray telephoned the hospital and managed to get the news we had been anxiously waiting for via the doctor assigned to my care. Nicolás was alive and well. The following day Ray arrived with Naomi, now to be admitted and brought the letter Nico had written. He had been interrogated at the University but, as he wasn't carrying any arms, was not arrested.

The care at Mildmay was of a high standard. The prayer and ward services were very special. However, I almost disgraced myself on coming round from the general anaesthetic. I was being wheeled back to Tankerville Ward and heard myself starting to say something, just what I don't remember, but what I do remember was that my mind and my speech were having difficulty co-ordinating. The next remarks uttered stayed indelibly on my mind as I heard myself say in a slurred voice:

'For the firshhht time in my life I think I know what it's like to be drunk!'

It's a wonder I wasn't discharged on the spot.

Lightly buttered toast four hours after the operation tasted so good, but sitting on the commode ended up with me promptly fainting.

I was reassured to know Naomi had come round safely from her anaesthetic. The 'mole' had turned out to be a particularly deeply imbedded naevus and the later biopsy report, to our joy, revealed no malignancy. We were so grateful that mother and little daughter were in the same hospital at the same time, as we were able to spend time together.

Entertainment was near to hand in a larger than life Cockney lady. She had the most amazing long, black artificial eyelashes imaginable and worked in a betting shop. We heard all about the interesting but somewhat doubtful characters she met in the course of her working day and night. My diary also records that I referred to one of the nurses that looked after us (not in her hearing) as '*Nurse Hale and Hearty*'.

On the third day post operation, together with the other patients able to be out of bed, we made our way down to the far end of the ward for morning prayers. It was the turn of Dr Hardacre to lead the short service.

'Are you sitting comfortably?' were his opening remarks.

All eyes turned to me as I sat perched gingerly on my rubber ring and we all burst out laughing.

This same day a record of eleven visitors came, including a number from the congregation of St Leonard's Church. Among these was Dave, the young Cockney husband who had originally said on our first meeting with him three years back, 'You'll never find me going in that there church.' He was growing in his Christian faith.

Another welcome visitor was my caring GP, Dr John Coleman. He was later to be seen on our television screens as he was taken hostage, together with his wife, in Iran. We kept in touch with him over many years until his death in the nineties.

The useful thing about keeping a diary is that many things long forgotten are recorded, waiting to be rediscovered. It was this same day that I unexpectedly was asked to take the Ward evening prayers. My 'drunken' remarks it would seem were forgiven and forgotten!

The following Saturday was time to say goodbye. My fellow patients were delighted to meet all the family. For me it was so good to see and cuddle Andrew and Julian after our enforced few days of separation. Andrew, in particular, remained very clingy. We made our way to our borrowed car, Naomi clutching her teddy bear and me clutching my new 'toy' from which I would continue to be inseparable for several days yet. With the rubber ring safely in situ, the five of us set off to the Leicester grandparents via Elaine's home in Rushden. Naomi was looking forward to spending the weekend on her own with Aunty Elaine.

For Ray, especially, it was a very busy time of speaking engagements at various groups and supporting churches. As usual my parents home was open to so many friends who visited, as well as small gatherings in which we continued to share what these past years in Chile had meant to us.

There was no way I could be back in my childhood environment without a visit to my favourite countryside place, Bradgate Park, where Elaine and I spent so many happy days. I introduced the children for the first time, as I had done their father, a few years earlier, to this wonderful wild and open space with its outcrops of rock, rust-coloured bracken (it was autumn) and deer. Naomi had now joined her brothers after her little holiday with her Aunty. The sun was shining, what more could we wish for? Photographs capture just a little of the pleasure we all felt, the three sporting their vibrant plaid South American ponchos against the gentler subtle green of an English countryside.

The days in Leicester were a time of catching up with relatives as well. Little did we realise that it would be the last time I would see a favourite Aunt. My Aunty Winnie, the younger sister to my mother, died after we returned to Chile.

There was to be no mistake. We were set to return despite the reaction of the democratic world to the events there, the horror stories (not always true) being pumped out by the media, and the natural concern of many friends. Chile was where God called us and Chile would be where we would return, unless God showed us otherwise.

'You're not going back to Chile, are you?' 'Will it be safe?' 'What about the children?' 'What freedom will you have?' Just some of the questioning reactions we heard.

Our parents remained very supportive throughout and never once tried to dissuade us at this point. After our next home leave, however, Ray's father did voice his desire that we might stay back in England, but at the airport, when we arrived from our flight from Barcelona on our first leave home, my mother said how she could see my heart was in Chile.

Increasing age, frailty and illness understandably can influence our thinking. At a later time, the advancing age of parents would be part of the equation in future decisions, but not in 1973.

There is a cost for parents when their families and in some cases their only son or daughter or their only grandchildren, in obedience to God's call, find themselves the other side of the world. Yet with the pain of separation is also the accompanying peace and satisfaction that godly obedience brings. We ourselves have been there not only as the ones to leave home for an adopted country but also to let go of some of our own family as in turn they too have responded to God's call to them. Nowadays with such advanced means of electronic communication it's so much easier to stay in touch within minutes, but nothing can take the place of the hugs and spontaneity of conversation.

Ray's father had been taken ill while we were sailing back. The news reached us in Tenerife from Ray's brother Howard that he had had what was thought to be a mild heart attack. Concern naturally tempered the excitement we felt the nearer we were to home, but all was well. Although he was unable to meet us together with the others at the airport, he was recovering well at home in Frinton.

For missionary families, being home on leave can be a time not only of joy in happy reunions, but also very stressful, with many visits to make and talks to give. For the children it can be unsettling needing adaptability as they move from one base to another.

We were fortunate initially to stay with Ray's parents in Frinton as our base, but this was only suitable for a short time, as the children occupied every spare bed in their bungalow and we were in the garden room at the back of the garage. A bonus at this time of year was that Grandma and Papa owned a beach hut and when we weren't travelling we made use of it. However, our faithful God had the best solution available.

The sea-front flat of 14 Garden Court was once again made available to us. It had passed ownership as a holiday home from Pelham and Gillian Clarke to the Rev. Will White, minister of their Church in South Woodford. The original owner, Mrs Wilderspin, a member of Frinton Parish Church, had prayed that God would use her flat in blessing for others. That prayer was wonderfully answered and we with others became the beneficiaries. It provided a much-needed haven and base from which we could give out in ministry and return to be refreshed and re-charged. However, before being refreshed, we had barriers of reverse cross-culture to overcome. I needed some paper tissues and walking into Boots the chemist in Connaught Avenue, not then being self-service, I asked for Kleenex tissues.

'Which kind would you like, Madam? We have carnaby tissues

…'. The shop assistant then reeled off so many varieties I was left in a complete daze and vaguely remember saying, 'Oh, just give me any box.' To think that even toilet rolls were scarce in the 'Land of Little'. We certainly found ourselves overwhelmed whenever we went shopping over the next few weeks in the 'Land of Plenty'.

We vacated Mother and Father's home ten days after arriving in England, cleaning and preparing the rooms we had occupied in readiness for my parents and Elaine who were coming to Frinton. The date was very significant. September 18th was Chile's national day of Independence. The children helped in making appropriate Chilean emblems – the national flag and the national flower, the copihue. It was also significant for on this particular '*dieci-ocho*' 1973, Naomi prayed a prayer of commitment to Jesus.

A trip to London was on the cards. Our cabin trunk from the *Rossini* was somewhere out there, but all enquiries had drawn blank. The only thing was to go down to the docks in person. Ray took the boys, much to their fascination, and mother and daughter preferred to go to the West End shopping. The luggage hadn't arrived!

We met up later and to the excitement of all three, took a London double-decker. We stopped off at St Paul's Cathedral, even climbing up to the Whispering Gallery. Unfortunately we were unable to go up the Post Office Tower, due to the recent IRA bomb. A later visit to the capital took in the Changing of the Guard.

Ray and I managed a much-needed break away on our own. We chose Scotland and broke our journey overnight with my parents. Without the children (they were staying with different family members) we had a few hours of quality time over a meal before setting off the following morning.

As we didn't have a television in Santiago, once back in Frinton it became quite a novelty to fill in gaps left by our itinerant life-style, not that there were that many gaps. Given the lovely November we had that autumn our preferred options were walks by the sea front or parks when away from the coast.

A special treat was to watch Princess Anne's wedding, but for the children this in no way matched the enjoyment they got from Basil Brush. Andrew couldn't stop laughing.

Our remaining days of home leave were spent in Frinton with the exception of a visit to Allen Gardiner House. This time, instead of being the students, we were now considered seasoned missionaries and held the platform, as we shared experiences and lessons learnt with the current recruits. What was very meaningful, after all the miles covered over these past two years and even on leave, was yet another focal place of stability. Whether by design or by accident we found the bedrooms we were given were in fact the very same ones we had occupied three years before. It might sound strange to my readers but little things like that, at least for me, meant so much and continue to do so in lives that have known so many changes.

Many years later, when we returned to Cambridge from three years' ministry in Ibiza followed by curacies in Lancashire, such an occurrence stands out for me.

Hengrave Hall, a Christian Conference and Retreat Centre in Suffolk, had been a place I would often escape to for a time of quiet reflection in the busyness of ministry. The resident community was ecumenical and the longer serving core members were Roman Catholic nuns.

This particular time in 1997 was my first time back after almost eight years. The welcome I received from the nuns who knew me was overwhelming. Especially Sister Ángeles (Angels) from San Sebastian, Spain. She was small and round with the most beautiful smile. Warmth exuded from her. When she saw me, she opened wide her arms and gave me such an embrace that only the *Latinos* could outdo their close cousins in! I was shown to the same room, the Wesley Room, named after the great itinerant preacher. As I sat at the small desk looking out of the same part latticed window, there in front of me was the same birch tree by now a little bigger. It's hard to describe the emotion I felt, a sense of deep peace and a feeling of coming home after all the changes, including three years on the island of Ibiza. Maybe this impacted me the more, because a severe debilitating illness, following on from a viral infection, had entered my life in 1995 and I was still struggling with fatigue.

After our return to Allen Gardiner House and the familiarity of our rooms, another co-incident happened which we prefer to own as a God-given incident. You will recall on the morning we first left for Chile I met Elena Goodwin Hudson, wife of Bishop Goodwin Hudson, in the launderette. In our first meeting we had been going out to Chile with the South American Mission Society. Now we were returning with Ray as the new Chaplain of the Santiago Community Church. This time I was to have coffee with both the Bishop and his wife (Ray was at a conference in Swanwick, Derbyshire). It was in the church hall of St Mary's Church, Frinton. I had gone with the three children to the church bazaar in the hopes of picking up some bargains as well as meeting with friends. Mrs Goodwin Hudson and I both recognised one another. She beckoned me over and introduced me to her husband.

'This is the young mother I met in the launderette I was telling you about on her way to Chile that same day.'

In the course of the ensuing conversation, I shared something of my misgivings with the complete change of ministry we would be engaged in on our return and my concern about the embassy functions we would be expected to go to. He smiled understandingly and shared how at a cocktail party he had been able to lead someone to faith in Christ. His final words were that they both would be praying for us.

Speaking engagements, haring over the country visiting friends and relatives were now at an end and with only a few days left before leaving these shores once again, it was time to wind down before winding up with all that a new appointment would bring.

The penultimate day of November started with a very early wake up call and the inevitable last minute packing. Mother and Father Smith took all three children by train to London. We followed with a car full of luggage. At Gatwick we were joined by SAMS personnel. This thoughtful presence, considering we were returning to Chile no longer as SAMS personnel, was all the more appreciated.

At the check in we waited with bated breath as our luggage was weighed. It was eight pounds overweight but this time we were not charged. By contrast with our initial Air France flight almost three years earlier the whole journey this time couldn't have been nicer: the attentiveness of crew, the food, and seeing the Andes in daylight. We had celebrated our fifth Wedding Anniversary under a cloud in Paris and now we were celebrating Ray's forty-third birthday above the clouds.

Our flight, starting the previous day, took us over the Atlantic and the continent of South America on St Andrew's day. As I looked out of the window on to a vast sea of white, interspersed with jagged snow capped promontories, my thoughts went back to an amazing story of survival among that inhospitable whiteness, only the year before, a story that we woke up to one morning in Santiago. It was the talk of the day and even replaced political headlines. The story has been well documented both in books and in a film. The first book, *Alive: The True Story of the Andes Survivors* by Piers Paul Read, was written shortly after the event and I draw upon this for the facts.

It was a Friday in October, the thirteenth of the month and some equated that combination with the events that followed. A Uruguayan Air Force plane had been chartered by a rugby football team for a match and holiday in Chile. Former students the 'Old Christians', from the Stella Maris College in Montevideo and relatives, together with the crew, made up the forty-five passengers the Fairchild FH-227D was carrying. The flight began the previous day but because of bad weather stopped overnight in Mendoza before crossing the Andes.

There was a crew of five, and both the pilot and co-pilot were experienced. The co-pilot, Lieutenant Dante Lagurara, aged forty-one, was flying the plane under the more experienced eye of the pilot and commander. Colonel Julio César Ferradas, aged thirty-nine, had served in the Air Force for over twenty years with over 5,117 hours of flying experience. In addition he had made twenty-nine flights over the dangerous Andes.

The youngest team member was eighteen, the oldest relative fifty. Among the mostly male passengers and crew were five women, mother, sister, wives and girlfriend. The passengers were drawn from the middle class, Roman Catholics in faith, and for the majority it was their first trip to Chile.

After resuming the flight in the afternoon, before long the plane was flying through a pass in the mountains. Due to an inexplicable navigational error, the pilot notified air traffic control in Santiago, that he was over Curicó, Chile. He was cleared to begin the descent.

Suddenly the plane lurched and shuddered violently as it entered an air pocket. Some of the younger men began to crack jokes to hide the obvious nervousness. One took the microphone at the back of the plane and said, 'Ladies and gentlemen, please put on your parachutes. We're about to land in the cordillera.'[2]

No sooner had he said this than the plane hit a second air pocket and dropped a few further feet. Soon the clouds lifted to reveal a most frightening sight to those looking out of the windows. Instead of the fertile plains of Chile, there in front of them, much too close for comfort was a wall of rock edge of a mountain. Screams and prayers were uttered simultaneously. The Fairchild's engines roared and vibrated as the pilot tried to pull the plane into a climb. But it was futile. There was a deafening crash. The right wing had touched the side of the mountain. It broke off immediately, and as it twisted and turned, cut off the tail of the plane. A few seconds later, the left wing broke away and the propeller fell into the ground but not before it had torn a gaping hole in the fuselage.

The plane, instead of smashing into the mountain face, amazingly landed on its belly in a steep valley. Some were sucked out of the plane as it fell, others died on impact. Still others died from their injuries the next morning.

Two of the team, Roberto Canessa and Gustavo Zerbino, were both medical students. Their training could never have

---

[2] *Alive : The True Story of the Andes Survivors* by Piers Paul Read, published by Secker & Warburg. Reprinted by permission of the Random House Group Ltd. p. 18

prepared them for what they were called upon to do. Some of the injuries were horrific. As it was spring and their stay was only for five days they were ill equipped for the harsh climate in the mountains. The survivors had no goggles to prevent snow blindness and their clothes and footwear inadequate to insulate them from freezing temperatures. In addition there was insufficient food and no medical supplies.

The resourcefulness of the less injured survivors came to the fore. Parts of the plane were used to make splints, sunglasses, using the sun visors in the pilot's cabin, and seat cushions acting as stepping stones to walk on the iced-over snow in an attempt to get from the back of the plane to the front. Insulating material wrapped around pipes was crucial to the final survival of some.

The small amount of food was rationed. Wine stored on the plane was measured out in almost thimble size amounts, and small pieces of chocolate served as dinner. They even tried to eat pieces of leather, ripped open the upholstery hoping the stuffing might be part straw only to find plastic foam.

One survivor, Nando Parrado, had lost both his mother and his sister. Susana Parrado, aged twenty, had sustained very serious injuries, but lived in and out of consciousness for eight days. Her brother massaged her frostbitten feet and sleep carefully huddled up to her to help keep her warm.

'On the eighth night on the mountain, Parrado awoke and felt that Susana had grown cold and still in his embrace. The warmth and the movement of breathing – both were gone. At once he pressed his mouth to hers and with tears streaming down his cheeks blew air into her lungs. The other boys awoke and watched and prayed as Parrado tried to revive his sister.'[3] Exhaustion forced him to give up, but his sister was already dead.

Food supplies from the plane had long since been exhausted and they were left with the hardest and most difficult decision they would ever face. If any were to survive at all there was only one solution, to feed off the corpses of their dead friends. A meeting was called to reach a decision. There were naturally

---

[3] Ibid: p. 43

varying reactions from the twenty-seven survivors. All of them were Roman Catholics. Canessa argued that they had a moral duty to stay alive and his strong religious belief carried weight.

'It is meat. That's all it is. The souls have left their bodies and are in heaven with God. All that is left here are the carcasses …'.[4] Zerbino added that if his own dead body would help the others to stay alive he would want them to use it.

'This argument allayed many doubts … There and then they made a pact that if any more of them were to die, their bodies were to be used as food.'[5]

Out of deep respect and sensitivity for the feelings of survivors who had already lost close relatives it was agreed not to touch the bodies of their loved ones unless there was no alternative.

Those who, while not in any way criticising the decision of the others, could not bring themselves to feed off such meat became weaker and weaker. It was the words of Pedro Algorta urging them to think of it as Communion that swayed the doubters. 'Think of it as the body and blood of Christ, because this is food that God has given us because He wants us to live.'[6]

During the night of October 29th a cruel twist of fate claimed the lives of eight of the original survivors. An avalanche enveloped them as they slept in the fuselage. What was particularly hard to accept was that several had bravely coped with serious injuries, some even healing, over the sixteen days they had already been on the mountain. It was a bitter blow for the remaining nineteen.

The stress and hardships took their toll. Flaws in personality surfaced, bitter arguments took place as well as acts of selfishness and deceit. Yet conversely, as always in times of great danger and adversity, generous and self-sacrificing acts, thoughtfulness, tenderness and sensitivity were in evidence. Gangrenous toes and feet were rubbed to aid circulation. The most coveted places to sleep were exchanged with those in greatest need. Friends would die held in the arms of friends. Such was Arturo Norgueira.

---

[4] Ibid: p. 61
[5] Ibid: p. 61
[6] Ibid: p. 61

He had had a premonition he would die at the age of twenty-one. The two passions in his life were his fiancée and his politics. 'His strong sense of justice made him a militant idealist – sometimes socialist, sometimes anarchist. He had more or less abandoned the Church of Rome in favour of Utopia.'[7]

Norgueira had worked in the slums of Montevideo and felt the problems of poverty could only be tackled through radical political methods. Now, although his broken leg and injured ankles were not as serious as some of the others' injuries, his mental state was causing considerable concern. His emotional state and political antagonism caused him to withdraw from the others. In an outburst of pent up emotion during an altercation he bitterly spoke out. 'You're all oligarchs and reactionaries, ... and I don't want to live in a Uruguay imbued with the kind of materialistic values that you represent ...'.[8]

Coche Inciarte, one of the gentlest of the group answered with indignation 'You may be a socialist, but you're also a human being, and that's what counts up here.'[9]

Later Norgueira told Carlitos Páez whom he had particularly singled out that he regretted what he had said.

It was Pedro Algorta, his closest friend, who drew near to Norgueira in his isolation.

A few days later Arturo Norgueira asked if he could lead the prayers. Páez handed him his rosary and he prayed for all their families, their friends, who had died, and their country. In the silence that followed, Arturo could be heard weeping. Pedro asked him why he was crying.

His answer was that he was nearer to God. In a weak hand he wrote on a bit of paper a letter to his parents and his *novia* (fiancée).

'In situations such as this, even reason cannot understand the infinite and absolute power of God over men. I have never suffered as I do now–physically and morally – though I have never believed in Him so much ... Morally and physically

---

[7] Ibid: pp. 120, 121
[8] Ibid p. 121
[9] Ibid p. 121

because of your absence and my longing to see you … and embrace you in the same way as my beloved Mama and Papa, to whom I want to say that I was wrong in the way I behaved towards them … Strength. Life is hard but it is worth living. Even suffering. Courage.'[10]

Two nights later after increasing delirium he became quieter as he slept in the arms of Pedro. It was in those arms Arturo Norgueira died.

The various search parties from neighbouring countries had been unsuccessful in locating the missing 'plane. The fact that it was white made it impossible to be seen from the air. When a 'plane was heard, the fittest survivors would dance and wave anything that would help to attract attention, but to no avail. After eight days the search was called off. Some of the parents and relatives had organized their own search party. Leaving no stone unturned, their determination, persistence and in some cases their unshakable trust both in God and in their own sons is a vital part of the story.

Initially on the mountain an attempt was made to use the cockpit radio but there was no power. Weeks later on November 17th with the weather getting warmer an expeditionary group of three of the survivors, Canessa, Parrado and Vizintín set out to try and find a way west through to Chile. They loaded up half of a Samonsite suitcase as a sledge with essential provisions. They had only been going two hours when they discovered the missing section of the Fairchild's tail. In the suitcases were items of clothing, alcoholic beverages, cigarettes, sugar and some chocolates. Stowed away in the tail section were the Fairchild's batteries.

Loading up their makeshift sledge with the extra provisions they set out. A huge mountain lay to the west and they calculated they would need at least three days to walk round it to find a valley that hopefully should lead them into Chile. The more they looked at the mountain in the changing light, the more it seemed to recede. Canessa began to question their strategy. The more he thought and the more he gazed at the huge mass of rock and

---

[10] Ibid: p. 123

snow, the more convinced he became they should return to the tail, load the batteries on to the sledge and return to the others in the 'plane.

Roy Harley had some experience of electronics and, as the batteries were too heavy for the sledge it was decided to return and bring Harley with the radio to the tail itself. The huge disappointment of the remaining survivors at the return of the three on whom their hopes for ultimate rescue had rested was replaced with further disappointment. The attempt to work the radio failed.

The two nights away had shown the three that unless they could find a better way to keep warm they would perish in the attempt. It was the insulating material that had been found in the tail of the plane that was now put to use. By day the temperature was mounting, only to plummet below freezing at night. A sleeping bag was made sewing the patches together, forming a large quilt in which all three spent the nights on their next attempt to get help.

On December 12th, the same three set out once again. After they had gone a short distance, Delgado staggering out of the plane waved in his hand a small statue of the Virgin of Lujan. Canessa shouted back not to worry, 'If she wants to stay, let her stay. We'll go with God in our hearts.'[11]

On the third day of the trek Parrado reached the top of the mountain ahead of the others. When he saw a small 'Y' in the far distance between the peaks, he gauged that the way out of the mountains would take more energy and therefore provisions than had been calculated. It was agreed that Vizintín would return to the others, leaving only two and not three mouths to feed.

Over the next days Canessa noticeably began to slow down, until each step became a great effort. 'Oh, God,' he prayed, 'by all means test us to the limit of our endurance, but please make it humanly possible to go on.'[12]

As Parrado, the stronger of the two, walked ahead he suddenly

[11] Ibid: p. 179
[12] Ibid: p. 218

found himself at the end of the valley and what a sight met his eyes. The snow had receded to reveal a veritable Garden of Eden, patches of grass, moss, rushes and, more wonderful still, purple and yellow flowers.

'As Parrado stood there, his face wet with tears of joy, Canessa came up behind him … both boys staggered off the snow and sank onto rocks by the side of the river. There, amid birds and lizards, they prayed to God, thanking Him with all the fervour of their youthful hearts …'.[13]

Nine days later Parrado was collecting wood to build a fire when Canessa suddenly shouted. He had seen what looked like a man on the other side of the river. At first Parrado thought Canessa, who was weak and ill from diarrhoea, was hallucinating. Across the river that divided them was, in fact, not one man but three countrymen all on horseback. They managed to convey their situation and one of the Chilean *campesinos*, (Sergio Catalán shouted back '*Mañana*.')

The following day the men on horseback returned. It was impossible to conduct an intelligible conversation across the wide fast flowing, cascading river. The *campesino* threw a piece of paper wrapped around a stone with a ball-point pen attached.

Parrado scribbled the essential details then added an SOS in lipstick, which the boys had been using to help protect their lips from the sun and wind. Safely thrown back across the torrent, Sergio Catalán unwrapped the paper, read the message and looking up indicated he understood the contents. Before riding off to get help, Catalán reached in his pocket and took out his daily ration of bread and threw it across to Parrado.

It was Thursday, December 21st, seventy days since the Fairchild had crashed, that Catalán rode for many hours to bring help. Eventually a team of *carabineros* and mountain rescuers arrived. On discovering the facts, helicopters were summoned to begin the airlift.

Meanwhile, back in the wrecked plane the remaining survivors had gone from despair to hope and back to despair, as the days dragged on, not knowing if the two had died in the attempt to

---

[13] Ibid p. 218

find help. Suddenly hope surfaced with a new intensity. Daniel Fernández and Eduardo Strauch left the 'plane, as usual, to tune in on the small radio they had to the news in Montevideo. Suddenly the news came through that two Uruguayan survivors had been found in a remote valley in the Andes. They tuned in to other stations.

'The words, once mentioned, spread over the air from one country to another until every wave length on the continent seemed to be carrying the sensational news that two survivors from the Uruguayan plane that had crashed in the Andes ten weeks before had been found, that fourteen still remained at the scene of the crash, and that their rescue was underway.'[14]

All sixteen were rescued, amid tears of some parents that had accompanied the rescue crew and the tears of three hundred soldiers of the Colchagua Regiment in Chile. After receiving medical treatment in a Santiago hospital the survivors were able to celebrate Christmas day with their families at the Sheraton Hotel.

The inevitable question of what they had eaten in order to survive was asked. They had decided to say 'cheese' that they had travelled with, until they could first speak to the relatives to explain the true facts. Unfortunately an ever intrusive and sensation-seeking media discovered those facts first.

For us in Santiago that December of 1972, those facts were visibly and shockingly expressed. Ray was visiting the centre of the capital. Staring at him from every newspaper hoarding he passed in bold headlines was the word '*Canibalismo*'.

This first book by Piers Paul Read was written after interviewing the survivors. In its opening the survivors explain why they wanted it to be written.

'We decided that this book should be written and the truth known because of the many rumours about what happened in the cordillera. We dedicate this story of our suffering and solidarity to those friends who died for us and to their parents who, at the time we most needed it, received us with love and understanding.'

---

[14] Ibid: p. 256

The Roman Catholic Church completely exonerated the survivors in the extreme necessities they had to resort to in order to survive. However, they did not concur with the parallel drawn to the sharing in the body and blood of Christ in Holy Communion.

The parents showed the same courage and selflessness that their sons had so valiantly displayed.

The father of Carlos Valeta, one of the youngest to have died went to a press conference. Afterwards in a statement to the newspaper, *El Pais*, he said, 'I came here with my family because we wanted to see all of those who were the friends of my son and because we are sincerely happy to have them back among us. We are glad, what is more, that there were forty-five of them, because this helped at least sixteen to return.' He went on to say that as a doctor he knew the only way they could possibly have survived was in the courageous decision they made. 'Now that I have confirmation of what has happened I repeat: Thank God that the forty-five were there, for sixteen homes have regained their children.'[15]

Another tribute came from the father of Arturo Nogueira in a letter to the media.

'Dear Sirs:

'With these few words, written in obedience to what is in our hearts, we want to pay tribute, with homage, admiration and recognition, to the sixteen heroes who survived the tragedy of the Andes. Admiration, because this is what we feel before the many proofs of solidarity, faith, courage and serenity which they had to face and which they overcame. Recognition, profound and sincere, because of the care they gave in every moment to our dear son and brother Arturo up to the time of his death many days after the accident. We invite every citizen of our country to spend some minutes in meditation on the immense lesson of solidarity, courage and discipline, which has been left to us by these boys in the hope that it will serve us all to overcome our

---

[15] Ibid: p. 304

mean egotism and petty ambitions, and our lack of interest for our brothers.'[16]

Not all survivors or relatives were able to accept as easily what had happened over those eventful seventy-two days. For a number, inevitable adjustments and coming to terms with their grief took a long time to work through. Although for the majority, their Christian faith had under-girded them through such suffering, not all were able to share the same belief in a loving God of justice.

As the 'plane we were travelling in continued its flight, looking out of the window at the whiteness interspersed with the hard granite rock face spread out before me, I had to acknowledge that we are not given all the answers to our questions this side of heaven.

We arrived at Pudahuel Airport, Santiago fifteen minutes early to be met with a small contingent of friends and members of the Trustees and Deacons of the Church. Derek Fernyhough saw us through customs and, no doubt because of his diplomatic status; there was nothing to pay – so very different from our first arrival in Chile.

The chaplaincy house in Las Violetas was stocked with food, and flowers adorned the lounge. Gracie Jones, a dear elderly lady had been living in the home for two weeks for security. We hastily found buried in our cases T-shirts and shorts for Andrew and Julian and a summer dress for Naomi. We had left England in early winter; we were now in late spring. Derek and Grace Fernyhough arrived the following day as we were unpacking with yet more flowers.

A very welcome noise interrupted us as we continued unpacking in the afternoon. The sound of a motorbike engine winding down and stopping outside the railings of our front gate heralded the arrival of a much-loved friend. A tall man clambered down from his bike and removing his crash helmet he revealed a shortened version of his dark curly hair. His handsome face broke into a beaming smile as we hastily unlocked the gate. We both flung ourselves, in turn, at him in a warm embrace followed

---

[16] Ibid: pp. 304, 305

by the three children doing the same. Nico had arrived. With a shorter hair cut he now looked a little less like Che Guevara! That was his prudent intention as we learnt the Military Junta had stipulated that young men should not wear their hair long. It had been the fashion for the leftist young men to have hair almost at shoulder length, if not longer.

It was now time to catch up with all the happenings since we had left for home leave, happenings of which there were many, momentous ones at that, for both friends and the country itself.

Chapter 26
New Beginnings

The next day, a Sunday, Ray was thrown in at the deep end. This appointment meant his first as overall minister. He had only served one curacy, but his maturity and wide experience over earlier years and a dependency on God served him well. The morning started with an Anglican 8.30 am Communion Service, although Ray had already been up two hours. After a rather rapid breakfast (the Manse was a car drive away) it was back for the morning service for all five of us.

The warm welcome was overwhelming. My diary records that there was also a baptism service in Spanish for Ray and later in the afternoon we paid an impromptu visit to our former neighbours, the Valdés family. Naomi was as pleased to see her little playmates, as they were to see her. As she was feeling apprehensive about returning to school the next day, we thought it would help to visit her best school friends the Arredondo twins. It paid off. The next morning Naomi returned to school very much happier. Andrew and Julian were excited to be going back to Los Dominicos pre-school.

Starting a new chapter in December was a mixed bag of positives and negatives. With end of school term activities, Christmas shopping and preparations and a full Christmas programme in the life of the Church community, it meant being thrown in at the deep end initially, as everything was reaching a climax before the wind down of the long summer holidays.

December was also building up to the hottest time of the year. Driving became even more erratic, if that was possible, finger on the horn more frequent and sustained. Tempers became frayed as the populace lost its more normal '*mañana*' approach to life and wanted things done immediately or even yesterday! Our time in the UK had been very busy. The prospect of a long quieter summer recess helped sustain us in these busy days of adjustment.

For the children, and for us too, the huge perk of free membership of the exclusive Prince of Wales Country Club was such a bonus. This provided years of enjoyment, of friendships and continuing ministry as so many of the English-speaking residents used the facilities. Playing tennis, swimming, sharing picnic lunches as well as occasionally a table in the restaurant or on the terrace under the veranda became the natural setting for a range of conversation.

It was on occasions like this and at other social gatherings that so much bridge building was achieved with non-churchgoers. Many genuine friendships developed, out of which conversations on issues of faith would often be expressed. A good number of friendships formed in this way would, over time, result in the lapsed churchgoer, the agnostic or the nominal Christian finding a new purpose as they came to put their trust in a personal Jesus.

Our way of life was changing, not least in the higher standard of living we became exposed to, although our salary didn't reflect this. However, there were privileges that went with the job, a nice house, car, school fees paid, membership of the Country Club and so many invitations that included meals. The Church had a gardener, Señor Orlando, who took care of the surrounding gardens to the Church and included ours. Neli also made contact, as she wanted to work for us again. As my own role would involve a higher profile within the English-speaking community, domestic help was not the luxury it would be back home. There were many official functions the Chaplain and his wife were expected to attend. Very many of these were embassy functions. For us to pay for domestic help out of the salary was quite a sacrifice, but it freed me to develop the ministry God was leading me into.

I didn't have to wait long before it became clear what God

had in mind, although I wasn't too sure at the time. One very warm summer morning towards the end of our first week in the new post the doorbell rang. There on the doorstep was Grace, our Consul's wife. She and Derek were already real friends.

'Gill, I wonder if you would be willing to start a group for the younger women in the congregation and community? As you know, there is the Ladies Guild but this caters for the more elderly.'

I knew this was the case. I also knew its nature was what its title indicated, a group producing sewing, knitting and hand made goods to raise money to support the residential home for elderly ex-pats.

'Perhaps we could have something on similar lines but perhaps with discussion and speakers ...' she continued.

' I will give it some thought and prayer but I'm not anxious to start something for the sake of it unless it meets a real need,' I replied.

I was not anxious to head up a group that met with little outreach in mission. My calling and training was teaching the Christian faith and my heart lay in reaching those who didn't know Jesus in a personal relationship.

I began to make a few soundings especially of one or two, who might share the same vision I had. Carol Reitz, an American who was on the Board of Deacons was the most obvious. Her faith and commitment was clearly seen. Carol was around forty-one or two, some eight years older than me, average height, with light brown wavy hair and a round face. She was married to Jack, a businessman. They had two sons in the States and their two daughters, Jen and Tracey, were with them in Chile. The two girls were in the Sunday Bible class for adolescent and teens. It was Jen, the elder of the two, who together with her friend, Sandy, came to me at a later date asking for their ears to be pierced!

I decided to invite around six women to discuss the possibility of forming a group. Among these were Grace, Carol, and Janice, Ray's future secretary. These three clearly represented the main nationalities that, in fact, became the future group: English, American and Anglo-Chilean. I'm not sure now who else was present but more than likely Frances, a Canadian, was among this initial exploratory group. We met in the sitting room of Las Violetas where I explained how my calling them together was the outcome of Grace's suggestion.

From the beginning, I made it clear if I were asked to head up something for the younger women it would primarily be with a teaching agenda. It's purpose would be the deepening of our faith and yet open to those who didn't claim to share a Christian faith. All were unanimous. Different suggestions were put forward as to what we should call the group, the nature of its programme and how often we should meet.

Grace, who at that time hadn't grown as deeply in her faith as she undoubtedly did later, was somewhat reluctant that we might make it too spiritual! She felt some of the titles expressed could put people off. A compromise was reached, but I remember saying:

'I don't believe in the sugar-coated pill. We should be very clear and unapologetic from the beginning as to what the purpose of such a group is about and clearly state this.'

From that meeting was birthed our title 'Women's Forum' with the aim clearly printed on all our publicity 'for women of all faith or no faith to discover the relevance of Christianity for today'.

We met every Thursday morning in the Church hall. The idea was that three of the four Thursdays each month would be teaching based on a Bible book. The fourth would be on topical issues like the Christian view on abortion, euthanasia, poverty and materialism. Then there was teaching on the Holy Spirit, Angels, the Devil and spiritual warfare. I undertook the majority of the teaching, as no one at that time felt they could! However, there was no way I wanted to encourage a group of passive participants.

I welcomed and actively encouraged anyone to butt in, disagree and ask questions as long as they were relevant. I was anxious not to rely on outside speakers other than occasionally by way of change and the stimulation of another input. My long-term goal was to train others in leadership. It was important for members to share not only the responsibility of the group but to own it. About twice a term there would be a book review taken by a different member.

The mix of participants was not only interesting but very revealing as I was soon to discover: lapsed churchgoers in their home countries, nominal Christians, agnostics, honest seekers, and Christians with a good deal of ignorance on biblical truth. What became apparent was that in the majority of those who continued in the group was a deep hunger, a hunger that their comfortable life-style and material advantage had failed to satisfy.

Ray and I had a large stock of Christian books and I used to give a willing member a choice of two or three to choose from for the review. When it was Grace's turn, the book she had was *Man Alive* by Michael Green. It was based on the resurrection of Jesus, answering in a lively way any objections to this that people put forward. The book also made clear that if the resurrection of Jesus was indeed true it called for a response from the readers – belief or unbelief. There could be no sitting on the fence. For the resurrection of Jesus completed what the crucifixion left incomplete. Christ's perfect sacrifice for our sinfulness was fully accepted by God. The way to relationship with the Father was now open for us.

On this particular Thursday morning after the welcome and opening prayer, Grace got to her feet. Her opening remarks were very honest which I greatly admired. Such was the atmosphere of Women's Forum that people felt free to express their opinions without a sense of judgement. There was room for disagreement.

'When I started to read this book, that Gill gave me, it wasn't long before I felt angry. I began to wonder if indeed I had my ticket to heaven.'

I wondered what was coming next!

'I was angry as I felt the writer was presumptuous to say the least but I carried on reading. The more I got into the book the more it challenged me to rethink some of my previously held views.' (Words to that effect.)

I seem to remember that she continued to give a fair and accurate review. This book marked a turning point in Grace's journey of faith, a journey that started in Chile as her daughter shared with me in a recent telephone conversation.

Rosalind, her daughter, and I had had a lively conversation in the swimming pool in the club one hot summer afternoon. She was a teenager and was visiting her parents for the Christmas holidays. In the course of conversation, Rosalind, in a forthright way, made it quite clear that she wasn't particularly interested in what it meant to be a Christian. We chatted for a time and she left the pool amicably yet unconvinced. Some years later when back in the UK she became convinced. To this day she and her family are very involved in their local church.

Perhaps my biggest challenge in the Women's Forum was a threatening open confrontation with an American member of the group. Her name was Janet and she was responsible for the Church's lending library, as she herself was a librarian. Both she and her husband were in their late twenties. They were regular worshippers in the church. We were good friends but on this particular morning something I said struck a discord for Janet.

'Are you actually saying that Jesus is the only way to God? Because if so, I think you are being very dogmatic!'

You could have cut the atmosphere with a knife. Some members looked down in embarrassment, others shuffled uneasily, as Janet's face and tone of voice expressed her obvious anger. I explained that, as we all arrived to Forum that morning by different routes, once there we had to enter through the one door into the hall, so was our journey of faith. Her face reflected very definitely that she was still unhappy with my answer.

I remember feeling very alone and vulnerable as no one chipped in, not even Carol, to give me any support. It was still very early days for the group. I shot up a prayer for wisdom and within seconds found myself passing the buck onto the one person able to truthfully and with authority answer that statement.

'Yes. I am saying Jesus is the only way to the Father ...' Then came the best answer I think I could possibly have given after turning to Jesus' own words in the gospel of John: 'And if you don't like it I suggest you take up your argument with him, as it was Jesus himself who said these words!'[1]

Then followed a palpable silence. There was no more arguing and I carried on with the study we were doing. Once home the reaction began to set in. My thoughts ran amok. Maybe I did come on too heavily? Perhaps it would have been better to have watered down my answer. Even as these thoughts surfaced I knew I was in spiritual warfare and that the Enemy was behind my thinking. I remember speaking out loud: 'No. I won't compromise the truth.'

However, for a time my relationship with Janet was a little strained. I prayed for wisdom as to how to build up the friendship we had had. We both enjoyed singing and one day I invited her to our home where there was a piano (church property, Ray and I don't play). She came and we spent a relaxed afternoon together. She carried on coming to Forum and over the consecutive months of continued bible teaching she grew in her relationship with Jesus. Janet, like so many in our congregation both then and in future places, represented those whose faith was still infantile, as a result of church affiliations that sadly had left them so untaught Biblically. There had been little growth in spiritual maturity.

John and his wife Margaret were such a couple. They too were American. He was a retired diplomat, having held a post as consul, and some years older than his wife who worked in the US Embassy in an administrative role. John, a dapper gentleman, was short, grey-haired, bespectacled and in his late sixties. He was sensitive, gracious and a talented musician. John was our organist, choir director and was well liked. Margaret, some twenty years younger, was more reserved and took a little more knowing before appreciating her own warmth and genuineness. She possessed a very dry sense of humour.

They became very good friends, a friendship that continued right until John's death well into his eighties. He never failed to send me birthday greetings right until his death and this is something Margaret has continued into the present. They

---

[1] The Bible: John chapter 14 verse 6

subsequently visited us in Cambridge and we, in turn, stayed with them in the States. Yet again their faith seemed very underdeveloped when we first met them. One evening I recall we were talking about prayer.

'I don't think we can bother God with the trivia of our lives, after all he's far too busy with all the far more important big issues of the world.'

'I think we can, John,' Ray replied. 'Aren't you, as father, interested in the details of Deb's and John junior's lives?'

It was such conversations with so many that showed a big gap between their believing in the existence of God, yet not knowing the intimacy of his fatherhood, a relationship made possible through Jesus.

It became very apparent over the following months that there was a deep hunger to discover more of what it meant to really know Christ. John initially and, in time, Margaret became regular members of our mid-week evening bible study group. Work commitments prevented Margaret from joining Women's Forum.

A stunningly attractive young mother, slim, brunette, with brown almond shaped eyes joined Forum. Her name was Penny. She was married to Jimmy, born in Chile but of Scottish descent, and nephew to Willie Reid who had interviewed Ray. Penny herself was born and brought up in England, an only child of an English ex-diplomat father and an equally attractive mother. On her mother's side there was Chilean blood, this without doubt contributed to the good looks of both mother and daughter, the fine facial bone structure, the warm brown eyes and good figure. Penny was in her late twenties, Jimmy in his thirties and their little boy, Andrew, the same age as Julian. I don't recall them attending church at this stage other than on special occasions. We would meet them at the Prince of Wales Club where our boys would paddle in the children's swimming pool with Andrew. Later we would make up tennis sets with them and others of their friends.

Jimmy, like his uncle and a number of the Anglo-Chilean men, formed the Fourteenth Fire Brigade, the '*Bomberos*'. Each member was a volunteer and the Fourteenth had a very reputable track record with a high standing among both British and Chilean communities. They looked incredibly smart with their navy trousers, bright red jackets and polished brass buttons, and helmets. On Remembrance Sunday they would join with the British Legion in presenting their respective standards.

Neither Jimmy nor Penny would claim to have any personal Christian faith. They had a vague belief that God existed, but gave him little thought and didn't see any relevance of him in their lives. Among their close friends were Neil and Philippa, known as Pip. Neil was also a *bombero*. They too, at this time were what we might call 'happy pagans'! Others among these Anglo-Chilean young couples with whom we were slowly building friendships were declared atheists. After we had returned to the UK years later some of this group, notably Neil and Pip, not only became Christians together with their daughter and son, but also have played a strategic part in the Anglican Church among Chileans. But that is for another chapter.

After time, developing my friendship with Penny, the day came when I invited her to come to Forum. It wasn't long before she started coming every week. It became obvious God was at work in her life and one day I invited her back to our home, by then we had moved to Avenida Holanda, next door to the church. It was a Thursday, after we had finished Forum. I had the privilege of acting as spiritual 'midwife' (being 'alongside woman'), as Penny prayed the prayer of commitment to Jesus as her Saviour and Lord. She's never looked back.

It was the long summer months, without the pressure of time as well as the many social occasions, that brought together the English-speaking communities that uniquely provided the setting in which key conversations took place. It all seemed so very natural. Mealtimes around the table were often the most conducive, helped at times by a glass or two of wine! Somehow all too often at home in the UK times like these are more difficult to find. Everyone seems to be in such a hurry and there is always such a proliferation of Church meetings that many Christians find themselves without non-Christian friends. All too often we make a false divide between the secular and the spiritual. The principle of the Alpha Course is thankfully opening many eyes to the importance of life-style evangelism.

We had begun to learn the value of spending time building bridges of friendship in our first term and out of these earning the right to share what our faith meant, yet had seen so little fruit – just one person we knew of who had through us opened a chapter of new beginning in her own life. We had now returned to a new ministry which would open for us a whole 'book' of new beginnings, although we had no idea then the size this 'book' would become under the authorship and editing of God himself.

The opening chapter of this volume occurred within three weeks of our return and the date was December 25th 1973 – and what a wonderful Christmas present it proved to be.

A letter home described this new beginning, one born out of a long drawn out painful and at times traumatic 'labour' for the one experiencing the 'contractions' as well as for Ray and I acting as 'midwife' in attendance. Our being in attendance for over two years echoed the apostle Paul's words to the Christians in Galatia: 'My dear children, for whom I am again in the pains of childbirth until Christ is formed in you ...'[2]

I wrote home: '*We spent Christmas afternoon between Lydia's parents, where we had Christmas lunch and Thea's house where we had tea joined by the Santiago SAMS team – but highlight of all and cause for real rejoicing and praise to the Lord is that on Christmas Day evening Nicolás was converted – in our home! He had brought a design student round to our home several times as she had expressed an interest in spiritual things and he was anxious for us to meet her. Her name is Lucia. They came again on Christmas Day evening and after 20 mins. In which we hadn't even spoken of spiritual things, Nicolás turned to Ray and said quite out of the blue "What must I do to receive Christ?" He then went on to say how much he had learnt in coming to our home and that he always left feeling more peaceful for having been! – and that he could no longer put off the decision. We explained and he prayed a most wonderful prayer in Spanish thanking the Lord for what he had*

---

[2] The Bible: Galatians chapter 4 verse 19

done and to come in and clean him right through and forgive his sins, and that he wanted his way in life to be God's way etc. After he finished praying he lifted his arms and shouted in English "I'm free!"'

My letter went on to say how he returned the next day to say how he hadn't slept for deep joy and that there was now such a real peace of heart and mind. This Christmas Day marked a new beginning for Nicolás. 'Labour' had started in earnest the previous April. You will remember that on my birthday, the day after our very worst experience of queuing, resulting in our going to bed mid-afternoon, Nico came round and expressed his desire to start reading the Bible with us. I mentioned how this led to a revolution, but not of a political nature. The radical change in which self government was ousted by the setting up of Christ's kingdom in his life was every bit as revolutionary as the coup the country had gone through, with the exception that this decision was unequivocally his choice and was permanent.

Chapter 27
Pinochet's Chile

What were the immediate differences we encountered on arriving back in a country that had gone through an upheaval of seismic proportions? My first two letters home referred to the cleanliness on the streets and less anxiety on the faces of many.

'We ... are enjoying a tranquillity and relaxation that we have never before experienced here although it is very evident we are under military rule with soldiers on guard all over the place.' Soldiers and police, armed with machine guns, had a visible presence on street corners and outside potentially vulnerable buildings. Some nights were punctuated by gunfire. We ourselves heard shots on at least four occasions in our first week: *'perhaps warning shots if people are lax about the curfew, which is operating from 11pm until 6am each night.'*

This meant that during our first Christmas in his new role, Ray was unable to conduct a Christmas Eve Midnight communion service. The curfew was limited from 11.00 pm to 1.00 am on New Year's Eve as a concession.

'Last night some incident must have occurred not far from us as we heard shots and helicopters flying very low encircling ... again and again, around midnight. In the week four soldiers were found shot dead together.

'Some of the gunfire was the shooting of stray dogs as the new government wanted to present a cleaner and more disciplined image, as well as controlling rabies as there had been some reported cases.'

I continued in my letter to say what a joy it was shopping, as queues were now a thing of the past. Prices, however, were high. These went up overnight with no warning and could be anything from double, which was less frequent; to five or even ten times more, which became more frequent. One example was postage stamps.

'*We heard that within an hour of the military intervening on the 11th, people were putting the Chilean flags outside their homes – it was evidently a very moving sight. However, there are incidents of torture occurring too, which, of course is very sad – but only in comparatively few cases we think.*'

These were first impressions and unfolding events over the next months and even years would inevitably prove this statement to be far from the case.

Colin Bazley who was assistant bishop in the south of Chile, later to move up to Santiago as diocesan bishop, was one of three pastors allowed to visit political prisoners in Temuco. Between the coup and my second letter home in early January he had seen around fifty prisoners who had embraced a personal faith in Christ and was reported to have said that '*for him personally it has been the most exciting evangelism of his life.*' My comments home went on to say that there were also '*cases of extreme and unjust measures being taken against some who supported the previous regime, although not actively involved with the "getting one's own back" policy.*' I asked my parents to pray that '*the pendulum will not swing in the other extreme.*'

Another letter written two months later shared how Nico was unashamedly telling his Marxist friends what had happened to him. By now he was speaking of his Marxism being in the past, yet naturally remaining left in his political persuasion with '*a very real social concern which we hope he will keep.*'

The military takeover resulted in a number of friends and acquaintances leaving the country. Some even before we returned. Alfredo and Marisa went back to Argentina, perhaps fearing the same abuse of human rights in Chile as in their home country. However, Argentina's track record of torture and the '*desparacidos*' (disappeared) has historically superseded that of Chile. We missed them. We heard that my communist dentist and her paediatric psychologist husband had fled in fear of detention or worse. Just how much they were involved in the political arena we never knew.

It was in these summer months when church meetings and commitments were at a minimum that Omar and Lía met with me for English lessons.

Very many years later from Canada, Omar wrote to me filling in many details from the days we first met over study books. The four of us had kept in touch from 1974 and we visited them in Vancouver in the late nineteen eighties. These are Omar's comments on those turbulent days in Chile's history. I quote exactly as he wrote in the third person and in his second language.[1]

'The military coup on September 11, 1973 changed Chile from centuries of democracy into 17 years of repressive dictatorship. The military halted the advance of Marxism and achieved an extraordinary economic transformation; at the cost of about 3,200 dead and missing persons. Inevitably there was a suppression of freedoms, a trampling of justice, and an increase in class differences.

'During the first months of military rule they took control of the enterprises that were nationalized and proceed [sic] to change the "guard." Under these new rulers, on September 24, 1973, Omar had to sign his "voluntary" resignation before a colonel with a pistol on his desk backed up by patrolmen with machine guns. In spite of the situation, he was paid his salary and compensations and no reprisal came upon him; this was not the case in other factories.

'This was a very difficult time for this family. It was a time of crisis, disappointment, tension, stress, depression, and lack of both direction and hope. All the dreams, values and democratic principles impressed on them through education and exercise as a citizen had disappeared in a violent take over. Their old friends and even relatives turned their backs on them, treating them with contempt in some instances. Not very much was left for them in Chile, a country divided by hate and violence, with a segment of victors lording it over people by the power of their guns.

'Chile paid the price for the cold war that the US participated in, by adhering to the American agenda of political overthrows. Chile had the

---

[1] Testimonial: The Faithfulness of God. Omar and Lia Martinez.

misfortune of having foreign and local politicians, with lack of moral character that plot and destabilize their government. Assassinations of Chilean leaders became commonplace. History has already revealed the truth, but the truth however does not reduce the pain of those who have suffered.'

For Omar and his family they had fallen on hard times; no work, loss of some friends, and little purpose left as their hopes in a utopia for their country were dashed. In the emptiness of their current existence he went on to say how at that time it was only the love of his wife and the welfare of his children that sustained him.

A few months after September 11th, aware of a 'spiritual vacuum' compounded by a bleak future for them if they decided to remain, they took the decision to emigrate. Canada, in keeping with the democratic world, had vigorously criticized the loss of democracy in Chile and opened its doors to a number of Chileans. After an interview and lengthy process Omar and Lia were given permission to emigrate but there was a condition attached. Omar had to go alone and only after finding work and a house could the family join him.

So it was that Omar left for Canada, with the Bible in his luggage that I had given him as a farewell gift. What happened there to him and what happened meanwhile in Chile to Lia is recounted in the next chapter.

While many left the country demoralized and bitter, many others within the country looked to a brighter future with hope and expectation. We returned to find the national flag flying from many a home. Pinochet was looked upon as the *salvador* (saviour) in many eyes, the very name given to Allende on his birth but which he had failed to live up to. However, Pinochet's Chile was every bit as polarised as Salvador Allende's had been. Feelings still ran high and families and friends remained deeply divided. Sadly in some instances divisions caused employees and even family members not only to ostracize those pro-Allende but also to report them to those currently in power. There was a palpable suspicion rife in some areas.

Within the community we were serving, these conflicting

views were held, although it would be true to say for the majority the bias was in favour of the military regime. Certainly those in the business world had a greater confidence, while those in the diplomatic services had to be more circumspect. Their own views had to be put to one side in favour of the governments they represented.

The secretary Ray inherited, Joanna, was married to a Chilean Presbyterian minister. One Friday in late April the Secret Police (DINA), descended on the Theological Community College and arrested the husband, who was known to have leftist views, along with a Methodist pastor, the secretary and three students. The charge was that they were holding 'clandestine meetings'.

By then churches, along with other organizations, were required to hold meetings only in public places after first submitting details of the purpose of those meetings. We complied. On first returning in the quiet summer months following the coup this wasn't law but just a few months later it became so. This was because arms had been found, hidden in various churches by priests sympathetic to the previous regime.

As we strictly kept to our mandate from the very beginning in Allende's time that we would be apolitical, we didn't feel in any way threatened, although on one occasion we remember coming out of a duly registered meeting on church premises, to find an armed *carabinero* on guard watching all who went in and came out. It did feel a bit unnerving.

What were our own reactions to the change of government? We felt at the time that, given the tense situation in Chile likely to erupt at any moment into civil war, a military coup was the lesser of two evils – a view we still hold to this day. Having said that, my opinion is that General Pinochet stayed in power far too long. History shows all too often how power corrupts and I believe this to be so in his case.

Personally I believe both Salvador Allende and Augusto Pinochet started off their respective terms of office with the highest ideals for the good of the people and the country. In the one case, a strong opposition, the involvement of an outside country in Chile's affairs, together with more extreme government members pushing for more rapid, radical change pushed Allende into a corner. In the other, while intervention was only undertaken as a last resort, the economic success that followed despite many democratic countries putting an embargo on Chile's exports, was an incredible achievement that led to inflated pride and misguided power with tragic consequences.

Chile had gone through a momentous crisis, albeit a short lived one, and inevitably there were deaths. In the immediate days and weeks after September 11th this was the case. Unquestionably some of these were not men and women of violence, but ideologists who passionately believed in their cause. In attempting to root out the 'cancer' drastic steps were taken by the military government and people disappeared without families knowing where or how. We met such a woman, a member of the church of our Roman Catholic priest friend, Kevin (known as Miguel) O'Boyle.

Her husband was taken from the marital bed at 4.00 am one morning at gunpoint never to be seen again. Some, thought to constitute a threat, were tracked down and assassinated outside the country. General Prats, the predecessor to Pinochet, had been allowed by the Junta, together with his wife to travel to neighbouring Argentina, four days after the coup. Agents, thought to be of the Chilean military regime, assassinated them both in Buenos Aires a year later.

'So ended the life of Carlos Prats, a tragic, poignant, and affecting figure in contemporary Chilean history. If and when political progressives govern Chile again, Prats will be remembered.'[2]

Orlando Letelier was another. He, like so many politicians from Allende's government, was imprisoned on Dawson Island. US Ambassador Davis was able to recommend a few former politicians, now outside Chile, for academic posts and other suitable employment. On leaving office during his farewell visit to Oscar Bonilla, the new Minister of Interior, he appealed for the release of Letelier and Clodomiro Almeyda. Orlando Letelier had been Allende's ambassador to the United States. Once back in the

---

[2] Nathaniel Davis: *The Last Two Years of Salvador Allende* I. B. Tauris. p. 371

States, with David Popper, the newly appointed US Ambassador, mediating in Chile and Davis in Washington, the two political prisoners were released after an even higher intervention coming from no less a person than Secretary Henry Kissinger. Sadly, in Nathaniel Davis' own words, 'considering Orlando Letelier's subsequent murder, the US government's humanitarian intervention in 1974 takes on a bittersweet taste.'[3]

Pinochet, like his predecessor, remained to a large extent an enigma. To the world at large and to Chileans in particular, he was regarded either as the great liberator of Chile or vilified as a devil in disguise. He was usually presented in the media in either of two ways depending on the bias they wanted to create: the ruthless dictator, seated between his 'henchmen', wearing dark glasses, in military uniform and jowl (which was heavy in any case), set in stone, or as a benign grandfather figure, clad in a suit and smiling, greeting his supporters. In fact he's both. The former image was the one portrayed in the early days, especially outside Chile. Mass graves and detention centres discovered some years after the coup would seem to confirm the ruthless dictator image. Undoubtedly he too is the family man. I had occasion one day to meet his wife, a charming lady. One of his grandchildren was in Andrew's class at school. It's hard to find an unbiased account of the man. I think Davis, with the knowledge he had, by reason of his diplomatic status, managed to do so with both opposing Presidents.

As there are conflicting views, it is unclear as to exactly when Pinochet's loyalty to the President and the Constitution deviated into planning the coup. It is interesting to know what General Prats' own view of Pinochet was. Pinochet had been his deputy as chief of staff of the army, since January 1972. After General Carlos Prats' resignation as Commander-in-Chief, following the humiliating circumstances concerning the woman who insulted him, General Augusto Pinochet took office as his successor.

According to Davis and his various sources Pinochet assured Allende on more than one occasion of his unequivocal support to both Allende and the Constitution. He was nothing but loyal

---

[3] Ibid: p. 386

to Prats himself at this time, and according to his Commander's conviction, only joined those planning the coup at the eleventh hour.

It also would seem that key politicians close to the President had no reason to doubt his allegiance. Civilians also involved with plotting the coup were equally of the opinion that Pinochet only came in at the last moment of the planning. However, after September 11th itself, Pinochet claimed that he had been planning it for some months and almost alone and that it was the June 29th incident that was the catalyst in his future decision[4].

Yet even as far back as 1971 he had threatened the media with judicial action for their reporting, which had criticized the armed forces for continuing to support the Allende government[5]. He categorically stated that military coups did not occur in Chile, which of course rang true in Chile's tradition historically. All the sadder that later circumstances proved this statement to be wrong.

I think the enigma surrounding the motives and decisions undertaken by Pinochet during these critical years in the seventies can be best summed up in Davis' words. 'I believe one should not let one's disagreement with a person's later public policies become the exclusive measure of his character at an earlier time.'[6]

We hadn't arrived back long before we heard about 'Plan Zeta' (Plan Z). Friends were a buzz with it. The Junta coined this name for an alleged pre-coup plot by left extremists. The disclosure of this was used to justify the military taking power. Undoubtedly radical leftists, dissatisfied with Allende's handling of the crises of these spring months leading up to the eleventh, were planning their own coup to oust him out and seize total power. Carlos Altamirano had hinted at such in a speech two days before the eleventh. Various dates, allegedly planned by various disaffected extreme groups, began to surface. One of these was for September 17th. The Junta announced on September 16th that it had discovered this in papers

---

[4] Ibid: pp. 227, 228
[5] Ibid: p. 228
[6] Ibid: p. 229

found in a safe in the office of the Subsecretary of Interior. The plan was to murder top military commanders and opposition leaders.[7] Some days later it was said there had been found a list of six hundred people to be assassinated in a notebook belonging to a Socialist leader in Concepción.[8]

Some of this seems authentic as a conversation with a former neighbour revealed. However, we will never know for sure if what we discovered was in fact true. When we went to visit our military neighbours, soon after we got back, we got into conversation with General Anderson. We asked him if what we'd heard was factual and he told us there had been documents found, which he had seen, of a dawn raid planned for the assassination of the military families in our *pasaje* (my memory doesn't recall which date but it was probably the plan for September 17th). The houses were all marked with the names of the various occupants and the precise time for the assassinations to take place. We asked what information was down for our house, his answer was that it had been left blank!

In October, the Junta published its 'White Book', a copy of which we have in our study. The claim is that the documents it contains constitute 'Plan Zeta'. According to Davis the authenticity 'is highly doubtful'.[9]

Over these quiet summer months the media recounted many incidents of former Allende supporters seeking political asylum in various embassies. It wasn't unusual for walls to be climbed over under cover of darkness, a risky business given the curfew and the policy to shoot those who disobeyed or were not showing a white flag.

Just around the corner from us was the Swedish Embassy. This had the reputation of being pro-Allende and anti-Pinochet. The Ambassador himself had to leave under strict security during the night not long after we arrived in Las Violetas. My diary referring to this incident adds that it was thought that they had been *'in league with the Cubans,'*.

[7] Ibid: p. 370 Davis quoting Sanchez and Calm p. 21; *Economist* 13 Oct 1973 p. 44; Sigmund p. 257; Taufic p. 208
[8] Ibid: p. 370 Davis quoting Sigmund p. 257; Freed and Landis p. 107
[9] Ibid: p. 370

The replacement Ambassador was the nephew of Dag Hammarskjőld, former Secretary General of the United Nations. His wife, Elizabeth, a Scot, was a member of our congregation.

An amusing incident happened some time later in their home. We had been invited to dinner along with diplomats and well known people in both the Anglo-Chilean and Chilean communities. There must have been around thirty of us sitting at the very long table in the dining room. The table was beautifully set with silver cutlery and crystal wine glasses. I don't recall who was on either side of me on this particular occasion but Ray remembers he was seated about two away.

On the table were small bowls containing what looked like blackberries. Near to each was another small bowl with what appeared to be whipped cream. Out from the kitchen stepped two immaculately dressed waiters in their customary black and white attire. One headed to the far side of the long table, the other approached me, as I was the first woman to be served at my end of the table. In his left hand was a large silver plate, on which were more than a dozen pancakes piled high, like a large tiered cake.

How unusual, I thought, to be served pancakes, blackberries and cream as a starter. But then this was my first experience of Swedish cuisine. The waiter handed me a large cake-slice and a fork. I had a sudden flashback to the East End some nine years previously. One Shrove Tuesday in Shoreditch, I had, by way of a change, layered a number of pancakes with savoury fillings in between each and piled them up in similar fashion. With this recollection in mind I took the cake-slice and attempted to cut a wedge.

The waiter barely disguising his consternation at this uninformed *gringa* yet trying to maintain diplomacy consistent with his environment came to my rescue. After a couple of my unsuccessful attempts he finally managed to communicate with me the method was to put the slicer underneath and with the aid of the fork just simply slide the top pancake on to my plate. How simple and how embarrassing! The next thing I discovered were that the blackberries and cream were in fact caviar and mayonnaise! From

'Cockneyland' to 'Embassyland' was yet another divide we were learning to cross.

When a nation, a family, or friends have become divided through fractured relationships, for reconciliation to take place, bridges have to be built. The fissure in Chile ran very deep and very wide. Bridges constructed to span the chasm from one side to the other would take time and effort. It wasn't until after we had left Chile, in 1980, that the Rettig Commission was set up once democracy was restored in the country. The purpose of this was to document human right abuses.

What was the church's response after the eleventh? At the time the official Roman Catholic Church took a neutral line but individual bishops like the rest of the people were divided in their loyalties. Shortly after, together with Protestant, Greek Orthodox and Jewish leaders, a co-operative was set up offering legal representation and economic aid to people suffering under the new regime. Thousands were helped.

Cardinal Silva was under pressure to close it in December 1975. In its place, however, he set up another 'bridge' across the political divide.

The *'Vicária de la Solidaridad'* came into being in January 1976, occupying a building next door to the cathedral. It was exclusively Catholic and, being under the Cardinal's supreme jurisdiction, the Junta was unable to force it to close. Its aim, like that of South Africa, was based on truth and justice in the long process towards forgiveness and healing. Our friend Juan de Castro, later to become a Monsignor, was part of the *'Vicária'*.

As more evidence of the *'desaparacedos'* and of mass graves came to light relations between the Catholic Church and the ruling military became more strained. The truth when it was uncovered made the Catholic Church, in a twist of historical reversal, more popular with the left than with the right. We found a number in our congregation had no good word to say about the Cardinal. Nathanial Davis is far more generous.

Increasing strain emerged between the military and other political forces of whatever persuasion. It seemed the military wanted to go it alone. General Leigh had the reputation of being more sympathetic and of wanting to return to civilian rule once the country was stable, but was overruled.

The personal 'bridges' we tried to build had as their foundation biblical truth and the sought after answer to the question 'What would Jesus do?' The power of the Gospel to change lives and attitudes was at work quietly but effectively in individual lives and relationships.

We well remember Easter of 1974 when Nico turned up on Good Friday. Having told us when we first returned how he hated the military for what they had done to his country, what he said and what he had done on this Good Friday showed a change that only God could bring about.

'Ray, Gill, I bet you can't guess where I've been today!' a smiling Nico exclaimed.

'I've been to Tómas Moro' (the Presidential residence) 'and started to talk to the soldiers on guard as to what Jesus had done for them on the cross that first Good Friday and how much he loved them. I then gave them a leaflet about becoming a Christian.' Another divide crossed.

Not long into the new regime both Ray and I met the top brass face to face. Ray had been asked to represent Bishop Colin Bazley on behalf of the Anglican Church in presenting a Bible to General Pinochet. He shook the President's hand in the former UNCTAD (United Nations Conference on Trade and Development) building. This modern building had been constructed especially to host a UN gathering in Allende's time and was opened shortly after we arrived in Chile. It was now government offices.

It was Pinochet's wife and the wives of the other members of the Junta I was to meet. As wife of the Chaplain of the only English-speaking Church representing the English-speaking international community, I was invited to a lunch at which Bill Bright, an American who headed up Campus Crusade, was the speaker. This Christian organization based in universities was international in scope.

Other wives of various Spanish-speaking churches were also invited. Our places were reserved and I found myself sitting directly opposite the President's wife. After lunch, while still at the table, Bill Bright got up to address us all. A young Chilean in her mid-twenties was sitting between the speaker and Lucía Pinochet, and was the translator. Unfamiliar with theological vocabulary there were one or two occasions when she found herself struggling to find the correct English words. Being diagonally opposite I caught her eye and was able to help her, being more familiar with such vocabulary. Afterwards she came up to thank me. We immediately took to one another and exchanged names and telephone numbers. This encounter was to symbolise a huge jump across the divide between right and left at a later date.

Another massive leap made was only discovered recently. I've already mentioned meeting up with four Chileans in the south of Spain when we were covering a locum recently in the Anglican Church. The other couple were Ricardo and María (not their real names). Ricardo had been firmly on the ultra right wing in his political persuasion in the 1970s and remains more to the right today. He was a disaffected Roman Catholic and had studied politics and Law at university in Santiago and became a member of Patria y Libertad. He left Chile in 1970 for Germany to study for a Master's degree returning in 1971 as a twenty-four-year-old. Within two weeks he was arrested by Eduardo Paredes, ('Coco'), and tortured with electric shocks. Paredes was chief of Investigative Police (DINA) in Allende's time. It was thought Ricardo had been involved in the assassination of General Schneider.

General René Schneider was already chief of the armed forces at the time Allende was elected President. In September and October 1970 a plot was hatched to kidnap General Schneider, 'a firm constitutionalist'.[10] The leading protagonists were the CIA, General Roberto Viaux and General Valenzuela. The reason behind it was the hope that the military would step in and seize power thus rendering Allende without office.

The CIA, instructed by Kissinger, allegedly pulled out of the plan but the Chilean conspirators continued, with the result of two failed attempts. The third attempt was on October 22nd.

---

[10] Ibid: p. 8

General Schneider's car was waylaid and he was fatally shot by a handgun. According to Davis, the CIA had provided submachine guns to Valenzuela's supporters and were therefore, implicated. The Church Committee ultimately absolved them of Schneider's death because they had in mind kidnapping and not murder.[11]

After four days in prison, Ricardo was released and in his own words told me that at that time he 'was filled with so much hate' that he 'wanted to give back what they had done'. He was trained by the marines to kill. By day he was a businessman and by night took part in assassinations on the orders of the Commanders. They selected who the targets were to be. He fought against the 'Miristas'.

After September 11th he was made redundant from his clandestine 'work' but 'instead of feeling happy I felt depressed'. Three months later he met María and his life changed.

Ironically María's grandfather, left in political persuasion, had held a high-ranking military post in the past and was acting Vice President when the President was out of the country.

One event that occurred in 1983 caused Ricardo to begin to question if in fact the military regime did have all the answers. Whilst acknowledging the good they had achieved economically, uncomfortable stories of abuse and ruthlessness could not be denied.

Sebastían Acevedo had doused himself in petrol outside the Cathedral fulfilling a threat he said he would carry out if the authorities wouldn't stop torturing his twenty-two-year-old son and twenty-year-old daughter. A large wooden cross was erected in his memory. The military sawed it off at its base.

Ricardo continued with his story.

'Neither of us was religious. After ten years of marriage and with two daughters we felt empty, our marriage was in crisis.'

In 1986 they went to the south of Chile for a holiday renting a motor caravan and took a boat trip on Lake Todos los Santos. When it began to rain they went inside the boat. Here they met a young couple laughing and cracking jokes. This encounter was

---

[11] Ibid p. 10

to have dramatic and life changing consequences. The happy couple were none other than Margarita and Lorenzo.

During the rest of the holiday the four kept on meeting up at the various popular tourist places. Ricardo couldn't understand how Lorenzo was so happy as he recently had lost his mother and every few words or so 'he was talking of the Lord'. It was obvious to Ricardo that Lorenzo and Margarita had a faith that had always eluded him. Curious to know more once back in Santiago, María and Ricardo went to their church in Plaza Egaña where a relative of Lorenzo, Eduardo Jacob, was the pastor. It was March 1st 1974.

'They were very humble people in the Church. I began to cry. I felt I'd arrived home.'

Ricardo was baptised, became a member of the Church Council, but after more than seven years they felt it right to worship in a church nearer to where they lived. The Anglican Church of La Trinidad became their new spiritual home. They became part of a team of married couples who, under the overall leadership of Alf and Hilary Cooper, were involved in 'Encuentro Matrimonial' (Marriage Encounter). It was at one of these occasions that they were sharing the platform with another couple who also had found Jesus and whose lives had been transformed too. The husband had been a Mirista. Ricardo and he embraced one another and asked one another for forgiveness. Such is the power of the gospel to bring healing and reconciliation.

Ricardo told me how he had spent years of nightmares, in which he recalled the killings he had taken part in. 'I knew God had forgiven me but it took a long time before I was able to forgive myself.'

He was involved in lay leadership in the church and began to study for the ordained ministry. This stopped when his business failed and he went to Spain looking for work and was joined by María later. In experiencing the power and enabling of the Holy Spirit today, he and his wife walk together in love and freedom in their new life in Spain, in continuing friendship with Lorenzo and Margarita.

His view on Chile today is that 'maybe twenty or thirty years more of socialist government doesn't matter because of the lessons learnt.'

At the time of writing Chile has a woman President, for the first time, continuing the socialist tradition of the last decade. All the more remarkable is that her father, an air force general, died following torture and she herself was tortured by Pinochet's secret police in the 1970s. Yet as Defence Secretary in Ricardo Lagos' socialist government, she has won the confidence of her commanders-in-chief. According to the Times, 'Political analysts believe that Señora Bachelet embodies the desire of many Chileans to move forward. "She symbolises Chile's reconciliation with its past," said Patricio Navio, of the Centre for Latin American and Caribbean Studies at New York University.'[12]

---

[12] *The Times* December 3rd 2005. Correspondent Hannah Hennessy in Santiago

Chapter 28

A First Harvest

'Rejoice in the Lord your God, for he has given you the autumn rains in righteousness.

'He sends you abundant showers, both autumn and spring rains …

'The threshing-floors will be filled with grain; the vats will overflow with new wine and oil.'[1]

Early this morning as I was sitting quietly in the conservatory I was reading these words in the book of the prophet Joel. My thoughts went back in time to Chile when we began to see the autumn rains bringing the beginning of a first spiritual harvest. They began to fall on that memorable Christmas Day with the turning point we witnessed in Nico's life.

I wrote a letter to my parents in the first autumn of our new ministry, which started in similar vein.

'As I'm writing this letter in the patio on a gorgeously hot Sunday afternoon, Andrew is helping me eat grapes which I've just picked from our own vine.'

With wine so cheap we weren't into making our own from the rich harvest gathered. As I continued my letter, Julian was riding back and forth along the pathway on his tricycle leading from the large back garden of Las Violetas, past the covered patio, down one side of the house and into the front garden, the security gate providing parental peace of mind.

Naomi had gone with her Daddy to Commonwealth House this particular Sunday afternoon. Both she and Andrew liked

---

[1] The Bible: Joel chapter 2 verses 23 and 24

to accompany Ray and help give out and later collect in the hymnbooks to and from the elderly residents.

It was in this letter I shared the news of Andrew giving his life to Jesus imagining how happy both sets of parents would be. Alongside the reaping of a harvest was the continuing planting of seeds. This was in the 'soil' of both Chilean and English-speakers' hearts.

Friendship with the Collingwood-Selbys was developing, first through the children themselves, although only Naomi was attending Redland, the boys having their names down for the following year. Richard now started to attend the morning service at the Community Church.

'Julian is still a pickle and is great friends with Benjamin ... (headmaster's youngest) who is every bit a pickle as Julian! In fact Richard said to us "Can you imagine both of them in the same class at school? Won't it be awful when I have to expel my own son from my own school!"'

Meanwhile both Andrew and Julian were building their own relationships with their teachers for the next year from the tree house among the branches of the large fig tree at the bottom of the garden. From this vantage point they bridged the dividing wall separating our garden from the grounds of the Convent. As a result they were the bridge in building relationships with so many Roman Catholic neighbours.

Such was the bridge built that eighteen nuns joined with many other friends in a showing we had later of a film *La Tierra Santa* (The Holy Land) with commentary by the famous and internationally respected American evangelist, Dr Billy Graham. We held it in the Church hall to which over 120 people came, including the Manriquez family and 'Supermarket' Doris, Dr Bennett, head of the Blood Bank of the El Salvador Hospital and Mónica, the President's secretary. Two people responded to the invitation to commit their lives to Christ. My diary records how impressed the nuns were, especially with the Biblical references given.

Attendance at the pre-school was a good preparation for starting at 'Colegio Redland' but with one drawback. Andrew was most unhappy at the outfit the nuns required all the children to wear. It was a smocked bright blue overall that he thought was better suited to his sister. We thought he had a point. He was so much happier with the standard overall requirement once he started school. At least it had trousers and was only worn by the boys.

It was two other comments in the letter home that were the catalyst for the harvest that was to be reaped, especially from the seeds planted and watered in Chilean 'soil'. In this letter I had written of my last significant English class with Omar and Lia before Omar left for Canada, complete with the New Testament I had given him.

Also in this letter I wrote of the desire of Nico and two friends to form a regular group to read and discuss the Bible. Their idea was to meet every week to study and for the first Sunday of the month to have a more open gathering to which they could invite their friends. Nicolás in particular wanted to invite his Marxist friends to discuss subjects like 'The existence of God – the only remedy for human nature?' In March of 1974 the military government hadn't as yet cracked down on home gatherings.

The meeting with both Nico, Omar and Lia were to have far reaching consequences that we could never have dreamed of at the time, both inside Chile and beyond. Simultaneously with this initiative was the beginning of the Women's Forum with my first Thursday on March 21st, having as its title 'Is the Bible Reliable?'

The nature of our international ministry meant we were privileged to welcome many visitors to the country from all over the world, bringing with them their own unique experiences and expertise. We were privileged to welcome to our home that autumn the well-known preacher, author and an Honorary Chaplain to the Queen, the Rev. Dr John Stott. He stayed for a week and was a most gracious and easy house-guest helping with the washing-up and delighting the children with his friendly and warm manner. It was Andrew who always addressed him as 'Uncle John Stott', something of a mouthful but retaining a balance between familiarity and respect.

John Stott was in Chile at the invitation of an international university Christian movement and was giving a series of lectures as well as kindly preaching to our congregation. Our Peruvian nun friend Sister Georgina and *Padre* Carlos Aldunate, together with other Roman Catholic leaders involved with the renewal movement in the Roman Catholic Church, attended those evening lectures sitting on the front row eagerly listening and writing notes, such was their hunger for Biblical teaching of the calibre John Stott always gave. Nico met him at our home. They hit it off immediately as JRWS (as often referred to) had such an affinity with students and young graduates. He kept in touch with this earnest young Christian by letter for sometime.

Letters were a valuable means of encouragement. They meant so much to us over these years, just knowing we were prayed for by so many friends and were a lifeline during the dark days of austerity and potential danger. Letters continue to bring encouragement three decades later as I re-read the originals and receive current updates from some already introduced in my writing.

It was a letter from Santiago to Vancouver, from an ex-Marxist to a dispirited Communist, from Nico to Omar, whom he hadn't even met, that in turn was the last link in a chain that led to Omar beginning the Christian journey. After he took the plane to an uncertain future in an unknown land, Lia started to come to our Sunday night small group. Here she met Nicolás among others.

I pick up the story from Omar and Lia's own words, written in the third person, in their Testimonial.

'Omar, Lia and sons have been living in Vancouver, Canada, since 1974. Recently, this couple celebrated 36 years of marriage; their sons are Omar Jr. and Daniel, were both born in Chile while John-Paul was born in Canada. They claim three nationalities, "Chileans by birth, Canadians by adoption, and subjects of the Kingdom of God by divine grace."

'Both of them grew up, were educated, got married and started a family in Chile. As a young couple they had a good life style as result of Omar's successful professional career. However, their spiritual life was nonexistent because they embraced atheism. But the political circumstances in the 70's in Chile brought Omar's career to an end getting the family into a crisis. Lack of hope for the country and for themselves led them into the decision of immigrating to Canada with their two small sons.

'It was during this time of uncertainty and doubts that Gill and Ray, Anglican missionaries in Chile, entered their lives for a short period of time. In retrospect, this was a divine appointment from God. Then a chain of circumstances started to unfold to the extent of transforming their lives forever [sic].'

The Testimonial continues with a biographical account of both their upbringings. Omar, born in Valdivia, southern Chile, had his childhood in a dysfunctional family with most of his education in boarding schools. Lia, born in Santiago was from a happier middle-class family with right-wing political sympathies. Both were brought up in the Roman Catholic faith, but whereas Omar dismissed any religious influence as irrelevant to his teen years, Lia, as a result of her mother's influence in taking her regularly to church remained receptive.

'She never had a Bible, only some Bible verses which were a part of the mass-book with the liturgy of every Sunday.'

The parable of the sower and the seed impacted Lia deeply, to the point of asking God with all her heart to allow her to be that fertile soil. That prayer was answered years later. As an adolescent she had hunger for knowing more about God and also a desire to serve in the Catholic Church. In pursuing her spiritual quest she got to know a priest who she asked to be her leader and mentor. He recommended for her to pray the rosary every day and to read some books that he loaned her. Her spiritual questions were not answered, the plan of salvation and purpose of Jesus Christ coming to earth were not taught, and so every day there were more questions that unfortunately were dealt with in a ritualistic manner.

'Finally in her late teens, Lia got disappointed with religion due to the wrong attitude of the mentor priest who tried to take advantage of her. Consequently, she stopped attending the Catholic Church, dropping her membership, and declaring herself a non-believer. Her

faith in religion was deeply damaged, affecting her trust in God for several years [sic].'

During the hard days immediately following the coup when Omar lost his job they moved from their rented house in Las Condes to Lia's parents' home. From here Lia managed to get temporary work in a friend's beauty saloon as a cashier. This was where I first met her.

'It was during this short time, that Lia had a glimpse of a foreign lady leaving the saloon, and thought to herself, "maybe she can give us a few English lessons." So, Lia approached the lady and made her request known … No phone numbers were exchanged, but Gill managed to get Lia's number from the saloon and gave her a positive response.

'Omar and Lia attended the private English classes for a month before Omar's departure in March. Lia continued attending for the next three months. During the last class for Omar, Gill explored their lives and asked if they had any religious belief. The answer was, "No!" Nonetheless, Gill gave Omar a New Testament (a portion of the Bible) for his trip; which Lia placed carefully in his luggage [sic].

'God in His grace sent messengers obedient to His will and created circumstances that led to both of their lives being touched by the gospel. God had a plan – to adopt them into His Kingdom.'

March 7th Omar left the family behind as he flew out from Pudahuel airport on his way to Vancouver.

'Later that day, Lia felt the effects of the separation, sadness, loneliness, anguish, and emptiness in her soul that were difficult to describe. Then, an opportune phone call from Gill brought words of comfort and understanding. She invited her to attend a meeting at her house the following day.

'Loneliness moved Lia to attend the meeting, where about seven persons were present. Someone read the Bible and discussion of the passages followed. This was a boring activity for Lia at the moment, and her mind was far away even when they were praying. Suddenly, when prayers were offered for her husband she was touched by the presence of the Holy Spirit. She asked herself, "Why do these people care about us?" tears rolled down her face.

'Next week, she was again invited to the meetings that Ray and Gill were leading at their home. In this occasion she had the desire to attend.

This time she started to remember the catechism classes of the Roman Catholic church, and began to consider God's existence. The other fact that impressed her was Gill's invitation to spend Easter with them at their home with the family. It was the first time in her life that she was in close contact with a Christian family, they prayed and gave honor to God in everything that they did. This impressed her and it became the desire of her heart to have a family that would practice the same principles.

'Bible studies became more and more interesting, the group grew, and people of various ages with different degrees of spiritual hunger and curiosity were attending. On one occasion, Gill asked Lia if she was ready to receive the Lord in her life. Lia hesitated because it was a very serious decision since she had distanced herself from the Catholic doctrine. This time if she were to make a decision it had to be forever. No turning back! [sic].'

This particular evening was indelibly printed on the minds, not only of Lia, Nico, and the others in our home, but it was a turning point for us as Ray writes in his letter home describing the events of that evening. The evening in which *'a Chilean Church was born in our home, a nucleus of four, including Nicolás …'.*

The Church was born out of human weakness and total dependency on God. Ray was ill in bed with typhoid and felt he was to spend the enforced rest in prayer. Meanwhile from his bed he heard the front doorbell constantly ringing as folk began to arrive. After a half hour or so I went upstairs, deciding to join him leaving Nico to continue the evening. I felt too tired after looking after an ill husband, family and Church needs, to be involved in the mental effort of a stimulating discussion in Spanish.

Ray continues in his letter home of his reaction to my decision:

'Ray said, "No", the Lord had shown him that she [Gill] was going to be needed downstairs … For 2 hours Ray was praying and not hearing anything that was transpiring below.'

Omar and Lia pick up the story in their Testimonial:

'That evening Ray was sick with typhus and was unable to attend the meeting. Gill led the group and after the testimony time, they prayed together. Gill prayed to Jesus Christ saying: "I know that there

are other people here tonight that also want to give their lives to you, I pray that they would have the courage to do so." Lia thought, "that is me, but I do not know how to do it." Gill opened her eyes to check any reaction and found Lia saying, "I want to do it but I do not know how to do it." Gill moved close to Lia and asked her to kneel. She felt uncomfortable, but as soon as she knelt she sensed that only God, Gill and herself were there. Lia repeated the sinner's prayer after Gill, and then she prayed for the conversion of her husband and sons, and asked for a Christian home [sic].'

Ray's letter home continues:

'When Gill had finally farewelled [sic] everyone, she came up to Ray and said, "What a wonderful evening it's been – 3 people have committed their lives to Christ." Ray said, "I know. Osvaldo, Lia and Lucia." Gill was staggered and said, "How do you know exactly who?" "They were the 3 that the Lord led me to pray for particularly," he said.'

With Ray ill, the reaping of the beginnings of a spiritual harvest among our Chilean friends, the ongoing family needs and the many things to see to within the Community Church, especially the Women's Forum, now bursting at the seams, little wonder I had no time to make any entries in my diary over these few weeks. It was during Ray's illness that the husband of Joanna, his secretary, was arrested and within a few weeks she left.

Added to this we had been given a new car, as the one we had acquired had long since gone past its sell-by date and was proving so unreliable. It fell to me to break it in! It was a *citroneta*, small, economical, high soft-topped roof and ugly in design. It looked like a giant ladybird although American friends referred to it as the 'cookie cutter'! They were very common on the roads of the capital. Certainly it caused some amusement as we arrived at our various embassy functions chugging up to park alongside the smooth-gliding Daimlers and Chevrolets! It was the gear stick that took the most getting used to. It was to the side of the steering wheel and operated by a pulling out and pushing in system.

Ray never reconciled himself to liking this car. I would tease him by saying it was because it was me who had to teach him its

Transform your scotch with water

26 Jan 08

From Mr Kevan Pegley.

Sir, Your correspondent Edward Brady (Letters, January 20/21) has adopted a curious position for a self-proclaimed Scot: he appears to think ice and water are equivalent. Chemically they may be, but in their effect on scotch they are as different as the stuff on which the Titanic was sailing to the stuff that sank it.

Water releases the flavour of scotch by weakening the bonds between its aromatic molecules; ice reduces its temperature, making those same bonds more difficult to break.

My formative drinking years were spent avoiding scotch completely. Much later in life an old friend – a Scot – introduced me to the transformation water effected. I urge your readers to try the difference.

Kevan Pegley,
Haslemere, Surrey GU27 1QJ

idiosyncrasies. In fact, apart from its appearance, I liked it and found it very good for bombing around, weaving in and out of the traffic, which was the only way to survive on the roads of Santiago.

Ray had started feeling unwell on April 16th and was in bed for over three weeks. Having kept up our vaccinations the typhoid itself wasn't too severe, but it was being compounded by acute tonsillitis. The doctor told him he couldn't resume duties until May 26th.

English members of our Church, who had the use of a holiday home for some weeks in the year, offered it for a much-needed convalescence for Ray and a rest for me. I had gone down with a high temperature preceding 'chileitis' just a day or so before setting out. Naomi then started running a temperatue and Thea diagnosed German measles. Nevertheless within three days we set out, but not before two more people had come to faith. Janice Raby, an Anglo-Chilean and member of the Women's Forum, later to become Ray's secretary, and Eduardo, a friend of Nico and Pato (Patricio) who himself, only a few days previously, had come to a personal faith.

Pato, like Nico was a university student and had been an avowed Marxist, but when we first met him was a disillusioned leftist. There was a difference in their political involvement, whereas Nico was a party member, Pato's radical left convictions, sprang out of idealism. It was in our home that they met for the first time. Pato came along to a discussion group brought by his girlfriend, Susan Macdonald, the younger daughter of Jeff and Bessie within our congregation.

The subject for that evening was a very current one in the 1970s. Eastern philosophies were filling the vacuum left by the collapse of left utopia among disillusioned students. Brought up in a nominal Roman Catholic background, Pato, very 'impressed' with the clear thinking former Marxist found himself siding with Nicolás in the discussion, although he 'didn't believe' in Christianity. At the end of the meeting, Pato turned to Nico, 'I found what you said very interesting. Would you talk with me?'

Winning co elusive for

STATE PRIMARY

None of the four main candidates can replicate the successful Bush formula to unify a diverse state, says Andrew Ward

It would take 13 hours to drive non-stop between Pensacola, in the north-western corner of Florida, and Key West, the state's southern.

fragmented John McCa ney in a t tory, whil and Mike stay in co As a 71 war hero, ular amon numbers retirees, w stance appeals to Mr Rom private-s before er the choic ida's b wealthy

Nico took him to his home and they met together for several weeks, after which Pato started to come to the Sunday night group. 'Six weeks later, I knelt by my bed saying, "If the Lord of Nico exists, come to me." From that moment "life began to change".'

Nico and Pato complemented one another in temperament. Whereas Nico was gregarious and smiled readily, Pato was more serious by nature, sensitive and somewhat melancholy. His deep sensitivity, which has caused him at times to be defensive and misunderstood, springs from a great heart of compassion and anger at social injustices. Physically they were very different too. Pato was shorter and stockier in build than his tall, slim dark friend, with light brown straighter hair, fairer skin and blue-grey eyes. His very European appearance reflected his ancestral genes, Ireland, Austria and Croatia. From that very first meeting these two students formed a deep friendship.

Zapallar, about three hours drive away was situated on the coast and a favourite spot for holidays. It lay to the north of Viña del Mar about halfway between the inland towns of Llay-Llay and La Ligua which had been the area of the epi-centre of the earthquake we experienced soon after arriving.

What should have taken three hours took us four and a half. We were only able to do 60 kmph. We were still breaking the car in. It had already broken down once on me when collecting the children from school. When we woke up that morning, there was a discernible change in the weather. Before long the much-needed autumn rains fell, falling torrentially within a short time. On went the windscreen wipers only to pack up, followed by the indicators. It was obviously an electrical fault. We pulled into the first service station on the Pan-American highway.

'We are sorry, Señor, but we don't have a mechanic here. You'll be able to get the *problema* sorted at Llay-Llay.'

The *problema* was that Llay-Llay was another 45 kilometres away. Not a good start to our convalescing holiday.

The last 10 kilometres were on a rough *ripio*, coastal road. Due to the heavy rain, puddles in the many deep holes in the road surface formed rivulets coursing down bringing silt in their wake.

The difficult start faded into insignificance in the light of our next encounters as Ray writes home:

'On arrival our troubles had not ended! No, we had brought the keys, the electricity was working, and so was the calor gas, but there wasn't a drop of water in the taps! Yes, the key was in the "on" position! We had been warned that the pressure drops a bit at certain times of the day during the summer ... but there was all this water bucketing down outside. That's it-buckets! So we searched for every imaginable container and put them outside the backdoor to catch the rain –"all good gifts around us are sent from heaven above, then" ... yes, as a family we did, "thank the Lord ... for all his love." Just enough to wash our hands, faces and teeth before going to bed, make some cocoa and coffee ... to wash up after supper-which was used to flush the toilet, partially! [sic].'

We fell into bed and still the rain was falling. Unfortunately Julian and I both found we had shared our respective beds with some unwelcome residents. The wooden house and especially the bare floorboards were the ideal environment for these established residents. Fleas continued to plague us for several days. My diary (which I had now picked up writing again) records the hunt was still on, five days later, for these tiny but determined little creatures. On this day we caught four in our bed bringing the grand total to around twenty. The bites were nothing in comparison to the havoc wrought by two little pests, of a Brazilian variety, that resided in the folds of a hammock, in which I was sleeping. The hammock was slung between two supports on deck of a small boat in which we were sailing down the Amazon thirteen years later. On that occasion I ended up with my back plastered from head to toe with three hundred and sixty-five bites, one for every day of the year! Ray actually counted them as I lay face down on our hotel bed two nights later.

It was on this Amazonian trip that my third fishing venture happened. We shared the small, basic boat with another tourist couple from the United States. Part of the attraction for this trip was that it was advertised as piranha fishing and alligator flashing. We were given a nylon line on a reel with chicken as bait. The American lady was the first to catch a piranha. Piranha are small, flat and pinky in colour. Their ferocious reputation lay in the fact they descend on their victim in their scores, if not hundreds. Their teeth are like a serrated knife and within a short time the flesh of whatever has become their target is ripped off leaving just bones! The one caught by the American lady was about seven or eight inches at its widest point.

'I think I may have got a piranha on my line!' I shouted out in excitement. 'Something is really tugging at my bait.'

It was. I landed it then kept a discrete distance, as the teeth snapped in no uncertain way. Our Brazilian skipper disentangled it from the hook. I actually caught five on my line over the next hour or so, but in my excitement only managed to land three. The two men didn't catch one! Their fishing success consisted in only small sardine like fish. The skipper's wife cooked the piranha and we ate them with rice. They tasted delicious and left us wondering what their own diet had been prior to becoming ours!

Our first full day in our holiday house was spent still without water on tap and no rain. Across the road was a building site and we managed to fill up the now empty containers. The next day a man turned up, having heard via the grapevine about our water problem. It turned out there was a problem with the motor system that the tanks depended on. He put it right and wouldn't take any money. He also went with Ray to the garage to help lift a full gas cylinder.

With warm autumn sunshine and vivid blue skies we set off with the children to walk along the sea front. Rounding the coast we came upon a very large shelf of flat rocks jutting out over the sea. From here in early evening we would watch beautiful sunsets. The evenings were becoming chilly and it became necessary to have a fire. It was our youngest that created the next *problema.*

Being the helpful little boy he was he switched the electric fire on, all three bars at once. All the electricity went off! It was

Sunday and with no shops open what were we to do? We prayed. Ray went out to see if by chance the local shop was open to get a spare fuse. It wasn't. Suddenly on turning a corner, he noticed, outside a house, a parked van marked *'electra'*. It was the local electrician who immediately came round and mended the fuse! No need is too trivial to bring to our Heavenly Father.

May 21st was a *feriado*. The whole village of Zappallar turned out at the local football pitch to celebrate the commemoration of the Battle of Iquique. It was a colourful event as the local firemen and schoolchildren, together with their respective bands, paraded in front of the mayor.

Once we returned home Ray gradually took up his responsibilities. Within a few days we celebrated Pentecost and what a celebration it was. The day started with three prizes being given to three young teenagers in the Bible class I was leading in the Community Church. After lunch several carloads of Chilean students, friends and families set off for El Arrayan. Our destination was the River Mapocho, not for a picnic but for baptism. It was still early days in Ray's full recuperation and the water, fed by melting snow from the lower hills on the Andean range, was very, very cold. It was mid-winter. Among those requesting baptism were Nico, Pato, Osvaldo, and Susan. As Ray and the candidates one by one entered the river, the rest of us stood under the trees on the rocks by the riverbank singing and praying. Twenty-two of us returned to our home for tea and to warm up. A couple of weeks later there were more baptisms and on June 27th on the eve of her departure to Canada, Ray baptized Lia in the thermal springs of La Colina.

While for Lia light and joy had entered her life, Omar meanwhile in Vancouver was becoming increasingly immersed in darkness and confusion. He was sharing rented accommodation with other Chilean political refugees. All were lonely and disillusioned. One evening as they shared their past, Gloria made a suggestion that was to have a profound effect on Omar. I record those events exactly as Omar wrote them.

'Gloria told them she had had some experience with spiritualism and séances. Omar affirmed that he was an atheist, his interpretation

of life and the spirits was a materialistic and scientific one, and did not believe in ghost stories. Nonetheless, if there was evidence, he wanted to hear it. She proceeded to start the "show" on the only table available at the kitchen. She wrote each letter of the alphabet on pieces of paper and distributed them in a circle, then placed an inverted glass in the center. Each person was supposed to slightly touch the glass with the index finger. With eyes closed, she begun to call the spirits. The glass moved frantically in the circle. Suddenly, Omar felt into a trance, a strong spirit took him over. He was in pain producing guttural groans and contortions. It was so bad that the others shook him out the trance. After a while, when he had recuperated he commented, "this seems very interesting, let us repeat the experiment and this time I will call a spirit in my mind so you do not know its name in advance."

'Again the glass danced in a circle and Omar fell into a trance once more. This time the trance was benign. When the glass stopped at each letter and formed the name of the person that Omar was thinking about, he was awaken. The name was Rosalia, the former nanny Omar had when he was a child, who he called in his mind to manifest herself this evening in Vancouver.

'That night, fear fell upon each one of the participants, at midnight the wooden floor was invaded by creaking noises as someone was walking on it. When Omar went to the bathroom and looked at his face on the mirror, he saw something horrific too difficult to describe. In terror he exclaimed "Jesus Christ help me." Right away his face turned to normal.

'This horrific experience had great impact in Omar's beliefs about the supernatural and the afterlife. He meditated "there is something beyond this earthly life and it seems there is a spiritual realm which I do not understand yet."

'Four months later, June 30 1974, Lia arrived with her two sons in Vancouver. This young family was united again, they had been changed in their inner persons, and they were not the same. Lia was a new person, she was radiant, joyful, peaceful, and something in her that was not easy to describe. Omar thought, "what am I going to do with this woman who is not the same anymore?" Both updated their lives with the happenings during the months of separation. Omar shared the spiritism experience, to which Lia objected. "This does not please God, *according to Deuteronomy 18:10-12, she affirmed, you should repent right away." Omar did repent [sic].'*

Lia's changed life and encouragement had a great impact on Omar over the next weeks and months. She encouraged him to listen to a couple of cassettes of a Puerto Rican evangelist.

He *'heard for the first time in his 36 years a Christian message that touched his inner being in a deep way. He felt that his life was exposed on this preaching, tears rolled down his face that day.*

'He understood the purpose of Jesus Christ dying a sacrificial death for the remission of his sins and the hope of eternal life. But when Lia asked him about making a commitment to Jesus as his Savior and Lord of his life, he objected saying that he was a great sinner and was unworthy of receiving him in his life. He was not ready [sic].'

A few weeks later a letter from Chile was the means by which God brought this atheistic scientist into his kingdom.

'... on Thursday September 26, 1974, both were again talking spiritual matters when the mailman knocked at the door and delivered a letter from Chile, addressed to Omar and Lia. The sender was Nicolás, a young college student full of passion for Jesus, who was part of the Bible study group with Ray and Gill. In a five-pages letter he made a theological presentation of the human condition, of this world full of injustice and slavery to a life of sinful behavior. He shared the calling to look for social justice not in human terms but through divine inspiration. "Blessed are those who hunger and thirst for righteousness (justice), for they will be filled." Jesus Christ is the only solution to the human misery, he died to redeem us from sin and give us abundant and eternal life. He is the peace and love God extends to us. At the end of the letter, Nicolás asked Omar directly to receive Jesus into his life, by praying with Lia:

'"Jesus, I repent of the kind of life I have been living, in which I have not known you. I want to receive you into my life and my heart, I want you to be my Lord and my Savior, the Master and absolute owner of my life, take control over it. Help me to follow your ways. Help me to bring clarity to my mind and help to others. Thank you Lord Jesus for taking residence in my life. Thank you. Amen."

'By means of this simple prayer that Omar prayed, he entered the

Kingdom of God and his name was written in the Book of Life. Lia's prayer for having a Christian family was answered that day [sic].'

Years later *'their parents and one of Lia's brother also made a commitment to the Lord.'*

Also many years later, Omar and Lia continue to serve the Lord in Canada and also in other countries, but that is the subject of another chapter.

Before long Ray was feeling overwhelmed with the harvest being reaped among the Chileans. Jesus' words in the Gospels took on new meaning: 'The harvest is plentiful, but the workers are few. Ask the Lord of the harvest, therefore, to send out workers into his harvest field.'[2]

Numbers for the Sunday night group by now topped forty. Help came in the form of Gordon and Beryl Whitehead who, after marriage, had joined the SAMS team in Santiago. Their brief, like our original one, was to church plant among the professionals in the Barrio Alto.

Ray felt rightly that the group should be Chilean led. The group was unanimous in choosing Nicolás and Patricio. They jointly led the group for four years. Gordon and Beryl, together with us (when we were able), would be there in an advisory and supportive role. We never tried to exert any pressure on our two leaders to form an Anglican church, understanding something of their innate mistrust of being 'institutionalized'.

'We don't like labels, only that we are Christians.' It would be later that they themselves discerned the need to become less isolated and to become more of an identifiable community within a wider body.

Alongside the reaping of God's harvest, our task was to continue the sowing and watering in the field of human hearts.

In a letter home Ray, wrote that forty copies of the *Living Bible* had been sold among the English-speaking members of the congregation, including one bought by our Ambassador's wife.

We needed to remind ourselves of St Paul's words to the Christians in ancient Corinth in these somewhat heady days. We are only servants through whom others came to faith. 'So neither

---

[2] The Bible: Luke chapter 10 verse 2

he who plants nor he who waters is anything, but only God who makes things grow ... For we are God's fellow-workers; you are God's field ...'[3]

Alongside the continued planting, watering and harvesting in the Chilean 'field' was the sowing of seeds in the neighbouring international English-speaking 'field'. This would in time bring a second harvest but the seeds took longer to germinate.

God in his graciousness had rewarded our obedience in following his directing of our lives even though my initial reluctance to move from Spanish into the English-speaking ministry was such a real struggle. We couldn't have imagined a crop of lives ripening so quickly into a harvest for God's kingdom after the previous three years of apparent drought.

---

[3] The Bible: 1 Corinthians chapter 3 verses 5-9

Chapter 29
Out from the Comfort Zone

Yesterday Ray and I walked across the fields to the morning service at St Michael's Church, Kirby-le-Soken, just outside Frinton-on-Sea. This is the church we now attend since moving from Cambridge. The path through the first field of wheat, beginning to turn from green to golden yellow, was clearly defined. This was not the case with the path in the second field. This field slopes down to the churchyard, and only a week or so earlier had been bright yellow, with rape-seed flowers in full bloom, but now was like a jungle. We battled our way down the ill-defined path, the tall plants, complete with green seed pods, reaching well above our waists, others that had fallen across the path entwining around our ankles. Within a few months from now, after harvesting, the plough would move in breaking up the ground.

In some ways the Community Church in Santiago had lain dormant and we needed the at times uncomfortable work of God's Holy Spirit to break up the fallow ground. This came about in a number of ways.

God uses various instruments to achieve his purposes. We ourselves were some of the instruments God was using to challenge the complacency we had discerned. I remember one member of our congregation telling us that the talk at all the cocktail parties she and her husband attended was the Santiago Community Church – not always in the most favourable terms!

'Why so much emphasis on the Bible?'

'There's so much talk on mission. Anyone would think we were heathens and needed converting!'

This supportive friend went on to say, 'At least we're on the map.'

Ray and I also were shaken out of our comfort zone, as we encountered a certain amount of opposition. Quite a few feathers were being ruffled. Freemasonry was an insidious influence within both the congregation and community.

The challenge for God to be first priority didn't sit too comfortably with those who thought of him as somewhat of an optional extra. We were in a spiritual battle and it was uncomfortable. I'll never forget during the following summer months when, taking the children to the Country Club, palpably feeling shunned by some and being gossiped about by others.

One of our chief opponents was a retired businessman who held office as Church Warden. In a letter home I wrote that he *'is openly opposing the work ... fortunately he is not liked within the community (although some are a little afraid of him – he's just a big bully really!) and had had numerous head-on clashes with others including Derek Fernyhough (our very nice and patient consul).'*

At one time the man in question sent around poison letters about Ray. The actual contents didn't leave us too anxious as they were so obviously untrue and we knew that truth would triumph. We were reminded of and encouraged by the Biblical Nehemiah, who on rebuilding the walls of Jerusalem encountered similar opposition in the form of untrue letters. I remember losing a night's sleep on first hearing about the letters, not because of their content, but more out of concern for this man's standing before God.

He had stopped coming to any services and only turned up to unlock the church and fulfil the bare minimum of his responsibilities. At the next AGM he was voted off the Board of Trustees and as Church Warden. Ray and I well remember his words, said publicly on that occasion.

'I think that's damned funny! Damned funny!'

However, it was the visit of Dr Michael Ramsay, the Archbishop of Canterbury, a few months previously that would shake the Community Church out of its comfort zone. He was, on this visit, God's 'plough' for us.

He had made some statements prior to his visit that had ruffled the feathers of those on the political right. There were some threats of his visit being boycotted. We had a bomb scare and the Church building had to be searched, although nothing was found.

On his way from the airport in the chauffeur-driven embassy car, he asked for the driver to stop when he saw a poor shantytown development on the outskirts of the capital. This had a profound effect on him to which he referred in his sermon the following day.

The Sunday started exceptionally early for us as he and Mrs Ramsey were coming to Las Violetas for breakfast after the early morning Communion Service. As Chilean grapefruits were, in our opinion, not very nice (small and on the sour side) I decided to treat the Archbishop and his wife to a Chilean starter, *chirimoya* served in freshly squeezed orange juice with icing-sugar, before the boiled eggs and toast. The children had already been breakfasted and were excitedly watching at the window for the arrival of our special guests.

A telephone call from the Church caretaker, Enrique, advised me 'the party' were on the way. Before long three excited children, noses glued to the window, gave the signal our expected guests were arriving and what an arrival it turned out to be. An armoured police car led the way followed by two limousines, flanked on either side by escorting police outriders. In the first limousine (the British Embassy car) were Dr and Mrs Ramsay and the Archbishop's Chaplain. Ray travelled in the second accompanied by a private detective. Police cordoned off the whole street such was the tight security. We wondered whether neighbours thought Ray was being carted off as a political prisoner.

While we ate our breakfast with our guests, the children were quietly colouring in their new painting books I had bought to keep them out of mischief. I personally wasn't relaxed in the Archbishop's company and found him somewhat distant. Perhaps it was the large white bushy eyebrows which made eye contact difficult that didn't help. He was an imposing figure resplendent in his cerise cassock showing off his hair in all its snowy whiteness. By contrast Mrs Ramsay was such easy company, as was the Chaplain. I had wondered if I should wear a hat for the special morning service but was pleased to note Mrs Ramsay wasn't wearing one. I took my cue from her.

Together with the children I followed the main party in our *citroneta* to the morning service meeting up with Mrs Ramsay to escort her into church and sit with her.

I had invited Mónica, General Pinochet's secretary to the service. She came and spent the rest of the day with us. In the evening she joined in the Sunday group, the first of a number she attended. We never ceased to be amazed that in the one group we had those who had been ardent Marxists, some having been tortured under the military, and Pinochet's secretary and others on the right politically. Rodrigo, one of our Chilean students, had spent a few days in prison immediately after the coup. While there he had been tortured with lighted cigarettes to his torso, but it was while in prison that he began his search for God.

The sermon Dr Ramsay preached was on Jesus washing the disciples' feet, but it was what the BBC did with that sermon that made me from then on somewhat suspicious of the media. Very little was reported as to what Dr Ramsay actually said and the media took his reference to stopping at a poor housing *población* out of context. They twisted and wove into this their own political opinions about Chile, which were one-sided, undoubtedly favouring the left. The Archbishop had been careful not to say anything criticising the present regime. Rather he kept within his spiritual role and rightly challenged his listeners as to how we were responding to the poor.

We needed to be shaken out of our comfort zone. The church was insular, many ex-pats never really integrating into the country of their adoption. The Americans tended to keep within their own culture too, even having their own dietary preferences airlifted in. Through the common language of English, bridges were increasingly built among the different nationalities represented within the congregation. We also discovered the richness of our diversity, reflected in the various church traditions members came from. Ray, together with his Board of Deacons, utilised this diversity by drawing together in worship the different elements contained in the various church denominations.

With the inevitable give and take, this meant for many a shake up from their familiar pattern and a willingness to learn from other traditions. It worked. It wasn't at all uncommon not even to know what church denomination people were from. It didn't really matter. What did matter was that each Christian would grow in spiritual maturity, reflecting Christ and those who didn't relate to him in a personal way would discover that relationship. We look back to the diverse mix, both international and interdenominational as the richest time of our ministry – rather like a diamond where each facet reflects a beauty that, together with all the other facets, makes up the full impact of the stone.

The bridge the congregation had been more reluctant to cross was seeing we had responsibilities to Chileans too. The Archbishop's visit helped that bridge to be constructed. His challenge to the Church resulted in a committee being set up, known as The Outreach Committee. Ray, together with two of his deacons, Lew Jowett and Derek Fernyhough, were the initial driving force. Lew had lived in Chile much of his life and was married to Alice, a French Roman Catholic lady and loyal member of the Women's Forum. It was Lew in particular who developed such a passion for this new venture. In a comparatively short time others caught the vision and a number of various embassy personnel came on board.

One of the first projects undertaken was helping a Chilean shoemaker. His sewing machine had broken down and was no longer repairable. The Committee bought him a new one, a supply of leather, and then bought from him the finished shoes. These were then given to those most in need. In this way he was set up in business giving him a sense of dignity. With work he was able to become self-sufficient without becoming dependent on the foreigner.

Someone else who became a right hand man for both Ray and

Lew was a tall, handsome Englishman whose connections with Chile went back several generations.

In 1890, as a twenty-year-old, William Strang had left his native Scotland bound for Valparaiso. Between the Great War and the Second World War he returned to his beloved Scotland, but not before two more generations of Strangs were born in Chile.

Grandson and great grandson Strang set up an Export Consultancy Partnership together. After the grandson's divorce, he, together with his son Nigel, set off from home near Colchester, for native Chile to start a new life. They arrived at Pudahuel airport on a lovely sunny mid-morning, December 21st 1975.

The first weekend in the New Year there was a knock on their front door. There stood the two daughters of their next-door neighbours. They had heard that an English father and son had flown in from England. They asked Nigel if he fancied going to a Young Christian Group held in the hall next to the Santiago Community Church.

'*El reverendo es un Inglés,*' referring to Ray. They also asked if Nigel happened to know Alf Cooper.

'Yes, we know of Alf Cooper!'

Nigel had been told of Alf back in West Mersea, near Colchester, when he had done some fact finding about the work of SAMS. Nigel recounted those details in a letter to me.

'*The following week, I went to Avenida Holanda 151 and was greeted by Ray and Gill … and introduced to Pato and Nico and the others.*

' *… by 1977 SCC was my home church, Ray and Gill had had me around to the "Chaplaincy House" where I met a number of fellow Christians who were to become dear friends. Lew Jowett can be singled out as it was with Lew and Ray and others that "Outreach" was formed.*

'*After the Marxist experiment of 1970-1973, the economy was still struggling. Lew and Nigel, both businessmen, supported by embassy personnel, found time even during the day, to visit contacts being established. This is how Bibles were supplied, wells dug, pumps installed, farmers encouraged, and links to local churches were established.*'

Most weekends at this time would see Nigel and Lew visiting

Lampa, a village lying northwest of the capital. It was here that Lew helped by his Roman Catholic French wife, Alice, worked unstintingly. Alongside the humanitarian help given they started a Sunday school among the local children as well as in one or two other areas.

'Later a dental clinic was set up, and a women's project was formed around a number of sewing machines in a building dedicated for the purpose on the mountain road from Lampa to Quilpué.'

Alicia, a Chilean dentist (whose American husband's funeral Ray had taken), gave some of her time voluntarily to give free dental care. Money was also found to provide storage tanks for water to some areas most in need.

The Women's Forum programme incorporated one Thursday each month a morning called, 'Coffee, Chat and Charity'. Our practical efforts ranged from bagging powdered milk, potting sticky honey from a huge barrel (not a pleasant job, especially when the bees and wasps visited to see what we about) and knitting squares for blankets. All of which were then distributed.

Nigel and Lew were both go-getters. Nigel was, and is to this day, a real net-worker and innovator, and gives unstintingly of his time to serving Christ in serving others. Currently he, together with his Chilean wife, Jimena, now living in England, are involved in their Anglican village Parish Church. Nigel is also a trustee on the Council of SAMS.

A stained glass window in the Santiago Community Church was commissioned by Lew before his death and remains a touching memorial for a man with a big heart for Christ and his kingdom.

Lew was a great enthusiast and had such a generous heart. Lew had come on a long way from his opposition to the initial appointment of Ray as Chaplain, because of our association with SAMS. Lew at that time was wary of those from an evangelical background, but after Ray's appointment, the friendship with us developed.

Often he would take our children, especially Andrew and Julian, to places of interest. Their favourite was to watch him parachuting. The only problem was that Lew would often turn up unexpectedly as we were having breakfast on a Saturday morning and ask to take them out without any prior arrangement. Usually we had already made plans, as it was our family day together. Living in Chile meant needing a much greater flexibility. For me, liking structure, this presented more of a challenge than it did for my laid-back husband!

One Tuesday, during the Archbishop's visit, he gave a talk on the person and work of the Holy Spirit, which I described in my diary as *'wonderful'*. That evening, together with our two Anglican bishops, David and Colin and their respective wives, we were invited to a dinner at the British Embassy. Also invited to meet the Archbishop and Mrs Ramsay was Chile's head of the Roman Catholic Church, Cardinal Silva Henríquez. I was well and truly out of my comfort zone when I discovered I was placed at the table between the Cardinal and Mrs Ramsay to act as interpreter!

With the passing of time I don't remember much about the conversation, but I do remember grappling not so much with the language but with the quail we were served! It was the first time Ray and I had ever eaten quail. Knives and forks seemed far too clumsy to try and prise the flesh off the small carcass. A few years later we discovered that we weren't the only ones who struggled with eating quail.

Peter Sellers in the film *The Party* encountered the same problem, but in his case with disastrous results that left us splitting our sides with laughter. He had found himself unexpectedly a guest at a celebrity party. As he tried to cut his quail, it shot across the table and impaled itself on a jewelled spike on a woman's tiara. When he managed to get the waiter, who was very tipsy, to retrieve the quail, it was lifted off complete with tiara and wig! Fortunately neither of us disgraced ourselves by shooting our quails across the dinner table but it would have been so much better if etiquette had allowed us to pick the small bird up and dismember it with our fingers.

A challenge to draw Ray from his comfort zone was an invitation to enter into a fortnightly dialogue with a young

Roman Catholic priest, Padre Felix, involving the top class of Redland School. After a few meetings together Ray felt not only unable to do justice to these discussions because of the language difficulties, but also he couldn't really spare the time. Both of us were operating on all cylinders. The work both in English and in Spanish was gaining momentum. Ray had to withdraw leaving the dialogue in the hands of a SAMS missionary.

By the end of the year inflation was 300 percent, down from the previous year. A letter home gives the price of a kilo of sugar as 1000 Escudos, equivalent to around a third of a pound then. In the same letter I refer to the fact that when we arrived in March, just under four years previously there were 32 Escudos to the pound and now there were 3,200 '...*you can see how it is that Chile tops the world record.*' Food was plentiful and queues a thing of the past but everything was now so very expensive, a hundredfold increase in less than four years!

We were really feeling the pinch financially, each consecutive month finding we were gradually running out of money before payday. After a time Ray had to ask the treasurer for an advance of the next month's salary before the current month had finished. This went on for several months. As a result, unknown to either of us, a small group met to discuss our financial affairs. The treasurer asked my friend Carol if she knew how I did the housekeeping.

Only a few days before this question I had shared with Carol how thrilled I was after shopping around to find the children's school requirements at bargain prices, including a new school uniform for Naomi as she had outgrown hers. Julian had to be kitted out completely as he was due to start Redland School in March and being so close to Andrew in age it was no longer possible to hand down Andrew's clothes. Carol was able to share this fact with the small group.

As a close friend she also shared with me that having to be party to the scrutiny of our financial affairs had left her feeling embarrassed. It also left me feeling exposed and very vulnerable. The previous Christmas with no money to buy Christmas presents for the children I had resorted to making candles, helped by Jimena, later to marry Nigel, and Nicky, his sister who was visiting Chile. Nigel and Jimena were to prove a real encouragement to us over the next four years and still are to this day.

We devised an innovative way to make the candles, which were sold enabling me to buy gifts for the family. Utilising old white stubs, we melted them down in an old saucepan on a low gas burner and added shavings of the children's wax crayons. When the wax was cool enough without setting too much, we layered different wax colours into old yoghurt containers, creating interesting striped effects. The most difficult part was inserting the wick. With the wax almost set we threaded the wick down by using a skewer and sealed the point of entry with a little melted wax.

In some cases we were able to recycle the original wick if it was long enough by trimming the burnt end. A professional candle-maker would be horrified by the method we used, but it worked.

Our American organist and choir director, also a member of the Board of Trustees, discovered after more than six months of financial difficulties and embarrassment for us that we were being grossly underpaid. Someone hadn't done his homework in keeping up with the exchange rate of the dollar to which Ray's salary was pegged. The ensuing windfall meant that when we went home on leave later that year we stopped over in the United States and Canada.

Part of the contract was the paying of our flights to and from Chile, with the cheapest route rightly being adopted. Any extra stopovers we would pay for ourselves. Some of our friends either home on leave themselves or whose contracts had terminated, invited us to stay as their guests. An added bonus was that we were able to take the children to Orlando, Florida. All three of them saved their pocket money to buy their own entrance tickets to Disney World. Nine-year-old Naomi was very embarrassed when Mickey Mouse took a fancy to her expressed in a big hug and kiss!

We spent three weeks travelling from Florida to Kingston,

Ontario stopping off at different friends' homes. Greyhound coaches were our means of travel, the longest journey being over twenty-seven hours that left me with a thumping headache. To keep three energetic children between the ages of six and nine in such a confined space was an incredible challenge to us both.

Julian was the most difficult to contain with his boundless energy. He kept on jumping up to go to the back of the bus where the toilets were. 'Gill, do you think Julian has a bladder infection?' was his father's concerned query.

This observation didn't hold water! He was too healthy to be harbouring any infection. 'I think I know what the reason is,' I replied as a perfumed smell caught our nostrils.

On investigating why the toilets had such a fascination for our six-year-old, it wasn't long before we discovered it was all the sprays, packets of soap and hand lotions that he enjoyed trying out!

However, it was on our second visit to Bolivia for the winter holidays that shook us completely out of our comfort zone. We were combining the holiday with a pastoral visit to the Anglo-Chilean Community in Antofagasta. There were three particular occasions in the fortnight.

The first concerned Julian, once again.

This was the train trip across the Atacama Desert of northern Chile and the High Plateau of Bolivia that we undertook, prior to Michael Palin taking his. We were on our way to stay with American friends from our Church who were now living in Bolivia. The husband, a Colonel in the American Air force, had been posted to La Paz.

We were to transfer from the bus between Antofagasta on the coast and Calama, deeper into the desert, to the train which would reach an altitude of 15,000 feet before dropping to just under 13,000 feet at La Paz. The bus had already broken down leaving us stranded for a couple of hours or more. Fortunately we were staying the night in Calama so apart from the nuisance of waiting for a replacement, we didn't have an urgent time constraint. What was so frustrating was the total lack of information. This attitude is very Latin American. What is expected is a patient passivity, usually present, except when a Latino is behind the wheel of his vehicle. As this particular driver was unable to beat it up along the highway, he had lapsed into a coma-like state. We just didn't know what was going on or how long we would be stuck in the desert before continuing our journey. We eventually arrived at our overnight accommodation.

It was early evening on the train the next day that I had my biggest ever scare with Julian, even more so than when as a thirty-four-year-old, he sailed around Cape Horn as a member of the Global Challenge yacht race.

Ray and the two boys had gone to the dining-section of the train to find out what was on the menu. There wasn't much choice. It was '*lomo a la pobre*' (poor man's beef). It certainly seemed misnamed. The beef, delicious in itself, was served up with an egg on top of a bed of rice. Ray had sent Julian back to our compartment to tell me he had ordered. After Julian arrived to tell me, I sent him back to 'tell Daddy I'll follow in a minute or two'.

On my way to the dining car just a few seconds after Julian, I passed from one wagon to the next down the length of the train. About half way along I was met by a blast of cold air and discovered the door of the train leading on to the track was wide open. There hanging on the outside of the door suspended over the single line track was a small blond boy.

'You naughty boy. What do you think you are doing?' I shouted in panic as I grabbed him and pulled him inside.

'I was only trying to shut the door, Mummy,' whimpered our precious six-year-old.

It was unlikely he would have hurt himself had he fallen out as because of the high altitude the train was travelling at a slow pace and, being single track, there wouldn't have been any danger from a train coming in the opposite direction. There was only one train a week! Danger lay in the fact that we may not have discovered him missing for some distance and we were miles from any civilisation. But the greater danger was that of exposure as, with the high altitude, the sun was fierce by day and by night the temperature dropped to freezing. It was winter and overnight our jug of water for washing had already frozen in our compartment.

Far from any interference from city lights, the dark inky night sky, with its myriad of stars never ceased to amaze us. They appeared so low in the sky that we felt we could just reach out our hands and pluck them from the horizon. After what seemed a never ending journey the train reached the end of the *Altiplano* (High Plateau) and there below us nestling in the basin, formed by the surrounding mountains, lay the twinkling lights of La Paz. Unfortunately we were all feeling too ill with the effects of altitude sickness to really appreciate the sight.

Our friends George and his wife Dudley were there to meet the weary travellers. On arriving at their home we crashed into our beds.

Once we had recovered and were adjusting to the altitude George offered to take us on a trip in his jeep up the Potosí Mountain and this resulted in the second challenge to our comfort zone.

Pizarro, in the sixteenth century, had sent his captains in search of gold. The *conquistadores* didn't find any gold. Instead they found silver and in such a bountiful supply that the name they gave to this mountain was 'Cerro Rico' (Rich Hill).

We set off up Rich Hill on a dirt track. About half way up the mountain (always snow-capped) the track began to narrow considerably so that there were only a few inches either side of the vehicle. At the same time the hairpin bends became more frequent and more extreme. Before long the engine began to protest, in a feeble way, as it encountered increasingly rarified air.

'I don't think we'll make it,' exclaimed our Air Force Colonel host, 'we'll have to turn back.' But that was the problem. We couldn't. With heart in mouth our driver began gingerly to reverse back the way we had come. All conversation in the jeep stopped as with bated breath we made the descent. We reached the bottom safely and greatly relieved.

We woke up on the last morning of our Bolivian holiday encountering our third challenge. Bolivia was having yet another coup. We discovered armoured tanks were surrounding the city. John Gunther in his book on South America mentions how a joke against Bolivia is that it is a 'nation where almost anything can happen and everything does'.[1]

Somehow we managed to get to the station and onto our train back home to Chile. Before we reached the border with their long-standing, unforgiven neighbour, armed Bolivian soldiers searched the length of the train confiscating all newspapers, to our amusement. They didn't want Chile to gloat over yet another uprising in the less developed neighbouring republic.

There was a desert adventure, from a previous occasion, that had also involved soldiers, this time Chilean, which shook us out of our comfort zone. It was a literal shaking!

In a previous chapter I made reference to a visit to the museum in San Pedro de Atacama. We had gone on our first holiday to Antofagasta, sadly having to leave Andrew behind in the capable hands of Dr Thea, as he was recuperating from pneumonia. Once the work part of the visit was over, we took a bus to Calama where we were booked in for three nights or so. This was the time when we visited the open copper mine in Chuquicamata. We very much wanted to visit the famous anthropological museum but there were no buses on the days we had available. We decided we would get there, by hook or by crook, if at all possible. The only way available was '*haciendo el dedo*'. Thumbing a lift for four wasn't going to be easy.

We left our two star hotel at the crack of dawn and began walking towards the road to San Pedro. It was extremely cold. At this time of the year the temperatures can drop to minus 20 °C at night and reach 30 °C by midday. Three quarters of an hour passed and still no offers of lifts, not that many vehicles were on the road anyway.

'If a car doesn't stop soon we'll call it a day,' Ray decided. We prayed.

The next two vehicles were Volkswagen dormobiles in convoy, very similar to the one that we used in our earlier days. They stopped. Inside were German families from south Chile. Their

---

[1] John Gunther: *Inside South America*. Hamish Hamilton Ltd. p. 389

destination was the museum. They could take us one way but as they were not returning to Calama, but continuing on to El Tatio, famous for its thermal geysers, they were unable to bring us back. Did we want to accept the one-way offer? We did.

Ray wrote to our parents:

'We stopped various times to admire the colours and pick up specimens of crystal salt, sulphur and copper salts. At 11:30am we arrived in this quaint village, with a quiet plaza and hardly a vehicle to be seen. We picnicked and looked around the famous archaeological museum and met the curator, who is also the village priest, Padre Lepaige.'

He went on to describe in graphic detail the well-preserved mummified bodies already referred to in a previous chapter.

It was then time to think about getting back to Calama. Ray continued,

'We spent about 2-3 hrs. in and around the plaza, by the obligatory police control post waiting for a vehicle to pass thro' [sic] the village to get us back to Calama. Two lorries came thro' in that time from the Bolivian border loaded with natural sulphur, with their cabs full of villagers from outlying parts. Eventually an army jeep drove up and two officer cadets started to chat with us and the outcome was we were offered a lift back.'

Ray didn't go into detail as to how the persuasion had come about. On approaching their officer in charge with our request he had shaken his head. Concern about being stranded with the children in such a way out place gave me Dutch courage (except I had not drunk any alcohol!) to approach the senior officer myself. Putting on my most engaging smile and mustering my best Spanish I explained how vital it was that we should get *los chicos* (the little ones) safely back. He relented.

Naomi and Julian sat in the front with one of the soldiers complete with machine gun. We were squashed in the back with the other, plus his gun and a huge drum of petrol. The senior officer was driving not only fast, but also in a cloud of dust, the flaps over the windows letting in dust and sand. The two soldiers were very friendly and to entertain the children on what was both a long and uncomfortable journey, dressed our two in their army helmets. We were driven right to our hotel and clambered out of the jeep covered from head to toe in dust. We hardly dared show our faces yet took some small comfort that with so much dust we might not be recognised anyway!

Chapter 30
Family and Extended Family

We always looked forward to visitors and there were many. What was even more exciting was when family were able to visit. The first family member to arrive in Chile was my sister, Elaine. She was to spend Christmas 1975 with us. The children were especially looking forward to seeing 'Tia' Elaine. Not having relatives living close was hard for the children when their school friends would so often talk about seeing their grandparents, aunts and uncles, but the very many friends, who shared our home and in some cases became extended family, did help to compensate.

Elaine was to travel to Buenos Aires by air and then overland by train to Mendoza on the border with Chile. While in Buenos Aires she was to stay a night or two with the parents of Pamela Yorston, a member of Women's Forum. The idea was that I would take a bus to Mendoza to meet up with Elaine and we would travel together over the Andes back to Santiago. I would take advantage of the rising inflation in Argentina to do some shopping. It was such a strange reversal for the Chilean exchange rate to work in our favour. Leather, of course, was high on my list of priorities, shoes and sandals for the family and my choice of Christmas gift for Ray was a new brief case.

My hosts in Mendoza were missionaries, Jim Hamilton and his Argentinian wife, Anna. They were kindness itself especially with what turned out to be an enforced stay, together with Elaine. Meanwhile in Buenos Aires, Elaine was receiving wonderful hospitality too. Mrs Prescott insisted on taking her breakfast in bed on two or three mornings.

Elaine wrote to our parents from Buenos Aires:

'I am now sitting in their back patio alongside an inviting looking pool, with a very friendly dog and cat, I can hear lots of exciting bird noises but cannot see them ... I am sitting in the shade of a lemon tree ... At the moment there are some ripe lemons, some smaller ones, some tiny ones and some blossom' all at the same time.'

Two days later, Pamela's father took Elaine to the station, where she caught the train to rendezvous with me in Mendoza. Then the problems began. In keeping with her neighbour cousin and with the rest of the continent, Argentina too had her fair share of *problemas*, in fact we were both to encounter a multiplicity before long.

What I hadn't reckoned with was the huge amount of people travelling or attempting to travel for the Christmas period and the incredible amount of frustrating bureaucracy involved. Perhaps I might be forgiven this lack of insight, taking into account that we never went away at the main Christian festivals for obvious reasons. As soon as Elaine arrived we went to the bus station to book our travel to Santiago. In Chile I had been unable to book a return ticket for myself. I already knew I couldn't get Elaine's ticket without her passport. On arriving, Elaine and I found a terrific demand for tickets – the queue reminiscent for me of past times – even though there was just over a week before Christmas day. The difficulty was that the bus station in Mendoza would not issue us with any tickets until the eve of the intended day of travel.

'I'm sorry, Señora, but I can't give you a ticket for two days time.'

'Can you, *please*, reserve two and I'll come back in two days to pick them up?'

'No, Señora, this is not allowed.'

We returned on the eve of our proposed day of return to find yet another queue and by the time I got to the front all available spaces on the coach were filled. This happened for the next two days, resulting in our enforced stay with Jim and Anna. With the date of our travel now passed the thought that the demand would be even greater the nearer we got to Christmas, left us feeling very apprehensive. The vision of being stranded in Argentina away from the family over Christmas left us both depressed. We prayed with our hosts. On the second day Jim tried every means of persuasion (bar bribery), appealing to the Latin love of family but to no avail. The official was obdurate. We continued to pray and Ray in Chile set up a chain of prayer. Looking out over the Andean range separating the two countries, our thoughts turned to Jesus' words about moving mountains. We needed the 'mountain' of unavailable seats to be removed.

Once again we set off for the bus station and joined the queue. This time we were able to get our tickets. How relieved and thankful we were. Prayers had been answered and we had been so well provided for by such generous and thoughtful hosts.

The time for departure was 7.00 am. We arrived half an hour before and were still sitting there at 11.25 am surrounded by our luggage. We left five minutes later.

Back home the Church Christmas dinner was scheduled for that evening. We wanted to get there in time but it seemed highly unlikely. It all depended on the amount of traffic to pass through the border control and customs. There were two ways by road of crossing the Andes from Mendoza to Santiago, one wound right over the mountains, the other some feet below through the tunnel. The latter is the preferred route by most drivers as it is normally that much quicker and the alternative route can only been used in summer when there is less snow. I asked the driver which route we would be taking. 'Through the tunnel, Señora.'

I was disappointed on the one hand because I really wanted Elaine to experience the amazing scenery and especially the famous statue standing sentinel between the two countries. Yet, on the other hand, the quicker route would mean there was a chance we could get back in time for the Church party. My next question left us doubtful on this front.

'Señor, we really do need to get back in time for an engagement this evening! Is it likely?' His expression and shrug of shoulders didn't give us much encouragement.

The seats we had were in fact the last two to be issued. Unfortunately they were not next to each other. I settled back to unwind after the tension of the past few days, just grateful to be on my way home.

When we arrived high in the Andes at the point where the two routes diverged, on looking out of the window to my dismay I saw a huge queue of traffic ahead, bumper to bumper as far as the eye could see. With a sigh of resignation I accepted that we were here in border territory for a very long time.

Then it happened! Suddenly, our driver changed direction. He was going over the top.

According to Pendle in the days of the Spanish Empire this route, named 'Camino de los Andes,' was the track used for trading. It was also the route by which in 1817, from Argentina, one column of General San Martín's army transported the artillery for attacking Spain's soldiers in the Chilean foothills. José de San Martín was Argentina's national liberator from the Spanish.

The original track was so narrow, made even narrower by the deep snow piled up, that not long after, English travellers from Mendoza would have to place their feet up on their mule's head, chewing garlic and onions as they went to help against cold and the altitude.[1]

I turned round in my seat, and mouthed to Elaine to look out for the statue. Christ the Redeemer stood high in the Andes, erected in magnificent scenery against the surrounding white jagged peaks; the highest mountain in the Americas, Aconcagua, forming the dramatic backdrop. The statue wasn't a crucifix. It showed a triumphant, risen Christ standing by the cross, feet firmly on the world, one hand touching the upright bar, the other raised in blessing. As a family, together with the Hunter family (SAMS) we had visited this special place four years previously for the first time. Leo Hunter had driven the Mission's minibus. The wind howling around on that occasion was so incredibly strong we could barely keep upright and didn't allow the small children out of the vehicle in case they were blown over the top!

What was also significant about the statue was what it meant

---

[1] George Pendle: *The Land and People of Chile.* A. & C. Black p 13.

for both countries, for it was here at the feet of 'Christ the Redeemer' that Chile and Argentina pledged everlasting peace, a peace not to be broken even if the mountains themselves should crumble. A plaque containing this sentiment was fixed to the base of the monument.

It was this pledge that was on the brink of being broken, as the two countries disputed over the ownership of three small islands way down in the South in 1978. And it was here at those same feet that hundreds of Roman Catholic young Chileans and Argentinians met at the invitation of the Archbishops of both countries to pray for reconciliation.

Chile had sent naval reinforcements down the coast. The army and air force were alerted. We heard that Argentinians were panic buying at the supermarkets and that the country had already amassed its soldiers at the border in the Patagonian region. We also heard that the order to cross the border was rescinded. Just at the last moment, war was averted.

Our bus reached the top of the Uspallata Pass and driving down the other side arrived much nearer to the head of the queue. The driver had made a wise move. We eventually arrived home and, with a fifteen-minute quick change, wash and brush up, walked into the Church Hall during the first course of dinner to a large round of applause. We fell into bed around midnight after an incredibly long and eventful day.

Naomi and Andrew had been unable to keep awake waiting for the arrival of Mummy and Auntie Elaine and had fallen asleep, but not Julian.

Elaine continued in her letter home, written the next day:

'This morning I saw the children for the first time ... they look fine and are so excited at having me here. They have very fond memories of you both and Naomi said she would like to have a birthday in England so she could invite her cousins and grandparents! Julian is a real pickle' (we agreed on that!) *' – he was so excited that he was awake when Gill and I arrived so I had a quick hug as we dashed out to the Church.'*

Elaine was thrown into a hectic schedule giving her a hands-on idea of what it was like living in a vicarage at Christmas, but in this case with very hot days. Elaine and I, helped by Naomi, made 160 mince pies to add to those already in the freezer for the open home evening we were to have for Church members.

It was the Chilean custom to have the family celebration on Christmas Eve. We had our cooked roast dinner then, which made a lot of sense given the midday temperatures. We had already done the rounds with the children delivering their presents to their friends. We sat down to our Christmas roast turkey. Before we opened our presents we had a tradition that we started in England and continued for a number of years.

Naomi to this day recalls the wonder of that tradition. In the centre of the dinner table was the 'Angel Chimes' mobile. This was made out of a brass coloured light tin, standing no more than 20 centimetres or 8 inches high. There were three or four candleholders in the base and in each stood a small, slender white candle. Above the candles clipped on to the central support were a corresponding number of angels, more like cherubim, each holding a trumpet. I lit the candles as Ray read the Christmas story. With the rising heat causing small convection waves, the angels began to move round and as they did so their trumpets touched a tiny bell like device, making a tinkling sound. The children, especially Naomi, were mesmerised.

Family traditions are so important. Another one we had profoundly affected the lives of all of us, not only the children. We had bought a paperback compendium of C. S. Lewis' Narnia Chronicles on our 1973 home leave. On the Boxing Day Elaine was with us, we took a picnic up San Cristóbal Hill and began reading for the first time *The Lion, the Witch and the Wardrobe*. Elaine, writing to Grandparents Williamson wrote how much the children loved it.

This then started the tradition of reading a few chapters every Sunday, as we remained sitting around the lunch table. Any guests for lunch, which was most Sundays, would be introduced to the exploits in Narnia regardless. Without exception they enjoyed not only the story but caught our three's enthusiasm. Thirty years later, this past Christmas, this first book in the series was out on general release at cinemas throughout the country, to popular acclaim. On chatting to Naomi, by 'phone, just before

Christmas I mentioned that we had decided to see the film that week.

'Mum, please can you and Dad wait until we're together as a family over Christmas and we can all go?'

Julian, it turned out, had already been to see the film in London with friends. Andrew and family were in Bolivia. Once Julian had returned to London, the two of us went, together with Naomi and husband Phil.

Ray had to make a quick plane trip to Antofagasta on December 27th. The Community there hadn't received their Christmas Communion. It's in situations like this we found the Anglican tradition of only ordained ministers being allowed to consecrate the bread and wine difficult to justify especially when there was a licensed layperson in the person of Phil Moneypenny. Once Ray returned, we had a holiday planned, to take Elaine down to the South. This was when she was stung by the *colihuacho* flying beetle.

American friends Sid and Marvann had lent us their own car, as we couldn't all fit in ours, swapping it for our 'cookie cutter', which they had so named.

We introduced Elaine to the beautiful lake and volcano region of southern Chile, or rather it should have been beautiful, had we managed to see the snow covered volcanoes. Unfortunately, we had overcast days and also rain and the tops of the various volcanoes were invisible. That is until the day we headed back to Santiago when we woke to a fantastic dawn and there against the red-orange sky were the silhouettes of volcanoes. On the dry, if not sunny days, we went for walks and picnicked by the lakeside of Lake Llanquihue, where we read, Elaine wrote letters and the children were happy skimming stones across the lake's surface.

When my parents visited us three years later, they were more fortunate with the weather in the south. We enjoyed blue skies and clear views of the glistening snow topped volcanoes across the lakes. One such volcano was Llaima. This is one of the most active volcanoes in Chile and when in 1957 it erupted, a large area of monkey-puzzle forest was destroyed. The flow of lava from the Andean volcanoes is very viscous and moves slowly, cooling as the flow descends the mountain slopes, eventually only advancing a few metres a day. As the edges of the flow cool they form natural banks, thereby channelling the flowing lava until the level is raised metres above the ground.

On our return from a post-Christmas holiday in 1978 with my parents, we stopped to explore the phenomenon of Llaima. It was very eerie. Uprooted trees contortioned at varying angles, lay to rest wherever the flow had deposited them, their stiffened roots pointing upwards and outwards as if reaching for help. Steep banks of dark grey molten lava containing rocks, stones, petrified branches, trunks and stumps of trees, lined the track on which we drove. Pockets of fresh green growth surrounded by blackened soil gave some respite to the dark landscape.

Grandparents Smith preceded my parents by just a few weeks. We were so excited. The children could now share with their school friends that '*Abuelo*' and '*Abuela*' were coming to stay.

Ray's mother, now seventy-eight, had suffered a few mini-strokes, and Ray's father, three years younger, had also had some health problems. Only a couple of days after they arrived they had a small accident. They had gone for a short walk round the block and Ray's father had tripped over the uneven pavement. As he fell he pulled mother down with him. Fortunately the only injury was a pulled muscle.

Respecting their age and health we had no ambitious plans to travel far from the capital, besides which it was term time for both the children and me.

I had a teaching job at the Lincoln Academy. The Head, Bob Seaquist, was an American and regular member of our congregation. His wife Veronica was Chilean and also a teacher. It was a small school and catered mainly for children whose parents were anxious for an English education, but following more an American educational bias leading to the international baccalaureate.

The school was one of two that came about with the demise, through scandal, of another school, in which I had taught two years earlier but had been forced to leave. This proved to be a blessing in disguise and fortunately was before the scandal broke. In 1976 I had agreed to teach a health course for the University of Nabraska to a mixed class of fifteen-and sixteen-year-olds and also religious education.

About six months into the year I was also asked to teach physics and chemistry. I knew I wasn't qualified to do this and said so. Pressure was put on me and an ultimatum was given that if I didn't take this on then they would have to replace me. Given that most of the students were American from diplomatic or business families whose parents were paying extremely high school fees they deserved the best. There was no way I could give them the best in these added subjects so I refused. Before being officially sacked I decided to hand in my notice. There were three months or so to the end of the school year and we were going home on leave then.

Within a day or so of our returning I received a telephone call from Captain Peter Archer, the naval attaché to the British Embassy and regular member of our congregation. He sounded concerned.

'Gill, are you still on the staff of … School?'

'No,' I answered. 'I handed in my notice.'

'Thank goodness,' he replied and went on to tell me that the Head and his administrator (two bachelor men) had fled the country taking all the school fees with them!

We kept sacrosanct our Saturday day off and borrowing the mission vehicle made some good trips out. The children were particularly anxious to introduce their grandparents to the snow of the Andes, so a trip to our nearest ski resort, Farellones was a must and on another occasion a visit to the beautiful Andean lake at Portillo.

For sheer beauty, spring was the best time of the year to visit. The winter snow still lay low on the mountains; the many fruit trees were in blossom as were the jacaranda, myrtle and acacia. It was also the month when we celebrated Chile's Independence, when the whole country parties: dancing the *cueca*, eating *anticuchos* (kebabs of barbecued meat), *empanadas*, and drinking wine or the more lethal *chicha*.

In between meeting many of our friends, enjoying the varied Church programme, receiving invites of hospitality, days out with the grandchildren and bedtime stories, they spent so much time relaxing in the garden. Grandma Smith writing scores of postcards and letters, which she so enjoyed and Papa spending hours reading. He shared with me how much he had appreciated all the reading he was able to do.

Writing to my parents on the morning of Ray's parents' evening departure I recount how much they had benefited from the rest their time with us had been and how they had endeared themselves to so many of our friends.

'... he [Ray's father] has particularly enjoyed meeting such interesting people here – professional and businessmen, coming from so many different backgrounds – as it's such a broadening experience.'

In just five weeks time Grandparents Williamson were to arrive and stay over Christmas and into the quieter month of January. Sandwiched in between were fraught times, health wise and work wise, and added to that the temperatures were gradually heating up. It all started when I had a routine medical check up prior to Ray's parents arriving. I was also booked for a radical haemorrhoidectomy at the end of the next month as the old problem had recurred and the consultant said he wanted to deal with them once for all. In the event his words proved true.

My Chilean-Jewish doctor had discovered a small lump in my breast. 'Is it malignant?' were my first words while lying on the couch.

'I don't think so, I think it's hormonal, but I want to be sure. I'll refer you to a leading Brazilian breast cancer specialist.'

That same evening we had a group meeting in our home of mainly Anglo-Chilean women, most of whom went to Women's Forum, and their husbands, for their part mostly agnostic, atheistic, or just plain apathetic to matters of faith. I shared with Penny my concern during the evening.

Within a few days I was at the hospital, only to be told that Dr Felix de Amesti was out of the country and wouldn't be back for two weeks. An appointment was made. It was during this interval that Ray's parents arrived. We didn't tell them our concern until we knew the outcome. I mentioned in a letter to my parents that there were health problems and that I had experienced a remarkable 'God incident' that I would share once they were with us.

The 'God incident' occurred during the night after we had our Anglo-Chilean couples evening, and the same day that the lump was discovered. We got to bed well after midnight and by 2.00 am I still hadn't had any sleep as the possible reality of the discovery kicked in. Eventually I dropped off only to be woken with a clear impression of words of encouragement and comfort. I remember thinking these were from one of the Psalms. I went back to sleep and was woken again with the very same words, seemingly audible. This happened three times, with always the same words clearly 'spoken' into my consciousness.

Around 8.00 am we were both awake. Ray's first words were to ask how was I feeling and what sort of a night I had.

'I couldn't get to sleep for a long time but eventually managed to drop off. Then an incredible thing happened. I woke up and heard these words ...' I was unable to recall them. 'I'm sure they are from one of the Psalms. This happened three times and always the same words but I don't remember what they were.'

To this day I've never been able to recall the words. I don't believe they were specifically from the Psalms, but rather were God's direct word to my heart and into my situation. Such peace flooded my being. I knew whatever the outcome God was in control. This kept me trusting over the next two weeks. I returned to the hospital and the Brazilian consultant, after examining me assured me there was no cancer.

We were under some pressure with end of term exams for our three and their mother to prepare for, in their respective roles of teacher and taught, following on from haemorrhoid surgery for me, and mounting pressure for Ray as Christmas was approaching. Our Christian friends rallied round and helped in so many practical ways. I had pulled out of any speaking in the Women's Forum until after the summer break. By now there were others who could fill the gap. My school teaching responsibilities at the Lincoln Academy involved lots of input as the end of the school year approached. My small class of twelve, thirteen year olds was a sheer delight. The boys outnumbered the girls and with only a couple of exceptions were Latin Americans whose fathers mainly worked in the diplomatic service. Such was their enthusiasm that we decided to put on a play for Christmas, by which time my parents were visiting. It was Charles Dickens' *Christmas Carol*. I must have been crazy! But it was Nigel to the rescue.

'Gill, who's your stage manager?'

'Me, I suppose.'

Nigel's face expressed sheer astonishment followed by incredulity at such naivety. 'You mean to say you haven't got one? You can't do that as well as direct the play! I'll be it!' I could have hugged him and probably did.

A few days later he arrived to plan with me. It was hilarious. At the end of the evening, the three children tucked up in bed and fast asleep, Ray, Nigel and I started to creep around the house. One of us was armed with our portable tape recorder, another had a bicycle chain. We hunted out every squeaky floorboard we could find and clanging the chain and dragging it across the floor we started to record. Our sound effects were most impressive for Marley's ghost. We edited out the accompanying muffled laughter.

One of Scrooge's speeches was so long I decided to make it easier for Carlos, who played the part of Scrooge. I pre-recorded him reading the part. At the performance itself, he sat on his bed and while appropriately miming we played his pre-recorded voice, as if he was thinking aloud. It worked exceptionally well.

The participating children came round to our home after school and together we made the props. Wire netting and papier mâché duly moulded, then painted, gave us a very realistic roast turkey. Old tights filled with cotton wool and tied at intervals provided realistic sausages. A deflated old football of our boys with a sprig of holly on top served well as a Christmas pudding. It was great fun.

Another huge risk I faced was that there was no understudy should any of the children fall ill! Fortunately they didn't. We put the play on for three nights, two in the school grounds and the final night in our church building. The children were fantastic and it proved a great success.

For Ray too, it was a very busy time but we had the two quiet months of January and February to look forward to. In January we were able to spend lots of quality time with grandparents.

My mother had taken up painting in her early sixties. Oil was her preferred medium and so it was that I had my first lesson in oil painting, from which I never looked back.

Introducing them to the relaxed atmosphere of the Prince of Wales Country Club was an added bonus. My father, addicted to swimming and sun was in his element. He was even more in his element when, borrowing the mission minibus, we drove them to the thermal waters in the Maipu valley. The children were so excited to share one of their favourite places with their grandparents. They were even more excited that it meant on this visit we would go even further into the mountains to the actual waters.

Among our many photographs is one of my father holding Andrew's hand, standing in the waters, surrounded by white mountain peaks, both torsos and faces covered with rejuvenating mudpacks. It's a reminder of a day of laughter and sheer joy.

These were good times and we were so fortunate to have both sets of parents experience something of the country and people of our adoption.

The good times weren't restricted to visits from only blood relations. Our lives were so enriched by extending our family.

I've already referred to the adopted uncles and aunts that helped make up to the children for missing their relatives. Undoubtedly some for us became like younger brothers and sisters. Apart from Nico, Lydia and others, who were frequent visitors, there were others who lived with us and shared in all the reality of family life with its laughter, tears, quarrels, and making up. Thea was one in our early days, but there were others whose stay proved to be an extended one.

First and unexpectedly to arrive was Hilary. Hilary was the third in a family of five born to SAMS missionaries, Tony and Peggy Barratt. Although their earlier years and Hilary's childhood had been in Chile, they were now living in Tucumán, Argentina. There had been a fatal accident of a member of a Chilean church who had gone to Argentina to look for work. His distraught widow wanted the burial to take place in Chile. Hilary, caring and sensitive by nature, offered to accompany the widow and her husband's body. Hilary herself was going through a personal crisis at the time.

One day in December 1975 the doorbell rang. I opened it to a young woman in her early twenties with long, dark hair. She smiled and introduced herself as Hilary Barratt. I knew of her by repute as, together with her elder brother Terry, and her two sisters, Rosemary and Patti they had formed the music group 'Los Picaflores' (the Humming Birds). I invited her in and in the course of conversation discovered she had nowhere to stay.

'I'll only need a bed for a few nights and really am so grateful for the offer.' The few nights turned out to be until her wedding over fifteen months later!

We simply loved Hilary. Naomi adored her big, older sister. I loved having a younger one. She brought so much laughter and joy, if at times a somewhat chaotic lifestyle. She was very Latin American in many ways, not surprisingly as all her life, right up to the present, had been spent in South America.

When Hilary first arrived we already had Lydia, on a visit to Chile for three months, staying with us. Her parents had returned to the United States. The children now had two adopted 'Tias'. The ratio of male to female in our home was suddenly changed and conversation reflected this! When we had our inevitable embassy functions it was so nice to draw on adult female thoughts as to what went with what rather than a well meaning but not fashion conscious husbandly opinion.

As Hilary was a PE teacher this gave her credibility with two little adopted brothers! Hilary had a small bedroom and ensuite (normally reserved for a live-in maid) off the kitchen in the Church House in Avenida Holanda.

We had moved from Las Violetas to next door to the Church

itself, a few days after Elaine had returned from holidaying with us. It was a cost effective decision by the Church Council.

Once Hilary had landed a teaching post and was here to stay for a time, there was a companion with which she needed to be reunited. Her inseparable companion was big and bulky but had the most melodious of voices. It was none other than her Paraguayan harp and took pride of place in our sitting room. An added bonus was to have live music of a different nature from the piano playing in which all three children were engaged. Hilary gave Naomi a few harp lessons over the next months.

We encouraged the children in the area of music and had brought back five melodicas from our second leave home. Each melodica (German in origin) had a set of notes like piano keys providing a range of octaves. It was held in the two hands and as the mouthpiece was blown the fingers played the appropriate keys. When Ray's parents were visiting we put on a concert for some of the elderly in the Church hall, all five of us playing simple tunes.

While God was in the planning of Hilary coming to live with us, he was also active in directing the thoughts and feelings of a young man who had returned to the country of his childhood. Alf Cooper still had relatives in Chile and was now back as an Anglican minister with SAMS. One day he had spotted the cover of a record showing the Humming Bird music group, dressed in national Paraguayan costumes: the three girls with frilly blouses and colourful flowing skirts, each with a flower in their hair, Rosemary and Hilary's flowers standing out against the background of their long, flowing dark hair, Patti's blending in more with her blond, shorter wavy hair, Terry standing resplendent in his waistcoat, baggy trousers topped at the waist by a sash. They were in a pose, playing their respective instruments, the oldest and youngest guitars and Rosemary and Hilary harps. Alf told us that it was Hilary's hands that first made an impact on him, as well as her face. He was smitten!

Sometime later he was asked to accompany one of the SAMS missionaries to a funeral in one of the shantytown churches. As they entered his heart skipped a beat, if not two, as his eyes alighted on the girl of the record, whose hands had held such an attraction for him. It was the funeral of the electrician and Hilary was sitting with the widow.

In April 1977 they were married. As part of Hilary's extended family we were very involved. Our home was a hub of activity. Ray gave her away as her father actually performed the wedding ceremony, Naomi was one of the bridesmaids, and my wedding veil was borrowed for the occasion. Fortunately we had been on home leave from December 1976 until the end of the following February and brought it back in our luggage. It was an extended family occasion in another respect as Nico was best man. In time I became *madrina* (godmother) to their second son, Jahnn.

Our house next door to the Church had many downstairs rooms and in this respect was more spacious than Las Violetas. The kitchen was large with a glass partition separating the utility area from the kitchen itself and leading off of here was the maid's quarters, that in fact Hilary occupied. An outside door from the kitchen led to a covered terrace leading down the steps to the garden. Connecting the utility part of the kitchen was a very small passageway leading into what we called the family room. As a family we had our inside meals here and played our table games. I had the bonus of my own study (Ray's study was off the church office). Next to this was another room which we made into the children's playroom and next to this a visitors' room. At the end of the corridor was the lounge. Another entrance from the lounge led through half wooden and half frosted glass concertina styled doors to the dining room from which was another entrance into the kitchen. Upstairs was smaller as the house was A-shaped. There were three bedrooms, ours having an ensuite, and a family bathroom. Outside the boys' bedroom was a large terrace. This was such a sun trap that here I used to dry apricots and grapes, picked off our tree and vine, on a long table borrowed from the church hall.

One day in the hectic time between Ray's parents leaving and mine arriving, my surgery and busy end of term, Ray put a question to me that brought a sharp retort in response.

'Gill, there's a New Zealander missionary that's looking for accommodation, could we help?'

'No! Definitely not!' I was adamant.

After Lydia, Hilary and Ray's parents I felt, understandably, that we needed some respite and to be together just as a family of five for a time.

'Well, I do think at least you should meet him. He really is nice. In any case it need only be for a short time until he's found somewhere suitable.'

Wearily I said, 'All right then but it won't make any difference.' Fortunately it did.

Alan lived with us for two years and was one of the easiest resident house-guests we've had – and there have been countless over the years.

He was in his late twenties, not very tall, had dark wavy hair and a moustache. He worked down town as manager of the Christian bookshop run by CLC (Christian Literature Crusade). Alan spoke Spanish and in addition to the bookshop he visited many national churches, mostly Pentecostal, preaching and setting up a bookstall. When not out on Sunday engagements, he would join the Sunday night group led by Nico and Pato as well as worshipping in the Community Church.

The children loved 'Uncle' Alan and he became for me a younger brother that I never had. In the very many evening conversations, when the children were in bed and Ray at a meeting, Alan shared his heart including, at times, the current girlfriend he was interested in.

He is now living with his family in Tasmania, where he is Director of the Bible Society. We still keep in touch and have been reciprocal guests in one another's homes. Julian met up with him in Sydney, on the yacht race just over a year ago.

Alan also introduced us to his 'Kiwi' friend, Ken, who visited Chile from time to time. Ken, like John Stott, in response to God's call on his life, involving as it did a very itinerant ministry, had accepted a life of celibacy. Ken was an evangelist and his main ministry, which often took him to Africa, was the training of church leaders, pastors and evangelists in the use of a sketch board to present the gospel in the open air. He was a tall man, an extrovert with a great sense of humour and a real tease.

Alf and other Anglicans were trained by Ken and subsequently teams used to go into the crowded streets of the capital using the sketch board as an effective means of presenting the Christian message, including upmarket Providencia as well as the poorer parts of the city.

It doesn't take much imagination for my reader to realise that even in the inevitable separation from family at home, God more than made up to us any losses we faced. Our lives have been so enriched by all the people with whom we have been privileged to share our home and our very selves.

Before finishing this chapter, there is one other most important person who shared in our family life becoming such a close friend to all of us. Her name was Nana. She helped me in the home.

Since Neli was no longer able to help there had been others who temporarily filled the gap. One of these was not a Chilean but an English young woman in her early thirties.

Joan had written to us through a mutual friend who received our newsletters. In one we had shared for prayer our need for domestic help. Joan, who loved to travel, had offered to come as a sort of au pair for a year helping me in the home in exchange for food, lodging and spending money. The added bonus was that she would also fill a gap in teaching in the Sunday school.

It was probably at least three years after Joan had left with a number of *empleadas* in between that Nana came into our lives. Neither Ray nor I can recall how this happened. I sat down at the table to interview a short, dark haired, Chilean woman only a few years my junior. She was married to Jorge and they had two children, a girl and a boy. They were from a Pentecostal church.

I took to Nana immediately. She had a deep faith and such a pleasant manner. She proved to be friendly, reliable, respectful and a hard worker. She worked Monday to Friday. From the beginning we made it clear that responsibility for the upbringing of the children was ours alone and that her role was to take much of the domestic load from me. Those boundaries were respected. We all became extremely fond of Nana. She was a true friend without compromising the work relationship – well and truly denying the claim that I'd heard from the middle-class Chilean woman previously that you couldn't be a friend with your *empleada*.

It was such an honour the day we were invited as a family to have tea with her and her family in their very modest home in a poor part of Santiago.

In time Nana even stayed overnight on the occasions we needed a childminder. She truly was God's gift to us and she has served all subsequent Chaplains and wives until her retirement when she received a generous pension.

Chapter 31

Treacherous Waters

The beauty of Chile comes at a cost. A price has to be paid for the dramatic landscape that makes this country so unique. Chile falls into what geologists define as the 'Pacific Ring of Fire'. This term refers to a band of volcanoes and fault lines circling the edges of the Pacific Ocean both on land and under the sea. Some of the most dramatic natural disasters of recent history have happened within the 'Ring's' arc, stretching from Chile, north to Alaska and then west to encompass Japan, South East Asia and the Pacific islands. Around the 'Ring of Fire' the Pacific Plate is colliding with and sliding underneath other plates. In Chile the ensuing instability causes the Andes to twitch and convulse, resulting in the very many earthquakes. Added to this there are volcanic eruptions, countless avalanches, landslides and floods. The most dangerous floods with the highest cost of lives are when an earthquake is followed, fortunately less frequently, by a tidal wave.

George Pendle noted that Charles Darwin in his diary extracts wrote of such a phenomena following the 1835 earthquake, one of many, that hit southern Chile. 'At Talcahuano a great wave, so common an occurrence with earthquakes, entirely flowed over the whole town, after the houses had been shaken down.' According to Pendle the wave, banking into a vast wall of water, was seen approaching the coast when still over five miles out to sea. Riding on its crest was 'a fine schooner' that was deposited inland, and when the water receded remained stranded in the town.[1]

[1] George Pendle: *The Land and People of Chile*. A. & C. Black p. 10 quoting Charles Darwin's diary extracts.

In the 1960 earthquake, which hit the south of Chile on May 22nd, a tsunami followed. Having seen on our television screens the terrible tsunami that hit so many Asian countries on December 26th 2004 none of us is left in any doubt as to the destructive nature of the sea. The 1960 Chilean *'terremoto'* followed by its own tsunami was the fiercest for the country in modern times, registering 9.5 on the Richter scale and was the largest earthquake ever instrumentally recorded at that time. It was so severe that, according to Gunther, it almost severed the narrow country apart at the coastal town of Valdivia.[2] Over several days, a 1000 kilometre section of the fault was ruptured. The main shock set up a series of seismic sea waves, not only destructive along the coast of Chile, but caused extensive damage in Hawaii and even across the ocean to Japan. In Chile, the Puyehue volcano erupted forty-seven hours later. There were more than 5000 deaths and over 350,000 citizens were left homeless. The map of Chile's southern coastline had to be redrawn as a result.

An eyewitness was the Rev. Reg Bartle. We had met Reg and his wife Thelma in our early days in Chile. Years later we spoke on the telephone and he recounted to me his own frightening experience of this tidal wave.

On a Friday night in late May he set out from his home in Temuco to visit the local Anglican Church in Nehuentue. This region of Chile is the heartland of the Mapuche Indians, the proud indigenous people who were never subdued by the Spanish *conquistadores.* Temuco is the provincial capital. Nehuentue was situated at the mouth of an estuary.

Just before leaving Temuco, the widow of Canon William Wilson, affectionately known as Struggles (maiden name Strugnall) had 'phoned from Nehuentue. She requested Thelma to buy a kilo of sausages, which Reg could bring with him. Southern Chile has an abundance of sausages, all flavours and all sizes, reflecting the German influence of this region.

Reg reached the church house after a two to three hour journey in a rickety bus along the bumpy, *ripio* roads. That

---

[2] John Gunther: *Inside South America.* Hamish Hamilton Ltd. p. 281

night, suddenly he woke up, as his bed started to move, hitting first one wall, then sliding back and hitting the other. He got out of bed and in a short time the movement subsided, so he made a cup of tea and took one to Struggles, by now also awake. The next morning minor tremors continued. On the Sunday, after breakfast, Reg was just leaving Church House to visit two Mapuche families from the congregation, who were not on speaking terms, to try and negotiate reconciliation. He hadn't gone far, when, 'Suddenly the ground started to heave up and down. I hung on to the fences and made my way back to the house. I found Struggles flat on the floor.' Shortly afterwards he ventured out again and found a boy shouting at the top of his voice, 'The sea has disappeared!' The estuary was empty.

'I knew this could mean only one thing. Then I saw it, a huge wall of sea 30-40 feet high. I shouted to Struggles to grab a blanket and to run. We scrambled over barbed wire and fences, along with five hundred others as we all headed for higher ground. We were marooned there for three to four days with only one blanket and one raincoat between the two of us. It was bitterly cold. A local farmer slaughtered some of his animals and fed us all opening his barn for shelter.

'Once the water had receded we returned to Church House on a borrowed horse, Struggles riding pillion.' While Reg was securing the horse, Struggles entered the house.

'I heard a terrible scream from the kitchen. The precious sausages were floating in the floodwater.

'"We're going to need these, you know," she said.

'"Oh, no we're not." I answered.'

As a matter of urgency they decided to return as soon as possible to Temuco. There had been no communication for four days. On arrival, Reg found two missionary colleagues completing the loading up of the Land Rover with basic rescue equipment. By their side was a distraught Thelma. With incredulity followed by joy they were greeted with the words, 'We were going to look for your bodies!' The BBC had reported them missing presumed dead.

The village was destroyed and the port of Savedra washed

away. The epicentre was out to sea. Financial aid had to be sought from abroad to enable the reconstruction of the districts of Concepción, Valdivia, Puerto Montt and the island of Chiloé.

The dangerous waters of the south replace the hostile desert landscape of the north, the more treacherous the further south you travel. The topography resembles that of Norway, with its many glaciers, islands, fjords and icebergs.

Very many sailors have come to grief as they rose to the challenge of these southern waters. Stories of shipwrecks abound and names given to bays and inlets reflect just how dangerous it is to sail the Southern Ocean, shared with both Atlantic and Pacific. We were immersed in such discoveries on our first visit to the southernmost city in the world. Although Argentinian Ushuaia is a little further south it is hardly a city, whereas Chilean Punta Arenas being that much larger does qualify.

Ray had been asked to conduct a Remembrance Day service and wanted me to accompany him. We would have to find the money for my fare and expenses. An American member of the congregation had suggested to me some weeks before that I should put on an Art Exhibition of my paintings. At the time I dismissed this suggestion but, now with this one and only opportunity to visit a completely unknown part of Chile, the idea of raising some funding began to take root. It would be the chance of a lifetime, as we were due to leave Chile to return to England for good within three months.

The next few weeks saw me pack up the 'cookie cutter' with easel, canvas, paint and brushes and set out to my chosen location – a favourite being Los Dominicos with its twin domes, nestling in the surrounding trees against the backdrop of the lower hills of the Andean range. Other paintings were done in my study getting ideas from pictures and photographs, including scenes from the desert with the snow-capped volcanoes. I loved painting the llamas, with their textured coat and haughty look. In my adolescence I was crazy about horses, as is Iloni, one of our granddaughters. In my childhood home we had a china wall vase in the shape of a horse's head, light chestnut in colour. To my indignation the opening of the vase was on the top of the horse's head between the ears. Most likely my feelings were taken on board because never once do I recall seeing flowers coming out of the top of its head, more suited to a donkey than a horse. I used to enjoy sketching and my favourite was this vase.

On the day of the exhibition, friends rallied round providing refreshments and sitting at the receipt of custom freeing me to mingle. It was well supported, the necessary money was raised with twenty-five percent given to Juventud para Cristo (the international Youth for Christ) to help in the refurbishment of a communal sports centre in a poor *población* within the city.

We left by air on Tuesday, November 13th 1979 bound for Chile Austral. This twelfth region of 'The Long Bean' is known as Magellanes, named after the famous Portuguese explorer. Beyond this lay the final region, Chilean Antartica itself. Our journey took us over the myriad islands (mostly uninhabited), the frozen glaciers, the fjords, sounds and lakes until we landed at Punta Arenas.

Our resident hosts of Scottish descent were there to meet us. Kenneth and Mayo Maclean were staunch members of the Anglo-Chilean community. We had already met Mayo on several occasions. Whenever she visited the capital she would make it a priority to worship with us as well as attend the Women's Forum. Her husband was a sheep farmer. Rearing sheep for both wool and meat was what brought many Scots out to southern Chile.

Given the scenery and climate of Brunswick Peninsula, where the southernmost city is situated, it's easy to understand how at home both Scots and New Zealanders feel. The wide open spaces, the unpolluted air, the sparkling clear water, the gentle hills and small mountains glistening with their snow covering made an impression on us coming from the smog laden capital. The contrast between the high Andean peaks in the central 'lumbar curvature' of 'the Spine', giving at times a sense of being hemmed in, was here replaced by the more flattened 'sacro-coccygeal' area, leaving a huge expanse of sky. We had never seen such expanse, even dwarfing that of the desert. Living now in eastern England and regularly travelling deeper into East

Anglia, with its wide open spaces, reminds me a little of that sense of wonder and freedom such skies give.

However, all is not beauty and tranquillity by any means. The inclement weather and the dangerous waters leave in their wake a catalogue of disaster, as we were to discover, on hearing and reading something of the history of this region. A quick look at the map gives the reader some idea of a history reflecting both bravery and tragedy. Islands, bays, lakes, sounds and water passages carry names such as Disappointment, Desolation, Useless, Famine, Last Hope, Fury, Risk and Destruction, to name some.

While we were there Ray and I wrote a potted history for our own interest. It was in 1540 that a total of twenty-one ships set out to use the South West passage from the Atlantic to the Pacific. Twelve of these were shipwrecked in or near the Strait. Of the remaining it was only Magellan's *Victory* that returned to Seville, Spain. Of the sailors who took part in the expedition more than 2000 perished and only some twenty percent eventually regained their native shore. A recent shipwreck occurred as recently as 1988. The *Logos*, a modern mission-afloat, sank off Puerto Williams across the Beagle Channel from Ushuaia, on January 6th. This boat was one of several that Operation Mobilisation, a Christian literature mission uses. Fortunately there was no loss of life as Puerto Williams is where the very efficient Chilean navy is based.

Two days after arriving we drove south of Punta Arenas following the coast until we came to Port Famine, 56 kilometres from the city. Nearby was the well-kept grave of Pringle Stokes, a one time Captain of HMS *Beagle*. Suffering from severe depression, he had committed suicide. Skyring, his next in command, temporarily succeeded him. Present day Port Famine was originally founded in 1584 by the *conquistador* Pedro Sarmiento de Gamboa (not to be confused with the later Domingo Faustino Sarmiento, the philosopher-President of Argentina). The port was named 'Rey Don Felipe' after King Philip of Spain. The earlier Sarmiento's task was to establish settlements to guard the Strait from enemy attacks on Spanish vessels, especially those of English pirates. His accurate surveys and chartings were two centuries ahead of his time. However, the big blot on his character was his ruthless persecution and killing of the last of the Incas. Because of his cruelty it was said a curse fell upon him and disasters marked much of his subsequent life. 'The luck of Sarmiento' became synonymous with disasters and misfortunes. Due to the harsh conditions and food running out before supplies could safely reach the colonists, all the animals and people, except one, died of starvation. Cavendish, Captain of the enemy English fleet, rescued the one survivor in 1586.

It was only towards the end of the same century that the English began their seafaring adventures in earnest. Legendary, within these waters in 1578 was Sir Francis Drake and his own ship the *Golden Hind*, previously named the *Pelican*. Piracy gained a mark of respectability in Elizabethan England because of her increasing hostility with Spain. Like his illustrious predecessor, Drake entered the Strait from the Atlantic, on August 22nd, at its northwesterly channel, at the Cape of Eleven Thousand Virgins. It had taken Magellan thirty-eight days.[3] Drake's fleet anchored off an Island, he named Elizabeth Island where they fed on the penguins already referred to in a previous chapter. It was in this section of the Strait that they encountered and made the first recorded contact with the canoe Indians, the Alakalufs (also spelt Alacaloofs).

They reached the Pacific on September 6th. Almost two hundred miles further south they were struck by such a severe storm, 'the like whereof no traveller hath felt, neither hath there been such a tempest, so violent and of such continuance, since Noah's flood, for it lasted full fifty-two days'.[4]

In the fierce storm the *Golden Hind* had become detached from the fleet and had drifted further south and then east right to the end of the Fuegian Archipelago. On October 28th, the storm subsided, Drake made his momentous discovery; beyond was a vast expanse of sea where the Pacific and the Atlantic met. He turned his ship westwards and anchoring off the most southerly

---

[3] Ibid: p. 316
[4] Eric Shipton: *Tierra del Fuego: the Fatal Lodestone.*

island disembarked taking his compass with him. With compass in hand he found the southern extremity of the island and lay with head and shoulders projecting over the sea. Returning to his ship he told the crew that he had been further south on land than any other man!

The day before we drove to Port Famine we took a ferryboat from Punta Arenas, south of Elizabeth Island to make the crossing of the Strait to Tierra del Fuego. It took the *Rio Cisnes* (River Swans) three hours to make the crossing to Porvenir, the Chilean regional capital on the west coast of 'The Land of Fire', a distance of around thirty-six kilometres. Just south of Porvenir is Useless Bay, thought to be so named after various frustrating attempts to find another way through to the Atlantic Ocean than that of the Strait to the north.

Dawson Island lies due west of Useless Bay. Such a location helps the reader to more readily understand the reason for the military Junta's choice of enforced accommodation for those deemed to be a continued threat. Surrounded by such hostile conditions and treacherous waters was considered incentive enough to prevent what in their eyes amounted to any further treachery.

Pendle refers to an act of treachery, rooted in these very waters that had its beginning in the early decades of the nineteenth century.

Pendle draws on Charles Darwin's journal and the memoirs of Lucas Bridges, whose own father, a Protestant missionary had first hand knowledge of those affected by such an act.

It all began in 1826, with Captain Robert Fitzroy being sent by the British admiralty to chart the coasts of the far south of South America. Anchoring HMS *Beagle* off Chilean Tierra del Fuego, Captain Fitzroy sent some of the crew on an exploration. They returned on a makeshift raft laying the blame for the loss of the small boat on the local Indians. Four Fuegian Indians were taken as hostages. Fitzroy decided to take the hostages back to England. His intention according to Darwin was 'to educate them and instruct them in religion at his [Fitzroy's] own expense'.[5]

---

[5] George Pendle: *The Land and People of Chile.* A. & C. Black. p. 83

The arrival of the hostages caused so much curiosity in London, perhaps more so because of the bizarre names the sailors had chosen for them: 'Boat Memory', 'York Minster', 'Jemmy Button' and the only girl of the four 'Fuegia Basket'. They lived with a clergyman in Walthamstow and were placed in a local school. King Willliam 1V summoned Captain Fitzroy, together with the Fuegians, to St James's Palace, where both the King and Queen Adelaide gave them gifts.

In 1831 HMS *Beagle* set out, under Captain Fitzroy, on a return visit to South America. On board, as different as chalk and cheese, were three apparently 'civilised' Indians together with Charles Darwin, the naturalist.

On arriving at Tierra del Fuego, the one-time hostages were set ashore among their own people. A year later the *Beagle* went to pay a farewell visit and to their huge disappointment found their protégés had reverted back to their former way of living.

Darwin wrote of a canoe coming alongside in which was 'Jemmy Button', hardly recognisable.

'It was quite painful to behold him; thin, pale, and without a remnant of clothes, excepting a bit of blanket round his waist; his hair hanging over his shoulders; and so ashamed of himself he turned his back to the ship as the canoe approached.' Darwin went on to write how this teenage boy had been so careful and particular in his English attire that by contrast 'I never saw so complete and grievous a change.'[6]

Darwin had originally described him 'as a universal favourite'.

At their invitation Jemmy did board the boat and was duly cleaned and suitably dressed. He then dined with the Captain and ate the meal 'as tidily as formerly' as he had been taught.[7]

During the pioneering discoveries in the natural world by Charles Darwin, another pioneer was praying and planning for an excursion into the same treacherous waters. He never looked back from his determination to fulfil the prayer he had made in May 1834 at the bedside of his dying wife. The prayer

---

[6] Ibid: p. 84
[7] Ibid

in which he promised he would spend the remaining years of his life dedicated taking the Christian gospel to those who had never heard. Since returning from the shores of South America, Captain Allen Gardiner had his heart set on the island peoples of one of the most inhospitable places on earth.

The following account is based on the well-documented work of Phyllis Thompson, *An Unquenchable Flame.*

Four years after founding The Patagonian Mission, Allen Gardiner got together a small team of men and a stack of provisions with the aim of setting up a base in the southern archipelago from which a work could begin. In January 1848 they left Cardiff on the *Clymene,* a merchant vessel bound for Valparaiso via Cape Horn. The plan was they would disembark at a suitable location, Staten Island (separated from the tip of the 'coccyx' of Tierra del Fuego by the Straits of Le Mair) with all their provisions, including two goats and a kid as well as plants suited for the harsh climate. The landing had to be aborted due to adverse weather. They turned westwards aiming for the Beagle Channel and Picton Island. They chose a small sheltered bay and named it Banner Cove after Gardiner had read Psalm 60, in which the fourth verse had really impacted him: 'Thou hast given a banner to them that fear Thee, that it may be displayed because of the truth.'

Within a short time of landing a couple of canoes approached carrying Fuegians. Bartering took place and initial contact seemed promising. The next day more arrived but this time the attitude was more threatening, as the men with no compunction grabbed at anything they could lay hands on including the clothes being worn together with the buttons. Before long the canoe visitors lit a fire and crouching down beside it watched all the stocks being unloaded and the hut being constructed. Gardiner and his companions instinctively felt too vulnerable in setting up a permanent base here.

Nevertheless, the next day the *Clymene* weighed anchor and set sail leaving them alone with their provisions. A decision had to be reached. Gardiner saw the need for a much bigger boat than the small ones they had as part of their essential provisions:

a home afloat in which they could keep all their vital equipment and in which the six of them could retreat if necessary. Reluctantly yet prudently all agreed.

There was no thought of giving up. The commission to go and make disciples in all nations was still valid. The tribes of South America were still waiting.

The hut and tent so recently put together was now hastily dismantled and reloaded back on board. Before departing he and two of his companions did a full reconnoitre of Picton Island, noting that there were cranberries, wild celery and patches of ground suitable for cultivation. He also left the goats and kid in the hope there would be more on their return!

He later wrote:

'Long after we had quitted our snug anchorage my glass was directed towards Banner Cove, and although both it and Picton Island have passed from my view, and are now sunk beneath the horizon, I trust it is not the last farewell which I have taken of those interesting shores, but that ere long, by the blessing of God upon our exertions at home, a mission upon a suitable footing may be established, and the banner of the Cross displayed …'.[8]

Two years after the failed attempt to found a permanent base for the Mission, Allen Gardiner set sail again. The *Ocean Queen* left Liverpool docks on Saturday, September 7th 1850. Comprising the six men who joined him were three young Cornish fishermen, Joseph Erwin, who had accompanied him on the previous visit as carpenter, John Maidment, a waiter, and Dr Richard Williams. The latter had left a flourishing medical practice in response to an advertisement he had seen, in which the vision had been outlined in a way as to leave no one under any allusion as to its attendant dangers.

'When I observed that it added that no one need apply who was not willing to risk his life in the service, my heart leaped within me,' he wrote. 'For here I thought was the very sphere of usefulness God had opened up for me.'[9]

Early in December the *Ocean Queen* let down her anchor in

---

[8] Phyllis Thompson: *An Unquenchable Flame*. Hodder and Stoughton. p. 127
[9] Ibid: pp.132, 133

Banner Cove. It wasn't long before the Fuegians once again displayed signs of aggressiveness and acquisitiveness.

So much so that this confirmed the need for the Mission initially to be afloat until such time as barriers could be broken down and mutual confidence established. A week before Christmas the mother ship cast anchor taking the precious letters the seven had written home, including one from Gardiner to Pakenham Despard, secretary of The Patagonian Mission.

'So the *Ocean Queen* sailed away, taking with them the precious missives, and heart-stirring memories of two little launches bobbing on the water, with seven men standing on them … singing hymns as they waved farewell.'[10]

What no one knew at the time was that she sailed away with the men's means of survival still in the hold, an omission that would ultimately cost them their lives.

When Gardiner had made his previous visit he had noted there was an abundance of fish and also wild fowl, mainly duck and geese. What struck him on this second visit was that for an unexplainable reason there were few fish to be seen. The Cornish fishermen would cast their nets only to find they were gathered in empty. It would be several days before they were to discover on completing a search through the unloaded stores that the essential gunpowder for shooting wild fowl was not there. It had remained somewhere on the high seas on its way up the west coast of Chile. They would have to survive on the stores until another ship arrived with fresh provisions and who knew when that would be?

The lack of ammunition for their food supply wasn't the only calamity they faced in the thirty-six hours after the *Ocean Queen* left. The two launches, *Pioneer* and *Speedwell* had been assembled, but there was still much finishing work on them to be done, one had already sprung a leak. Gardiner decided the wisest course of action would be to sail them to a sheltered bay and away from the prying eyes of the native inhabitants, where they could work on the boats. Unfortunately the additional dinghies were too big to be accommodated in the larger vessels so had to be towed.

---

[10] Ibid: p. 146

The *Speedwell* got into difficulties and became separated from the *Pioneer,* in which their captain was sailing. With the hostile waves tossing them around like a cork, and finding the launch entangled in seaweed and perilously near the rocks, Williams was amazed at his calmness; a calmness '... for God had the ordering of this as well as of any other circumstance which should betide us.'[11]

They managed to free themselves after several hours and ran aground in Banner Cove, with some damage to the boat but not themselves. It would be almost twenty-four hours later before the two boats with their crew were united in the Cove just in time to celebrate Christmas Day with preserved food from their precious stocks.

The next five weeks were dogged by storms forcing them to shelter on the coast for two weeks, leaving the boats grounded among the rocks. The Fuegians had appeared inquisitively and at times aggressively on and off leaving no alternative but to try and dodge them. It was agreed that to deliberately land where the tribesmen were gathered would be foolish. Dr Williams wrote in his diary that 'to do so would be displaying as much trust in God as for a man to rush over the edge of a precipice and expect not to be injured.'[12]

On the other hand they were unwavering in their trust that God had not brought them so far for no purpose and they were not going to give up. What they sought was that in time this purpose would be revealed.

Williams continued:

'The captain offered up a prayer, a prayer breathed in simplicity and godly sincerity and in firm reliance upon the goodness and providential direction of our heavenly Father ... it was the prayer of a child who knew the Father heard and heeded ... Never did the captain appear to more advantage. There was a man of God, the praying, sincere devoted servant of the Lord.'[13]

When Dr Williams had first set out, his impression of Allen

---

[11] Ibid: p. 147
[12] Ibid: p. 156
[13] Ibid.

Gardiner was not so positive. To this warm hearted, sensitive medical man, Gardiner's stern and reserved nature bordering on an apparent aloofness left the doctor initially concerned and vulnerable. It took some weeks before the initial impression was exchanged for a greater understanding.

The decision was made to proceed eastwards to Spaniard Bay. The two boats set out. For a while the weather was extremely favourable: blue skies and gentle wind. The captain and his crew of two, Maitland and Williams in *Pioneer*, disembarked. Gardiner went off to explore the area to see how suitable it might prove to be for a base and for how long. Overnight the weather changed so dramatically, so much so that the *Pioneer* lost her moorings and was dashed irreparably against the rocks. A couple of days later they were able to drag it onto the shore. It would never sail again and was only fit for sleeping quarters on land. After the storm abated, they were able to make contact with their friends on *Speedwell*. As they talked over their predicament, it became clear that the only course open to them was to stick it out until the ship bringing them replenishing supplies arrived in three or four months time.

They would then head for the Falkland Islands and put into action a revised plan for achieving their goal of setting up the Mission.

The hostile climate, the wearing of damp clothing, and the more serious lack of adequate food began to leave their mark. Illness hit and Dr Williams was the first to succumb with the symptoms of scurvy. Space does not permit to write in any detail about the next few weeks: the sailing in difficult waters in a heavily laden *Speedwell* with all on board, including a sick man, to Banner Cove on Picton Island, and the messages left in bottles and written on rocks in the hope that when the supply ship arrived they would be discovered. The messages advised that they would be in Spaniard Harbour (present day Aguirre bay).

Despite the near capsizing of the boat being so heavily laden, they sailed safely into Spaniard Harbour. Gardiner writes:

'We have experienced the good hand of our God upon us, in

carrying out and bringing us back in safety, and enabling us to do in Banner Cove all that was necessary for insuring, as far as instrumentality is concerned, the due arrival of the vessel which is expected to bring our supplies.'[14]

Meanwhile back in England, Pakenham Despard was facing problems in finding a ship willing to risk her insurance by sailing in such treacherous waters with a comparatively small cargo of provisions on board. In Montevideo, Uruguay, Samuel LaFone had sent a vessel down the Patagonian coast of Argentina with instructions to call in at Picton Island to find out how Gardiner and his men were faring and to give them help if needed.

By June the Antarctic winter was closing in. The hardships the seven were facing were unimaginable as slowly illness and starvation claimed their lives. Gardiner and Maidment were berthed in the wreck of the *Pioneer* for the nights and by day made a cave their base. The other five were cramped but secure in *Speedwell*. The two parties were separated from one another when the tide was high.

Allen Gardiner, in spite of their present predicament never gave up on the vision they all shared. He wrote an outline of his plans for the Mission, drawing on the experiences encountered, in an exercise book while in the cave.

'To transfer the station to East Falkland, maintaining there a few of the natives from Picton Island, for the purpose of enabling the missionaries to acquire their language, which it has been found impossible to do among the islands.'[15]

It would fall to others to take that vision forward. By September all seven had died from illness and starvation. The bravery, the concern for one another, and their unwavering faith in the God they loved and served right up to the end is the legacy handed down to those who followed in their footsteps. In incredible weakness one or two from each grouping had managed to stagger over the beach separating the two parties in an effort to find how the others were faring.

Maidment, having painfully made it to the *Speedwell*, found a

---

[14] Ibid: p. 165
[15] Ibid: p. 169

distraught Pearce, the young twenty-one-year-old Cornishman, a weak and delirious Williams and two of the men dead. Before returning to the cave he summoned up what strength he had to bury the two men. He himself, reminiscent of Oates of Scott's expedition to the Antarctic years later, knowing his end was near chose to die away from his captain.

The last entry in Allen Gardiner's diary written slowly with a hand numb with cold reads,

'Yet a little while … the Almighty to sing the praises … throne. I neither hunger nor thirst, though … days without water … Maidment's kindness to me …

'Your affectionate brother in …

'Allen F. Gardiner.

'6 September 1851.'[16]

It was four months later that HMS *Dido* arrived and found the bodies on Spaniard Harbour.

Some would later claim that Gardiner acted naïvely and without sufficient thought. But a true pioneering spirit is prepared to take risks as so many down the centuries have proved. When those risks have, as the underlying reason, a passion with an eternal perspective in view then only the eternal God himself is best qualified to make the judgement. The written documents left by these brave men are full of trust, gratitude, and a sense of deep peace in the God they served with such sacrifice.

Their endeavours were not in vain as others picked up the mantle and followed in their steps. However, more deaths were to occur and this time not through starvation but through an act of treachery, as Pendle writes from the memoirs of Lucas Bridges. Jemmy Button, one of the four Fuegians taken to England by Captain Fitzroy, instigated this treachery, according to Pendle's account.

Lucas Bridges, the son of a missionary, was born in 1874 in Ushuaia, on 'The Land of Fire', where he grew up and played with the local Indians. His parents had arrived three years earlier and established a mission among the Fuegians. It was his

---

[16] Ibid: p. 184

father who 'was closely connected with the victims of Jemmy's culminating and unexpected act of treachery'.[17]

A few years after the deaths due to starvation of Gardiner and his friends, another pioneering group of missionaries left England bound for the islands of these southern waters in the hopes of making contact with Jemmy Button to enlist his help in establishing a friendly contact with the Fuegians. Crossing the dangerous waters that divided so many of the islands, on October 1859 a group anchored in a sheltered bay. Canoes of Indians came out to meet them, among them Jemmy Button. All seemed well. The missionaries went ashore, with the exception of the ship's cook, and erected a small hut as a church. At the end of the week they decided to hold their first service. Three hundred Fuegians arrived but after the singing of the first hymn, they fell on the missionaries 'with clubs, stones and spears and … beat every one of them to death'. Only the cook remained and his life was spared. It was on his evidence that Jemmy Button was implicated as the ringleader. It seems that he became 'more demanding, and seemed resentful that the Englishmen were bestowing on other Fuegians the favours of which he himself was accustomed to have a monopoly'.[18]

Almost a century later, again in South America, this time in the jungle of Equador, five American men were also killed by those with whom they had come to share the good news of the Christian gospel. Today, in both places, there is a thriving Christian witness.

A recent chaplain of the Intercontinental Church Society (ICS) writes of an historic event. On December 17th 2001 a visit was made to Keppel Island, now the uninhabited island of West Falkland. An invitation to the Falklands had been given to a former bishop of Chile and the present one to represent the then Archbishop of Canterbury, Dr George Carey, also Bishop of the Falkland Islands. Bishop Colin Bazley, former successor to Bishop David Pytches, and the present national Chilean bishop, Tito Zavala, spent a few hours on Keppel Island.

In 1855 the Patagonian Missionary Society established this

---

[17] George Pendle: *The Land and People of Chile*. A. & C. Black p. 82
[18] Ibid: p. 86

island as both a farming settlement and a mission base. For the next forty years the missionaries brought the Christian gospel to the Yaghan Indians of 'The Land of Fire'. Undeterred by the hardships, reversals and sacrifice of life, the brave missionaries continued to reach out to those to whom they were called. Notable among these early pioneers was Waite Hockin Stirling, who arrived as Superintendent in 1862. In 1869 he went to live alone among the Indians of the Beagle Channel, building himself a house in Ushuaia.

A short time later others joined him, among them the parents of Lucas Bridges born five years later. Stirling became the first Anglican bishop of the largest diocese in the world – the Falkland Islands and South America.[19]

It was fitting that two Bishops of Chile as representatives of the South American Mission Society, formerly the Patagonian Missionary Society should make this historical visit. On speaking of the visit to Keppel Island, Bishop Tito said,

'It was an emotional visit, especially as I thought about all those who had died in the past trying to be faithful to the lord's mission to South America. I want to help the Christians in the diocese of Chile realise that people gave their lives to reach South America with the gospel, and that we must continue with that mission.'[20]

---

[19] Alistair McHaffie: *ICS News*, March 2002 'An historic moment …'
[20] Ibid

Some members of the Sunday night Chilean student group,
Back row: Ray, Nico, Pato. Front row: Me, Jackie, Heather and Susan Macdonald.

Some of the same members 26 years later!
From left: Pato and Susan, Luz and Nico, Ray and me, Hilary and Alf.

'Lydia' with Andrew.

Hilary and Alf's wedding. Nico as Best Man.

'Los Picaflores' - Hilary 2nd from left.

The Santiago Community Church (formerly St Andrew's Anglican Cathedral).

Visit of Dr Michael Ramsey, Archbishop of Canterbury together with his wife.

Members of the Women's Forum - Pamela Yorston on left and Penny kneeling.

Women's Forum bagging milk powder.

Mary Trum - Women's Forum.

Our 'kiwi' friends Alan and Ken.

Jimena and Nigel with Abigail in their mountainside home. Andrew and Ray on either side during 1988 visit.

An extension of the Outreach programme, Sunday school at Caleu - Lew on left, Jimena and Nigel far right.

John and Sandi with Richard.

John and Margaret Heyn.

Omar and Lia with their three sons in Vancouver.

Keith Haskell addressing audience on the occasion of Craighouse Speech Day.

British Consul Derek Fernyhough with Grace - Santiago.

The Caledonian Ball (St Andrew's Society). Left to right: Ray and me, Neil and 'Pip' Maclean and opposite Penny and Jimmy Reid.

425

Revd. Dr John Stott on Ray's right, Nico on Ray's left and Oscar Canales front right.

Mónica Ananías, President Pinochet's personal secretary, next to the church notice board. Penny on the left.

Moorhead and Louisa Kennedy on tour. Photograph Robert F. Rodriguez.

Together with Phil and Naomi seeing Julian off at Portsmouth on Global Challenge Yacht Race.

'Stelmar' heading out into the Solent.

Julian on board.

Derek with Julian in our home in Cambridge, 1989.

'Pato' and Susan visit us in Cambridge, 2004.

Nana with Peter and Brione Goodwin-Hudson - Santiago, 2000.

Omar and Lia (standing far right) with team of Canadians in Costa Rica, 2003.

Chapter 32

A Second Harvest

'We are therefore Christ's ambassadors, as though God were making his appeal through us. We implore you on Christ's behalf: Be reconciled to God'[1]

Parties! I love to party, with one exception. The one exception is when the music is so loud that two-way conversations become impossible. In the gospels we find that Jesus himself enjoyed celebratory occasions. Neither before nor since have we had such a whirl of dinner parties as the last six years of our nine in Chile. This was due to the nature of our calling among the upper echelons of society, a calling initially resisted, and a far cry from the beginning of our ministry in East London.

My nursing training equipped me well to get changed in mere minutes. After getting the children to bed, reading and praying with them, we would get changed into our party clothes. In the nineteen-seventies this meant a long dress for the women and usually black tie for the men. I had bought two very attractive dresses in the sales when home on leave and a seamstress made other outfits as necessary.

Minimal make-up would be hurriedly applied as Ray started up the 'cookie-cutter'. With Ray driving we would offer a quick prayer that we would be Christ's ambassadors during the evening's proceedings.

One day in the garden during the early weeks of living in Las Violetas I was thinking about our new calling within the Santiago Community Church and the wider English-speaking community. I was lost in thought. Into my mind came a strong

---

[1] The Bible: 2 Corinthians chapter 5 verse 20

visual image and words that immediately I felt immediately were from God's Holy Spirit. I had a picture of a lighthouse with the light beaming out in all directions from the convex windows of its rounded tower. Simultaneously words impressed themselves deeply into my inner being.

'This is how the Santiago Community Church will become, beaming my light throughout the world.'

Apart from sharing this with Ray I told no one else for some time, and then only a chosen few. Two or three years later Nigel remarked on how that prophetic statement was indeed being fulfilled.

We always enjoyed being invited to the New Zealand Ambassador's home. David and his wife Rowena were always so warm and relaxed. They were regular members of our congregation. We were invited to the Residence on the annual celebration of New Zealand Day. As it always fell in summer, the party, complete with full house and a live band, was held in the garden. Floating on the surface of the tastefully lit swimming pool were numerous candles in the shape of water lilies – a magical setting. Dancing took place on the large terrace. Ray and I were chatting with a small group of friends on the periphery away from the band. Suddenly Ray said, 'David's looking around and seems to be coming in our direction. I think he's looking for a dancing partner.'

It had been obligatory for us, at the Wyggeston Girls' School, to have ballroom dancing lessons. Those years were well and truly behind me. Subsequently and regrettably ballroom dancing was not a pastime I had indulged in. But how do you refuse an ambassador? Thus it was that I found myself not dancing a romantic waltz, nor a fast moving foxtrot, not even a sensuous Argentinian tango. In fact I ended up dancing rock and roll with David to the sound of 'Rock Around the Clock' made famous by Bill Haley and the Comets!

On another occasion at the New Zealand Residence just one tiny particle of light, from the 'lighthouse', made its appearance. In time this would become a beam extending from Chile to Iran. It was at a small dinner party hosted by David and Rowena that we met Moorhead known as Mike and his wife Louisa. He was number two in the United States Embassy. During the course of the evening he took Ray aside and totally out of the blue suddenly said, 'I wish to be confirmed.'

Once home Ray recounted the conversation to me, adding that at the time he thought Mike had had too much to drink! We had never met either Mike or Louisa before and had never even seen them in church. However, Ray decided he would go along with this somewhat bizarre request and said that he would be starting a confirmation course in the autumn. They agreed to be in contact nearer the time. Meanwhile we still didn't see any sign of them at any church service during the summer months.

True to his word Ray contacted Mike's secretary at the US Embassy. On the appointed evening a chauffeur-driven car was the first to arrive and out stepped Mike. He never missed one evening of the course and now would be seen every Sunday in church. Louisa rarely accompanied him. Family concerns with one of their sons had been the catalyst for Mike's spiritual search. Mike was later confirmed. A year or so later his time in Chile was at an end.

The Sunday before they were due to leave he invited us to join him and Louisa at the Country Club (the PWCC) to lunch. In the course of conversation he turned to Ray and said, 'I want to thank you both for all you've done and my prayer is that Louisa,' turning to look at his wife, 'will find the same faith that I have.'

As Moorhead was an expert in Arab affairs, his postings would take him to the Middle East. Initially he was on temporary assignments, including Beirut and the Department of State. It would be several months later that he, together with fifty-one others, hit the world headlines.

In September 1979 he was assigned to Iran, as acting Economic Counsellor to relieve the regular incumbent who was home on family leave. His department tried to persuade Louisa to accompany him, but as it was only a temporary assignment they decided it would be more prudent for only one parent to face the risks that such a posting involved. In addition, Louisa herself had returned to a thriving real estate practice in Washington.

The overthrow of Muhammad Reza Shah Pahlevi by an Islamic revolutionary government earlier that year had led to a steady deterioration in Iranian-American relations. Moorhead in communication with me wrote,

'Teheran could perhaps be typified by students chanting "Death to America", as they marched past the main entrance to the American Embassy, while also lining up at the consular entrance for student visas. We knew, but resisted the idea, that we were in deep trouble.'

What had ignited the flame of anger for the students was the admission to the United States of the Shah for medical treatment. A crowd of about five hundred, mostly students, overran the Embassy on November 4th. Fifty-two hostages were taken. Mike was among them. His new-found faith helped to sustain him during those tense, anxious months. The first full day in captivity was his forty-ninth birthday. I pick up Moorhead's account, *'At first, convinced that we were about to be released, I declined to remove my jacket and tie. This was a case of sartorial denial. Finally a bed-mate whispered, "Wouldn't you be more comfortable if you removed your jacket?"'* Mike heeded the advice. The treatment varied: on the one hand he was subjected to a mock execution, on the other the student captors provided some items of comfort. Among the latter were New Testaments that had been sent out by a missionary organisation. *'With my hands tied, I managed to turn to Second Timothy, where St. Paul, a prisoner in chains, points out that Jesus Christ ... was raised from the dead and his word is not bound. Whatever happened to me, God's word would last and was my comfort throughout 444 days.'*

Prayer was being offered worldwide. Meanwhile in Santiago, a short time after the hostage taking, we were alerted and a chain of prayer for the hostages was set up among church members.

For her part, Louisa was involved in shuttle diplomacy to a number of European countries, organizing prayer support and campaigns for the release of the hostages. This brought her to England and an interview with Margaret Thatcher, as well as a visit to the Pope.

President Carter resorted to the application of economic pressure on Iran by halting oil imports and freezing Iranian assets. Alongside the economic sanctions, he began a number of diplomatic initiatives to free the hostages but to no avail. One initiative that had disastrous results and contributed in large measure to the downfall of his government some months later was a failed attempt at rescue. On April 24th 1980 the United States sent in eight helicopters, three of which were damaged in a sandstorm, eight people were killed. Subsequently the operation was aborted. Cyrus Vance, Secretary of State, who opposed the action, resigned after the mission's failure.

In 1980, the death of the Shah, whilst exiled in Egypt, and the invasion of Iran by Iraq persuaded the Iranians to resolve the hostage crisis. Ronald Reagan's defeat of Carter, together with intermediary assistance from Algeria, led to the beginning of negotiations. On January 20th 1981, the day of President Reagan's inauguration, the United States released almost $8 billion in Iranian assets. The fifty-two hostages were released after 444 days in captivity. We, ourselves, having now been living back in the UK for one year, together with so many others worldwide greeted the news with both joy and great relief.

Following his release, Mike left the diplomatic service to work at the Cathedral of St John the Divine in New York. This proved to be very disappointing. His faith, having been refined in the crucible of danger and suffering, was further tested as he encountered in a number of colleagues a very watered down faith. *'Many of the Episcopal "Liberal Clergys'"' concerns were totally secular, often political.'* The Cathedral experience led him to write a book entitled *The Ayatollah in the Cathedral: Reflections of a Hostage*, which I've yet to read.

He and Louisa now live in Maine where they have both continued to serve locally in their Episcopalian Church and also on the Diocesan Council. They keep very busy in retirement on various boards and societies. In addition, Moorhead lectures at Acadia Senior College. He teaches a seven-week course on Islam

– the Faith, the Law, the Political System and Islam as a way of life.[2]

There was another Mike, this one with a New Zealand connection and a recent graduate. We met 'kiwi' Mike as a result of a telephone call. The voice at the other end was Stella, who with her husband ran the Christian bookshop in downtown Santiago. This was before Alan, also a 'kiwi', who shared our home had arrived in Chile.

'Gill, a young man has just left our shop on his way to your house. He's back-packing in South America and unexpectedly has an enforced stay in Santiago. He's anxious to get hold of some books in English. I gave him your address as your Church has such a good library of English books. I hope that's okay?'

A short time later our doorbell rang. I opened it to a tall young man, in his early twenties. He was clean-shaven with a fresh complexion, light brown hair shot through with touches of auburn. We introduced ourselves as I invited him in. Ray was out at the time, but in those days you didn't think twice about any risk in inviting a stranger into your home, especially a tourist.

He told me his name was Mike and that he had developed a skin condition that meant he had to remain in Santiago extra days than planned. Ray arrived home and we chatted more to Mike. I had made an assumption that, as he had gone into a bookshop that specifically sold Christian books, he had a Christian faith. It so happened that that evening we were having our weekly group of study and discussion of a Bible passage. We invited him to join us for the evening meal and to stay on to the discussion.

'I've never been to a Bible study group. What happens?'

I guess time on his hands and feeling a bit lonely persuaded him to stay. At the end of the evening Mike left us armed with several books he had chosen from our own collection of books. Three days later, on Saturday, he joined us for a family picnic. Sunday morning, he was in church, causing some perplexity to our Ambassador's wife.

Ray had just finished giving out the notices when suddenly a

---

[2] A mere couple of months after I wrote this chapter, Mike informed us that Louisa had died.

voice from the back of the church said, 'I have a notice I'd like to give.' It was Mike up on his feet. He started by acknowledging the welcome he had been given, went on to say how he thanked us for the way we had opened our home and lent him books and finished with these words, 'I just want to say that, in my protracted stay here, I've read several books and talked to Ray and Gill and have now committed my life to Christ.' We had had no idea, but were of course thrilled.

As Catherine Secondé left church, she turned to Ray and with her own personal faith then in such infancy said, 'Ray, what was that young man on about?'

Mike never looked back. Some years later, in addition to both his and his wife's involvement in their local church, Mike had an input into the organisation World Vision. This has taken him to a number of developing nations. We remain in touch with Mike and his family and have stayed in their home just outside Wellington.

In addition to the home of David and Rowena we visited among the high-ranking diplomats, was the home of Derek and Grace Fernyhough. It was here, at a cocktail party, that we first met John and Sandi Burley, who had arrived in Chile on the second anniversary of the military coup. John was a Cambridge graduate in mineralogy and was in Chile on a United Nation's contract at the Mining Laboratory of COPEC. Immaculately dressed waiters were serving the cocktails and canapés. Suddenly Grace came up to us and said there was a young couple she would like us to meet, adding, 'You might be able to get them to come to church.'

John's account of what happened during six weeks of the following January and February, culminating in this particular cocktail party, might cause incredulity in the minds of some cynics. I will recount these events in John's own words. To put this into context, very many years later a Cambridge agnostic asked me, how I had heard God's call to me as a nineteen-year-old. Was it an audible voice? Was it just an impression? How would I define God speaking to me? For me, the best way I can describe it was as a very clear inner voice. For John it was more clearly audible.

When we first met them he described both he and Sandi as unbelievers. He had moved away from his childhood faith as a chorister at Hereford Cathedral. Once at Cambridge, as an undergraduate, he described himself as '*a convinced atheist/ scientist.*' This view he held for the following twelve years until he found himself, like us, the other side of the world in late summer of 1976. He described what happened in a letter to me, as if they occurred only days ago. He was on his way, with a work colleague to a cocktail party, when '*I heard a voice behind me say, "I am going to make you a priest in my church." I turned around but no one was about. (It was in the Calle Marchant Pereira in Providencia).*' Over the next six weeks he heard the same words on two further occasions – '*always when I was alone. I began to worry about my sanity and made a doctor's appointment! Two days after hearing the voice for the third (and final) time I was at a cocktail party ... There I met Ray and we chatted amicably. I explained I was not a churchgoer, but felt prompted to ask if there was a choir. I remember Ray saying – "yes, but we are in need of altos and basses." The fact that Sandi sings alto and I sing bass struck me as no more than an amusing coincidence!*'

In March, once the long summer and Chilean vacations were over, church activities started up again. John and Sandi turned up to choir practice and the following Sunday to their first church service. John continues, '*I had armed myself with a book (Agatha Christie!) to read during the sermon, but never got past the first paragraph. I remember looking up and Ray's voice (a pleasant background drone up to that time) suddenly became sharp and focussed and I had the strange sensation that he and I were the only two people present. He was preaching on John 3 and I think I really heard the gospel for the first time. I don't know how I felt at the end of the sermon – we just sang out the service and went home.*'

The sermon was based on Nicodemus, a religious leader, who sought a nightime interview with Jesus. It was during the ensuing debate that Nicodemus was confronted with the fact that although religious, his faith was not grounded in reality. There was an outward observance of ritual but not a changed inner life.[3]

Over the next three Sundays John was so *'similarly gripped by the message'* that he was left wondering why the church wasn't in fact bursting at the seams. At the end of those three weeks John arranged to see Ray for a chat about the Christian faith. Ray lent him *Mere Christianity* by C. S. Lewis. *'It was reading this at home later that I realised what conversion was about and finally decided to give my life to the Lord (it was the chapter on "Pride" that clinched it for me!). I invited Christ into my life at midnight on 1st April 1976 and nothing seemed to happen. When I awoke the next morning it was a new world ... even the colours were brighter – an extraordinary sensation! I decided to say nothing, but Sandi quickly noticed something was different, and ... went to talk with Gill. I have no idea what passed between them, but the upshot was that Sandi gave her life to Christ about ten days later. Since then we have always shared our walk with the Lord and have worked together.'*

Another milestone for John in his journey of faith was about a year later. Through Alf Cooper we had a visit from a Christian men's duo. Don Double and Michael Darwood were from the charismatic branch of the Christian church. They were booked for a time of preaching and ministry in the Community Church as well as to Chilean groups. It was during this visit that John *'was filled with the Holy Spirit'* resulting in a desire to serve God.

This couple over the following months and years were among the most committed within our Church fellowship. When his English contract with the UN came to an end John opted for a UN Chilean contract. This meant a large drop in salary. His reason was that he was learning so much on the journey of faith while with us that he wanted to remain in Chile. He became a deacon, then part of a ministry team and began to share in preaching. It was no surprise when sometime later John felt God call him to the Anglican ordained ministry.

Meanwhile Women's Forum was going from strength to strength. One Sunday, a Canadian, Charles Cooper, by now on

---

[3] The Bible: John chapter 3

the Board of Deacons said from the pulpit how much a number of the men in the church owed to the Women's Forum. His wife, Frances, had grown so much in her Christian faith, as had many others, yet even more had come to a personal faith for the very first time. What, for me, was such an encouragement was the way, the women themselves were inviting their friends. They were living out the 'Andrew principle' of wanting to introduce others to Jesus. And they came!

Attractive looking Penny brought along another attractive young mother, in this case not a brunette but a blonde, the Anglo-Argentinian whose parents had been so very kind to Elaine.

Pamela was a nominal churchgoer, so it wasn't long before on her arrival to Chile with Gordon, that she made her way to the Church. She was duly recruited to Women's Forum and, short of any unforeseen circumstances, never missed a Thursday.

Their home was on the way to Redland School and I would often drop in. What I remember on those visits were that her blinds and curtains were inevitably drawn – something at first I thought strange until she explained what in reality was so logical. 'It's to keep the rooms cooler from the heated glass from the sun's rays.' This was sound advice that I took on board and to this day have put into practice whenever necessary.

We inevitably talked about the Christian faith and, with Pamela always full of questions, conversation was stimulating, even more so given her propensity to debate and act as devil's advocate! It was a very joyful Sunday when, together with just around a dozen or so, she was confirmed. I'll never forget thinking what a good advertisement for Christianity she was. The candidates were occupying the front two pews of the church and were given an opportunity to share their stories of faith. Facing the congregation and leaning on the back of the pew in front, perhaps for support, but with a posture fit for a model, long blonde hair falling onto her shoulders, she said what Christ had come to mean to her, free of clichés and in-house jargon.

A few years later, Pamela with her husband Gordon, left for Uruguay. It was in Montevideo that she introduced a Bible study course that I had used with an increasing number of women from Forum. The women Pamela taught were in the English Anglican Church, hungry for spiritual food.

Another model-like young mother was thirty-two-year-old Mary. An American, she was married with three young sons. Her husband was financial manager of the American Embassy. Mary was not only striking in looks but especially in height. She was around six feet tall, with a good figure and light brown-blonde hair. She was gentle by nature with a soft American drawl. On her husband's posting to Chile, like others, they gravitated to the English-speaking church looking for friendship among those sharing a common language. A friend invited Mary to Women's Forum and it wasn't long before I realised that Mary was looking for meaning and purpose in life. She was having marriage difficulties and recalling those days she writes, *'I desperately needed to find strength and hope for my life ... I needed to know how to get in touch with God, so I asked Gill.'*

Mary had been brought up to go to church yet knew she didn't have the same faith in God that her grandmother had shown. *'Gill and I knelt down to pray ... that was the day that I met Jesus. On January 24, 1979 in Santiago, Chile I entered into a personal relationship with Jesus Christ that filled me with the greatest love, joy and peace I have ever known.'*

During Mary and her husband's subsequent posting to Africa their marriage, as a result of her husband's alcohol excesses, broke down completely. Sadly, later, they divorced. In the difficult days ahead as a single mother with three boys her faith never wavered. *'My walk with the Lord, which began in Santiago, Chile has led me through deep valleys and onto glorious mountaintops and God has used all things to work together for good in my life. He has called me to love and obey Him and be on mission with Him as He works to fulfil His purpose ...'.*

Back in the States Mary felt God was calling her to train for the ordained ministry within the Methodist church. After undertaking a Master of Divinity degree she served as minister in a North Carolina church. We met up with Mary and her second husband, Bob, some years later when she was doing a 'pulpit exchange' in Yorkshire. On returning to the US she became involved in prison ministry. In a visit to our home several years later, in 2007, with her husband Bob, Mary recounted to me something of her passion in reaching across the racial divides within her own country. She had led a privileged life as a member of the diplomatic community. As a white person growing up in a southern state she enjoyed cultural advantages that many black Americans did not have. The call of God led her to become a volunteer chaplain in the men's prison in Raleigh NC where most of the inmates were black.

'Jesus led me to step with him across the cultural and racial divisions that divide my society to minister healing and hope.'

Mary was yet another example of a beam of light radiating from 'the lighthouse'.

Grace and Joan were especially pro-active in recruiting to Forum among the British: Grace's environment was especially among the diplomatic staff and Joan's in the business sector. These two women unashamedly put their own reputation on the line and left no one in doubt as to their faith in Christ. Little wonder that all the many dinner and cocktail parties we attended together with so many within the English-speaking community became the natural environment in which conversation turned to spiritual matters. We would inevitably meet up with several from our congregation at these occasions.

The St Andrew's Society was a very popular organization that drew in not only Scots but also others who shared our common language and who enjoyed dancing. Joan, was from Yorkshire, and together with her Scots husband Douglas, had recently arrived in Santiago. Douglas was managing director of Coates thread and textile firm. They were leading lights in the St Andrew's Society. Douglas later came on to the Board of Trustees while Joan was active in Forum. They hosted a Bible study group in their home led by an American couple, as well as leading a Bible class for young teens. Joan was from the Christian Brethren and Douglas 'the Kirk'. Their two sons, Hugo and Nicky, became friends of Andrew and Julian. Our paths were to cross very many years later as it was through their recommendation that we found ourselves last year serving the Costa del Sol West Chaplaincy, where we met our Chilean friends.

Another couple with Scottish connections and who, in fact, headed up the St Andrew's Society, were Andrew and Dorothy. They were churchgoers, but like so many we discovered, went more out of a sense of community and 'the correct thing to do'. It was Women's Forum in particular that challenged Dorothy to review her relationship with God and his church. In time the whole family, including daughter, Lucy, and son, David, would speak of their time in Chile as the turning point in their faith commitment. Dorothy and I both remember sitting in my car chatting about what it meant to have a personal relationship with Jesus, after which she prayed a prayer of commitment. Recently in a letter she described the impact of those years, '... *for both of us, our time in Chile drew our faith more into the foreground of our lives – made what had been implicit, explicit, it was a time of renewal, refreshment and great blessing.*'

With a number of the couples it was the growth in faith of the women that was the challenge to the men. One very real drawback for some of the men to commit wholeheartedly to Christ was their allegiance to Freemasonry. This was particularly the case with the British and Anglo-Chileans, not so the Americans. Ray had a choice, either to confront head on or to wait for the power of the gospel and the work of God's Holy Spirit to rebuke, convince and challenge them to a greater loyalty. Given Ray's temperament and reluctance to confront, he chose the latter. I'm sure, given that our Church was the only English-speaking Church in Santiago at that time, this was right. Subsequently some of these men severed their allegiance to Freemasonry, as their commitment to Christ deepened. Andrew, Dorothy's husband, was one of these. He subsequently renounced his membership. The change in Andrew was remarkable over the ensuing months and years. Earlier he had been one of those who, for a time, had initially kept us somewhat at arms' length.

Another challenge for Ray in our early days that involved risk-taking faith, was inviting those whose spirituality was still undeveloped to take positions of responsibility on church committees and councils. These were risks that other church leaders might not be prepared to take. In our situation there was a great turn-over of personnel. Many were only on a two or three year contract so we could not afford to wait until such individuals showed great spiritual maturity. The amazing thing was that in several of the men it was exactly because they were entrusted with responsibilities that they took the first big step on their faith journey – a case of belonging before believing. In still others what was an infantile belief matured.

Nigel Strang referred to the days at the Community Church to be ones of growing in spiritual depth and responsibility. In a recent communication he wrote, '… *Ray formed a Ministry team to which five of us were invited … Training was given and opportunities were provided to preach both from the pulpit, with friendly de-briefings, and at Commonwealth House …The Lord poured many blessings on us those days.'*

Andrew, John Burley, Lew, Nigel and Moorhead were the five. Nigel recalls how he and Moorhead worked on the compilation of a new Songbook for the services. It was to Andrew, the tall, dour and totally reliable Scot that Ray left the main leadership of the Church while we were home on leave.

The training and leadership responsibility was the catalyst that led him, after he left Chile, to becoming the Interim Moderator for the United Reformed Church in Redcar.

In her letter, Dorothy, wrote how much Andrew '*loved his lay preaching dearly, gaining great satisfaction and inspiration from his study and involvement with struggling churches in the area'*. He was very involved also with the Gideon Movement, distributing Bibles and taking assemblies to schools in North Yorkshire. Andrew died a few years ago.

Ray reminded me of an incident concerning Andrew I had long forgotten. One Sunday after the service, Ray went to collect his jacket hanging in the vestry only to find it had been stolen. As this was his one and only suit, it was quite a loss. Within a week Ray received a telephone call from Andrew. Would Ray meet him at such and such a shop in Providencia. They met up at the agreed time and destination.

442

'I'd like you to choose the material for a new suit,' said Andrew. The material was top quality and, with measurements taken resulted in what was probably the best suit Ray ever possessed, thanks to this generous Scot.

As we look back over those years we are very humbled at the privilege that was ours in sharing in the lives of so many – such a rich investment in the kingdom of God. The labour of breaking up hard ground, the sowing of the precious seed of the gospel, the watering and nurturing of tender plants was costly especially on our time and energy, but the joy of seeing the harvest God's Holy Spirit was reaping was without measure. At times life was tough, but never dull.

Years later a friend in Cambridge said to me, 'Gill, you've had such an exciting life; all the places and the type of ministry you and Ray have enjoyed.'

I well remember my answer, an answer that I frequently give when such sentiments are expressed. 'You're right, we have had an exciting and privileged life, but there has been inevitably a cost involved. With such an itinerant and pioneering type of ministry we've been called to over the years, we have always had to be saying goodbye and starting afresh.'

This doesn't get easier the older one becomes but with heaven approaching sooner now I shall meet so very many friends and, as our American friends would say, 'We'll have a ball!' I've got my dancing shoes on! And this ball will be for eternity!

Chapter 33
A Diplomatic Crisis

After the coup, relations between Chile and England's Labour government cooled considerably. Chilean exports were boycotted and among other items, wine was withdrawn from major supermarkets.

It was a difficult time once again for British investors. Under Allende's nationalisation programme and subsequent economic chaos, investors had been reluctant to further invest. Now with a change of government, foreign policy back home was dictating the terms. For diplomats it was also an uncertain time. Embassy social events continued as normal on the surface, but underneath the surface anxiety simmered.

In our new ministry we wanted to continue giving hospitality, which had always been part of both our upbringing and our married life. The fact was that our salary by no means reflected that of the vast majority of the congregation. I was faced with a choice to invite business and diplomatic personnel for dinner or not. We were not in a position to provide the kind of spread we would receive in their homes. In fact it really was no choice. I was not prepared to try in any way to compete. I liked cooking and, blessed with a creative flair, we decided that some good home cooking, attractively served in an atmosphere of genuine friendship was much more important.

Eventually it was the turn of our Ambassador and his wife. Knowing something of the strain they were under, we decided not to invite our usual numbers of anything between four or twelve or more. We really felt we wanted to provide a home in which they could let go of their official cover and just be themselves. So it was that on an early spring evening in 1974 Mr and Mrs Reginald Secondé arrived at the railings of Las Violetas in their chauffeur-driven car. The wine we chose for the evening was Concha y Toro, which we ourselves enjoyed.

'I say, Ray, this is excellent wine,' said our distinguished guest during the course of the dinner. 'What make is it? I must get my *mayordomo* [butler] to purchase some.'

Ray and I didn't dare look at one another. We knew we would find it hard not to burst out laughing. This wine was among the cheapest on the market. We could just imagine the look of horror on the *mayordomo*'s face when the Ambassador gave his request.

After dinner and an hour or so conversation, Mrs Catherine Secondé turned to me saying, 'Before we leave let me help with the washing up.'

'Oh, no,' I replied. 'I wouldn't dream of it. It won't take long.'

'But I'd like to. I don't do it very often.'

'Why not?' I thought. 'It's true. She wouldn't wash up very often, given all the staff they employed.'

'Thank you,' I replied.

We moved into the kitchen. Handing her the tea towel, reserve was broken down, as we chatted woman to woman. It was in the ordinary task of washing up that she told me to drop the Mrs and to call her Catherine. Her husband was to receive his knighthood in 1981 as Ambassador to Venezuela, just before retiring from the Diplomatic Service. That evening was very special to all of us, as we relaxed in the privacy of an ordinary home with no veneer to mask reality.

It was late December 1975 and once again we were at a cocktail party in the home of our Consul and his wife. Grace took us aside as soon as we arrived.

'Ray, Gill, I'm afraid Derek isn't here.' She looked around and lowering her voice continued, 'He's visiting a British woman in prison who has allegedly been tortured.' Thus it was that we heard about the detention of Dr Sheila Cassidy. The knock-on effect involved a huge political storm. She wrote her story in her autobiography *Audacity to Believe.*

Like so many of us, when we first arrived in Chile, she was naïve in her political awareness but also like us, living during those turbulent years of the nineteen seventies, naivety gave way to political awareness. For Sheila she was right at the cutting-edge.

She arrived in Chile December 1971, nine months after us, at the invitation of Consuelo, a Chilean woman doctor she had worked with in England. Through this friend, who was pro-Allende's government, Sheila found herself exposed to relatives and friends on the political left. Like us too, she found many of them to be caring, compassionate and with a deep sense of justice. Inevitably some were extreme and more radically involved politically than others. This brought them into direct conflict with the military and the secret security forces after Allende's fall.

As a result of her friend's *conocidos* (known contacts), being a national and knowing the system, Sheila was able to practise as a doctor. Initially this had to be under supervision. All foreign professionals, in order to practise their profession, had to revalidate their degrees by further study and examinations. This was done and Sheila subsequently was able to follow her professional calling. Another calling, which had recurred from time to time, had been put on the back burner.

Brought up as a Roman Catholic, she had had early stirrings of becoming a nun, stirrings not always welcomed. During her graduate years she had dropped her church attendance and on arriving in Chile, God did not figure large in her thinking. Her friends' political positions and her medical work undertaken among the very poor and disadvantaged of the capital exposed her to injustices never before encountered. Gradually she began to re-examine the faith she had been brought up in. It was after a period of deep loneliness, depression, culminating in the death through illness of Consuelo, that Sheila reached a turning point.

'Sad and lonely I sought refuge at the feet of the God to whom I had given little thought for many years and quietly and naturally returned to my undergraduate practice of daily attendance at mass and communion.'[1]

She found solace, support and friendship among American nuns and the Columban priests. Alongside her spiritual quest was the continuing ministry of seeing to the physical needs of the poor living in the shantytowns.

Like our Columban priest friend, Kevin, known also as Miguel, living and working right among the very poor led many a sensitive, compassionate person to question an orthodox faith which in its history had favoured the elite and privileged. This was by no means restricted to the Roman Catholic Church, as our own Archbishop had challenged us. Also, like Kevin, Sheila turned to the authentic Jesus of the gospels and his teachings for answers. At this time the unbidden call to take her vows that had pursued her over the years returned. Another 'Jonah' eventually capitulated. Crunch time for Sheila came as a result of going on a retreat as her Dutch priest confidant had wisely advised her. It was the same retreat house in which I had had my deep spiritual encounter through the ministry of Sister Georgina; the respective experiences taking place within a year or two of one another.

I write in the words of Sheila's own account of her surrender to God's call.

'How can one convey the agony and the ecstasy of being called by God? At one moment one is overawed by the immensity of the honour, ... and in the same breath one screams, "No! No! Please, not me, I can't take it!"

'As I lay there in tears ... I knew that this was the end of the chase. I had chosen to come to this place and I had invited God to speak and he had. Of course, I was free to say, "No, I don't want to", but this would be a clear and deliberate refusal. I thought about it, and knew that I did not want to say "No" and that, however much it hurt, I could only humbly accept.'[2]

Her priest advised her to remain in Chile to test the call. Her medical work during her time in Chile had taken place in

---

[1] Sheila Cassidy: *Audacity to Believe*. Darton, Longman and Todd p. 71
[2] Ibid: pg. 123

hospitals, clinics and *postas*. The latter two were situated in the shantytowns and in these she continued attending to the needs of the sick and malnourished poor.

The next months were building up to the crucible in which both her faith and her calling were to be tested to the limit. But first I must fill in some details.

One morning in October 1974, we woke up with the news that the top *Mirista* had been killed. The gun battle between the left revolutionaries and the government security forces had happened the previous afternoon in a plaza only a fifteen minute walk away from our house in Las Violetas. We had driven past there with the children just minutes before. Others were ready to take the place left by the assassination of Miguel Enriquez.

A year later, during the night of October 15th 1975, the security forces closed in on the headquarters of this outlawed revolutionary party. Malloco, a small country town lies about 15 kilometres outside of Santiago. In yet another gun battle, this time lasting around four hours, one man was killed and another amazingly managed to escape even though he received two bullets in his leg.

It was this man, Nelson Guttierrez, Sheila was asked by a Chilean priest to treat. The stories she had heard from those she encountered daily in her work in the poor *poblaciónes*: of the disappeared, the imprisoned and the tortured had faced her with the fact that sooner or later she might well have to treat a fugitive.

'So now it had happened. The moment that I neither looked forward to nor dreaded had arrived, as I had known that it inevitably would. Without hesitating I said "Yes", knowing quite well that this might well mean the end of my work in Chile. I did not weigh up the pros and cons: a doctor faced with a wounded man does not weigh as on a balance the worth of that man against the worth of other possible patients. In a disaster with multiple casualties, of course, priorities must be assigned, but when faced with one patient who is sick, the doctor treats. On reflection, perhaps this is a Christian ethic rather than a purely medical one:

the value of the individual as against the state. Anyway, I had no doubts; it was not my place to judge this man but to treat him.'[3]

Sheila was taken to a convent where the wounded man was sheltering. She did not know initially that he was one of the two from Malloco. Due to the seriousness of his condition it was arranged that he should seek asylum. Guttierez was told he would need to hand over his arms, and then was taken under cover to the house of the Papal Nuncio (Apostolic Delegate). Once there another doctor treated him, freeing Sheila from further responsibility.

A week later Sheila was visiting the home of missionary priests. Suddenly without any warning a sudden scream pierced the quietness. One of the priests and Sheila moved together in the direction of where the terrible scream had emanated. Lying in a pool of her own blood was the maid, Enriquetta. At the same time bullets were coming through the French windows from the street. The firing continued for sometime. A few moments later men's voices demanded that the door should be opened. It was men from the DINA (the Directorate of National Intelligence). Sheila was the one they were after, having discovered that she had treated Nelson Gutierrez. The priest was able to give the last rites to Enriquetta before she died. Roughly bundled into the waiting car, Sheila was blindfolded then struck on the face as the car drove off. Just before leaving the house she was able to cry out to the priest to contact the British consul. The destination was the Casa Grimaldi, one of the main centres of interrogation.

The night of November 1st 1975, the same night of her arrest, the torture took place. Stripped and tied to a lower metal bunk bed, electric shocks were systematically applied. The questions came furiously one after another. The interrogators were determined to know who else was implicated. Uppermost in her mind was the need to protect her priest and nun friends. Sheila resorted to giving false information. She had made up a false story with false names and false addresses of where she had treated the wanted man.

After the interrogation, badly shaken and in pain, she got

---

[3] Ibid: p. 157

dressed. Once more she was bundled blindfolded into a car, which sped away in the direction of the Central Station that she had mentioned under interrogation.

The next half hour was spent doubling back and going round in circles as she tried desperately to stall. The armed plain-clothed security officials became increasingly angry and accused her time and again of lying. The false trail could have led to serious consequences for the unhappy couple, not even the owners but only the caretakers. The house fitted coincidentally the made up description given under torture. Fortunately for them, unfortunately for Sheila, her deception was uncovered. She was taken back for further torture.

In all she was tortured on and off during three separate occasions in Casa Grimaldi. Back in her cell a practice she had first started in her journey back to faith became an important point of reference. While waiting for a bus or on duty in the hospital she had looked for 'the sign of the cross in doors or windows and all things square, for it reminded me of Christ and helped me to focus my attention on him …'.[4] Looking up at her bunk bed she focussed on the metal strips supporting the mattress.

'As I lay now and looked at the cross above my head I longed to leave some Christian sign upon this terrible place and wondered how I could mark for others the cross that I could see so clearly in the metal above me.'[5]

She began to pull out the threads from a black woollen cloth that had been a blindfold and began to weave the upright of a cross. When asked by the young women who shared her cell what she was doing courage failed her, but later she shared openly with them her Christian belief and her vocation to become a nun.

'… it came as a surprise to find that these girls, although they no longer believed in God, understood the concept of commitment

---

[4] Ibid: p. 210
[5] Ibid: " "

and total giving far better than the average Christian, for they, too, had made the decision to give themselves without reserve.'[6]

Another opportunity came later on in her detention. It was on her first day at Tres Alamos. She was approached by a small group of prisoners asking if she would hold a service. Perplexed by their request, considering the majority were Marxists, she nevertheless agreed. Feeling vulnerable by exposing her faith to those who confessed none, she put up a notice informing the other prisoners of her intention. She chose a simple liturgy incorporating New Testament readings, a selection from the Psalms and prayers. Around twenty women gathered under the trees. During the sharing of the sign of peace Sheila took the hand of the woman guard and 'for a brief moment the barriers between captors and captives were lifted.'

The pattern adopted by the DINA for political prisoners was arrest, followed by interrogation and torture, a period of incommunicado and finally detention at Tres Alamos, if death or murder had not already occurred. Thus it was that she was transferred to Cuatro Alamos, situated within the grounds of Tres Alamos.

Here on Friday, November 7th she had her first visit from an Englishman. It was our friend and Consul Derek.

I recount that meeting in Sheila's own words:

'When I saw Derek Fernyhough standing there looking so incredibly British, all the bottled-up anguish of the past week overflowed, and I burst into tears on his shoulder.'

The guard, none too pleased, insisted they conduct the interview in Spanish. 'In that small office with the doctor and the colonel looking at us and the men with the machine guns just outside the door, I knew that Derek was just as helpless as I was … I realized from his manner that he was completely powerless to rescue me by force and that we must both resort to the famous diplomacy of the British.'[7]

As she choked back tears she asked him for a handkerchief that became her treasured possession. The clean white handkerchief

---

6 Ibid: " "

7 Ibid: p. 223

was a link with a country far away 'where policemen were one's friends'.

Somehow she needed to convey the fact of her torture but how? The Spanish words for torture and for electricity were too similar. With the telephone conveniently ringing at that moment she managed to lean across the table to Derek and whisper,

'Mains, Derek, mains.' The bemused look on Derek's face indicated he was not at all sure exactly what she was trying to convey. He did, however, pass this on to the Foreign Office in London. They knew the significance and the diplomatic wheels were set in motion at an increasingly fast rate.

Sheila returned to her cell with the precious gifts Derek had brought, cologne, soap and cigarettes.

The next weeks meant escorted visits to the Military Court where, here at least, she was treated more humanely and with greater respect.

It was almost eight weeks later before she was finally released and put on a plane to England: eight long and fraught weeks of uncertainty, but no further physical torture. Throughout this time the consulate in Chile and the Foreign Office in England were carefully monitoring the situation.

News at last came that she would be released on December 29th. The day before, Boxing Day, Derek together with Grace visited her, bringing cold turkey and ham.

The next day Sheila arrived at the airport escorted by an embassy official and three armed men. Inside the airport lounge were among others Mr Reginald Secondé, the British Ambassador and Derek Fernyhough. Derek accompanied her right up to the door of the plane.

'Slowly I climbed the ramp and at the plane door said goodbye to Derek Fernyhough who had been so good to me during the past two months. I have not read the code of behaviour laid down for guidance of British consuls in dealing with foreign nationals in trouble but it is difficult to imagine that it includes the provision of handkerchiefs for weeping, novels, bibles, food, clothing and the care of the subject's dog while he or she is in prison!'[8]

And so this naïve, but brave and compassionate doctor left Chile. She looked out of the tiny window 'at the long, narrow strip of land that is Chile; at the land where war and peace, riches and destitution, hatred and love live side by side, and where paradoxically, in losing [her] life [she] had found it again.'[9]

As soon as the plane had taken off, the top diplomats in the whole saga, drove immediately to the Foreign Ministry to lodge a formal complaint. The next day, December 29th, Mr Secondé himself, in response to the summons from Downing Street, boarded the plane, to take him back to the UK.

Once home the full story of Dr Sheila Cassidy's imprisonment and torture was told. Harold Wilson retired soon after and it was Jim Callaghan, assuming the premiership, who made that recalling permanent. For the first time in history between the two countries, Britain now had no ambassadorial figure in Chile. A history that traditionally had enjoyed positive and friendly ties was breached, a breach that began with a large crack when Allende's democratically elected government was overthrown.

In place of Mr Reginald Secondé, Keith Haskell was chargé d'affaires, signifying a downgrading of diplomatic ties between Chile and Britain. Immediately following Mr Secondé's departure, Keith called a meeting of all the top diplomats of the European Community giving the full details surrounding the recall.

Keith and his wife, Toni, had only arrived in Chile three weeks before. They involved themselves in the life of our Church in a way that our Ambassador was not able to, as he was a practising Roman Catholic. In temperament our new ambassadorial representative couple were both warm and more approachable. Keith was tall with dark wavy hair, Toni, of Portuguese origin, was average in height had long dark hair and an attractive face. They had small children, which, no doubt, helped in creating such a family atmosphere. Their home, although rather grand,

---

[8] Ibid. p. 332
[9] Ibid: p. 333

in keeping with their diplomatic status, was always warm and 'normal'.

After the baptism of their small son, Paul, which Ray took, the invited guests went back to their home. By now they had moved into 'the Residence', as the Ambassador's house was referred to. We were enjoying drinks before lunch in the beautiful garden, when we were interrupted with the news that Naomi and their daughter Lysa, the same age, were stuck in the lift. We ran inside to find Keith, used to handling emergencies, patiently giving detailed instructions to two eight year olds through the closed doors of the lift. In a short time the two girls were safely out. A gentle lecture followed on not going into the lift without an accompanying adult.

Toni was a superb cook. To this day I've never tasted a crème brûlée like the one served in their home. Our paths have crossed over the years and we still remain friends.

On speaking to Keith recently, he recalled an amusing incident that stayed indelibly in his mind. It was the occasion when Ray dressed in his clerical robes hobbled slowly into the church building ready to take the service. All decorum vanished as Ray had to explain why he was hobbling on two bare feet! We had been to the coast on our day off with the children and Ray managed to get both feet sunburnt.

With Mr Secondé now back in the United Kingdom it was an uncertain time for his wife. She didn't know whether he would be returning or not. Some months after his recall they were due to celebrate their Silver Wedding. The day arrived, he in England and she in Santiago. Our hearts went out to them.

One evening around this time I suddenly said to Ray, 'We should visit Catherine. Let's go this evening.'

'We can't do that,' was Ray's reply, 'we can't just turn up. What about protocol?'

'Blow protocol,', I replied, 'she needs our support.'

We arrived at 'the Residence'. We stood outside the imposing railings, rang the bell and over the intercom Ray informed security that the Chaplain and his wife wished to visit *la Señora* Secondé. We waited while the message and answer were relayed. The big gates swung open and we drove up the drive to the open front door with butler in attendance. We had of course been on many other occasions and were recognised.

Catherine came to greet us. That evening she was able to let go of her normal official façade and the tears flowed. Before leaving, we prayed with her and I handed her a book that had been avidly read by many in Women's Forum. Catherine Marshall, wife of Peter Marshall, one time Chaplain to the US Senate, had written many books. This particular one *Beyond Ourselves*, had helped many in their Christian journey of faith. It helped this other Catherine.

Sir Reginald never returned. It was with sadness we said goodbye to Catherine as she subsequently left Chile, sadness too that for them their leaving of Chile had been under a cloud.

Chile was without a British Ambassador for the remaining years we were there. The Secondés, after further postings abroad, retired to eastern England. We ourselves returned to that part of the country and our friendship was renewed. After lunch one day, Catherine asked Ray what he could recommend to help her in the reading of the Bible. From then on she started to take daily Bible reading notes. Their maid, another Consuelo, came to live with them. We've known of several cases where maids have built up such a friendship and loyalty with their employers that they've chosen to live here. Consuelo gave such loyal service and in turn received such loving care right until her death.

Chapter 34
An End of a Chapter

Last night, I was watching the 11.00 pm news on television. It was Sunday, December 10th 2006. I called to Ray in another room. The headlines were about Chile. General Augusto Pinochet had died in the Military Hospital. This was not surprising as he was ninety-one and had suffered a heart attack the previous week. We tuned into the World Service news on our radio at midnight, anxious to know if the news of his death would create riots in the streets. Certainly old wounds would be reopened, but with so much healing having taken place over the years it was unlikely for any disturbances to be more than relatively short lived. As predicted, supporters of Pinochet and antagonists turned out on to the streets of the capital, the former to grieve and the latter to celebrate.

This morning Ray went to buy two newspapers. We hoped to get two representing both right and left views. Our local newsagent did not have such a wide choice as we would have liked. In place of *The Guardian* Ray bought *The Independent* with a full impressive photograph filling the front page with the headline 'He took his crimes to the grave' while *The Times* only gave coverage on page two with the obituary on page forty-eight.

Amnesty International's reaction was that his death 'should be a wake-up call for the authorities in Chile and governments everywhere, reminding them of the importance of speedy justice for human rights crimes, something Pinochet has now escaped.'[1]

---

[1] Reported in *The Independent* December 11th 2006

456

While it is true so many questions remain unanswered with Pinochet's 'going to the grave', leaving many dissatisfied that he had never been brought to justice in this life, he will not escape the ultimate court of final justice before God, the Judge of all. News from Chile on the radio this morning was that he would be given a funeral befitting a former Head of the Armed Forces, to be held in the Military Academy Chapel but not as Head of State.

General Pinochet was ousted from the government in 1990. He had called for a plebiscite two years earlier. This was organised fairly by the Chilean Electoral Tribunal, and closely scrutinised by international observers. Pinochet thought he would win, but in fact lost by 43 percent to 55 percent. The following year the right suffered another defeat at the hands of a broad coalition led by the Christian Democrats. Pinochet had to accede defeat to Patricio Aylwin. However, he remained Commander-in-Chief of the nation's armed forces until 1998. He had ruled his country with an iron fist for seventeen years, during which he was implicated in the deaths and disappearances of over 3000 Chileans, a charge he denied. But the Truth Commission verified that over 3000 were indeed killed during his reign and 250,000 were locked up, some having been tortured. Many of his former supporters lost faith when it came to light that he had amassed as much as $27m in various foreign bank accounts. Some of these supporters who had helped in the financial reconstruction of the country in Pinochet's early days in office, rightly felt anger at such betrayal.

Central to Pinochet's nationalism was an intense hatred of communism, a hatred shared with his strong ally, the United States. Leaders of nations are often products of their era. The cold war between the US and the Soviet Union was being fought out across Central and Latin America, Cuba being an important protagonist. Although heavily implicated in stirring the flames of opposition in Allende's presidency, America held back from directly ordering Chile's military coup. It was General Pinochet's sincere belief that as Commander-in-Chief it was his duty to prevent Chile's descent into communism and further chaos.

What he didn't sufficiently reckon on was the strength of Chile's democratic tradition, putting it head and shoulders above the majority of its neighbouring republics. It was the intense respect for democracy that forced Pinochet ultimately to bow to the will of the people as expressed in the referendum.

A legacy of the military era, that brought Chile from being a developing nation into the orbit of a developed, one was the application of a free-market economic policy and eventually a stable return to democracy. Not long after coming to power, Pinochet gave his support to the 'Chicago boys', the Chilean economists who had trained in the University of Chicago. Their anti-Marxism, entrepreneurial policies and unconditional support for the coup ensured his full support, even though two severe recessions followed in their wake, 1975-76, which we, of course, experienced, and 1982-83. He survived both, as did the economy. He also survived ever increasing international hostility as the Roman Catholic Church continued its sustained campaign in defence of human rights. His mistake, like so many in high office, was holding on to power. It was thought, given the country's democratic history, that the military would soon hand power back, but with the creation of a powerful authoritarian government and an intensely loyal military this hope was soon quashed.

It was a visit to England and ensuing events that led up to the final chapter in the life of this most well known of all South American dictators.

A relatively newly elected Labour Government was in power in the autumn of 1998 when Augusto Pinochet arrived in England, supposedly on an arms purchasing mission. In fact, he came for surgery on his back. He had previously visited London, always as a welcome guest of Margaret Thatcher, who remained indebted to him for the support given during the Falklands War. The political climate had now changed. News soon got round of his presence and it was a Spanish judge, Baltasar Garzón, who issued a warrant for the General's arrest. The charge was the murder and torture of Spanish citizens during his rule in Chile. The British police arrested him on October 16th in the London Clinic pending extradition to Spain. The next eighteen months lawyers argued over his fate, during which time he was under house arrest at the exclusive Wentworth Estate in Surrey. By 1999 other European countries were also requesting his extradition on the charge of abuse of human rights against their own citizens. Angry protesters joined in, the majority being Chilean or connected with Chile: some were in favour of his release, the majority demanded a trial. Margaret Thatcher gave her voice to the side demanding his release.

The House of Lords voted in favour of his extradition, later to be overturned when one of the Law Lords had too close a connection with Amnesty International. In March 1999, the Law Lords ruled on a more narrow interpretation of the law. Crimes committed after 1988 (when both Chile and the UK signed international treaties outlawing the use of torture) could lead to extradition.

Jack Straw, as Home Secretary, accepted the ruling and extradition proceedings were begun. However, the General's ill health and increasing frailty overturned this decision. He had suffered two mild strokes while on English soil. Jack Straw arranged a medical examination to see if Pinochet was fit to stand trial. The medical panel reported that there was extensive brain damage, memory loss and difficulty in communication. The Home Secretary announced in January 2000 that he was 'minded' to release the octogenarian on humanitarian grounds due to his failing health. This was greeted with uproar.

On March 2nd, a Chilean Air Force plane took off from Waddington, Lincolnshire to return the General to his own country. As we watched the news on our television screen the following day, like many others we were left with questions unanswered, as we saw Pinochet rise from his wheelchair once back on home soil and wave his crutch in triumph to his gathered supporters.

In Chile his opponents continued to pursue him through the courts and these hearings were very acrimonious as feelings on both sides ran high. In time, in August 2000, the Supreme Court did strip him of his immunity as a Senator for Life. His defence counsel argued that his mild dementia made him unfit to state his case.

Last month on his 91st birthday he tentatively accepted 'political responsibility' for what had happened during his time in power, but insisted that he never personally ordered the killings of any of his opponents. The truth of that now remains between him and his Maker. Although death has ended the chapter of Pinochet's earthly life, there are still very many who have been denied appropriate closure to their sorrow and grief.

In 1979, as a family, we were facing the end of a chapter, our own time in Chile. Ray's second three-year contract was coming to an end and we had to make a decision whether it was right to renew or not. With much prayer we arrived at the conclusion that it was time for us to return home. There were two contributory factors in making this decision. One was the secondary education of the children: Naomi was, by now, twelve, Andrew ten and Julian nine: the other was the age and health of our four parents.

Bishop Colin Bazely asked if we could meet with him, as he wanted to discuss our future. His proposal was for us to return as full SAMS mission personnel and for Ray to have an Archdeacon's responsibility. Although we felt it to be God's will not to renew the contract with the Community Church, we had now another alternative that we needed time to think and pray about. The two factors of the children's education and the parents' situation remained the same. What were we to do? Over the next few days we both felt increasingly that we should return home and it was a verse in the Old Testament that confirmed our decision making. The Israelites had been journeying in the Sinai desert under Moses' leadership and had known God's guidance again and again even as we had. At a given point on their journey God spoke to Moses all those centuries ago with words that now spoke to us in the winter of 1979.

'You have made your way around this mountainous country long enough; now turn north.'[2]

---

[2] The Bible: Deuteronomy chapter 2 verse 3

Ray had to give sufficient notice to the Church Council for them to start advertising.

The timing for the three-year contract (Ray had served two) couldn't have been more ideal. The children were able to see out their current academic year, followed by a busy Christmas and the winding up of many church activities for the long summer recess. Once the news broke there was an endless round of *despedidas*. With the holidays immediately following on from Christmas, when there is a large exodus out of the city, farewell parties were hastily crammed in during those early spring months. The Chilean custom of *despedidas* meant not only did our food bills go down considerably but also we were laden with farewell gifts. The Church Council arranged our farewell in the garden of the Church House. Inevitably some friends were missing due to holidays, but had already ensured their own personal leaving hospitality for us. The children had their own *despedida* parties as well as a number of invitations with us.

Willie Reid (trustee of the SCC) and his nephew, Jimmy had made a proposition. If the Council was willing to use their Air Freight business for our luggage all the family would travel back free. It seemed a good deal. Financially it was good for the Church and hassle free for us as the packing would be taken care of, so unlike our arrival nine years previously! There was only one draw back. The five passengers would have to accompany the luggage and their business cargo. Their cargo was crates and crates of fruit – apples and peaches, stored at 4 °centigrade!

For some reason, forgotten with the passing of time, the larger plane was exchanged for a smaller DC 8. This meant we would have to split up as only two passengers could travel at any one time. As two trips of two passengers didn't add up to five, Naomi, being the eldest, returned alone on a British Caledonian scheduled flight – a big journey for a twelve-year-old. Her Uncle Howard met her at Gatwick.

Next to travel home were Ray and Andrew. We were to be based once more in Frinton until Ray found a living.

What excitement when the day came for their unusual journey home. Andrew was very excited, the thought of the cool temperature not dampening his enthusiasm one little bit. The aircrew were Icelandic and had never flown from Santiago over the Andes before. Both father and son were invited into the cockpit. Ray recounts his reactions.

'*It was terrifying. The navigator was poring over a map identifying the huge peaks as they came into view. As the respective peaks began to fill the cockpit window, I had to shut my eyes. Suddenly a command would be given to turn right or left to negotiate a way through! I couldn't look any more and had to return to the cabin.*' Meanwhile as Ray rejoined his 'cool and fruity' passengers, Andrew remained in the cockpit fascinated with the proceedings.

The plane's destination was Luxembourg. From there Ray and Andrew would take a train to the Hook of Holland and continue by ferry to Harwich, a stone's throw from Frinton, where Grandpa Smith would meet them.

An enforced grounding of one of the CargoLux DC 8 planes in Luxembourg, due to a small landing accident, meant the plane that should have flown Julian and me home was unable to leave for Chile. It was six weeks later before we arrived back, not as planned by CargoLux but by British Caledonian.

Adjusting to reverse culture shock proved to be a huge challenge and one that we didn't find easy. Undoubtedly we had left our hearts in Chile, but there were compensations. For the children to be so near to all four grandparents was a bonus. In fact once again kind friends lent us a holiday home. This time it was a bungalow only a few yards from grandparents Smith and a ten-minute walk from grandparents Williamson. We remained Frinton-based until Easter when a new chapter of ministry opened to us, not in a capital city the other side of the world, but in a sleepy village on the Essex-Suffolk border, not in a practical town house, but in a Georgian vicarage of more than twenty rooms counting the cellar and an acre of land! The contrast couldn't have been greater.

Chapter 35
Passing on the Baton

In common with many families whose children spend their formative years in another country, there can be the question of which culture they belong to. For Naomi this was a big question. To find the answer she had to return.

At the age of twenty-one, after a three-year course in Foreign Languages and Business Studies, she went back to Santiago for a year. Her secretarial work took her each day high into the Andes. Her work destination was a copper mine, La Disputada de las Condes. A minibus would pick her up at a given point in the city at 6.30 am and she would travel with the miners, the only female, for the next couple of hours up and around the hair-pin bends. This was the only secretarial job she had with a dress code that demanded denim jeans, which suited her down to the ground! In addition she had to wear a helmet every time she went out of the office. She loved the daily journey, as the scenery was so stunning with the ever-changing light and seasons.

Her year gave her time to catch up with many friends: it also provided the answer she went out to discover and for which we anxiously waited. The four of us met her at Gatwick with such joy, in marked contrast to the pain of separation a year earlier.

'You know, Mum and Dad, I've loved being back in Chile but I know where my roots really lie, in England.' Sixteen years later, Naomi introduced her husband, Phil, to the country of her childhood.

Andrew decided to return to Chile during his gap year before going to Manchester University to read Law. We ourselves made our first visit back during this same time, eight years after arriving home. For Ray it meant combining a sabbatical leave of absence from the Parish of St Philip, Cambridge, with covering a temporary vacancy in the Santiago Community Church. His study leave project was research into the pros and cons of cross-cultural marriages. I joined him a month later, once Julian had finished his A levels. The only slight drawback was that we exchanged the summer months for the winter ones.

Speaking of marriages, I digress to recount an invitation Ray had, to be interviewed on Chilean TV. We often found ourselves inviting lots of interest among our Roman Catholic friends because Ray, as an Anglican priest, was in fact married with a family. Without doubt the majority thought this was good and wished the RC priest could have the same choice. This then was the subject of the TV interview. I was returning from taking the children to school, and as I drew alongside the house, I saw Ray on the steps outside the church surrounded by TV cameras and microphones. Suddenly Ray spotted me and to my consternation beckoned me over, the crew also joining in. I thus found myself alongside Ray in front of the daunting cameras, facing questions delivered and answered in Spanish. I didn't even have time to put a comb through my hair!

Before Andrew left, I felt some concern that his childhood memories might not match his present expectations. We had a chat. His first letter home quashed these concerns. '*You remember our chat Mum, well you needn't worry, Chile hasn't changed a bit, and you'll both love it when you come out ... One thing that really surprised me, however, was how small the Country Club seemed, especially the swimming pool.*' Andrew by now was over six feet tall!

It was less than two years ago that Julian, while not actually landing on Chilean soil, did technically visit. This was the occasion when *Stelmar* entered Chilean territorial waters into the Beagle Channel, just north of Cape Horn, to evacuate a sick crewmember at this southernmost naval base. It is customary to hoist the flag of the host nation on entering their waters. The problem was this was an unscheduled stop and there was no Chilean flag. Julian to the rescue. Taking an A4 size of sail repair cloth and using permanent markers he designed the flag of his childhood country. With the flag proudly displayed the yacht sailed into Puerto Williams and moored alongside a Chilean naval vessel. The naval crew on seeing the flag suggested a swap should take place. 'Each of us should sign our flag,' said Julian. Clive, *Stelmar*'s captain, then presented the signed flag to the Chilean Naval Officer and was told it would be put up on display in the Mess. After seeing Karen safely into Chilean hands the yacht had to do a quick turn around to continue racing.

In July 1988 father and son met me at Pudahuel Airport. As the chaplain's car turned into Avenida Holanda nothing had changed. There before me lay the familiar iron gates, open to receive us, behind which were the cream coloured walls of the Church House. A smiling Nana was waiting in welcome. After a warm *abrazo* (hug) with her, a lengthy chat and some light refreshment I went upstairs to the familiar bedroom and lay down to sleep in the same bed I'd last slept in eight years previously. I had returned home.

To enable us to make a second visit to Chile in the new millennium, I ran an art and craft exhibition, helped by Naomi and others, to help towards our fares. The original lesson in painting my mother gave me once again brought its own reward.

This visit was mainly holiday, although we both did preach once each in our 'old' church, the first time an ordained woman had done so! Once again we were in the familiar surroundings of Church House, with the ever-faithful Nana. The difference was this time we were house-guests of the resident Chaplain and his wife and here my story goes full circle; yet another of those remarkable God-incidents. The resident Chaplain was none other than Peter Goodwin Hudson, the son of the lady I first met in the launderette in Frinton, almost thirty years previously. It was his father who had been the first Anglican Chaplain of the present building; he was also its architect. The baton had passed from father to son.

Another baton passed from father to son was within our own family. Andrew, who together with Carol gave up their professional careers to serve God in South America, returned to the sub-continent. Their destination was not Chile or Brazil, where each had been brought up, but in the connecting republic. They left for La Paz, Bolivia in October 2003, with our, by now, four grandchildren, the youngest eighteen months and the eldest eight years.

They arrived at an incredibly difficult and dangerous time. Bolivia was in a state of political turmoil with the Andean High Plateau (Altiplano) cities and surrounding areas the focal point of the disturbance: the area with the greatest concentration of the indigenous Aymará. These were the very people they had on their hearts to work amongst. Their particular passion was for the street children. The 'Alalay' (Aymará word meaning 'out from the cold') Project had been running for a number of years providing a communal home, education and spiritual direction to these disadvantaged and often deeply traumatised young people.

As part of the team Andrew and Carol set up a resource centre, took services, ran 'discipleship courses' and generally drew alongside both staff and young people. Underpinning all was the love they offered, love and acceptance reflecting the Father heart of God, which in fact was the basis for much of their teaching. It was a very humbling experience for me when I visited one year from their arrival. (Currently they are on Study Leave, each working for an MA in Global Mission at Redcliffe College, Gloucester.)

Out of their involvement with the Alalay Project sprang another vision – the Kainos Project. Before leaving they were able to see the gestation period of that vision, which had been conceived twelve years ago in the hearts of an indigenous Bolivian couple, Juan Carlos and Fely Mamani.

For Andrew and Carol, seeing first hand '*the profound scar of fatherlessness … hampering many young people's maturing in their Christian faith, especially those young people who have lived on the streets of La Paz*' impacted them deeply. Alongside this '*is also the passion we have come to see in some young people, to serve God, both here in Bolivia and across the world.*'

To enable this growth the house they lived in, with its outhouses and surrounding land, has been left to the Mamani family to carry the vision forward through 'labour pains' to full birth.

Alongside them, acting as 'midwives', in this process is the Kairos Church and Alalay itself with which this fledgling vision is closely connected. The Church *'is committed to providing the additional pastoral care and discipleship as well as training opportunities.'*

Kainos House is located at a height of over 12,000 feet right at the heart of the rural Aymará community. It is situated a half hour car journey away from the two major Altiplano cities of El Alto and the capital itself. The acre of land provides for the growing of vegetables and fruit. When I visited, the fruit trees were only just being planted. Two years later they are producing an abundance of fruit – a sign we hold on to of spiritual fruit in the lives of the young people who live there.

We count ourselves extremely privileged that, after so many years since leaving Chile, we have been able to continue to accompany on the journey of faith those whose lives we mutually touched. Many of these are still in Chile but others are scattered throughout the globe, yet others have exchanged their earthly life for the greater reality of heaven itself. That journey, common to most of us, can lead into dry and arid desert places, as well as oases of fruitfulness.

What happened to Omar and Lia? Since leaving Chile they have continued to make their home in Canada. In 1990 we made a second trip to the USA and Canada visiting many friends. Once again our Canadian hosts were Charles and Frances Cooper from the Santiago Community Church congregation. They had now moved from Kingston, Ontario to Vancouver, where Omar and Lia were also living. It was a whistle-stop visit and we only spent the Sunday with Omar and Lia.

In their initial days in Canada they not only went to an English-speaking church but, because of the language, started a Bible study group in their home in Spanish in 1975.

Omar wrote, *'… it was a multi-denominational bunch of people in unity. Their one focus was Jesus Christ.'* The Church born in their house grew to over thirty members and became the 'core group' for the first formal Evangelical Hispanic Church in Vancouver, in 1978.

Today an Argentinian family has the oversight of 'La Iglesia Esperanza' (Hope Church). This church is still active, together *'with forty other churches that started'* during the influx of Central American migrants in the 1990s. In conjunction with this was the downtown Hobbit House Mission for Hispanics that Omar and Lia led.

Over the years, Omar, with a passionate heart for mission, has headed up Latin American ministries of humanitarian and evangelistic outreach. Two other church plants this couple helped initiate, were another Hispanic Church and a Vineyard Church in English. Sadly this second Hispanic Church had to be closed due to the serious misconduct of the young pastor.

To date this Chilean couple continue in their mission outreach, taking students with them from Campus Ministries International and working with the local churches. For the past three years they have made annual trips lasting six months to Costa Rica and to Cuba. A container went by sea with fifteen tons of items for the disadvantaged: this *'was distributed among 25 charitable organizations that reached about 5000 people. Also we did street evangelism, and went door to door to share the gospel ...'*. They work with other teams of Christians and, in two campaigns, over one thousand people responded. At the time of writing this chapter they are again in Costa Rica and will be visiting Cuba, where they support and encourage local pastors.

In common with so many of God's servants *'not everything has been rosy'* in the lives of this couple. In 1979 while testing with cyanide in the chemistry laboratory of BC (British Columbia) Research, some gases leaked. For over twenty-four hours Omar was at death's door in intensive care at Vancouver General Hospital. He was *'placed in an Isobaric Chamber to extract the gases from his body, a painful experience.'* Two years later, intense work pressures, insomnia and depression, compounded by hypoglycaemia led to a nervous breakdown. He was not a diabetic but for some reason was suffering from a bio-chemical imbalance of insulin. This affected the normal functioning of the brain and subsequently Omar was advised to give up work. The following year Lia's mother died and she, together with their two sons travelled to Chile. Omar had reached rock bottom. Kneeling down and with tears he prayed for release. God heard.

'It was a clear, sunny day in mid August, when he was praying that he saw a vision in the sky. A cumulus of clouds that appeared from nowhere formed a black tunnel toward which two human figures were running. Toward the end there was a gleaming light waiting for them. There is hope! "You are my lamp, O Lord; the Lord turns my darkness into light." 2 Samuel 22:29. Then, in a few seconds the clouds took the form of two gigantic hands that were holding this human shape. God cares! The clouds disappeared as fast as they had come. "You are my God. My times are in your hands …" Psalm 31:14-15.'

After two years out of work, he was offered a permanent job back with BC Research. Amazingly they allowed him to work just one hour a day, increasing to full time over a period of three months. Gradually his health improved. Three years later he attended a conference on God's healing. He was prayed for, simply and with humility. Lia writes, *'That night, for the first time in four years he slept like an angel without medication. All his illnesses were gone. Jesus Christ was the divine healer.'*

It was on our first return visit to Chile that we caught up briefly with yet another 'enemy' who had become a life long friend. Nico was now married to Luz, who he had met in the Sunday night group. By now, a fully-fledged geologist, his work had taken him to various mines in the central region of the country, but more often in the arid Atacama Desert. However, on this particular reunion with him it was at their home in Rancagua, just over an hour's drive south of the capital. He was in a semi-arid place spiritually and was not involved in any local church. The spiritually dry time for both him and Luz lasted a number of years, although as he told us subsequently, in that time he never ever really lost his love for Jesus. He had, for a number of reasons, become somewhat disillusioned with other Christians.

It was during our second trip out, in 2000, that God's Spirit provided the much-needed refreshment for Nico. By now, together with Luz and their three teenage children they were back in the suburbs of Santiago. They opened their home for a reunion party. Some of the former students from the Sunday evenings were present, including Patricio and Susan. Although Pato and Nico had never lost touch completely, it was as a result of our being there that they decided they needed to meet together on a regular basis for mutual encouragement – perhaps a reminder of former times?

While Nico was in his semi-arid spiritual desert, in Rancagua, Pato had had his own. When he and Susan visited us in Cambridge he shared with us something of their continuing journey of faith. In 1987 after years of leadership he reached a time of 'burnout' In an effort to rightly guard 'time for family and me' he ended up for a time in a wilderness, leading to a crisis.

He and Susan attended a Marriage Encounter weekend the following year that proved to be the oasis in their desert. Pato decided to return to the Anglican Church, in which he had become involved in the intervening years. Without Susan, he attended La Iglesisa de la Trinidad, where Alf was the minister – 'just listening'. After two months, Susan joined him, but with one condition that he wouldn't be involved 'in the leadership'. Six months later he was a member of the Church Council, confirmed and in 1989 was licensed by Bishop Colin as a lay preacher.

In 1990 John Burley started a service in La Reina, in the Barrio Alto and Alf asked Pato to head up the house group John had started in La Reina. This he did for two years and in that time God 'planted in me the vision to plant an Anglican Church there'. Pato was ordained deacon in 1992 and priest six months later. While Alf was on home leave, Pato led Trinity Church. Two years later the Anglican Church of San Andrés in La Reina was planted under the leadership of Pato.

Meanwhile, Nico's suspicion of the Roman Catholic Church had left him over many years still with a reluctance to get too involved in any institutional church. He has often recalled how much he appreciated that '*not a tiny suggestion was made by you to enter the Anglican Church … because you were focussed on me, on us, to be looking to Jesus Christ Himself. The rest were details.*'

In the same letter from Nico written sometime after our

millennium visit, he wrote of his returning to regular Bible reading and other Christian books *'that have helped me to feel more free in terms of committing myself to a community. With Luz, we have been participating in a Catholic group and in Pato's community, in house groups and Sunday worship.'*

Today Nico and Luz are regular members of San Andrés Church with Pato as minister. Nico is also on the Church Council and leader of a home group. These two life long friends support and encourage one another in their journey of faith as they did in the past when they were joint leaders of the Sunday night group.

Pato, not only pastors the church of San Andrés, in La Reina, he also serves the wider church. In 1999 he became Chile's Director for World Vision. This Christian organization provides relief in developing nations. By the end of this same year, he became President of World Vision for the whole of Latin America. In 2004, in Nicaragua, he was elected to the Board of World Vision, covering Asia and Africa as well as Latin America

Today San Andrés is just one of many Anglican churches scattered throughout the capital. Church planting has been and continues to be, the passion and commitment of both Alf and Hilary together with teams of faithful men, women and young people. Alf is now Archdeacon and in a recent letter he recounts those early years. He and Hilary initially worked with an Anglican Church plant in La Florida, a poorer area on the outskirts of Santiago. As this part of the city was well served by several Pentecostal congregations, Alf questioned the need for starting yet more Anglican congregations; the Barrio Alto was calling them. In the capital itself and wider region there are today thirteen Anglican churches. One of those, in the wider region, is in Caleu an hour or so drive northwest of Santiago, and another in nearby Batuco. Lew and Alice had bought some land in Caleu using it as a 'bolt-hole', a *'poustinia'* (a Russian word meaning a place of refreshment) This area, including Lampa was where Lew and Alice, together with Nigel, had combined a social programme with running a Sunday school for the children and the giving of Bibles.

These thirteen Anglican Churches do not include the rest of the country both north and south (where the Anglican work began) or the coastal region. Five of the thirteen are in the Barrio Alto.

It was the passionate vision we had initiated for a Protestant work among the Barrio Alto that first impacted Alf and Hilary. By now they were involved in the Sunday night student group. In addition, with Alf's own Anglo-Chilean family connections and Hilary having lived in our home, they witnessed first hand the potential within the Santiago Community Church. The core of stability within a congregation of transient members on short contracts came from the resident Anglo-Chilean community. The future generations of these were far more integrated into Chilean culture. This was so obvious to us. We had increasingly held a vision for a Spanish-speaking congregation to be formed within the building of the SCC and shared this with Bishop Colin. Alf wrote that it was while on home leave, *'we received a surprise visit from Bishop Colin Bazley* [himself on leave], *informing us of a vision Ray and Gill had had involving our posting to the SCC to start a Spanish Anglican service. Colin gave us his consenting blessing and we were suddenly preparing for a new adventure.'*

So it was in the early 1980s, back in Chile, that Alf and Hilary devised a strategy. Other colleagues had already started house churches in the Las Condes area, namely Gordon and Beryl Whitehead and Colin and Barbara Bazely. The strategy Alf and Hilary adopted was an intense visitation programme based on the church register. They visited all Chileans and Anglo-Chileans they could locate who had been baptised, confirmed and married at the SCC, but not yet buried! This took them as far back as when it was the Cathedral Church of St Andrews as well as after the more recent merger.

The first service was in September 1978, two years before we left. Thirty-five attended, about half were those from the small house churches, the remaining had never been to an Anglican Spanish service before. *'We asked for a sign. If it was God's move and not merely man's idea, would someone be converted to Christ on that day. Hilary who was at the door welcomed a young lady, María*

472

Eliana, who had left her house praying, "Lord, I am going to look for one more church. If I don't find you there today, I will never again go to church." She heard the singing, was welcomed by Hilary and that day she found the Lord!'

Alf has always stood out for us as a man with a great passion to see the kingdom of God expand. We often smile as we recount his exuberant enthusiasm and at times have said, 'Come on, Alf, you're exaggerating. Isn't it a bit OTT?' But those who know him would agree we could all do with more of his Holy Spirit inspired enthusiasm and great heart of humility. Together with his team of leaders Alf set out goals for church growth. *'The thirty barrier when we began to "make disciples". The sixty barrier when we began to go out and evangelise the neighbourhood ...The one hundred barrier when we began to train young leaders.'*

The links with our own ministry involving the passing on of the baton began to merge within this new Chilean outreach.

'We were never far from Ray and Gill's pioneer work ... It was a real move of God that took place as their life-style evangelism led couple after couple to Christ. Several of these became involved with our work.'

Notable among these couples were John and Sandi. They had returned to Chile in 1981 after John had completed theological training at Trinity School for Ministry in Pittsburgh, USA. This was as part of the SAMS team. John joined Alf, later taking over the Iglesia Anglicana de Providencia as minister of the Chilean work in the very church he and Sandi had come to faith. Meanwhile the never flagging Alf was busy with further church planting. *'When...we left to plant the Las Condes church, God had graciously given us ... John Burley, whose brilliant teaching ministry consolidated the church, now a good 130 adults strong on a Sunday morning. A good number of these went with us to start the Las Condes church.'* The principle of dividing in order to multiply is a known strategy with its example rooted in the early church.

John is currently a vicar in Surrey and over the years, together with Sandi and others, has been involved in short term missions in Spain.

Alf borrowed a vitally important tool that has had an enormous impact for building the kingdom of God. It was borrowed from the Roman Catholic Church and used by the Anglican Church in Chile (as was '*Cursillo*') not only in its own outreach, but also in other parts of Latin America and Spain with amazing results. It was Marriage Encounter. '*I had heard of the wonderful way God was using Marriage Encounter in Brazil.*' But it was on being introduced to Eduardo Villagrán, a Roman Catholic priest, who was '*willing to give his Catholic Marriage Encounter to the Anglicans that the whole concept took off.*'

Gordon and Beryl pioneered the very first 'Encuentro Matrimonial Anglicana' (EMA) while Alf and Hilary were on home leave. Once back the team worked together to continue with more of these special residential weekends away with married couples.

Alf wrote. '*Among the pioneers over those foundational years were several of the couples that Ray and Gill had led to Christ, young couples full of zest and zeal ... it has developed into one of the most fruitful evangelistic outreaches that we have known, winning hundreds if not thousands of people to Christ over the past twenty years. I say thousands because over blood, sweat and tears the ministry was gradually handed over to many denominations, sent over to other countries and taken as far as Russia and Hong Kong by the Alliance Church.*'

Sometimes I have remonstrated with God as to why we have so often been involved in a pioneering type ministry, the breaking up of fallow ground and the planting of the seed, only to move on when things really took off. Yet I am once again reminded of the apostle Paul's words that in God's harvest field, some sow and others water the seeds in his kingdom, but it's God alone who brings about life and growth. We count it an immense privilege to have been part of the process.

When Christians are prepared to reach across the denominational divides that separate them, majoring on what unites rather than what divides then we will become the answer to Jesus' prayer:

'May they be brought to complete unity to let the world know that you sent me and have loved them even as you have loved me.'[1]

For this very ordinary couple with our three precious children, it was our going to Chile that enabled us to cross so many divides.

---

[1] The Bible: John chapter 17 verse 23

MELROSE BOOKS

If you enjoyed this book you may also like:

The Nazareth Route
Cecil Hargreaves

The Nazareth Route by Cecil Hargreaves focuses on the themes of "challenge" and the "form of vulnerability which consists in a willingness to get hurt and wounded." It is also about human dilemma.

The author outlines as many as thirty people across the world who have been seen to be among Jesus' modern Nazareth 'route-makers' and 'route-finders'.

Size: 234mm x 156mm   Pages: 224
Binding: Hardback with dust jacket   ISBN: 978 1 906050 44 3   £13.99

Biafra The Memory of the Music
Jim Malia

How many now remember Biafra, the first such conflict that television brought into our homes, people staring in wonder at the sight of suffering unseen since the days of the Holocaust? Jim Malia spares the reader little in telling the tale of the nightmare that was Biafra: tribal conflict crushing the hard-won fruits of Independence; military coup followed by massacre, secession, blockade, starvation.

Yet as they gave, many asked and still ask: "Why? Why this suffering? Why the turmoil of post-colonial Africa? This book is an attempt to answer that question.

Size: 234mm x 156mm   Pages: 192
Binding: Hardback with dust jacket   ISBN: 978 1 906050 00 9   £12.99

Kiss The Hand You Cannot Sever
Adrienne Brady

Libya 1993. A time of extreme tension. In the wake of Gaddafi's failure to meet the UN deadline and hand over the Lockerbie bombing suspects, Adrienne Brady, accepted a teaching post in Tripoli. A month after her arrival, the UN renewed and tightened sanctions, an attempt was made on Gaddafi's life and political upheaval turned into chaos. Against a backdrop of arrest, interrogation and constant surveillance, Adrienne found herself living through a slice of history.

This then, was the world behind the headlines: the real world, sometimes menacing, occasionally comic, frequently bizarre. And yet, in spite of everything, including the authority's best efforts to make travelling difficult, if not impossible, Adrienne's passion for exploration remained as powerful as ever. The Tuareg people have a saying: "Kiss the hand you cannot sever", which dates back to the days when it was more than a traveller's life was worth to refuse help from these self-appointed guardians of the Sahara.

Size: 234mm x 156mm   Pages: 304
Binding: Hardback with dust jacket   ISBN: 978 1 906050 60 3   £12.99

St Thomas' Place, Ely, Cambridgeshire CB7 4GG, UK

www.melrosebooks.com   sales@melrosebooks.com

ANGOSTURA P140 lower left
WORLD VISION P435

SHEILA CASSIDY